The Best of *THE* Raven

150 essays from Algonquin Park's popular newsletter
~ in celebration of the Park Centennial 1893–1993 ~

by Dan Strickland and Russ Rutter
Illustrated by Peter Burke

The Ontario Ministry of Natural Resources published *The Raven* from 1960 through 1992. These 33 years of service and the Ministry's financial assistance in the publication of this book are gratefully acknowledged by The Friends of Algonquin Park, the new publisher of *The Raven*.

Published in Canada by The Friends of Algonquin Park
P.O. Box 248, Whitney, Ontario K0J 2M0

First edition 1993
Second edition 1996

Credits:
Editor: Heather Lang-Runtz
Book Design: Deborah Burke and Heather Lang-Runtz, The HLR Publishing Group
Text Preparation and Formatting: Tracy Sparling, The HLR Publishing Group
Word Processing and Proofreading: Tracey Wojcik, The Friends of Algonquin Park

Canadian Cataloguing in Publication Data

Strickland, Dan

The Best of *The Raven*: 150 essays from Algonquin Park's popular newsletter: in celebration of the Park Centennial 1893–1993

2nd ed.
Includes index.
ISBN 1-895709-19-9

1. Algonquin Provincial Park (Ont.)   I. Rutter, Russell J.   II. Friends of Algonquin Park
III. Title.

FC3065.A65S87 1995   333.78'3'09713147   C95-920931-X
F1059.A4S77 1995

Printed on Luna matte 120M (text); Cornwall coated 10 pt. (cover)

Printed and bound in Canada by Love Printing Service Ltd., Stittsville, Ont.

Dedication
For Sarah and Louis-Matthieu, whose delight and wonder at the natural world have been a delight and wonder for *The Raven.*

Contents

Foreword

It gives me great pleasure, on the occasion of Algonquin Park's 100th birthday, to introduce this long-awaited collection of essays from the Park's famous newsletter, *The Raven*. For 34 years now, *The Raven* has been informing, edifying, and amusing a whole generation of Park visitors. Every week in the summer hundreds of copies go out to lodges, camps, newspapers, and radio stations, where their contents are passed on to countless numbers of people who might otherwise remain unaware of the Park's enormously rich natural and human heritage. Every fall thousands of complete sets of all 12 issues for the year are mailed out to people around the world who, through the pages of *The Raven*, will relive their visit to the Park and gain further insights into its ecology and history. And yet, because *The Raven* is a weekly newsletter, most of its articles, however interesting they may be, quickly disappear from view and become unavailable to succeeding Park visitors and the general public. Only a few well-organized people can boast of having a complete set of all the original issues, and even in these cases, individual articles are difficult to index and retrieve for subsequent reference. Understandably then, there have been numerous requests over the years for a collection of *Raven* articles in book form. The Board of Directors of The Friends of Algonquin Park needed no convincing about the merits of such a project, and the result is what you are now setting out to enjoy.

I have an additional, more personal, reason for being so pleased to introduce this book. As someone closely associated with Algonquin Park for over 35 years — including five years as chief park naturalist — I have seen *The Raven*'s development from its unsung beginnings back in 1960 right up to the present. It was my boss and immediate predecessor as chief park naturalist, Grant Tayler, who came up with the idea for a park newsletter and the name "Raven." Today, just about every sizeable provincial or national park has a newsletter (often

PHOTO BY DAN STRICKLAND

Russ Rutter.

modelled after *The Raven*), not to mention an array of other publications. But back in 1960, Algonquin Park quite literally had no publications at all, except for a map, and no one had even heard of a park newsletter.

Grant's idea, therefore, was quite original and innovative at the time, however obvious and modest it may appear today. Indeed, it seems amazing to look back now at one of the original issues, mimeographed on the most primitive of equipment and barely legible by today's standards, and to think that something so unprepossessing was going to be the start of an enduring Park tradition that would soon reach "circulation" levels of over 135,000 copies every year. As any long-standing *Raven* reader will tell you, whatever success *The Raven* has achieved has been in spite of its appearance — certainly not because of it. Indeed, for its first 12 years *The Raven* was typed on flimsy paper stencils that produced a woefully fuzzy, hard-to-read final product. Even worse from the staff's point of view, it had a soul-destroying, frequent tendency to turn to ink-saturated mush and disintegrate before the end of the print run. When that happened there was nothing for it but to sit down, often in the middle of the night, and type up another paper stencil from scratch — and with no guarantee that it would last any longer than its predecessor. In 1972 we acquired the ability to produce tougher rubber stencils by electronically scanning clean, original typescript, but it was another 15 years before the Park was finally able to abandon the mimeograph process and have *The Raven* printed by commercial printers in nearby towns. Even then, *The Raven* continued to be produced from typewriter originals, and only in 1989, when The Friends of Algonquin Park bought a computer for the Park Museum, did *The Raven* finally join the modern era of desktop publishing and achieve its present, reasonably professional appearance.

I think it is worthwhile to recall the less-than-impressive visual appearance that *The Raven*

PHOTO BY LYNN BALL

Dan Strickland.

had through most of its history because a case can be made that it was precisely the poor appearance that made a major contribution to *The Raven*'s success. *The Raven* has had only two writers, Russ Rutter from 1960 to 1973, and Dan Strickland from 1974 to the present. Both Russ and Dan were acutely aware that, in attempting to communicate their insights into the natural world through *The Raven*, they had almost nothing going for them except their own writing. There was no glossy paper or four-colour printing; there was no professional layout or design; and, until very recently, there was no time or talent to produce first-class illustrations — and no way to print them satisfactorily even if they had been available. No, the only hope Russ and Dan had of capturing and keeping the interest of their readers was to choose fascinating topics and write about them in the warmest, most engaging style possible. There were no crutches, no gimmicks — only the writers and the readers linked through those terribly hard-to-read, mimeographed sheets. I personally believe it was these less than ideal circumstances that brought out the very best in both Russ and Dan.

Of course, good writing consists of more than just an engaging style, and both writers of *The Raven* brought a second just as important ingredient to their work. Both

were true, self-taught naturalists (the only kind there is) with a long-standing and deep knowledge of the flora and fauna of Ontario in general and Algonquin Park in particular. This meant not only that they were personally familiar with all the main actors in the Algonquin ecosystems, but also that they had deep and often quite original insights into how the system operates. You will see examples of these insights throughout this book, and they, just as much as the warm personal style, are what set *Raven* articles apart from most contemporary writing in the natural history field. Indeed, Russ and Dan almost made it a point of honour never to write a *Raven* that merely repeated the basic, well-known facts of a plant's or animal's life history. To be sure, such facts might well emerge during the course of an article — and usually did — but there would always be a more fundamental principle or newly discovered phenomenon that would be discussed as well. I daresay this combination of fresh new information and original insights, illustrated through the example of familiar Algonquin animals and plants, is what makes *The Raven* just as popular among naturalists and biologists as it is among the general public.

Of course, not all the new slants and interpretations contained in *The Raven* over the years have been due to original insights by Russ or Dan. Indeed, they would be embarrassed to hear anyone suggest such a thing. Still, as keen naturalists, they were always quick to recognize an intriguing new idea, whether from their readings in the scientific literature or from personal contact with other naturalists and researchers, and they deserve credit for using *The Raven* to bring those ideas to a much broader public in a simple, interesting style. In particular, they have written many a fine article based on research done right in Algonquin Park at one or another of its three renowned research stations.*

I have mentioned Russ Rutter and Dan Strickland several times now, and I know many people will want to know about them, especially since no author's name has ever appeared on *The Raven* (except for a few issues in 1971). Russ was born in 1899 and grew up near Utterson, southwest of Huntsville. He fought in the First World War and worked for Ontario Hydro in Toronto until his retirement and return to the Huntsville area in 1957. Entirely self-educated in natural history, he was already well-known and respected in naturalist circles before he joined the Algonquin Park Museum staff as a summer naturalist in 1959.

He had many published natural history articles to his credit and was the natural choice among the staff to write *The Raven* when Grant Tayler came up with the idea the following year. This period was also the heyday of the

---

* *The three stations are the Harkness Laboratory of Fisheries Research on Lake Opeongo, the Wildlife Research Station on Lake Sasajewun, and the Forestry Research Station on Swan Lake. In addition to various articles in* **The Raven**, *readers are referred to the Hemlock Bluff Trail Guide, which summarizes several of the more notable research projects undertaken in the Park. A complete Algonquin research bibliography is also available from the Visitor Centre.*

first Algonquin wolf research program, and Russ became passionately interested in wolves and their preservation. He and the chief scientist in charge of the program, the late Dr. Douglas Pimlott, collaborated in producing one of the first and best books on wolves (*The World of the Wolf*, Lippincott & Co., Philadelphia) as a means of educating the public about the true nature of wolves and their role in the natural world. Back then the subject of wolves aroused almost violent emotions in many quarters, and I suppose it is a measure of the success of Russ and Doug's book, among many other initiatives, that today the subject hardly seems controversial anymore. Russ wrote *The Raven* until 1973 and died in Huntsville in 1976.

Dan Strickland was born in 1942 in Toronto. He grew up in Burlington and Mississauga as a keen amateur naturalist and was educated in Toronto and Montreal. After four summers as a summer naturalist in Quetico Provincial Park, he came to Algonquin in 1965 and went on permanent staff in 1970. He took over writing *The Raven* in 1974 and is still going strong 19 years and over 225 issues later. Some readers may recognize his name as principal author of the Park's well-known series of ecological trail guides, larger books, and map brochures, now published by The Friends of Algonquin Park.

Besides their authorship of *The Raven* over the last 34 years, Russ Rutter and Dan Strickland had another important thing in common. Shortly after he began working in the Park, Russ became intensely interested in Gray Jays — otherwise known as Canada Jays or Whiskeyjacks. Gray Jays live in the north woods of Canada all year 'round and actually nest in the late winter when the snow is still almost a metre deep. Russ applied the new technique of putting unique combinations of coloured bands on different Gray Jays so that he could recognize individual birds and follow their movements. He soon succeeded in finding nests (something very few people had ever done before) and began to flesh out the story of how, through the storage and recovery of food, this remarkable and most quintessentially Canadian bird makes a living amid the hostile conditions of the boreal forest. Russ's interest and early work on Gray Jays was so fascinating and raised so many interesting questions that Dan joined the study and has continued it to the present. Today Dan is recognized as the foremost authority on Gray Jays but will be the first to tell you that he never would have even begun to study them had it not been for the pioneering efforts of Russ Rutter. Thus, there is an interesting if entirely coincidental parallel in the history of Algonquin Park's newsletter and one of its longest-running biological field studies (on the Gray Jay). That both were started by Russ Rutter in the early 1960s and have been continued by Dan Strickland is one reason why the pictures we chose to present here of our two *Raven* authors show each man interacting with Gray Jays.

The purpose of this book is to introduce some of Russ's and Dan's best *Raven* articles as a fitting contribution by The Friends of Algonquin Park to the celebration of the Park Centennial. The following versions are much easier to read than the mimeographed originals, and I am delighted to add that the entire collection has been beautifully enhanced by the outstanding illustrations of Peter Burke. Peter is one of Ontario's finest wildlife illustrators and one of a long list of keen young naturalists who have worked in their formative years in the Algonquin Park interpretive program. Peter contributed many fine drawings to *The Raven* during his Algonquin stint (1988–1990), and we are most pleased that he was available to illustrate this special centennial collection. So, please, sit back and enjoy *The Best of The Raven*. Savour its insights, enjoy the puns, admire the drawings and, above all, treasure the great Park from which *The Raven* and this book draw their inspiration.

William C. Calvert
Chairman, The Friends of Algonquin Park (1983–1993)

How This Book Is Organized

For your convenience and ease in relocating specific articles, the 150 selections from *The Raven* that appear in this book have been presented in chronological order, by decade.

Footnotes and explanatory notes are added where we thought them useful. A Table of Contents appears on pages iii and iv and an index on page 220. Authorship is indicated by initials following the article (i.e., RR = Russ Rutter, DS = Dan Strickland).

The Loon

It would probably be correct to say that the Common Loon is the best known bird in Algonquin Park, that is, the one most often seen or heard by the most people. Nearly everyone who spends time here sees it, and it is almost impossible to be here long without hearing some or all of its loud, wild notes. For all that, the loon is seldom seen in detail close at hand, and few of us know much about its private life, where it goes in winter, and so on.

The loon belongs to an order of diving birds that also includes the grebes and auks, peculiarly adapted for an almost completely aquatic life. Their skeleton is long and somewhat rounded in outline, and is constructed so that it can withstand the great pressure encountered in deep water (loons are said to have been taken in fish nets 60 feet beneath the surface). When swimming under water they use both wings and feet, and they need to be very fast, as their food consists largely of fish, which are caught alive. Their wings are comparatively short but powerful, and their legs are attached to the body so far to the rear that they are unable to walk on land. They are also unable to take off from a hard surface, but must have a running start on the water before they can rise in flight. Our loon is quite a large bird — up to three feet from the tip of its bill to the end of its tail — and its wingspread may be close to five feet. This is considerably smaller than a Canada Goose but larger than our largest wild duck.

The loon makes its nest on the ground close to water, often so close that the sitting bird can slide off and swim away without any land travel. Sometimes there is a considerable nest of sticks and marsh grass, but not uncommonly just a hollow in the soft ground. Into this are laid two greenish or brownish eggs, and when the young loons hatch, in about 28 days, they are coal black and take to the water almost at once. From then on they follow their parents, bobbing around them like little black corks and sometimes stealing a ride on their mother's back. Loons' nests are subject to predation by such animals as coons and foxes, and although there are two eggs, we see a pair of loons with one young more often than with two. They hatch late — usually after the middle of July — and it is a race against time while the young birds grow sufficiently to be able to leave the home lake before freeze-up.

The migration of loons in Algonquin Park is largely regulated by ice conditions on the lakes. They may be seen here until November, and in spring they appear as soon as the lakes are open. There seems good reason to think that they would stay here all winter if there was sufficient open water, as they do not go to a warmer climate but spend the winter in the ocean off the east coast. There they find the kind of weather that seems to suit their wild and hardy nature, and the following quotation from an eye-witness on their winter territory gives us some idea of what it is like:

"Here, midway of the wide bay where the seas are running high and wildly tossing their white tops, with a wintry gale whipping the spray from them in smoky gusts, the loon rests at ease, head to the wind and sea, like a ship at anchor. The tossing and tumult disturb him not, as he rides, light as a birch bark canoe, turning up his white breast now and then as he reaches unconcernedly backward to preen his feathers. Often toward nightfall I have heard his wild storm-call against the black pall of an approaching tempest, like the howl of a lone wolf coming down the wind. Such is the loon in his winter home off our coast."

The food of the loon, as we have said, is largely fish, but it also takes frogs, crayfish, and water beetles. Most of the fish it catches are small, non-game species, but if it does occasionally catch a small trout or bass, we think there are few Park fishermen who would not gladly contribute a few fish to a bird that adds so much to the spirit of Algonquin.

August 30, 1961, Vol. 2, No. 11 (R.R.)

Algonquin Spring

How does spring come to the Algonquin Highlands? Not with a rush, as in more moderate climates, but slowly, little by little, with many setbacks and fresh starts, giving us an opportunity to see the whole process in detail and at leisure. From the time in late February when we first become conscious of lengthening days and a warmer sun until the last ice goes out of the lakes toward the end of April, what with recurring snowstorms, freezing nights, and snow still deep in the bush, there is no point at which we can say, "This is Spring." But there are enough signs to make us hopeful. Deer appearing again along the highway, a chipmunk track on a sunny hillside, a coon at the garbage pail, reports that somebody has seen a crow, a robin, or a Red-winged Blackbird. Then on some sunny morning we hear what we have been waiting for, the wild call of a returning loon, coasting down to his summer home on some newly opened lake, and we know that we are "in business" at last. Every morning now we hear the distant thunder of drumming grouse, the volume of bird song increases as more songsters return from the south, and it is time to look for the first flowers.

To those who are accustomed to wildflowers in the neighbourhood of Toronto, or Detroit, or Philadelphia, or even at Huntsville, only 25 miles from the Park boundary, their comparative scarcity on the Highlands of Algonquin could be disappointing. But when we know that the average altitude above sea-level here is from 500 to 1,000 feet higher than the surrounding country, which results in the average mean temperature being a few degrees lower, there is added interest, for we realize by what a narrow margin plants are able to survive and how the whole picture can be changed by what seems like a minor difference in external conditions. A good example is the White Trillium, which grows in abundance almost up to the Park gates and then stops, as definitely as if it had been denied entrance. Others that thrive outside but seem unable to climb the hill are hepatica, Wild Columbine, and Squirrel Corn.

It is really a little difficult to prove just what prohibits these plants from thriving here, but there is so much evidence in favour of altitude that it can hardly be doubted. Besides wildflowers, it affects certain trees and shrubs and some animals. Only this spring it was noted that when the early frogs were in full chorus both east and west of the Park, they were only beginning at the boundary and had not been heard at all in the central part. Many of our birds are a few days later arriving on the height of land in the vicinity of the Park Museum than at the East and West Gates.

All this may suggest that the Algonquin Highlands is a barren place, unrelieved by the beauty of spring wildflowers, but this is far from the truth. Those that do flourish here are hardy breeds, in keeping with their surroundings, and usually make up in numbers what they lack in variety of species. This makes it an ideal place for the beginning botanist to get a start.

Some of the most interesting early spring flowers are on shrubs and trees. Before the snow is gone, Red Maple, Hazel, and Alder are in bloom, and through April and May there is a steady succession of bloom. You will find an element of discovery in noticing a tree flower for the first time — they so often go unnoticed — as when you first see the strings of little golden bells hanging from Striped Maple, the tasselled flowers of Sugar Maple, or the unlikely looking candles that decorate some of the evergreens. Most of our herbaceous plants are of low growth, a typical adaptation to a harsh climate. Trailing Arbutus is a feature of Algonquin, especially on the east side; the tiny Twinflower and Flowering Wintergreen, or Fringed Polygala, both flourish abundantly, and Bunchberry, Canada Mayflower, Foam Flower, Star Flower, and Spring Beauty carpet the ground in many places. There is an invigorating quality about these tough little plants, blooming so soon after a long winter of deep snow, which seems to give them a character unknown to the larger and more luxuriant blossoms of softer climates.✐

May 1962 (Spring Issue) ,Vol. 3, No. 1 (R.R.)

The White Trillium, floral emblem of Ontario, is very rare on the highlands of Algonquin Park.

The Good Old Days

Back in 1893, the first year of Algonquin Park's official life, Park Headquarters was on Canoe Lake, and there were only two ways to reach it from Huntsville.

Both of them started out from Huntsville by steamer and proceeded to Lake of Bays, and there you had a choice. You could take a wagon at Dorset and ride over 22 miles of lumber road (said to be "wretchedly made") to South Tea Lake, from where you could paddle to Canoe Lake; or you could start from Dwight by canoe and paddle all the way up the Oxtongue River. First, you portaged seven miles to Oxtongue Lake, then around two falls and countless rapids, and after 10 and one-half hours work you had reached South Tea Lake. If you still felt like it, you could go on to Park Headquarters, but you could stay at a lumber camp on South Tea if necessary. The Park highway doesn't look so bad after all.◦

July 25, 1962 ,Vol. 3, No. 6 (R.R.)

Forty Years Ago

"A summer day is long in Algonquin Park, inviting to outdoor pastimes of all descriptions. The nights are cool and restful, with clear lakes reflecting the great stars that hang low in the northern skies and there is silence, except for an occasional fluted call, the dip of feeding trout or bass, and the subdued song of water and stirring leaves. If you would experience such summer days as these, visit Algonquin Park, drink in with your lungs the air of its heights, with
your eyes behold its manifold beauties, and you will become a lover of this big unspoiled forest of the Ontario Highlands."

The above was written just 40 years ago, in 1923, as publicity for the Canadian National Railways, which at that time provided the only access, at least in the southern part of the Park. It fits today's situation reasonably well, but some things were different. Stage coaches carried passengers from the Highland Inn, the railway's big hotel at Cache Lake, to Smoke Lake and Burnt Island Lake, for a fare of $1.00 each way. Visitors had free camping privileges anywhere, but no motor boats were allowed in the Park. Strange to say, a resident fishing licence cost $3.00 and a non-resident $5.00, 40 years ago. Of course, fishermen were allowed to catch more fish and there were more fish to catch than there are now, but the record bass then was six pounds, and we heard of one of the same weight being caught just the other day.◦

July 17, 1963, Vol. 4, No. 5 (R.R.)

Oldtimers

As far as we know, the record for summer camping in Algonquin Park is held by Mr. and Mrs. James Gross of Guelph, Ontario, who are now at Two Rivers Campground for their 18th consecutive year. Even in that far-off time they came here on the recommendation of some friends who had travelled the winding dirt road through the Park and reported back full of enthusiasm for its scenery, climate, and wildlife.

On their next holiday they stopped off at Two Rivers and hacked out their own campsite on the heavily wooded shore where the present crowded campground is now located. There were five tents there at that time, and the only charge was $1.00 for a travel permit.

Mr. Gross recalls there was a path through the woods around the shore of the lake, and that this led to a long log bridge that crossed the marsh at the west end of the lake to the saw-mill, which had been operating there a short time before. The site of the present beach had long been used as a dump for logs on their way to the mill, and the ground was covered by a thick layer of bark fragments.

The Gross's have watched the present campground grow up around them but have no complaints about the changed condition. They have made many friends among "repeaters" such as themselves and have no intention of making a change, although they have paid brief visits to many other Ontario campgrounds.

Can anyone tie this record?◦

July 31, 1963,Vol. 4, No. 7 (R.R.)

Wolf Hunt*

A new feature in Park interpretation will be introduced by the Park naturalist staff on Thursday, August 15, when campers and other Park visitors will be invited to take part in an evening of "wolf-listening" along Highway 60. This will not be a strenuous outing. Those taking part will be able to remain in their cars most of the time, simply joining a cavalcade along the highway while Park naturalists try to establish contact with wolves by the use of vocal and recorded wolf howls. Fortunately for students of these animals, wolves will usually howl when they hear other wolves, and this method of locating them — by playing recorded howls — has been in use for some time.

An interest in the wolf and a desire to know more about it has been evident for some time among our summer visitors, and Park naturalists believe that an important element of the Algonquin environment is being neglected if people do not become better acquainted with what is perhaps the Park's most interesting animal. In Algonquin Park, where there is no hunting, wolves play an important part in regulating the deer population. They also contribute much to that spirit of "wildness" that is one of the attractions of the Park. To hear a wild pack howling in the night is a never-to-be-forgotten experience.

Present plans call for meeting at the Two Rivers Picnic Area, Mile 22, at about 9:00 p.m. on August 15. If the weather is unfavourable, the program will be scheduled for the following night. Wolves are unpredictable, a perfect illustration of the old saying, "Here today, gone tomorrow," but we think there is a better than even chance of hearing them howl before the evening is over. Final plans will be confirmed in next week's *Raven*, and announcements will also be made at evening programs and conducted hikes.

August 7, 1963, Vol. 4, No. 8 (R.R.)

---

* This short announcement launched the Park's famous program of Public Wolf Howls. Now, 30 years later, over 65,000 people have participated in such expeditions, with a success rate of over 66 per cent. It is probably safe to say that more people have had first-hand contact with wolves in Algonquin Park, thanks to this program, than any other place in the world.

Should We Still Be Pioneers?

It has always been the fashion to admire our ancestors for their resourcefulness in carving homes out of the wilderness and for their ingenuity in improvising tools, furniture, and other needs to make themselves comfortable in a land completely covered by forest. But the modern camper too often shows his admiration by demonstrating that he, too, can live at least partly off the country, by building a lean-to of branches or making camp furniture from green poles cut from the woods. What harm can these few things do to a vast wilderness?

The fact is that today real wilderness is not so vast as we may think, and what we carve out of it to show our pioneering spirit may spoil other people's opportunity to enjoy it as wilderness. The scars of our woodcraft may last a lot longer than we do.

We who grew up believing that the best camper is the one who knows how to make the most things out of the small trees surrounding his camp have some unlearning to do. Our admiration today should be reserved not for the person who makes his mark upon the country but for the one who knows how to camp without leaving a mark. Today, we need to make our mark on the wilderness as obscure as possible; our ideal should be to leave the wilderness as we found it. We have to learn — and help others to learn — how to enjoy wilderness by adapting ourselves to the environment rather than adapting the environment to ourselves.

Our ingenuity and resourcefulness should be spent on making up camping equipment we can take in with us and bring out again that will keep us comfortable while we are there, without interfering with native materials. We need greater skill in covering up our tracks than in establishing a permanent reminder of our having been there. The next user can better enjoy a campsite if he or she can maintain some illusion that no one else has camped there before.

Not the least of the benefits of wilderness is the concept of immortality that one may gain in contemplating an ecologically balanced community — an area in which plants and animals live out their lives undisturbed and then return their substance to the soil for the support of new life.

Whether he likes it or not, man is still a part of the natural community. It is a saddening thought that he is just about the only living creature who often sets out to deliberately destroy his own environment. We should think about it.✎

August 28, 1963, Vol. 4, No. 11 (R.R.)

La Belle Bonnechère

If you would see the headwaters of the Bonnechère River, which rises near White Partridge Lake in the east central part of the Park, you must be prepared to travel far with a canoe on your back. There is good water there, but the portages are long and the hills are high, and it is no place for the easy traveller. You should also know something of the country because travel off established routes in Algonquin Park can be extremely frustrating at any time if you are unfamiliar with the lay of the land. There is always the unexpected beaver pond or the stream that looks big on the map but will not float a canoe.

We were lucky when we went in, for we had as a guide a man — whom we shall call The Woodsman* — who had known this country years before and had roamed over it literally foot by foot. He had a phenomenal memory for landmarks, and knew not only the gross features of the landscape but many individual trees, rocks, beaver ponds, deer trails, and other marks that help a man to find his way in the bush.

---

* The "woodsman" referred to here was Emmett Chartrand, a colourful lumberjack and trapper from the village of Madawaska south and east of Algonquin. For years Emmett worked at the original Pioneer Logging Exhibit and shared his knowledge of the bush with Park staff and visitors alike.

One of the purposes of this trip was to look for (The Woodsman would have said "to bring out," for he never doubted his ability to find them) a pair of skidding tongs from the old square timber days, which he had found and hung in a tree more than 20 years before. We paddled across lakes, threaded our way over little-used portages, and walked across beaver dams, and at last found the clue we were seeking — the remnant of an old logging road that started at the base of a huge heavily wooded hill, sloping up steeply on our left. From here it was easy — for The Woodsman. First there was an ancient skidway, then a faint deer trail leading up the hill, then a skidding trail, grown up with trees and filled with dead leaves, and then the tongs, looking as if they might have been hung there yesterday, except for a groove in the limb on which they hung, caused by the continuous weight for 26 years.

For the benefit of the uninitiated, perhaps it should be explained that dragging a log through the bush to a convenient loading place is called "skidding," and a skidway is a framework of logs flat on the ground on which the skidded logs are piled and from which they are loaded onto a conveyance that will take them the next stage of their journey to the mills. In this case they would have been dumped on the ice of the Bonnechère, to be floated downstream on the spring floods. All log hauling was done in winter in the early days of lumbering, since it was much easier to make a sleigh road in the snow than to construct a road for wheeled vehicles, and much heavier loads could be pulled by horses on a sleigh.

This Bonnechère country is dotted with rotting skidways, for it was on the timber limits of the McLachlin Brothers, one of the earliest companies to penetrate deep into what is now Algonquin Park in the days of the Big Pine. A mile from the tong site we located one of their camboose camps, now outlined by 40-foot long mounds of earth that once were walls, and in the centre the camboose itself. Originally made of wood and stones, it now supports a luxuriant growth of round-leaved dogwood, apparently thriving in the deep accumulation of ashes, as we saw it nowhere else in the neighbourhood. The ashes puzzled us for a moment, for they had hardened into a semi-solid material resembling low-grade concrete. A couple of worn-out crosscut saws, the rusted skeleton of a pail, parts of a tobacco box put together with square nails, and a crumbling river-driver's boot were all we could find to tell of the roaring activity that once went on here when the lumberjacks gathered around the camboose to dry their sox (sic), smoke their pipes, and play their lusty games.

This is still pine country. Red and White Pine of medium to large size grow to the water's edge around the lakes and cover the beautiful islands. Surely it should always be peaceful here, we thought, as we paddled down the last pine-rimmed lake on the way out, past a pair of loons that were serenading us with their wild music, a family of seven mergansers lined up on a log to see us off, and a mother otter with three kits playing among the driftwood in a little bay.

There are lakes here that have never heard the sound of a motor boat, much less the roar of highway traffic, and we shuddered to think of what these lakes might become if the human pressure for more and more recreational space continues to grow and is not controlled. It is protected now because it is all but inaccessible, but every realist knows that it can happen here without controlled access. As we beached the canoe under overhanging Red Pines and took a last look at the flat-topped dome of Bonnechère Bluff, we speculated on the possibility of some kind of guided tours into this kind of country, so rich in

human history and at the same time a sample of pure wilderness. Something, perhaps after the fashion of the pack horse tours of the western mountains but using canoes instead of horses. Just a dream, but a pleasant thought on which to end the day.⌀

August 28, 1963, Vol. 4, No. 11 (R.R.)

Emmett Chartrand, woodsman.

Highway Deer

In the past two or three years there have been increasing enquiries from visitors to Algonquin Park about the noticeable decrease in the number of deer to be seen along the road. Since this highway was completed in the 1930s, the popularity of Algonquin Park as a camping and general holiday area has grown year by year, and along with this has been established what now amounts almost to a tradition — the practice of feeding and photographing roadside deer tame enough to take food from the hand. This practice continues, but there is no denying the fact that it has greatly diminished, simply because the deer are not where they used to be and many of those now seen are less tame than formerly. This has been a matter of real concern to the Wildlife and Parks people of the Department of Lands and Forests, who would be as pleased as summer tourists if the deer would continue in their old ways. There are, however, a number of reasons why this cannot be so, and we thought a summary of the whole situation would interest readers of *The Raven*. We think most people would prefer to keep the forests and wildlife of Algonquin Park as natural as possible. So let us consider briefly the food and habits of a natural deer.

The White-tailed Deer, which is the correct name for our species, is a forest-dwelling animal, living on a wide variety of vegetable food — beech-nuts, acorns, wild mushrooms, grass, clover, aquatic plants, and the twigs of a great many kinds of shrubs and trees. This last item, generally called "browse," is the deer's only food in winter and forms a large part of it through the year. For that reason deer thrive best in young forests, such as might follow lumbering or forest fires, where there is plenty of fresh, low growth. As the forest matures and the growing parts of trees get beyond their reach, the deer feed mostly about the edges or along roads and other clearings. They are to a large extent nocturnal, feeding mostly in late evening, night, and early morning and remaining undercover, often lying down, through the day. Keen senses and a great running ability protect them from enemies, and in completely natural surroundings we are

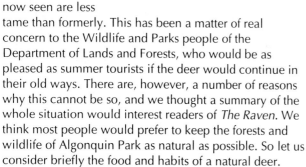

The Algonquin Park version of a drive-in restaurant.

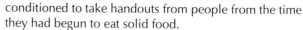

lucky to catch a glimpse of a deer, even where they are plentiful.

For many years before the highway was put through, the business and social life of Algonquin Park was centred on Cache Lake. Administration buildings, homes of permanent staff, a railway station, and the Highland Inn made a sizeable community. Local deer soon acquired the habit of eating scraps from the hotel and department kitchens and of being fed by guests who came in by rail to the Inn. An important point is that this went on 365 days in the year for a long period, and gradually built up what became known as the Cache Lake deer herd. Even with good luck, few deer live to be more than 10 years old, so by the time the highway came, most of the deer in the Cache Lake herd had been born and raised there, and had been conditioned to take handouts from people from the time they had begun to eat solid food.

When people started driving through the Park, the deer soon learned to associate cars with food, and the people learned that the place to look for deer was near Cache Lake. Then Highland Inn was torn down, diverting more deer to the highway, but at the same time kitchen scraps from the department staffhouse encouraged many of them to stay around all winter. Up to 1960, deer were to be seen along the road all winter, and if a car so much as slowed down they came running for food. But in 1960, Park Headquarters was moved to the East Gate, and what remained of the Cache Lake deer herd had only visitors to rely on for the apples, carrots, bread, cake, soda biscuits, and all the other items that were quite unnatural for a deer but to which they had become accustomed. Even this was available for only three months of the year. In the other nine months the deer were obliged to revert to a natural life, which included withdrawing from the highway to sheltered "yards" in winter, wandering farther in search of their natural foods in spring and fall and retiring to secluded cover during the day. It is safe to say that there are now few "cultivated" deer left, and the animals we see this summer are more natural than those we have known in the past.

We believe that the circumstances just described have had the greatest influence on the so-called scarcity of deer, but this is not the whole story. Many things about the food and habits of deer are not yet well understood, and studies are constantly in progress to improve our knowledge. Inevitable changes in roadside vegetation could be an important factor, as could the extensive construction work of the past few years. It is too early to finally assess the effect of the cut-back forest; theoretically, at least, it should be beneficial because of the new growth arising from the removal of trees. This would not necessarily result in seeing more deer, if they have lost the cultivated habit of coming out to look for food in the daytime. In a co-operative effort of the Departments of Highways and of Lands and Forests, clover was planted on selected areas of roadside last year, but the reaction was not all that was hoped. During last fall and even far into the winter, deer ate the clover extensively — pawing large holes in the snow to reach it — but although the clover has grown luxuriantly this year, it has had little if any effect on the number of deer seen. Systematic road surveys, mostly at night, indicate that there has been no significant decline in the number of deer over the past five years, but they are now

distributed from one side of the Park to the other and not concentrated in one place. Late last fall, after most people had left the Park and following a summer when complaints of deer scarcity were heard every day, deer were abundant every night along the highway from the East to the West Gates. All this seems to confirm the idea that it is a change of habits rather than an absence of deer.

Then there is the question of wolves, but we are not going to go into that controversial subject. We will say, however, that if there is one thing professional students of wolves and deer are sure of, it is that wolves are not an important factor in the current situation.

It is likely there will always be deer to be seen along the highway through Algonquin Park, and there will always be some that will learn to take food from the hand during summer. Perhaps we should learn to appreciate the difference between winning the confidence of a real wild animal and feeding a lot of tame deer who might almost as well be in a zoo.❧

July 1, 1964, Vol. 5, No. 2 (R.R.)

Thirty Years Ago

With all the new blacktop road in the Park at present, it seems a good time to mention the transportation situation of 1936. Then we were still concerned about encouraging people to come here and to lease land for cottages, a practice that has long since been discontinued.

In June 1936, the new road in from Huntsville was said to be in fine condition, maintained by a grader that operated three times a week. From Cache Lake to Whitney the road was rough but passable, except after heavy rain. Little work had been done toward the

preparation of campgrounds, but for the benefit of leaseholders it was planned to build 15 garages at Cache Lake, 15 at Canoe Lake, six at Smoke Lake, and eight at Whitefish Lake. During the summer of 1936, 3809 cars checked in through the West Gate.

Canadian National Railways was still operating three passenger trains a week between Cache Lake and Scotia Junction, coming into the Park on Tuesdays, Thursdays, and Saturdays and going out on Mondays, Wednesdays, and Fridays. Trains from the east came in as far as Lake of Two Rivers, from where passengers had to arrange their own transportation. There were two freight trains a week with no regular schedule.❧

June 29, 1966, Vol. 7, No. 2 (R.R.)

In the early days Highway 60 was a highway in name only.

Thoughts From Abroad

*A recent visitor here was a lady from Glasgow, Scotland, and when we learned she had come to Algonquin Park particularly to see or hear our timber wolves, we thought her impressions of the Canadian environment would be of interest to readers of **The Raven**. The result is the contribution that follows.*

The last wolf howled in Scotland in 1743. Bear, moose, and reindeer had already gone by the 13th century, and beaver by the 15th.

Yet even 250 years ago a writer described Sutherland — a remote area of the northwest mainland — as rich in game and general wildlife. He mentions Red and Roe Deer, marten, weasel, fox, wolf, polecat, eagle, osprey, and several kinds of falcon. Generous woodlands then gave them cover, but today there is scarcely a tree left in that region, and little can be heard but the croak of ravens and the interminable bleating of sheep that can barely make a living from the eroded landscape. Visitors come from all parts of the world to admire the scenery, but, picturesque as it may be, what they are looking at now is chiefly a manmade desert. The pine forests have gone; the beaver dams are broken; and the silt they held washed away to the sea long ago.

Hunters and fishermen from the south demanded the removal of all predators, in the mistaken idea there would then be more and more grouse to shoot and more salmon to catch. They were successful in removing the predators, but they are now reduced to consulting scientists of the Nature Conservancy, seeking a reason for the continued decline of the grouse. During the winter, starving and overcrowded Red Deer, stunted from lack of proper food elements, raid the farmers' potato pits, and in their frantic efforts to reach this food, expose what they do not eat to frost, often causing heavy losses.

There are few parks in Britain such as you know here — none larger than a few square miles. I have sat on a hilltop there and absorbed the beautiful scenery, but there was always something lacking. A wolf or two would make all the difference, or even a bear. Then one day a sympathizer sent me a clipping from a Canadian magazine describing the research being done on wolves in Algonquin Park. Why, people even went wolf-howling for a pastime! I decided then that I must go as soon as circumstances permitted to hear for myself the song of a wild wolf pack.

Perhaps I have been more lucky than some, but within two weeks of landing in Canada I had experienced the lifetime thrill of hearing a wild pack answer the call of an expert howler. I had even been introduced to the captive wolves and had my nose licked by these most loving and lovable creatures. During the next few days I had seen a bear (not the garbage dump bear, but my own bear) and watched the beaver swimming with a load of poplar branches. All three animals have not been seen in Britain for hundreds of years.

You in Canada have such wonderful opportunities to see and hear wildlife at your own doorstep. It is all there, if you will take the trouble to find it, but it should not be taken for granted. The forces that destroyed so much in Britain are still active, only the momentum of change has increased so much in recent times that what took hundreds of years in Scotland might be accomplished in a few years on this continent. If you are content just to drive through the Park and feed the deer, picnic at the roadside, or camp overnight, you have little to worry about. The facilities could not be better. But I think everyone should sometimes ask the question, "What is a national or provincial park? What is its prime purpose?" I liked the definition that I read recently: "to maintain or restore to, as nearly as possible, the original condition that prevailed when the area was first visited by white men; these areas to be for the perpetual enjoyment, the educational and spiritual enrichment, of Canadians and their guests."

The amateur naturalist today is no longer typified as the "absent-minded professor" with a butterfly net. We are recognized as a group of people concerned about the preservation of wilderness areas as national treasures, and perhaps our greatest danger is that we may be too absent-minded.

Other interests have formed powerful groups so that their combined voices might be heard, and we might very well do likewise. As a visitor it is not my place to say what you should do here — I do not even know the extent of the need for such action. I do know what has happened in many places throughout the world, and that you do not want the time to come when you, too, will be looking at an empty landscape with the nagging feeling that something has gone — forever.☙

July 22, 1964, Vol. 5, No. 5 (R.R.)

Bands Right and Left

Although attempts had been made as early as 1750 to place some sort of identification on migratory birds in order to learn something of their travels, organized banding — the placing of serially numbered aluminum bands on birds' legs — did not play an important part in bird study until the late 1800s in Europe and the early 1920s in North America. Today there are tens of thousands of banders spread over nearly every country in the world, most of them working on a voluntary basis, and it would be difficult to exaggerate the importance of information obtained from banding, both to those administering our game bird resources and to those who study birds for the advancement of pure knowledge.

Banding is not a big operation here, as this Park does not attract large numbers of migratory waterfowl. It is ideal, however, for studies of the day-to-day living habits of many kinds of birds, and banding is widely used in such work. For several years now a banding project originating at the Park Museum has been marking Gray Jays with numbered aluminum bands and coloured plastic bands, and much new and interesting information about these fascinating birds is being accumulated.* The Gray Jay is the gray, black, and white bird that comes so boldly around our picnic tables, and it is known to many people as Canada Jay or Whiskeyjack (from the Indian

---

* In this short article Russ Rutter alerted Park visitors to his pioneering study of Gray Jays and to the newly applied technique of colour banding. See a much later article (Sept. 5, 1991, page 198) for some of the discoveries eventually made during the study.

"Wiskedjak"). Among other things, it has been learned that these birds do not travel very far from their home range, and there are banded birds around now that have been in the same area for at least seven years.

You may see Gray Jays with just one aluminum band, usually on the right leg. Others have a coloured plastic band on the same leg with the aluminum, or either one or two coloured bands on the left leg. For example, a jay with a green band above a white band on the left leg and an aluminum band on the right leg has been reported several times from the Kearney Campground area. This bird was banded in March, 1967, opposite the entrance to Pog Lake Campground. It is known in our records as GOWL (green over white on left leg). Since we use green, orange, white, blue, yellow, and red bands, we come up with some odd names for our birds. What we are leading up to is that if you see OOGL, BOBL, GOYL, BOYL, YOBL, or any others and report the time and place at the Park Museum, you will be making a real contribution to ornithological research.⤳

July 19, 1967, Vol. 8, No. 6 (R.R.)

The Adventures of Phoebe

Phoebe is sometimes used as a girl's name, more commonly a generation or two ago than now, but the Phoebe whose adventures are related here is a gray, sparrow-sized bird that raised two families this year in nests fastened to museum buildings.

The Phoebe is a flycatcher, and its name is pronounced "fee-bee." But one of our tree-nesting flycatchers, of similar size and colour, is called a Pewee, yet in each case the name is an attempt to imitate the bird's song. One says "pee-wee" and we call it a Pewee; the other says "fee-bee" and we call it a Phoebe. All of which suggests that the American Ornithologists' Union, the learned body that changed the name of our well-known Canada Jay to just plain Gray Jay, is not as consistent as it seems to think. The name "Phoebe" has nothing to do with the goddess of that name in classical mythology, but that's from where the curious spelling comes.

Although it is widely distributed throughout Algonquin Park, the Phoebe can hardly be called a common bird here. It makes its nest on buildings, bridges, rock ledges, or cut banks, but in the last 10 years it has nested at the Museum only three times — 1962, 1967, and 1968.

Their first nest this year was on a beam over the door of the ladies' washroom (where they built last year), but this effort came to a bad end. Before the first egg was laid, one of the pair was found dead on the ground near the nest. As there is no difference in plumage between male and female Phoebes and the dead bird was past the stage where dissection was possible, we could not be certain which one of the pair had been lost. The remaining bird

A Phoebe's nest on the washroom building of the old Park Museum.

stayed nearby but did not pay any attention to the nest, and in a few days it was seen with a new partner.

But they didn't go on with the old nest. Instead, they went away over to the other side of the staffhouse and built on a narrow ledge above an upper window, far from the reach of anything without wings. In just over a month, young flew from that nest, and within days, while the male looked after the fledglings, the female returned to the abandoned nest on the washroom and soon had another set of eggs incubating. As *The Raven* goes to press this week, the young of this brood are sitting on the edge of the nest, ready to try their wings any time. So the museum Phoebes have added eight or 10 young birds to the population this year, in spite of their early setback.

The Phoebe may not know how to spell its name, but it knows how to say it, and does so, loud, clear, and often, in spring and early summer. Bird watchers would be happier if all other birds would do the same.✎

July 24, 1968, Vol. 9, No. 6 (R.R.)

The Question Is:

should the deer of Algonquin Park be allowed to interfere with the defence of our country?

About a week ago a couple of long military convoys drove through the Park, and after the main body had passed we saw two or three of their vehicles parked beside the road near Smoke Lake. Surely a mechanical breakdown, we thought. But no; along with the other folks the boys were feeding a deer.

Come to think of it, our defence is probably in good hands; but we wonder what explanation they had prepared for their Commanding Officer.✎

July 16, 1969, Vol. 10, No. 5 (R.R.)

A Sad Story

About the first of December 1970, a pack of wolves killed a deer 100 yards from the highway near Mile 25 in Algonquin Park. The ground had been snow-covered a week before, but there had been mild weather with rain, and it was bare when the kill was made. Although workmen had reported seeing wolves chasing a deer near this place, news of an actual kill did not reach Park authorities until nearly a week later. At that time an immature Golden Eagle and several Ravens were seen feeding on what was left of the deer, by then under nearly a foot of snow.

There is nothing unusual about wolves killing a deer. It is a perfectly natural part of the Park's ecology, and except for those engaged in some kind of research involving these animals, no attempt is made to investigate every kill that is reported. So it was chiefly with the idea of

Poisoned wolves, December 1970.

checking on the eagle, which really is unusual, that the Park naturalist went to the scene. After verifying the eagle, he decided to examine the remains of the deer but soon found more than he had bargained for. In the snow near the dismembered carcass were two dead Ravens and a third that was dying. An ominous picture had begun to take shape and was soon completed by finding the tip of a wolf's tail sticking up through the snow and the uncovering of its frozen body.

Subsequent laboratory analysis showed that the wolf had been killed by strychnine, a powerful and deadly poison that attacks the central nervous system, causing fairly quick but extremely violent and painful death.

There was only one way this could have happened. Somebody with more hatred for wolves than concern for Algonquin's wildlife had found the kill soon after it occurred and had scared the wolves from their meal long enough to insert a generous quantity of poison.

Frequent snowfalls hampered further investigation, but repeated searches over the next few weeks brought the final score to five dead wolves, four Ravens, and one fox. As all meat-eating animals are attracted to wolf kills, it is almost certain there were others that have not been found.

We have called this a sad story, but the sadness is not for the animals killed. They live in a harsh world, where sudden death often is commonplace, and they have long since learned to cope with such losses. The sadness is that there are still so many men who ignore all the facts of scientific research and think that dead wolves will make live deer. In Algonquin's early years, Park Superintendent's annual reports always referred to the abundance of deer and wolves. But wolves were shot, poisoned, snared, and trapped, and a great amount of money was wasted on useless endeavours to eliminate them. The number of deer available regulates wolf numbers more than wolf predation regulates the number of deer. There will not be more or fewer deer in the Park next year because five wolves were poisoned. There may be, however, fewer wolves to howl next August for the thousands of campers who get their most vital Park experience by going out with us to hear them.

A more immediate loss is two Raven nests that we found each year. At this time they should contain young birds, but neither site is occupied.

Ravens come back year after year to the same cliff, often repairing last year's nest, and although they may range widely in winter in search of food, like all permanent residents they tend to remain near the home territory if food is available there. Both sites were within a few miles of this kill, and the reason they are not in use this spring seems obvious.

Fifty years ago wolves were being poisoned by Park rangers, and the Raven population was all but wiped out. It is only in recent years that they have come back to normal numbers.

And although the Golden Eagle was able to fly away, it seems doubtful that it escaped a lethal dose. This eagle, known around the world as the King of Birds, is now so rare in Ontario that the loss of even one bird is a matter of some concern.

All of which should surely add to the self-esteem of the man who did the job.⇨

May 7, 1971, Vol. 12, No. 1 (R.R.)

A Peek at the Past

At the present time discussions are going on all over the world on how best to administer undeveloped areas so that full use may be made of their natural resources without destroying their natural aspect. With the ever-growing pressures of human populations and demands for outdoor recreation, this situation is likely to continue indefinitely, or as long as there are wild places left to administer. Discussion and controversy on such matters are not new, and it is interesting and at this distance sometimes amusing to look back at some of the difficulties, now long outdated, that had to be overcome in our own Algonquin Park.

As everybody knows who has seen the audio-visual presentation at the Visitor Centre, this park was established in 1893, when it had been penetrated only by hunters, trappers, and lumbermen, and large parts of it remained almost untouched.

The original reserve covered only 18 townships, compared with 32 and parts of six others at present. The only access, other than by canoe, was over the rough roads of the lumbermen coming up from the Ottawa Valley. But the village of Dwight on the west already had a steamboat service on Lake of Bays, 15 miles from the Park's west boundary, and it was from this direction by canoe up the Oxtongue River that the first Park Superintendent came with his staff of four rangers in 1893 to establish the first headquarters on Canoe Lake.

The setting aside of such a big area as a wildlife and forest reservation created an acute problem. There was no trouble with the lumber companies, for it was never intended that lumbering would be stopped in the Park, and the lumber industries welcomed the protection from fire that would result from the change. But there were several hundred men in the surrounding country who had for years derived a good part of their living from hunting and trapping, and they strongly resented any restrictions.

Attempting to control poaching made up a large part of the early Algonquin Park ranger's work, and this was strenuous when the only means of travel was by canoe and on foot in summer and on snowshoes in winter. Things were made even worse in 1908, when the Department decided to harvest Park furs as an addition to revenue by having the rangers trap during the fall and winter. It was apparent that this not only aroused the poachers to greater efforts but opened the way for various malpractices often involving the rangers

themselves. This unfortunate situation was allowed to continue until 1920, when all trapping in the area was made illegal. Poaching continued to be a serious problem, however, through the depression of the 1930s, but now that the Park is patrolled from the air and the eastern half divided into registered traplines, it is only a minor annoyance.

During the First World War, two other ventures that seem to us with our current views of Park use almost incredible were undertaken. By 1917 the war had been in progress for three years, and there was a great shortage of fresh meat both in Canada and the United Kingdom. There was a tremendous deer population in the Park at the time, thriving on the young forests that followed lumbering and the ensuing fires, and the Park Superintendent suggested using deer to help relieve the meat shortage. His report for the year 1918 shows that 650 deer were shipped that year to dealers in Toronto and other southern cities where the meat scarcity was acute.

In the last year of the war the shortage of coal was being felt, and the cutting of wood for fuel was then undertaken by a number of municipalities. Again, Algonquin came to the rescue, and new railway sidings were built to facilitate shipping. Not only did local contractors take advantage of this opportunity, but other municipalities were granted the privilege, and cutters soon arrived from places as far away as Guelph and Hamilton. Fortunately, the war ended in the fall of 1918, the ensuing winter was mild, and that was the end of the wood-cutting.

Times change, and for all our problems now, we think the Park is safer today than it was then.☙

June 30, 1971, Vol. 12, No. 3 (R.R.)

A wagonload of deer waiting to be shipped by rail from Algonquin to alleviate the meat shortage in Toronto, 1917.

Bird-Waiting Pays Off

Goshawk eating a nestling kingbird.

The Goshawk is one of the more unusual hawks in Algonquin Park, and we have only one definite record of its nesting here. This is a large, powerful bird, one of the accipiters hawks that hunt by low, direct attack rather than the watchful waiting for prey common to most large hawks. Its strength and boldness made it a favourite in the ancient sport of falconry. If we see more than one or two in a year, we consider it exceptional.

The other day one of our young naturalists, prowling alone in the Sunday Creek bog, sat down in a dry spot to see what might turn up if he stopped looking for it, and a few minutes later an adult Goshawk appeared and perched on a nearby stump. Presently it dropped into the grass and caught something, which could not be identified, and after eating this it returned to the stump. Here it was being attacked by a pair of kingbirds, which made it duck from their swooping but could not drive it away. Then it was noticed the kingbirds had a nest close by in a tree, and at this point the Goshawk flew up to this and removed a young bird, which it carried back to the stump and ate. It then returned for a second helping, but after eating that it flew away across the marsh and disappeared. It seemed not the least concerned about the man who sat watching, a few yards away.

This was one of those once-in-a-lifetime things that bird-watchers live for, but as might be expected, our naturalist, although skilled in photography, had for once gone out without his camera. So he can only tell us about it, like the fisherman who tells of the big one that got away; but we believe him.

This little story is a superb illustration of one of the useful techniques of bird-watching. To see birds close-up, going about their normal chores, find a comfortable place in bird country, cover yourself with fly dope, and just sit there. The only equipment needed is patience, if possible a pair of binoculars and, if you take pictures, a camera.◌

July 7, 1971, Vol. 12, No. 4 (R.R.)

"Hew to the Line"

As with many old "sayings," the above has become a part of our language, but its origin has been forgotten. Saws for cutting the trunks of trees into various shapes are of comparatively modern origin, but axes have been used since earliest recorded history. Long before saws were invented, logs could be used more efficiently if they were square instead of round, and the practice of hewing off the rounded sides to form a square timber came into general use. The first crop of big pines that were removed from the Algonquin region were squared in the bush, built into huge rafts, and floated down the rivers to the outside world.

The first step in squaring a log was to draw a straight line along one side and with an axe hew off all the wood outside the line. The axeman had to be skilled enough to cut in to the line but no further. Thus, "hewing to the line" came to mean consistently following a straight course.◌

August 18, 1971, Vol. 12, No. 10 (R.R.)

Felix Luckasavitch of Whitney preparing a timber for squaring at the old Pioneer Logging Exhibit.

Wilderness Opera

Is wolf-howling to become a part of the general field of entertainment, like opera, symphonic concerts, and ballet? How can we maintain a wilderness atmosphere when the audience breaks into applause, as it did on our last howl after the wolves responded with a stirring encore? Will the time come when an applause meter to measure our success will be necessary equipment? Whether or not, we found the incident inspiring but suggest that applause be withheld till after the encore, to make sure the wolves are not distracted from giving one.

Anyway, surely this was a "first." Was there ever another occasion, anywhere in the world, when 1,000 people applauded the howling of a pack of wolves in their native habitat? We think not. We have frequently emphasized how much the difference between success and failure in wolf-howling depends on luck, that is, on the behaviour of things beyond our control. If it doesn't rain; if it is calm; if the wolves are in the right place. … Considering all the ifs and the way the wolves have kept us guessing between howls, we have been almost unbelievably lucky this year. Two good answers out of three tries equals a batting average of .667 in any league, so, although luck is nothing if not fickle, we just have to try again. So far we have had standing room only crowds, so next time come early if you like to sit. ∞

Aug. 30, 1972, Vol. 13, No. 11 (R.R.)

A New Algonquin Feature

This Park does not lie within the "tornado belt," which, according to a reliable reference book, is "within a 500-mile radius of southern Missouri." However, we do have meteorological phenomena that fit into the definition of a tornado, which is "a localized violently destructive windstorm occurring over land." On the ocean a tornado turns into a waterspout; on the desert, a dust devil; and on snow, a snow devil. The word is also a synonym for "whirlwind," although usage confines it to a particular kind of whirlwind. Small whirlwinds are seen quite often on areas of light sand, dry snow, or the surface of a lake.

Although we know it can't be literally true that "Algonquin Park has everything," we sometimes make that claim to emphasize its many attractions, and are always glad to add any new feature that may bring it nearer to the truth. So we quote the following colorful description from a recent news release supplied by our District Office:

"Late in July the Great Wind God puffed up his cheeks and blew a smashing blast across Algonquin Park. He started near Big Crow Lake and flattened the forest in an almost straight line south and east across Thomas Lake, Hardy Bay of Lake Lavieille, Little Crooked Lake, and finally sputtered out near White Partridge Lake.

Pine, hemlock, maple, and birch trees were uniformly flattened, sometimes in straight lines, sometimes in circular patterns. The direction of the wind was clearly indicated by the rows of fallen White Birch. Among the casualties are several trees in the Big Crow pine stand, whose ages range up to 300 years. We hope to salvage as many of the merchantable trees as possible."

We have presented this as a new Algonquin feature, and to our knowledge it is the first time a similar incident has been given publicity. But it should be pointed out that such small tornados are well known to occur from time to time in forested country, and although they seldom cause extensive serious damage, they are "features" we could well do without.∞

September 6, 1972, Vol. 13, No. 12 (R.R.)

The Low-Down on Lost and Found

Taking a core of bottom mud through the ice of Found Lake.

Just about everybody who has come to Algonquin Park has seen Found Lake beside the Park Museum, but very few have ever given it a second thought. True, if you had asked one of the rangers about Found Lake, you might have learned that until Highway 60 went through in 1935–36 the lake was called Lost Lake. With the new highway running right beside it, the old name no longer seemed very appropriate, so some wag renamed it Found Lake — and the new name has stuck ever since. Apart from this odd (and true) story, however, there was nothing very special about Found Lake. It looks very much like any one of hundreds of other small lakes in the western uplands of Algonquin Park.

As things have turned out, however, Found Lake is without doubt one of the most interesting lakes, not only in Algonquin but in all of Canada. The reason for this is that the mud at the bottom of Found Lake contains a remarkably precise year-by-year record of the forests that have grown and died around the lake for the last 9,500 years — in fact, right back to the departure of the last glacier. The importance of such a record can hardly be over-emphasized in our day and age of increased concern and interest in how natural environments functioned before modern man began to exert his strong and sometimes devastating influence. In Algonquin Park, for example, we know the forests have been significantly modified by early logging and the unnaturally large and frequent forest fires of the late 1800s and early 1900s. However, we do not know exactly what the forests were like when white man arrived, and we are even less clear on the sequence of events that led to the establishment of the original natural forests. We have always had lots of unanswered questions about the history of our forests. For example, did the big White Pine always tower above hardwoods on the west side of Algonquin, or were hardwoods growing up under and replacing an earlier, more nearly pure, pine forest? How important were forest fires in the natural turnover of Algonquin forests, and how often did they occur under natural conditions?

Until recently, it seemed we would never have answers to these questions, but last summer a preliminary test indicated that Found Lake might be a key to the past.

You may legitimately wonder why Found Lake is so special in this regard. If Found Lake can tell us about past forest history, why can't other lakes? To understand why Found Lake is different, you have to know that it is amazingly deep for such a small body of water, over a hundred feet deep, in fact. This great depth, plus the fact that very little water flows into or out of the lake, means that the deep water doesn't circulate. It just sits there, and the oxygen it originally contained was used up thousands of years ago. The lack of oxygen results in a total lack of living things — living things that could stir up the mud on the bottom.

In every lake, material is continually settling out on the bottom-silt brought in by creeks, the dead bodies of tiny plants and animals living in the warm water near the surface, and pollen and leaves blown onto the lake from the surrounding country. In the summer these sediments are naturally richer in organic material than in winter, when the lake is covered with ice and life in the lake is at a low ebb. In other words, the material that settles on the bottom in summer can be distinguished from the siltier material that settles out in winter. If things stayed that way, every lake would have a year-by-year layering of its bottom sediments. In most lakes, however, the neat layers are destroyed by the movements of bottom living organisms. So it is only in a truly exceptional lake such as Found Lake that the layering is preserved — winter layers alternating with summer layers for the last 9,500 years.

In a core taken from the bottom of Found Lake through the ice last winter, these layers were clearly visible. Since only a half dozen such lakes have been found in the whole world up until now, it will be understood that there were a few happy faces out on the ice of Found Lake when the core was finally brought to the surface.

The painstaking work of identifying the preserved pollen grains has only just begun. This will tell us what trees were growing around the lake and their relative abundance over the centuries. Fragments of charcoal will tell us when and how often forest fires occurred. Already four different species of arctic plants have been identified from leaf fragments from the 9,000-year level, indicating a tundra type of environment in the Highway 60 region following the retreat of the last glacier.

And, oh yes, one other major event is recorded in the bottom of Found Lake. The highway construction back in 1936 kicked up quite a bit of dust. Enough fell into Found Lake for a white line to be clearly visible in the bottom mud at the 1936 level. That was the year that Lost became Found, but we think 1973 will be the year this unique lake really got on the map. ◌

May 1973 (Spring Issue), Vol. 14, No. 1 (D.S.)

The Old Railway

When J.R. Booth and his associates decided in 1888 to build the Ottawa, Arnprior and Parry Sound Railway across the Park, they were far-sighted businessmen with an eye on the soaring trade in timber from the Park and grain from the west which would take advantage of this shortened route to the markets of the world.

Apparently their idea was sound. The first train went through the Park in 1896, and for the next 25 or 30 years it was one of the busiest lines in Canada. Standing at what is now known to all Algonquin "regulars" as "the old railway crossing" at Mi. 14.6, it is difficult to picture a train passing every 20 minutes, but that's the way it was in the early 1900s. There were no roads into the Park then, except the remains of some of the old lumbering "cadge roads," which were not suitable for passenger traffic, and the very considerable number of early cottagers and canoeists also used the railway, adding to its volume of traffic.

By the early 1920s, however, competition from the improved highways outside the Park and a decline in the lumber industry made it apparent the era that had brought success to this small railway was coming to a close. The construction of Highway 60 in the middle 1930s settled the question. The first section of the line to close was between Two Rivers and Cache Lake in 1935, and this was because of the deterioration of one of the trestles

During the First World War the now-abandoned railroad across the southern part of Algonquin was the busiest in Canada.

between Lake of Two Rivers and Cache Lake. Trains continued from Whitney to Two Rivers up to 1944 and came from the west as far as Cache Lake until 1959. In that year all the rails were taken up, and the right-of-way settled down to growing up with grass and weeds and trees, as we see most of it today.

Now many Park visitors take pleasant walks along the old line, and parts of it are included in three of our present conducted hikes. Here and there it is used to facilitate the opening of roads by lumber companies or to give access to lodges or private cottages. Everywhere it forms a highway for the permanent Park residents — moose, deer, bear, wolves, and many others — who appreciate a good trail as much as the rest of us.

To the present generation it seems to be contributing quite as much to our lives as it did in its busy and noisy days of old, and it provides a fine example of how nature works to repair the scars of man's activities. ∞

July 4, 1973, Vol. 14, No. 3 (R.R.)

Your Friendly Neighbourhood Moose

We suppose there is hardly anyone who doesn't derive great pleasure from seeing a wild animal — especially if the animal is "friendly" or at least tolerates our presence at close quarters. Except for the occasional fleeting glimpse, we commonly see animals only in pictures or on television. In fact, we are so far removed from the day-to-day lives of most wild creatures that when we are lucky enough to share a moment with one, we treasure the experience but seldom stop to wonder what the animal's life is really like.

Such a situation arose this past winter. One fine February day we were informed that a large bull moose was lying in the snow at Mile 25, placidly chewing his cud and watching the cars go by. This was not so terribly unusual in itself, but the prospects of a few good winter moose pictures seemed fine, so down we went. Very conscious of how big he was and how small we were, we cautiously approached the moose, always watching for the laying back of the ears, which signals the displeasure we had every intention of respecting.

But there was no sign of displeasure. The moose behaved as if we weren't even there. He took slow careful steps through the snow; he browsed methodically on hazel and Red Pine, the crunching of twigs quite audible; he lay down six feet in front of us, closed his eyes, and calmly chewed his cud once again. This scene was repeated many times over the next few weeks for us and for dozens of winter campers and other visitors to the Park. Many had never seen any moose before, let alone one that was totally unconcerned by their presence.

The visitors' enthusiasm was so great that we almost hated to mention the possibility that something might be seriously wrong with the "friendly" moose. True, he looked healthy enough, but for some of us it was just too much to believe a normal moose would be so indifferent to humans. Offended human conceit? Perhaps, but one of the hard realities in the lives of all wild animals is the existence of parasites. In this case we suspected a tiny worm that has no English name but only the following mouthful in Latin (*Parelaphostrongylus tenuis*). This worm is transmitted to moose, via a snail, from deer (which are not affected). In moose the worm destroys nerve tissue in the spinal cord and in the brain, causing a progressive loss of co-ordination, blindness, and death. Not a pleasant subject but a very important one to moose, which share the same range with deer (as in Algonquin). The deadliness of the worm to moose helps explain why moose are rare where deer are common.

We watched our moose carefully over the next couple of weeks for any sign of deterioration, but saw none at all. In early March a solid crust developed on the snow, and the moose was able to walk around on top of the snow instead of sinking deeply at each step. For a few days more, he stayed around his old haunts, treating more passersby to the magnificent sight of a huge bull reaching high up in the alders to browse on the most tender twigs. It was obvious that he was quite healthy and, with the new mobility that the crust afforded, he soon wandered away towards Whitefish Lake.

Perhaps we had been too pessimistic about our moose. After all, he had survived living beside Highway 60 for several weeks and he was not fatally parasitized as we had suspected. Maybe he was just a "friendly neighbourhood moose," after all. We have to say "was," however, because near the end of April we found him drowned near the shore of Whitefish Lake. His great weight had probably broken through a weak spot in the ice, and he had been unable to break through the ice to shore. … Hardly any wild animals die of old age.⋄

May 15, 1974, Vol. 15, No. 1 (D.S.)

We'll never know whether this moose was sick or tame.

Budworm Bulletin

This is the fourth time in as many years that we have devoted space to the continuing Spruce Budworm population explosion in Algonquin Park. First-time visitors to the Park may be wondering what all the fuss is about, so for their benefit we might just provide a little background information before we bring everybody up to date on the current budworm situation.

Actually, even people who just drive through the Park without stopping see the effects of the budworm, although they may not recognize them as such. Almost everywhere you look east of Cache Lake, you see patches of Balsam and spruce whose foliage has a purplish-brown cast. A closer look around such places as Mew Lake, Lake of Two Rivers, the Outdoor Theatre, and farther east will reveal thousands of half dead trees with tangled clumps at the ends of their branches.

All this is the work of the budworm. If its effects are obvious, the budworm itself is just the opposite. The adult budworm is a drab, fluttery little moth less than an inch long. Normally, they would be very easy not to notice, but right now there are thousands of them busily searching for still-green spruce and Balsam foliage in which to lay their eggs. The eggs will hatch out into tiny larvae, which will spin minute silken cases where they will spend the winter. Next spring they will emerge to feed on the new needles grown by the trees at the ends of their branches. As they munch away, the little caterpillars pull the twigs together with strands of silk, and this, along with the consumption of needles, makes for the tangled sickly appearance the heavily budwormed trees in Algonquin now have.

When the Spruce Budworm attacks a tree, all the new foliage may be eaten. The old needles are left largely untouched so the tree is not killed by a single year of even an overwhelmingly heavy budworm attack. The trouble is that the old needles don't last forever; as a rule they live about four years and are then shed by the tree. This means that if a tree loses all its new needles to budworm larvae for four years in a row, the tree won't have any needles, old or new, at the end of those four years. At this point, the now defoliated tree is doomed, and this is precisely where much of the Balsam and White Spruce in Algonquin find themselves this summer. They have been hit hard by the budworm every year since 1970, and

Normally rare Cape May Warblers become common during outbreaks of the Spruce Budworm.

there is no doubt that many stands of both tree species are now dying.

The prospect of large stands of dead trees in Algonquin fills many people with a kind of horror. Perhaps this is understandable, but we think it worthwhile to examine this attitude a little more closely. If our concern in "saving" a forest from the budworm is to save against economic loss, then it is right to view the budworm as a serious enemy. Millions of dollars worth of timber are destroyed each year in North America by this insect. But in Algonquin this is not our concern, because neither Balsam Fir nor White Spruce is very important commercially in the Park.

We might still condemn the budworm just because we don't like the look of dead trees. Hopefully, however, we have enough ecological sophistication to realize that more is involved in a budworm outbreak than just budworms and trees. For example, when the trees are being attacked there is a spectacular increase in the local bird population. The abundant budworm caterpillars make it possible not only for greater numbers of birds to live in the area but also for different kinds of birds — kinds that wouldn't be there if it weren't for the budworm. Two of these birds are the Bay-breasted Warbler and the Cape May Warbler. The Cape May, a jewel in the treetops, has been common in budworm areas during the last four years, but when the outbreak is over, you will be doing well to see even one anywhere in the Park. If we ever eliminate the budworm, we will eliminate the Cape May Warbler.

After a budworm outbreak peaks and the trees begin to die, they are attacked by wood-eating insects, fungi, and woodpeckers while, down on the ground, the increased sunlight makes possible a flush of new green growth supporting a variety of animals ranging from Red-backed Voles and their predators to bear and deer.

The periodic destruction of spruce and Balsam forests by the budworm, along with the attendant benefits to other plants and wildlife, are natural parts of the Algonquin environment going back many thousands of years. In fact, both the trees and the budworms were here long before modern man came along and presumed to decide one was "good" and one was "bad." Personally, in a day and age when few natural agents of change are allowed to function normally, we consider ourselves rather lucky to be able to witness firsthand a major spruce budworm outbreak and all its fascinating details.

Not everyone will share this view, of course, but for the benefit of the Doubting Thomases we might recall what happened in the last budworm outbreak (1940–45). In the Highway 60 area at that time, virtually 100 per cent of the Balsam, 50 to 90 per cent of the White Spruce, and 20 to 40 per cent of the Black Spruce were destroyed by budworms. Yet, in spite of that destruction, the Park "managed to survive," just as it had during the thousands of years before and just as it will this time. Toward the end of the 1940s outbreak, DDT became available and, comparing its benefits to those of penicillin, the Ontario government rushed to try it out on the budworm — in Algonquin.

In hindsight, we know how foolish this was and believe our present "hands-off" attitude to be wiser. We have made one exception by spraying 1,700 acres along Highway 60 with Zectran (a short-lived but effective insecticide) in June to protect campgrounds until the outbreak is over.⌖

July 10, 1974 ,Vol. 15, No. 4 (D.S.)

A New Fern for the World

One of Algonquin Park's greatest appeals is that you can never know all its secrets — there are just too many. You can spend a lifetime enjoying the rewards of discovering some of these secrets, but only if you make the effort to see and understand.

Exactly one year ago today, a discovery was made in Algonquin Park that illustrates this point rather well. The scene was remote Greenleaf Lake in the northeast part of the Park. Two Park employees, Dan Brunton and his assistant, Paul Keddy, had spent an exhausting day conducting a biological inventory of the rugged 350-foot cliffs that dominate the lake. They had pitched their tent near shore, eaten supper, and were more than ready to turn in.

But it wasn't dark yet, and tired though he was, Paul still hadn't had enough of Greenleaf's impressive scenery and amazing botanical richness. So he paddled across the lake to explore some more while there was still light. When he returned to the campsite he had a frond from a fern that didn't "fit" anything he knew. Dan looked at the specimen and, while admitting it looked strange, managed to convince Paul it "had to be" just an odd form of the very common Marginal Shield Fern. What else could it be? Besides, it was time for bed and they had another long day ahead of them. More as a reflex action than anything else, Dan and Paul put the frond in their plant press and didn't give it another thought.

Months later, back at the Park Museum, Dan was cataloguing the botanical collections from the previous summer and came upon the specimen once again. We presume Dan hadn't climbed any cliffs that day because, although he still thought the specimen was probably Marginal Shield Fern, he didn't find it quite so easy to be sure the second time around. The specimen began to annoy him. It was Marginal Shield in some ways; yet in other ways it was not. Finally, the non-conformist fern got the better of Dan, and he sent the "offending" plant off to a world expert on ferns, Dr. Donald Britton of the University of Guelph.

Dr. Britton's reply was not long in coming, and it was a bombshell. The fern was new to science, apparently a hybrid between Marginal Shield Fern and the Fragrant Cliff Fern. With the benefit of Dr. Britton's insight, the mystery fern began to make sense. It looked a bit like Marginal Shield Fern because, in fact, it was partly that species. The features that didn't fit were in turn strongly suggestive of Fragrant Cliff Fern, and both the suspected parents were known to be common at Greenleaf Lake.

But just because a thing looks right doesn't necessarily mean that it is right. More work needed to be done before we could be sure, and so Dr. Britton launched a bit of an international detective story. First, he took the specimen to Harvard, where another leading fern expert supported Dr. Britton's opinion. Second, a portion of the frond's leaf-stalk was sent to Dr. Carl-Johan Widen in Helsinki for chemical analysis. If the fern was, in fact, a hybrid between the two suspected parents, it should have predictable concentrations of all the various chemical compounds normally found in each (but not necessarily both) of its parents. Right? Right! For example, our fern contained "phloraspidinol," which could only have come from Marginal Shield Fern, but also "aspidin BB," which could only have come from Fragrant Cliff Fern. These and

other results from Finland strongly supported the identification of our fern as a hybrid between those two species.

So much for biochemistry! The final test had to wait until this past June because only then could we get fresh material suitable for an examination of the fern's spores and chromosomes. There was some concern whether the plant would still be alive and whether we could find it again because only Paul had actually seen it, and at the time he had no idea how important his discovery was.

The rediscovery expedition took place on June 15 and was quickly crowned with success. Back in his lab at Guelph, Dr. Britton found even more evidence to support the hybrid theory and is now ready to formally describe the new fern for the world's scientific community. The official Latin name of the new fern will have to await the formal description, but we can tell you it will translate into English (which is of more use to most of us) as Algonquin Wood Fern.

Only fitting, we think, that it should be named after the Park that has so many secrets to reward those who look.↩

July 17, 1974 , Vol. 15, No. 5 (D.S.)

See the footnote to the later article "Eternal Life — Here and Now" (July 24, 1986, on page 138) for an update on the Algonquin Wood Fern.

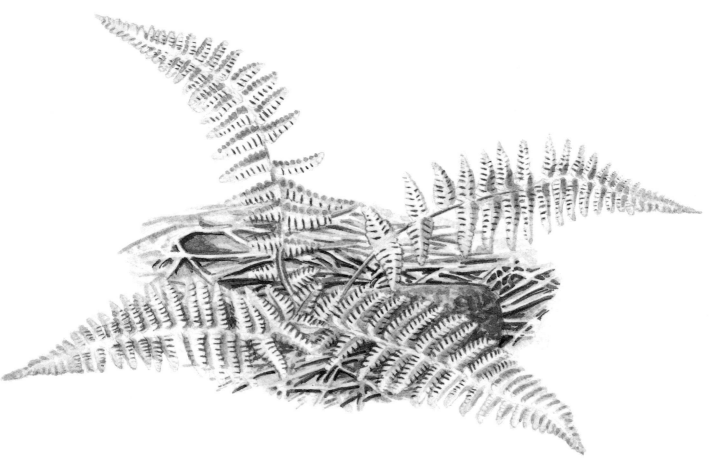

More on Deer

Last week we briefly commented on the difficulty of estimating the numbers of animals in Algonquin, and we made particular reference to last winter's estimate of 2,600 deer in Algonquin. While we stressed this figure was only an estimate and could be considerably off the true figure, space did not permit us to explore more deeply the implications of that number.

The number can tell us one piece of useful information because, whatever the shortcomings of the method and whatever the error involved in arriving at our population estimate for deer in the Park, we should at least be able to discover the year-to-year trend of deer numbers if we use the same estimating method every year.

When the figures for the last several years are compared, there can be little doubt that the trend in deer numbers has been a steady decline. In 1969, for example, we estimated 7,900 deer in the Park, and this year only 2,600.

But even the 1969 figure is far lower than the numbers in the 1950s or in the early part of this century. Incredible as it seems today, it is said that one ranger shot over 100 deer during two months' casual hunting in 1917, when Algonquin deer were being used to alleviate war-time meat shortages in southern Ontario.

Knowing this, we all ask the question, "What's happened to all the deer?" For many years the standard answer was that wolves were responsible, and even today many people refuse to believe otherwise. But quite apart from the fact that deer have co-existed with wolves in North America for thousands of years, there is another even more serious problem with the wolf theory. The decline in deer in Algonquin is by no means a local phenomenon. There has been a similar decline in Nova Scotia, where there are no wolves; in New Brunswick, where there are no wolves; in Michigan, where there are no wolves. In fact, the drop in deer numbers has occurred right across their northern range, and in most of this area there is not one wolf. So the onus is on those who cling to the wolf theory to explain why wolves must be blamed for the low deer population in Algonquin when something else has to be responsible. It must also be explained how Algonquin deer, which escaped predation by wolves, would somehow be spared from the factors that are apparently operating to reduce deer numbers right across the northern range of the White-tailed Deer — wolves or no wolves.

Well, if the wolf theory doesn't make much sense, we are back to square one and must examine other possible reasons for the decrease in Park deer numbers. A number of such examinations have been made over the years, but one of the most serious has been that of Rae Runge of the University of Waterloo. With financial and other assistance from the Ministry of Natural Resources, Rae spent two years carefully studying the production of deer food in Algonquin and hundreds of old records concerning the presence of deer and the condition of the forest in the Park. In our remaining space, we would like to relate some of the highlights of Rae's summation of this extremely interesting subject.

To many people, the most startling fact to emerge is that deer were very rare, if not totally absent, before the 1800s. Archaeological studies reveal no deer bones in Indian campsites, and while early explorers referred to caribou, they do not mention seeing any deer in our area. The reason for the deer's absence was the rarity of suitably extensive areas of young forest growth that deer need for food. The wild forests were simply too mature, with thick canopies blocking off the light that could have promoted the growth of shrubs and other deer food — if it had been able to reach the ground. Natural disturbances such as wind and insect outbreaks apparently did not occur frequently enough to open up the forest, and although perhaps a dozen lightning fires started every year, they didn't burn well enough in our hardwood forests to destroy them and create good deer range.

All this changed in the 1800s with the arrival of the loggers. The "shantymen" not only cut down trees but also left a lot of highly flammable debris. Add to this the fact that loggers started fires accidentally, and the Park area soon had more and much bigger fires — fires that devastated considerable areas of Algonquin. We often think of fire as the deadly enemy of wildlife, but if deer could talk they would tell you just the opposite. Here in the Park they demonstrated this by moving into the new environment and thriving as never before in the young forests springing up in the ashes of the old.

Big fires continued to produce good future deer habitat long after the Park was created, with an average of 25 square miles being burned every year between 1921 (when accurate records began to be kept) and 1936. After this date, however, more men, planes, and other efficient means of fire-fighting came into operation, with the result that the average area burned each year dropped to less than two square miles.

You often hear it suggested that the virtual disappearance of fire may not be all that important because we still have logging, and it too creates openings in the forest, which encourage new growth for deer. But Rae has found that typical logged areas (with only scattered big trees removed) produce only about 7,000 stems of new growth per acre, while severe burns produce as much as 24,000 stems per acre. What's more,

the aim of most modern forest management is to grow new trees as quickly as possible, so the new trees in a logged area should grow out of a deer's reach much faster than they did in the old burns (where competing shrubs slowed down the growth of new trees).

The upshot of all this is that modern forest management and the virtual elimination of fires have combined to transform the scrubby forests of 60 years ago where deer abounded back to a condition more like the original one — where there were very few deer or none at all. The heyday of deer is over. But all is not lost; moose are increasing and who knows? — perhaps someday we can bring back the caribou.∞

July 31, 1974 , Vol. 15, No. 7 (D.S.)

The Egg of the Osprey

Nowadays the vast majority of people enjoy wildlife, especially birds, simply by looking and listening. But this wasn't always true. In the 1800s and the early part of this century, for example, the consuming passion among many amateur ornithologists was egg-collecting. Some of these oologists (as the egg collectors called themselves) went to extraordinary lengths to procure full clutches of such difficult-to-get eggs as those of the Gray Jay or the Saw-whet Owl. But the prize in any collection was the egg of the Osprey, one of the most beautiful known by man to be laid by bird. Osprey eggs have a pale pinkish cinnamon ground colour, heavily splotched with rich chestnut — irresistible to the diehard oologist. The point was proven a few years ago when, after an absence of over 50 years, Ospreys nested once again in Scotland. The nest was promptly robbed and, after that, conservationists felt obliged to mount a 24-hour guard to prevent further losses.

As far as we know, the magnificent sight of an Osprey soaring high above an Algonquin lake, or closing its six-foot wings to plunge to the surface with a tremendous splash and then emerging with a fish tightly gripped in its razor-sharp talons, is no rarer today than in the past. As far as we know, there has always been the present thin

population in Algonquin, and oologists haven't been a problem for the eggs in the great stick nests built high up in towering dead White Pines.

But this doesn't mean that we shouldn't worry about the egg of the Osprey in Algonquin Park. For the fact is that in some areas of North America the Osprey has all but disappeared because of egg shell cracking brought on by the adults eating fish contaminated with pesticides. This wouldn't seem to be a problem here, but you must remember that in winter the Ospreys are forced to leave Algonquin for areas to the south, which have open water and, unfortunately, contaminated fish. In 1971 we attempted to survey from the air the success of Algonquin's known active Osprey nests (seven at that time) by flying low over the nests and counting the young or the eggs. After a near collision with an adult that rose to attack the plane, however, we decided such a survey was too risky for man and bird alike.

We haven't given up completely though. We all want the egg of the Osprey to remain a part of Algonquin.∞

August 7, 1974, Vol. 15, No. 8 (D.S.)

In Defence of Blackflies

To begin with, Algonquin blackflies should not all be tarred with the same brush because there is not just one kind but well over two dozen. Of these, only five bite human beings. The others include species that bite only birds or amphibians; still others never bite animals at all.

At this time of year the air is normally filled with two things. First, there are millions of blackflies and then, flying in hot pursuit, are almost as many quite unprintable words.

We do not know if a word, oath, or bellow has ever succeeded in catching a single blackfly, but we can report that for whatever reason, the flies are much less numerous this season than they have been for many years. With human tempers therefore that much calmer, the time has come to say a word on behalf of this tiny speechless brethren.

Our blackfly species have distinguishing differences in structure, markings, and life history, but they all share in common certain basic strategies for success. We believe these strategies are so ingenious that even the most rabid blackfly hater must grudgingly admit that the little b------- have some clever tricks up their non-existent sleeves.

Blackfly eggs are laid in running water, either at the surface from where they drift down and become lodged in the stream bed or attached to rocks or vegetation. With some species the eggs pass the winter in a resting state and do not hatch until the following spring. Others hatch shortly after being laid, and the tiny "worm-like" larvae are active, though slow-growing, throughout the winter. (It is a simple matter, by the way, to see blackfly larvae even on the coldest Algonquin winter day merely by looking closely at rocks and pebbles in unfrozen streams.)

The key thing is that the larvae live in running water. At first glance this might seem to be a rather unpromising place to choose. After all, the risk of being swept downstream should be considerable for a tiny larva only a few millimetres long. Blackfly larvae solve the problem, however, by spinning sticky, silken mats of saliva attached to submerged objects. Larvae attach themselves to the sticky mat by means of hooks at the rear end of the body. They can move about by alternately gripping the mat with their mouthparts and the rear-end hooks, or by drifting downstream on lifelines of silken saliva.

Normally, however, a blackfly larva stays put, with its rear end holding on and the rest of its body trailing in the current. If the current poses a danger to a tiny insect larva, it also brings substantial rewards to any that can remain stationary. To feed, the blackfly larva just holds its two fan-like arms up into the current and intercepts bacteria, algae, and other debris being swept along by the stream. Just how profitable such an arrangement can be may be appreciated by the fact that the number of adult blackflies emerging from just one square yard of suitable stream bottom in just one season is typically in the range of 30 thousand ... yes, 30,000 blackflies from one square yard!

The way they emerge is no less amazing. Blackfly larvae transform to adults in open-ended silken cases. When the time comes to emerge, the case fills with gas and the adult fly rides in a bubble up to the surface. There, the bubble bursts and the adult is liberated into a new world.

It may come to you as a surprise that adults of all blackflies feed on nectar (chiefly, that of blueberry flowers). The catch is that the females of some species must have a meal of blood to ensure development of their eggs, and as we said earlier five species regularly bite humans to get the "donation."

Especially at their peak in June, biting blackflies are no laughing matter, and many a tortured human has asked, "What good are they?" The question is understandable, of couse, but it's a bit like asking what good is a carburetor. The answer, in both cases, is no good at all except as part of a system. Just as a carburetor

If you like blueberries, you have to like blackflies, right?

is a vital ingredient in the system of parts that make up a functioning car, blackflies too are an integral part of a system — in this case, a living community. As adults, blackflies are a major food item for fly-catchers and swallows, and they may be one of the most important pollinators of blueberries. As larvae, they remove huge quantities of bacteria and debris from the water. They also constitute food for fish. One of many blackfly studies conducted here in the Park showed that 16 per cent by volume of the food taken by Brook Trout in the Oxtongue River consisted of blackfly larvae and adults.

So the next time you pick a blueberry or catch a trout, lift your hat to the blackfly — but not too long or they'll get you! ✐

June 25, 1975, Vol. 16, No. 2 (D.S.)

We'll Never Know

Wapiti, introduced to Algonquin in 1936, survived for at least three years.

The other day, while looking through some old superintendent's reports for Algonquin Park, we came across the following:

"Ten Wapiti, or American Elk (four males and six females) were transported from the Petawawa Game Preserve in trucks of the Department of Game and Fisheries and were liberated at Algonquin Park Headquarters (Cache Lake) on January 10, 1936. They have remained during the winter in the vicinity of Cache and Canisbay Lakes, and will be an added attraction to tourists."

Having been thus reminded of this intriguing experiment, we then read on to refresh our memory of subsequent developments.

In 1937, the elk were deemed to be "thriving," and in his newsletter of March 19, 1939, the late Superintendent Frank MacDougall wrote that animals had been seen at many places in the Park, including Smoke, Source, and Burnt Island Lakes, and that "tracks of several young have been reported from Cache Lake, Lake of Two Rivers, and Joe Lake."

MacDougall went on to say that it was too early to predict the success of the introduction, but noted that elk seen at Source Lake were browsing higher than deer could reach and speculated that a large increase might bring a clash between the deer and elk populations for winter food.

Strange to say, there is no further mention of the Algonquin elk — not even a word — in any of the newsletters or reports from the years that followed. The probable reason is that there were simply no elk left to report. Today, at least, it has long been apparent that the introduction was a failure. Most people would now say that this is just as well for it is surely not the purpose of Algonquin to try out poorly conceived introductions of exotic wildlife. If such introductions fail, they are pointless, and if they succeed, they almost always have far-reaching and disastrous effects on the native wildlife a park is supposed to protect.

Most of us now realize that intact wildlife communities are too precious a resource to play around with and are quite content to restrict our elk-viewing to the western states and provinces where they are very much a part of the natural scene. In fact, hardly anything could evoke the Rocky Mountains more than the thought of a spectacular 1,000-pound bull elk tilting back its head and magnificent antlers, and sending its high, squealing bugle rolling across a golden October valley to challenge its rivals.

Few scenes could be more wildly exotic in the Algonquin Park we know today. Incredible as it may seem, however, there is a possibility that we once did have such scenes, not just 39 years ago with introduced elk, but as recently as 150 years back with native elk. It is a surprising and little-known fact that when European explorers reached the Atlantic shores of North America, they found elk along with the familiar White-tailed Deer. There is no doubt that these eastern elk occurred in southern Quebec and Ontario as well. They were seen in the Ottawa Valley well into the 1800s, and old elk antlers have been occasionally unearthed by farmers there, even as late as this century.

As close as the Ottawa Valley is, we still have no solid proof that elk actually occurred in Algonquin itself. There is at least one piece of evidence, however, that we regard as intriguing, if considerably less than conclusive. Written over the Algonquin Park area, on a map prepared by Samuel de Champlain in 1653, appear the words "Grand chasse de cerfs et de caribous." This translates as "Good hunting for stag and caribou." Just what Champlain meant by "stags" might be open to question, except that on an earlier map of the Kingston area he used the same word, this time accompanied by an unmistakable portrait of an elk. Champlain never set foot in Algonquin, however, and we have no way of knowing how accurate his information was.

Whatever the virtue of this evidence, there were certainly no eastern elk in Algonquin by the mid-1800s, or anywhere else for that matter. The race had become completely and mysteriously extinct. No one knows why. While the disappearance of the elk generally coincided with logging and clearing of farms, it is difficult to understand how elk would have suffered from this since they feed on a wide variety of vegetation, by grazing in meadows, browsing in forests, and even by stripping bark from the trunks of aspen trees.

In spite of this adaptability, they did disappear, and there is plenty of room for speculation. The theory we like best is that the elk owed their decline to the rise of deer, which occurred during (and because of) the same period of forest-clearing. Deer carry a parasite which, while harmless to the deer, is fatal when transmitted to moose or elk. Perhaps the increased numbers of deer ensured that all elk sooner or later were infected with the parasite and died as a result. This might also explain why elk can be kept quite easily in enclosures in eastern North America and yet so many attempts to establish wild populations in areas where deer had become numerous ended in failure.

This brings us back to the elk introduced to Algonquin 39 years ago. We don't know what happened to them. Even more important, we don't know whether elk were native to Algonquin in the first place. We probably never will know.

July 9, 1975 , Vol. 16, No. 4 (D.S.)

Bears Having Bad People Year

When you read this, the chances are quite good that someone has already told you the latest gossip about bears in your campground. It may be a story about "the people two sites down, who had their cooler smashed last night" or about "the family who packed up in the middle of the night after hearing a bear noisily emptying their garbage can."

Sad to say, there is no shortage of such stories and, especially if you are among those who have been "hit" by bears, you are probably more than ready to conclude that we are having a bad bear year.

Well, *The Raven* begs to disagree. People are not having a bad bear year; the bears are having a bad people year.

Consider for a moment what a bear really is — a very large animal that must eat to live but in many ways is surprisingly ill-equipped to get food. It survives by being an opportunist, grazing on grass, browsing on leaves, eating berries, grubs, roots, and any carrion it comes across. A bear lives by one unconscious rule: "Anything edible is acceptable." Human food or garbage is no exception to this rule, and the bear's unthinking brain is untroubled by such abstract human notions as private property or right and wrong.

We do not blame a rock for falling if we drop it, and we cannot blame a bear for taking our food if we make it available. In both cases, we are responsible. If we don't want the rock to fall or the bear to raid our campsite, it is entirely up to us to prevent it.

In the case of bears, there are thousands of campers who have never had any bear problems and never will. They follow the three simple "bear rules," which appear on every campground office bulletin and in the Park folder. Other people, unfortunately, choose to ignore these rules by not storing their food in the car truck, by not keeping a clean, odour-free campsite, or by not burning their scraps and other garbage. Sooner or later, of course, these people pay the price by being "hit." Not too long ago we even heard of a bear-wise camper who amuses himself by accurately predicting which of his neighbours is going to be visited.

This might strike you as a somewhat morbid pastime, but we too must confess to having very little sympathy for bear "victims." Their self-inflicted scares or losses of food and equipment are quite minor compared to what happens to the bears. We said earlier that bears are opportunists. While they aren't born with the habit of foraging in campgrounds (indeed they are quite shy of man naturally), they are obviously capable of learning just what a bonanza a campground can be. Once learned, this lesson is never unlearned.

This leaves us with little choice but to remove the bears to whom campers have given the campground habit. This is done by trapping them in a large culvert trap on wheels and releasing them at least 20 miles outside the Park. The hope is that they won't return. If they do, rather than risk repeating the same sad and expensive routine, we destroy them. As of this date, we have trapped and relocated 14 bears from the Highway 60 Corridor and have destroyed 10 returnees. Another seven have been destroyed in the interior (where trapping and relocating are not possible).

In other words, the bears are indeed having a bad people year. We don't like being forced to destroy bears that have been corrupted by careless campers. We also recognize that we must do much more, especially in our on-going program of constructing bear-proof garbage facilities. But even without them, there is still no good reason for any unhappy incidents (for you or the bear) provided you follow the three bear rules.

And, oh yes, you must follow those rules to the letter and then a little bit more. We will always remember the man who came to us a few years ago and reported (rather bravely we thought) that he had returned to his campsite and found a bear eating his food. The man had been told to put it in the trunk of his car, and in fact he had done so. The trouble was no one had told him that you also have to close the lid.❧

July 23, 1975, Vol. 16, No. 6 (D.S.)

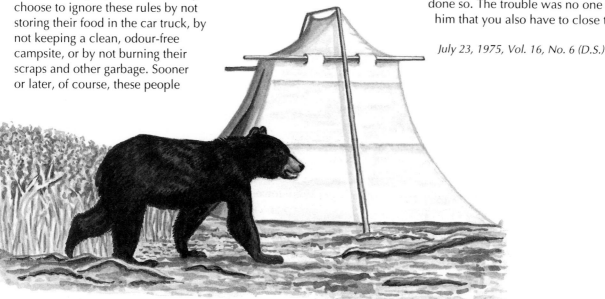

An Afternoon's Paddle

At this time of year the campgrounds along Highway 60 are filled to capacity, and the result may be that you are having a little trouble seeing the Park for the people. Even on the trails you may not do much better unless you go early (you'd be surprised how empty the Park appears at 9 a.m., not to mention 7 or 8).

But even in the afternoon of the busiest day, it is a simple matter to have a whole lake to yourself — provided you use the Park map with a little imagination and are willing to paddle and portage a canoe.

A few weeks ago, we went on such an excursion, and we think you might be interested in hearing about it. What we saw was typical of the quiet rewards that await anyone who takes the time and trouble to do a little off-the-beaten-path exploration in Algonquin.

In this case, our lake had the usual pair of loons, gliding across the water with no apparent effort and occasionally disappearing below the surface to hunt for fish. Above the loons, a billion-year-old cliff rose in angular, weathered grayness until it merged with the needles and straight trunks of Red Pine, born in the ashes of some unknown fire many years ago. Beyond lay an island, and as we drew near, a kingbird spluttered overhead in frantic but needless alarm at our close approach to its nest, just visible at the top of a broken stub. As we rounded the island, our eyes stopped on a large, black shape on a blueberry-covered point of the mainland. Did it move or didn't it? Yes, it did move, and during the time it took to paddle quietly over, the mother bear was joined by her two cubs, all of them intent on the berries. At a distance of 40 feet we made the mistake of bumping our paddle on a gunwale. She looked up, and in

a flash was thundering into the woods with the cubs bouncing along behind her just like two rubber balls.

On the same afternoon we saw a brood of 10 baby mergansers skittering over the water and riding on their mother's back; Great Blue Herons making ungainly landings at their treetop nests at the edge of a beaver pond; carnivorous sundew plants growing with hundreds of Club-spur Orchids on the lakeshore; five ravens doing aerial acrobatics high in the sky; and two Broad-winged Hawks at their nest.

All this, plus a swim and a sun tan in five hours and within three miles of Highway 60. Any guesses as to where we were? ꙮ

August 6, 1975, Vol. 16, No. 8 (D.S.)

The Stuff of Legends

The name "Booth" should be at least vaguely familiar to most Park visitors. There is a large lake east of Opeongo named Booth Lake, and of course there is the Booth's Rock Trail near the Rock Lake Campground. But then, there are hundreds of places in the Park named in honour of now obscure historical figures, and you might well wonder why we are singling out Booth for special attention at this time.

As a matter of fact, there are two excellent reasons for doing so. The first is that John Rudolphus (J.R.) Booth was a truly remarkable man who had a tremendous influence on Canada and Algonquin Park; the second reason is that this year marks the 50th anniversary of his death back in the year 1925.

However unknown J.R. Booth may be today, you could hardly have helped knowing about him half a

century ago. His death at the age of 98 removed the still-active head of a huge business empire. Newspapers all over North America ran front-page stories and headlines. From the Prime Minister of Canada on down came tributes to the courage, fairness, and unaffected ways of the great man.

But none of this tells us who J.R. Booth really was, how he came to such prominence, or anything about his influence on Algonquin. In the space remaining to us, we would like to at least touch on the major points of his career.

J.R. was born in 1827, the son of a homesteader, in the eastern townships of Quebec. As a boy, he worked on his father's farm, received very little schooling, and apparently had no greater ambition than to become a carpenter. Even this goal was at odds with the will of his authoritarian father, and after an unsuccessful attempt to run away and join the California gold rush, the young J.R. resigned himself to life on the farm until he was 21. He then moved to Vermont and worked as a carpenter until he had saved enough money to come home, marry, and settle down. But it was not much later, in 1852, that J.R. pulled up stakes and moved to Ottawa with his wife, a newly born daughter, and nine dollars to his name.

Living in rented rooms, he walked three miles to work each morning, back again in the evening, and then turned out shingles in the backyard. With all the money he had saved and all he could borrow, J.R. soon went into business for himself full-time, buying the timber rights to small areas of woodland and leasing a succession of mills. Only three years after Booth arrived in Ottawa, the little town of 8,000 people was chosen as capital, and a contract was let to supply wood for the new Parliament Buildings. Booth landed the contract and made a profit of $15,000, thanks in great measure to his innovative use of horses to haul his logs (oxen had been used until then) and his recruitment of unemployed longshoremen from Montreal. J.R. had to teach them personally how to use an axe, but he also secured their labours for much less money than was demanded by the professional axemen. (Those original Parliament Buildings, incidentally, burned to the ground in 1916, all except the Parliamentary Library, which still stands today.)

Although J.R. Booth was a success by this time and had acquired outright ownership of his first mill in 1860, he was still a rather small operator, with very small timber limits and nowhere near enough capital to acquire any really big areas. He did have one very important asset, however. This was his credit, based on a solid reputation for hard work, determination, and good judgement. He capitalized on this credit in 1867 by outbidding the established lumber barons in the auction of the "Egan Estate," 150 square miles of prime pine now lying mostly in Algonquin Park. It cost J.R. Booth $45,000 of borrowed money to get these limits, but the profits he reaped were many times this amount. These and subsequent profits were poured into greater and greater expansion of his holdings.

By 1894, Booth owned close to 4,000 square miles of timber and produced one million feet of sawn lumber each day in the world's largest mill, employing some 1,500 men. Booth himself was one of the continent's richest men, a millionaire many times over.

He was also in the process of building a 264-mile railway from Ottawa west to Georgian Bay at Parry Sound, crossing the new Algonquin Park on the way. Booth had been in the railroad business since 1878 when he had

acquired a line running from Vermont to Ottawa, but it was not a money-maker. It was fairly typical of Booth that he decided it could be profitable if he spent more money on it — hence the 264-mile extension. J.R. reckoned that the line could carry not only the timber from his own Algonquin limits but also western grain shipped across the Great Lakes. As usual, he was right, and the new line, whose abandoned roadbed can be seen at Canoe, Source, Cache, Two Rivers, and Rock Lakes, was for a time the busiest in Canada. For many years it was the only practical means of access for Park visitors, and for this reason alone, it had an incalculable influence on the development and history of Algonquin. But the new line did more than make the Park accessible. Until then, the only trees cut in Algonquin had been Red and White Pine because only they could be floated out on the rivers. The railroad changed that and may have led to the policy change that in 1900 allowed all tree species (not just pine) to be cut in the Park.

Although Booth had made himself the sole owner of an industrial empire worth millions, he always rose at 6 a.m. and preferred working in overalls out in the millyard — a fact much appreciated by his employees. They also appreciated his generosity, but soon learned that he could not be pushed. One man, a driver who had received a 50-cent tip from J.R., mentioned that Mr. Booth's son always gave a dollar. "That's different," replied old J.R., "that boy has a rich father, but I'm an orphan." ∞

August 13, 1975, Vol. 16, No. 9 (D.S.)

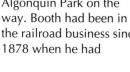

The Moose Explosion

If you have attended a few of our evening programs or conducted hikes, you have no doubt learned that moose are on the increase in Algonquin.

This may be no consolation if you haven't seen a moose yourself, but the increase is nevertheless a very real and very interesting one. Mind you, a few years ago, we couldn't really put any firm figures on our moose population, and our belief that it was increasing was really based on our subjective impression that we were seeing more and more moose and moose-sign each year.

Today, however, we are in a position to give you more than just guesswork. For the past two winters now, our Fish and Wildlife staff have conducted aerial moose surveys that have enabled us to arrive at the following moose population estimates. In the winter of 1973–74, we estimated the population at 931 moose, plus or minus 380. Last winter (1974–75), using the same procedure, we arrived at an estimate of 1,800 moose, plus or minus 345. For the first time, the surveys gave us some measure of the size of our moose population and indicated that it had almost doubled in the year's time that separated the two surveys.

The days of guessing about our moose numbers would appear to be over. But if somebody asks you how many moose there are in the Park and you answer "1,800," you will be almost certainly far off the true figure. No, we have not just contradicted ourselves, but we wish to point out a couple of traps into which most people fall when it comes to animal numbers.

The first trap has to do with the fact that a survey done last winter cannot tell us what the moose population is this August. Since the survey was done, an unknown number of moose have been eaten by wolves or died from starvation, disease, or accidents. Even more important, in late May or early June the cows give birth to calves, but we don't know how many cows had young or how many had twins as opposed to single young. Nor do we know how many calves have died since they were born. For all we know, at this moment Algonquin's moose population may have doubled again since last winter's survey. In other words, the figure of 1,800 moose from last winter's survey could be badly out of date even now, only six months later.

The second trap into which people often fall is misreading the figures in the first place. For example, we did not say there were 1,800 moose in the Park when the survey was done last winter; we said there were 1,800, plus or minus 345. Put another way, the survey indicated that the real number could have been as low as 1,455 or as high as 2,145 (and we're only 90 per cent sure about that)!

At this point you may be ready to throw our moose figures in with the three famous categories of lies (lies, damn lies, and statistics). If you are, you have plenty of company, but we think this is because many people unreasonably assume that animal populations are easy to count. It would be nice if they were, but in most cases they just aren't.

With moose it is impossible to do a census at this time of year because of the leaves, and in fact, the only real chance we have is during the winter when the trees are bare and the tracks of moose in the snow can be spotted from the air. (The animals themselves can be seen too, of course, but not when they are standing under thick conifers.) The trouble with tracks is that there aren't many to see until 24 hours after a snowfall, and by 72 hours after new snow, there are so many tracks the task of following them to the animals is hopelessly confusing. What this boils down to is that moose can only be surveyed one to three days after a snowfall. With only so many days falling into this category and almost 3,000 square miles of Park to cover, it is impossible to do all of Algonquin.

As a second best, we survey about 12 per cent of the Park instead.

This sample consists of 28 randomly chosen plots, each of which measures four miles by four miles. When conditions are right, we fly low over each plot in parallel lines a half mile apart. Every time moose tracks are spotted, they are followed to the animal or animals, whose positions are then recorded on the map before we resume flying the parallel lines. This is a reasonably good way of finding all or nearly all the moose in the areas we survey, but the numbers of animals seen vary widely from one 16-square mile plot to another. For example, some plots had no moose at all, while the numbers on others ranged right up to 39. This variability is the reason we can't just take the average figure of 9.9 moose per plot and apply it to the whole Park and arrive at the "exact"

figure of 1,800. We have to take into account the possibility that areas of high moose population density are over- or under-represented in our randomly chosen 12 per cent of the Park. This is the reason behind the "plus or minus 345" mentioned earlier.

Whatever the uncertainties about the figures obtained by our moose surveys, one thing seems certain. Since we are using the same method from one year to the next, with the same plots, observers, pilot, and aircraft, we should at least be in a good position to detect trends in our moose population.

With the dramatic, almost twofold increase in our census figures between last winter and the year before, our present "trend" is more like an explosion. We'll report next year on the explosion's progress and hope in the meantime that you get some "fallout" in the form of good moose-viewing.⌁

August 20, 1975, Vol. 16, No. 10 (D.S.)

A Landmark Passes

Many of us were sorry to see the disappearance of one of the Park's more interesting landmarks this past summer. This was an old fire tower located on a hilltop overlooking the west shore of Smoke Lake. The tower was special because it consisted of a platform, complete with railing and room for three men, mounted eight feet above the topmost branches of a 102-foot tall White Pine. Because of its unique construction and long disuse, we had always assumed it was the oldest fire tower in the Park. Not so, we learned, when we talked to one of the two men who built it back in 1925. The first towers in Algonquin were all steel, erected in 1922 at Farm, Cache, and Trout Lakes.

The treetop version at Smoke Lake was improvised because it was handy to the fire ranger headquarters located there. First the pine was inspected by felling a nearby Sugar Maple into the pine's lower branches and climbing up the "ladder" thus formed. The platform was built of peeled spruce poles hauled up to the pine top by rope and then cut there with axes and fastened into place with angle braces. All this derring-do soon paid off with the discovery of a fire at Ragged Lake several miles south of the tree, and many others were spotted during the years that followed. The treetop tower was not used after the 1930s but did stand for a full 50 years until the ancient tree crashed to earth in a storm last July.⌁

September 3, 1975, Vol. 16, No. 12 (D.S.)

Winter Notes

Every season of every year has its memorable features and events. Last winter was no exception, and since so few of our visitors know Algonquin in winter we thought it worthwhile to record a few winter happenings.

The maximum snow accumulation was only about two feet, and there were very few nights when the thermometer reached 30 below. So the winter was on the mild side as Algonquin winters go, but in spite of this there were remarkably few birds. This really showed up on the second annual Algonquin Christmas Bird Census. Thirty-one observers (including many summer students who came up just for the occasion) tromped through the bush all day on January 3 in a 15-mile circular area centred at the Museum. Even though they started out at 6 a.m. when it was still pitch-black (to listen for owls) and stayed out until it was dark again, the total bird count was only 722 individuals of 21 species. Only the year before, just 15 observers had seen at least 5,240 individuals of 31 species.

Why the big difference? In most cases the birds that were absent this past winter were winter finches — wide-ranging seed-eaters that depend entirely on the seed crops of certain tree species for their winter food and survival. The trouble is that most trees produce a good crop only once every several years over large areas. For example, the winter before last there were thousands of Pine Siskins in our Yellow Birch trees all winter long. In fact, the 1,748 seen on our first bird census was a high for North America. There were also good numbers of Goldfinches visiting White Birch trees and White-winged Crossbills extracting seeds from the cones of White Spruce. This past winter we saw no Pine Siskins, no Goldfinches, and only seven Crossbills, so it seems clear that the preferred seeds of these birds had utterly failed, forcing the birds to search elsewhere.

Thus, our intrepid census-takers straggled in, cold and hungry, having learned a fundamental lesson in winter ecology — but with precious few birds on their lists.

They did not come back empty-handed, however. Everybody had had an invigorating day, one party had had a good view of a mink, two had seen otters, and almost everyone saw or heard at least one wolf — at Canisbay Lake, at Source Lake, near Smoke Lake, and right at the Museum bird feeder.

Rosie, a wild but fearless Timber Wolf, visiting the bird feeder at the staffhouse of the old Museum.

Now, it may seem a little unusual to have a wolf come to a bird feeder, but for the last two winters it has been visited by almost as many mammals as by birds. There have been Red Squirrels, Flying Squirrels, Deer Mice, a Short-tailed Shrew, foxes, martens, and fishers. But heading the list has been a wolf who, perhaps once a week on the average, at any time of the day or night, would saunter up to the feeder, help itself to whatever suet or food scraps were there, and eat them, even with people sitting inside less than two feet away watching through the window.

Lest *The Raven* be accused of telling tall tales, we hasten to add that we have ample proof of these visitations. Not only do we have photos showing wolf, armchair observers, and feeder, but also the feeder's base of quarter-inch plywood is missing two wolf-size bites. It seems that on at least two occasions the wolf arrived to find only a thin, frozen layer of food on the plywood so it … well … ate part of our feeder. If you have squirrel problems at your feeder back home, we are not impressed. ∞

May 12, 1976, Vol. 17, No. 1 (D.S.)

Underground Flowers

"I must not forget to mention that delicate and lovely flower of May, the Fringed Polygala. It is a rather shy flower and is not found in every wood. One day we went up and down through the woods looking for it — woods of mingled oak, chestnut, pine, and hemlock — and were about to give it up when suddenly we came upon a gay company of them beside an old wood-road. It was as if a flock of small rose-purple butterflies had alighted there on the ground before us. The whole plant has a singularly fresh and tender aspect."

This quotation from the writings of Mr. Burroughs, an early American naturalist, rather nicely sums up our impressions of one of Algonquin's most beautiful flowers. His comparison of the flower to a small butterfly is not at all far-fetched because there really are two purple-pink "wings" on either side of the flower's central structure. In fact, the Fringed Polygala is known to many people by the much simpler and more descriptive name of "Gaywings."

Unfortunately, Gaywings is a spring flower, and not many Park visitors get to see it at its best. Even now, in the last week of June, you will be doing very well to find more than a few scattered plants still sporting their fantastic blooms. The rest have all been pollinated by bumblebees and have melted into the summer greenery.

But, however confusing this may seem, our Algonquin Gaywings are nevertheless at the peak of their flowering season — right now. The catch is that the Fringed Polygala has two kinds of flowers, the rose-purple "butterflies" described by Mr. Burroughs and which are now all but finished for the year, and a second, less obvious type of flower. Even though these other flowers are doing their thing right this week, you aren't likely to see them without a special search because they are very small (about half the width of your little fingernail) and for the even better reason that they grow underground.

Now, there are many perplexing things in this world, but underground flowers have surely got to be near the top of the list. How can they open? How can they release their pollen or receive pollen from other flowers? How can any seeds produced get to new sites suitable for germination and growth into new plants? These questions have interesting answers, which we know, thanks to a painstaking study carried out here in the Park a few years ago. To begin with, the underground flowers do not open, and there is no question of cross-pollination with other flowers. They pollinate themselves instead. This means that the seeds will grow into exact copies of the parent plant, with almost no chance of producing new, perhaps better-adapted individuals. This might seem to be a disadvantage, but, in fact, it is not so very different from many other plants that reproduce by suckers or underground shoots and very rarely produce any seeds at all.

We still have the question of how the seeds produced by the underground flowers of Gaywings are dispersed to new locations. The answer is that ants do the job, not out of the goodness of their tiny hearts but because on the outside of each seed is a transparent, sac-like appendage filled with an oily liquid the ants find particularly appealing. So appealing, in fact, that at least three species of ant make a regular practice of cutting the seeds out of the ripe fruits resulting from Gaywings flowers (both underground and aerial) and carrying them as far as 30 feet back to their nests. There, the ants chew on the transparent, outside appendages of the seeds and eat the oily food they contain. Then, having no further use for the seeds, the ants carry them out of the nest and drop them in nearby refuse dumps. None of this has damaged the seeds which, thanks to the ants, often end up in new locations suitable for the development of new Gaywings plants.

So, underground flowers make some sense after all. Developing just below the surface, they result in the production of "baited" seeds in just the sort of place where ants will find them. The ants get fed, the seeds get dispersed, and we come to the end of our story. ∽

June 23, 1976, Vol. 17, No. 2 (D.S.)

Ants are attracted to the underground flowers of Fringed Polygala.

Algonquin Battle Scene

Anyone walking in hardwood bush on the west side of the Park these days may well wonder what has "hit the place." Virtually all of the Sugar Maple seedlings that carpet the forest floor have only a few tattered leaf remnants, and in many cases this is true of the bigger trees also.

The cause of all this was the Bruce Spanworm, a small, three-quarter-inch long moth caterpillar that munched away on our maples until the middle of June, at which point they entered their summer-long cocoon stage in the soil. This is actually the second year in a row that the spanworm has been at such high population levels.

When we described the outbreak last year, we said that we had it on good authority that no damage was foreseen and that predator build-ups would stop the outbreak this year or next.

Well, part of this prediction came true in a spectacular and, in a way, gruesome manner. Last month, when the hardwoods were full of spanworms, they were

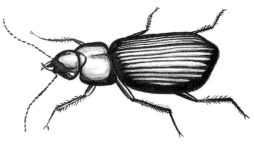

also full of big (an inch-and-a-half long) rather ugly black beetles. At first we did not see the connection, but observations soon showed that the beetles were relentlessly stalking and voraciously devouring the spanworms. The caterpillars were helpless before the onslaught of the black "monsters," which sought out their prey everywhere — on the ground, on tree trunks, and high among the branches. Coming as it did a year after the first spanworm outbreak, the dramatic buildup of the beetle population was a beautiful example of the principle that predator numbers depend on the abundance of prey.

We still don't know the whole story, however, because in the middle of June the beetles abruptly and almost completely disappeared. Did they starve when the spanworms went into the cocoon stage and became unavailable? Had the beetles significantly reduced the spanworm population before they both disappeared from view? We don't know.

July 7, 1976, Vol. 17, No. 4 (D.S.)

A Page From the Past

Those who have taken us up on our suggestion to walk the Whiskey Rapids Trail will know that the Oxtongue River was the scene of intense human activity just 80 years ago. Still, in contemplating the peaceful river of today, it takes some imagination to picture the log drives that took place each spring or the lives led by the men who cut the logs in remote winter camps back in the 1890s. We believe, therefore, that you will share our interest in the following account of logging camplife along the Oxtongue, taken from the *Bobcaygeon Independent* (Feb. 22, 1895).

"A considerable number of men arrived this week from the Gilmour shanties, the winter's cut having ceased about 10 days ago. The company have about 11 camps and two jobbers, averaging about 55 men to the camp. Supplying this little army of men, together with over 150 pairs of horses, was in itself a large undertaking. Dorset, on the Bobcaygeon road, is a depot point at which provisions and supplies are gathered from Haliburton County and Huntsville,

and are then cadged to the camps over the company's tote road of 47 miles. On an average, 65 cadge teams have been engaged all winter drawing in supplies for the camps from Dorset, and occasionally a camp would get down to pork and bread before a team could reach them.

About half the camps are situated along the Canoe Lake river (the Oxtongue – ed.) which is about 10

River drivers on the Oxtongue River around the turn of the last century. ➤

rods in width and between four and five miles in length. The men were sent in early in the fall and had a fine season for cutting up to Christmas. Since then the snow got deeper, but as soon as it became troublesome, the skidding of logs was stopped and the men were put to work close to the river, so that the teams drew from the stump to the dump. One of the camps having 75 men had 14 teams, and each team made 17 trips a day, drawing an average of six logs at a load.

In the old days the system was to pick out the best trees, and the same ground was gone over year after year. The rule now is to make a clean cut as they go, that is, every live pine over 10 inches in diameter is cut down, and whatever is of any use is taken out of it. The cross-cut saw is now used much more than was the case, and the axe less, the felling being done with the saw. A great saving in timber is made in this way, especially with large trees. They cut closer to the ground, and there is no waste in butting. It is usual for three men to work together, one measures and chops, and two saw. The chopper puts a cut four or five inches in depth on the under-side of the tree indicating the direction it has to fall and marks out the work for the saw on the fallen tree, making the logs of various lengths according to the peculiarities of the tree. Sixty-five logs a day is the customary allowance for each gang of three, and if they cut more it is usual to 'bank' the extra ones, so that on a stormy day the men need not go out if they have enough 'in bank'.

The old-fashioned camboose, or great log fire in the centre of the shanty, with the swinging jack and steaming kettle, and cheerful flames dancing up through the stack in the trough roof, has become a memory of the past, and the cooking is now done on a large stove and in an attachment to the shanty, which also contains the bunks of the cook and foreman. The shanty is heated with a stove. Square box stoves were used until this winter, but the men broke them so frequently in putting on pots to heat water for washing their clothes, that this year round stoves were adopted so that nothing could be put on them, and the men built a fire outside between two stumps, suspending a pot from a pole when they wished to luxuriate in a clean shirt.

There are at present only a few men in the woods, river 'drivers' who are filling in time cutting boom stuff and preparing for the opening of the lakes, when the enormous accumulation of logs, some 300,000, or about 50 million feet of pine will be floated down the streams, rapids, lakes, slides, falls, and dams, passing Dorset, Minden, Bobcaygeon, and Peterboro (sic), and in the end bringing up at the great saw mills of the company, at Trenton on the shore of Lake Ontario."

To this old account, written just two years after the Park was established, we might add that although the camplife described above was typical of those early days, the ambitious scheme to float logs from Algonquin to Lake Ontario was not. The amazing thing is that it actually worked — except for the fact that the logs had started to rot by the time they got there. This little miscalculation led, a few years later, to the bankruptcy of the Gilmour Lumber Company and the abandonment of the village of Mowat at the top of Canoe Lake — but that's another story. ∞

July 7, 1976, Vol. 17, No. 4 (D.S.)

Missing for 76 Years

Two years ago we reported our failure to find a bog "near Catfish Lake" where, way back in 1900, the great botanist John Macoun had collected nine species of orchids, including three that had never been seen since.

The one we wanted to rediscover most was the rose-magenta Dragon's-Mouth or Arethusa because, in the opinion of many people, it is the most beautiful of all our native orchids. As another early naturalist put it, "We shall never forget the moment when our eyes first fell on its blossom in the lonely depths of a sphagnum bog. The feeling was irresistible that we had surprised some strange, sentient creature in its secret bower of moss; that it was alert and listening intently with pricked-up ears."

As in many areas, success in orchid-hunting often comes when you least expect it. And so it was with us when we discovered some 30 stunning Arethusas last June 7 in a little bog near the Park's southeast boundary. Our surprise was total, but having once broken the "Arethusa barrier," it wasn't too hard to do again — one of our staff found another one five days later right on the Booth's Rock Trail. After the passing of 76 years without a single record, Arethusa had been rediscovered twice within a week.

Arethusas are finished blooming for this year, but several of Algonquin's 33 other orchids are in flower right now. ∞

July 14, 1976, Vol. 17, No. 5 (D.S.)

Arethusa, Algonquin's missing orchid from 1900 to 1976.

Sphyrapicus and the Freeloaders

"Who or what is a sphyrapicus?" you ask. Well, even if you aren't a Latin scholar, you probably already know the subject of this article, at least by its English name, the Yellow-bellied Sapsucker. The trouble is, the name sounds so ridiculous and has been used so often to poke good-natured fun at bird-watchers, that many people aren't really sure if the bird actually exists.

To any Doubting Thomases we give our solemn word that the Yellow-bellied Sapsucker is alive and well throughout the northeastern United States and south-central Canada, including Algonquin. In fact, here in the Park the sapsucker is the most common of our eight species of woodpeckers and, as such, is probably seen most often by Park visitors. It is about eight or nine inches long and mostly black above but with a conspicuous white stripe on the wing. The belly is (sure enough) yellowish-white, and the head has black and white stripes, which rather attractively set off a bright red patch on the crown and, in the male, another red patch on the throat.

But even if this description doesn't ring a bell, you don't have to go far to find convincing proof of the sapsucker's presence. Chances are good that there are telltale, evenly-spaced, vertical rows of holes on a White Birch near your campsite. These are the holes made by the sapsucker in its quest for the sap flowing in the tree's conductive tissue just below the bark.

The Mourning Cloak butterfly, the White-breasted Nuthatch, and the Ruby-throated Hummingbird all benefit from the holes made by Yellow-bellied Sapsuckers.

White Birches seem to be the trees most often tapped in this way, but they are far from the only ones.

Maples, alders, some spruces, and the Yellow Birch all get attention as well. Some species are used at certain seasons. For example, White Birches do not leaf out until a month after sapsuckers return to the Park in late April. During this period when there is little sap flowing in their favourite tree, sapsuckers often attack hemlocks instead.

So far, we have neglected the question of how a sapsucker sucks sap. The answer is that it doesn't. It licks the sap oozing out of the holes with its brush-like tongue or drinks it like water

— by taking a beakful and tilting its head back. Even more common is its habit of catching insects (the major part of its diet) and "dunking" them in the sap. Sapsuckers often mush mayflies or ants in their sap-holes for several minutes before finally eating them or taking them to their young. This certainly doesn't get sapsuckers any marks for good table manners, but it does get them a significant dietary supplement in a simple and unique way.

Even more interesting, however, is the influence the drilling for sap has on other members of the forest community. In effect, what's sauce for the sapsucker is sauce for the neighbours, and a whole host of freeloaders capitalize on the sap flowing from the sapsucker's not-so-private wells. Flies, wasps, ants, and butterflies (especially the beautiful Mourning Cloak) are all attracted to the sap. So are warblers, other woodpeckers, nuthatches, and Red Squirrels. Many of these larger visitors not only drink the sap but eat the insects that have been attracted as well. Hummingbirds find active sapsucker trees to be such a good thing that they visit more often than sapsuckers themselves. Often, a female hummingbird will construct her tiny nest on a nearby branch, from which she can make short trips to gather sap and insects for her young. The activity goes on all night, too. At sunset, flying squirrels arrive for their share of the sap, and so do moths — if they can get past the bats that patrol back and forth in front of the tree waiting for just such visitors.

At favourite trees, sapsuckers keep the sap flowing by drilling more holes above the old ones. Occasionally they pay a price for their weakness for such liquid refreshment by drinking fermented sap — and more than one observer has reported seeing sapsuckers that were quite definitely drunk.

But the real price paid for all this revelry is the one paid by the host — the tree. Repeated drilling can effectively girdle the tree, killing the part above the holes. Or, death may be indirect as when fungal spores enter through the sapsucker wounds and infect the wood, causing it to slowly rot. Even when the tree survives, it may be permanently weakened. One of the commonest defects in hemlock, for example, is "ring shake," a splitting of the wood between adjacent annual growth rings. For many years, the cause was unknown, but then someone noticed that even on shakes over a century old there were discoloured patches in a pattern of "tell-tale, evenly-spaced, vertical rows." The shakes were caused (you guessed it) by sphyrapicus, who, along with the freeloaders, had visited the hemlocks over 100 years earlier.

July 14, 1976, Vol. 17, No. 5 (D.S.)

"Long-Leggedy Beasties"

Everybody who comes to Algonquin Park wants to see wildlife — by which most people mean mammals. We all see Red Squirrels and chipmunks, of course, and with a bit of luck you should spot fox, beaver, and White-tailed Deer. You always have a chance of seeing others as well, but the fact remains that well over half of our Algonquin mammals are usually active only at night.

This puts us in the frustrating position of only being able to guess at the identity of whatever is causing those intermittent rustlings and scurryings that we hear in the blackness surrounding our tent. When this happens, we have two choices: we can snuggle deeper into our sleeping bag and recite the old English prayer "From ghosties and ghoulies, long-leggedy beasties and things that go bump in the night, good Lord deliver us!"; or we can analyze the situation (calmly and rationally, of course).

Now it is true *The Raven* does not have all the answers in this area, but we can help you with at least one common night-time sound in Algonquin. The animal responsible for the "hop, hop, hop" we often hear in the dead leaves on the darkened forest floor is one of the Park's most beautiful and most interesting mammals — a jumping mouse.

We realize the words "beautiful" and "interesting" may seem a little too extravagant to be applied to mice, but this is because the only mouse many people have ever seen is the unwelcome, dirty-brown House Mouse, which our ancestors unintentionally brought from Europe. Our eight native mice are really quite different, not only from the House Mouse but also from each other. They range from the large, aquatic muskrat, to the small-eared and small-eyed Red-backed Vole of our coniferous forests, and, in the hardwoods, to the Deer Mouse, with its large, appealing dark eyes and attractive white underparts.

Most different of all are the jumping mice, which most authorities now place in a separate family of their own. We have two kinds, the Meadow Jumping Mouse, which prefers beaver meadows and grassy stream banks, and the Woodland Jumping Mouse, which tends to be found among brushy vegetation near forest streams or lakes. The one you are most likely to see in Algonquin (or rather hear hopping by in the night) is the woodland species. If you are ever lucky enough to actually see one in good light, no matter what may have been your previous opinions of "mice," you will have to agree that this one is beautiful. It is white underneath, golden-yellow on the sides, and buffy-brown on the back. The tail is often a good six inches long, accounting for over half the total length, and is tipped with white.

Our local race of Woodland Jumping Mouse was described from a specimen captured at Smoke Lake back in 1940 and named in honour of the Park, *Napaeozapus insignis algonquinensis*. The *Napaeozapus* part of this

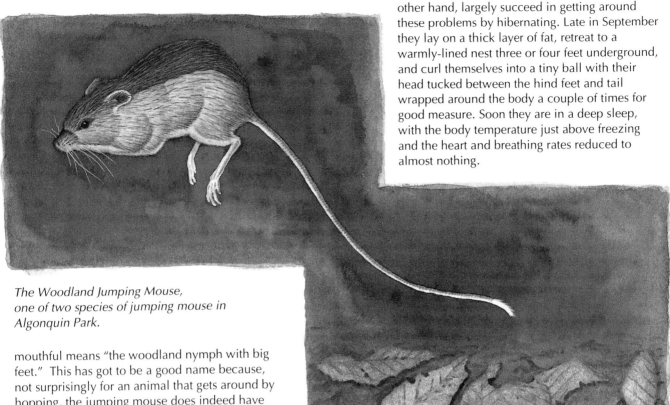

other hand, largely succeed in getting around these problems by hibernating. Late in September they lay on a thick layer of fat, retreat to a warmly-lined nest three or four feet underground, and curl themselves into a tiny ball with their head tucked between the hind feet and tail wrapped around the body a couple of times for good measure. Soon they are in a deep sleep, with the body temperature just above freezing and the heart and breathing rates reduced to almost nothing.

The Woodland Jumping Mouse,
one of two species of jumping mouse in
Algonquin Park.

mouthful means "the woodland nymph with big feet." This has got to be a good name because, not surprisingly for an animal that gets around by hopping, the jumping mouse does indeed have big, strong hind legs and feet.

Most of the time, jumping mice move along in short hops less than a foot long, but when hard-pressed they can cover astonishing distances. We remember one that we discovered in the Museum lobby one morning a few years ago. When we tried to shoo it out the door, it became a lightning-fast pingpong ball, zinging around the lobby in 10-foot "hops," literally bouncing off the walls before finally escaping. Such remarkable ability must give jumping mice an advantage not enjoyed by more conventional mice when attacked by their many predators.

Superior escape ability is not the only advantage possessed by jumping mice. All other mice remain active during the winter, and although they are usually out of sight in tunnels beneath the snow, they are still regularly detected by sharp-eared owls and foxes or chased down right in the tunnels by weasels. Jumping mice, on the

Since they spend almost two-thirds of every year out of harm's way, asleep underground, jumping mice commonly live to be three or four years old, which is a ripe old age for a mouse. They do not emerge until well into May to resume their nightly quests for the berries, seeds, and insects that form their diet.

So the next time you hear a "hop, hop, hop" in the dead leaves outside your tent late at night, don't pray for deliverance from "ghosties" or "ghoulies." It's only a long-leggedy beastie called a jumping mouse. … But then … on the other hand … it just might be a … ??!*☜

July 21, 1976, Vol. 12, No. 6 (D.S.)

Midgets and Midges

We don't know anyone who hasn't stopped, at one time or another, to admire the grace and beauty of swallows. Few creatures can match these aerial midgets in sheer elegance, let alone in effortless, buoyant flight.

And yet, because swallows are so common, we are probably guilty, more often than not, of taking them for granted. We all note their arrival as soon as the ice goes out in the spring, but very quickly we accept them as part

of the everyday Park scenery and only suddenly realize one day that "all the swallows have gone."

Now it may come as a surprise, but that day isn't very far off. As we write this, Barn Swallows still have young in the nest (their second brood of the year), but our four other common species have all finished nesting and are now flocking up. In fact, after next week, you won't be able to see any Barn Swallows in the Park at all, and most of the others will disappear during the few weeks that follow.

In this day and age we all know that birds disappear because they migrate (usually all the way to South America in the case of our Algonquin swallows). While

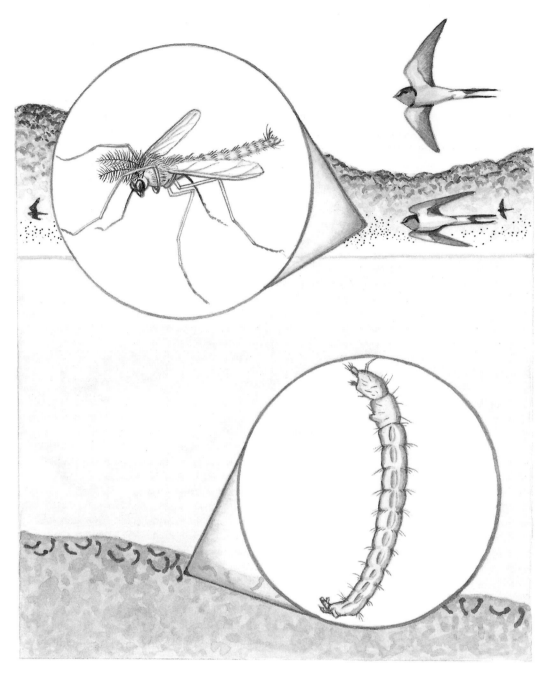

Midge larvae living in the bottom mud of our lakes become food for swallows when they rise to the surface and take wing as air-breathing adults.

Actually, there are at least two reasons why we should not laugh at the idea. The first is that Sam and his contemporaries had some circumstantial evidence in support of their idea. Why, after all, should swallows always appear just after the ice goes out unless that was what enabled them to return, and why should swallows form such large flocks over water in late summer if they were not preparing to "take the plunge"?

The second reason for not laughing is that, crazy as it may seem, there really is a very close and vital link between swallows and lake bottoms. Since we would probably have no swallows at all without this link, it is well worth giving it a close look.

Why, in fact, do swallows spend so much time skimming over the waves, or, putting it another way, why are the insects the swallows are obviously catching found in such great numbers out over open water? After all, there is nothing for an insect to eat out there. Well, if you can manage to get a good look at those insects, you will see that they are midges, tiny mosquito-like creatures (don't worry, these don't bite) with long legs and antennae. In good light and at certain times, you can see tens, if not hundreds, of thousands of them dancing in the air just above the lake surface. The reason they occur in such numbers over water is that they have just emerged to begin their adult life in the air after spending one or two

we regret their departure, we don't find it particularly mysterious.

Once again, we are guilty of taking something for granted — this time the comparatively recent knowledge that even very small birds can and do fly thousands of miles each year. It was not so long ago that most people thought such an idea was preposterous, and everybody "knew" that swallows, for example, spent the winter buried in the mud at the bottom of lakes and rivers. Even the great British man of letters, Samuel Johnson, writing 200 years ago, said, "A number of them conglobulate together by flying round and round and then all in a heap throw themselves under the water." Today, we all smile at the quaint language and dismiss the supposed association of delicate, aerial swallows with cold, murky lake bottoms as totally ridiculous.

years as worm-like larvae half-buried in the murky ooze on the bottom far below.

Many of the larvae are red and are given the rather gruesome name "bloodworms." They make a rather gruesome living, too, down there in the sunless depths, because they feed on corpses — the tiny dead plants and animals that gently rain down from the sunlit, productive zone just below the lake surface. There are many different kinds of midges, often 50 or more species in the same lake, and each one has its own preferred depth. Those that live in shallow water have plenty of company in the form of living plants and other insect larvae, but those found in the cold, deep parts of the lake are almost the only living things to be found there. As such, they are extremely important to Lake Trout, which in summer are confined to the cold depths and do not have access to the more varied and abundant food supply in the warmer, shallower sections of the lake.

The different midge species also emerge to the surface and adulthood at different times of the year. Some appear just after the ice goes out in the spring, and they are what sustain the first swallows. More species emerge in June and early July, and these are used to feed hungry young swallows in the nest. The numbers of emerging species and individuals start to tail off at the end of July, which helps explain why the swallows are already starting to "conglobulate."

The close and vital link between swallows and lake bottoms will soon be broken, forcing the swallows to leave on their long journey to South America. While there is still time, it might be an idea to stop and admire them — and also the intricate web of nature on which they depend — just once more.☞

July 28, 1976, Vol. 17, No. 7 (D.S.)

The Big Pine

Recent mention was made of the Park area's only two remaining stands of virgin White Pine, and we promised to return for a closer look.

Before we do, however, we should point out that big old White Pine can actually be found in many other places in Algonquin. For example, you can see a fair-sized tree right on Highway 60 at Mile 18.6 (km 28),* and there are many places in the Park interior where the horizon is broken by a giant old pine towering high above the surrounding forest. But, although such trees are not really rare, the fact remains that they are the isolated, scattered, individual remnants of the White Pine that grew here when the pioneer loggers first pushed up from the Ottawa Valley over 100 years ago.

This is what makes our two old pine natural zones so special — they are the only places left today where you can go and see what the original old forests of Algonquin were like. Only there can you see reasonably extensive stands (as opposed to isolated individuals) of ancient White Pine.

The first of our stands (set aside back in 1938 by Superintendent Frank MacDougall) is located almost exactly in the centre of the Park, just east of Big Crow Lake. It is about 180 acres in size and can be reached by following a mile-long trail starting at the dam on the Crow River.

The other stand is actually just outside the Park at Dividing Lake on our southwestern boundary. The best way to get there is by paddling south from Smoke Lake.

If you do visit either of these stands, be prepared for a surprise. Although they are both among the finest remaining stands of White Pine, not only in Ontario but in all of North America, it is quite possible to stand in the middle of either one and not see a single pine. But don't give up. As you explore further, in a forest of Sugar Maple, Beech, and Yellow Birch, your eyes will suddenly stop on a massive column rising from the forest floor and disappearing into the hardwood forest canopy above. Then, away off in the forest you will see another ponderous column, and perhaps a third in a different direction. These are the huge trunks of the 300-year-old pines, many of them over 40 inches in diameter. Only if you find a break in the hardwood canopy and crane your neck will you be able to see the first branches on these forest giants, let alone their towering crowns 130 feet or more above the forest floor.

While there is no denying that these old pine are mighty impressive, many people find it hard to believe that the stands themselves, with only one to three pine per acre, can be truly representative of Algonquin's original forests. We have all heard the old accounts of the Ottawa Valley being "blue with pine," and so we conjure up the mental picture of vast, solid stands of White Pine. This may have been accurate in some areas, but in most of Algonquin the pine grew just as we see them at Big Crow and Dividing Lakes today — as individual giants scattered among mature hardwoods. The distribution of old rotting pine stumps, still visible today in our west-side hardwood forests, is much the same.

The stumps are all that are left of most of the Park's original big White Pine. The loggers of the 1800s, toiling with axes and horses, felled the great trees, squared them (you can see an example of this at the Pioneer Logging Exhibit), and floated them out of the Park each spring. In spite of their primitive technology and the remoteness of the Park area, it took the pioneer loggers less than 70 years to take almost all the big pine in Algonquin. It is

---

* This famous tree, unofficially called the Grant Tayler White Pine after a former Park naturalist who saved it from a highway-widening program, finally fell in November 1992.

only due to some fluke of history that our two stands were spared.

Today, of course, they are protected as official natural zones, but we should be under no illusions as to their eventual fate. Like all trees, the big pine will die someday — probably within the next 100 years or so — and the prospects are not good that they will be succeeded by more big pine. Young pine can rarely establish themselves in the thick layer of dead leaves in hardwood forests and, even if they do, cannot tolerate the shade of the trees overhead.

You might wonder, then, how the original big White Pine got established. Well, all indications are that lightning-caused ground fires occasionally burned off the dead leaves and killed some of the bigger trees, thus allowing more light to reach the forest floor. These are precisely the conditions that would permit White Pine to get established and put on good growth before the hardwoods could recover enough to shade them out. Even if such fires occurred only once every two centuries in any one given area, they would nicely account for the scattered presence of giant pine among our original hardwoods.

The catch is that today we put out all fires — whether they are natural or not — and this does not bode well for the return of White Pine to most of our hardwood forests. Exceptions to this are the primitive zones and watershed natural zones where the Ontario government has announced its intention to allow natural, lightning fires to burn.

This policy is not yet in effect, and even if it were, we cannot expect to see any really big old pine in those zones for another 200 years. If you don't want to wait that long, go see the stands at Big Crow or Dividing Lakes. They're open for business now.↩

August 11, 1976, Vol. 17, No. 9 (D.S.)

The Frank MacDougall Parkway

If you are a regular visitor to Algonquin you have probably already noticed new green, white, and blue signs along the highway showing a stylized canoeist and the words "Frank MacDougall Parkway." On August 21 a special ribbon-cutting ceremony was held at the West Gate to honour the late Mr. MacDougall and to name the Parkway (that part of Highway 60 lying in Algonquin) in his memory.

As you may not know who Frank MacDougall was or why his memory should be so honoured, we therefore offer the following brief highlights of his career.

Mr. MacDougall was Superintendent of Algonquin from 1931 to 1941, which was a time that saw more important developments in the Park than any other comparable period. Chief among these was Frank's personal introduction of the plane to Park management. Patrolling Algonquin in an open cockpit biplane, our first flying superintendent almost single-handedly turned the tide in the battles against poachers in the winter and fires in the summer.

The era of modern recreation in Algonquin also began in this period with the opening of the highway now named in his honour in 1936, and Mr. MacDougall was the first to see the coming conflict between loggers and canoeists. He did much to alleviate this problem by reserving shorelines and other special areas from logging (for example, the Crow River White Pines). These reservations were a revolutionary concept back in the 1930s, but they are the direct forerunner of the zones established in the 1974 Algonquin Master Plan and that appear on this year's new canoe route map. MacDougall also foresaw the greatly increased pressure on Park fisheries that came with the opening of the new highway, and it was his efforts that led to the establishment on Lake Opeongo of what we now know as "the fish lab" — the centre for Brook and Lake Trout research in Canada.

Frank left Algonquin in 1941 to become Deputy Minister of the Department of Lands and Forests (the

forerunner of today's Ministry of Natural Resources). He held this post for 25 years, a record for Ontario deputy ministers, during which he directed the development of many services we now take for granted. The most important of these was the widespread, efficient use of aircraft in fighting forest fires, an area in which Ontario is an acknowledged world leader.

In recognition of this accomplishment (and other contributions, such as being a major influence in the design of the deHavilland Beaver aircraft), Mr. MacDougall was elected to the Canadian Aviation Hall of Fame in 1974.

Frank retired in 1966 but continued to fly for another eight years. He died on June 27, 1975, at the age of 79. ∞

August 25, 1976, Vol. 17, No. 11 (D.S.)

Heavenly Ecology

Everybody, in this day and age, has heard of "ecology." In fact, it would be fairly difficult to pass even a single day without coming across the word some place or another. All the same, we suspect that many people aren't really comfortable with the term, and we think we know why.

Ecology is the study of the relationships between living plants and animals and their environments. Most of us, however, are a little skeptical about such a definition

because most relationships aren't especially obvious, and deep down inside we suspect they can't really be all that important.

To be sure, we can all admit that deer and hemlock trees have an important relationship in Algonquin because snow is less deep under thick hemlock branches, thus permitting the deer to move around and reach food more easily. We can also agree that rocks are important to Algonquin trout because they are the source of nutrients like calcium and phosphorus, needed by algae, which are eaten by small water animals, which are eaten by the minnows, which support our trout.

Be that as it may, it is one thing to see an ecological relationship between a hemlock and a deer directly below or between a trout and the rocks that hold the lake water. It is quite another thing to see relationships that stretch over thousands of miles, and ecologists are always telling us that our planet is one single system of related parts.

It may be hard to believe, for example, that anything in the jungles of the Amazon can affect anything in Algonquin, but in fact there are many such influences, and others that originate even farther away.

Right now, for example, we are seeing dramatic ecological adjustments being made by almost all of Algonquin's plants and animals. Red and Sugar Maples

Guided by faraway stars.

from time to time, you will hear thin call-notes of birds passing invisibly overhead. Strange as it seems, there is a very real connection between the stars, trillions of miles away, and those tiny songsters winging their way through the night on the planet Earth.

The birds, of course, are undertaking their annual fall migration — a trip that takes many Algonquin thrushes, warblers, and finches 4,000 miles or more from their summer haunts to exotic tropical winter quarters. That tiny warblers, weighing only 20 grams, can have the energy to fly such long distances is fantastic enough. What is even more amazing is that they can find their way, especially since many of them are young of the year making the southward trip for the first time.

The extraordinary navigational prowess of migratory birds was a complete mystery for many years, but recently a few secrets have been unravelled. It was found, for example, that caged migratory birds had a strong urge to fly south on clear, starry nights but had no real preference when the sky was overcast. When the same birds were exposed to an artificial sky in a planetarium, they could be fooled into orienting in any direction chosen by the researcher merely by a change in the orientation of the artificial night-time sky.

These birds were obviously capable of reading the stars and adjusting their flight direction accordingly. Further experiments showed that the part of the sky that really matters is the part we pay attention to as well, the northern sector, which includes such familiar constellations as the Big and Little Dippers. The birds aren't born with knowledge of these star patterns, but during their first summer somehow learn to associate them with "north" by observing their nightly rotation around the North Star. (Actually, of course, it is not the stars but the earth that rotates, and because the North Star is directly above our North Pole, only it "stands still" in the sky and identifies "north.")

If all this seems to be heady stuff, it's because it is. The unerring fall flights of Algonquin migrants are guided by unimaginably distant stars twinkling down on us from the blackness of space. This gets our nomination as the ultimate in ecological relationships.

September 1, 1976, Vol. 17, No. 12 (D.S.)

are starting to shut down the sugar manufacturing machinery of their leaves — which by the end of September will reach a peak of blazing colour — and then fall brown and lifeless to the forest floor. Beavers are hauling branches down to mist-shrouded moonlit ponds. By day, the crystal stillness of Park forests is broken by Red Squirrels clipping pine cones for winter storage. Bears are gorging on beechnuts and laying on the last pounds of fat, which will sustain them during their long winter sleep. … All these changes are in response to the shorter and cooler days of fall, which in turn result from just a few degrees of difference in the tilt of the earth towards the sun, 93 million miles away.

This might seem to be the extreme in long-distance ecology, but it isn't — not by a long shot. Try going out in the Park on a clear fall night. With luck, you may be treated to the ghostly, shimmering Northern Lights or to the wild music of wolves rolling over ancient Algonquin hills. But even without these bonuses you will see a spectacular mosaic of tens of thousands of stars, and,

Waking Up

As we write this in early May, each day brings new signs of spring. Warm sunshine floods down through the leafless hardwoods to carpets of Trout Lilies and Spring Beauties. Bumblebees lazily work their way from one blossom to the next, and the drumming of woodpeckers echoes through the slowly stirring forest. Faint music drifts to earth from high, straggling lines of geese returning to the far north, and distant hills are washed with the scarlet of flowering Red Maples and the pastel green of leafing Aspens.

All these are sure signs that Algonquin is waking up at last from the long, long winter, and each, when you stop and think about it, borders on the miraculous. To us, however, one particular sign of spring is more amazing than all the others. The return of the groundhog to grassy clearings throughout Algonquin may not seem outstandingly noteworthy, but we have a good, although partly personal, reason to think it is. As everyone knows, groundhogs spend the winter asleep in burrows. What many people do not realize, however, is that unlike bears and chipmunks, which merely go into an intermittently deep sleep, groundhogs go into a true hibernation that is hard to tell from death itself. A hibernating groundhog, covered with a thick, insulating blanket of fat and curled into a tight ball, has a body temperature as low as 45°F and may breathe only once every five minutes. The blood pressure is drastically lowered, as is the heart beat — to four or five a minute. Of course, it is not hard to see the advantage in this to the groundhog. By lowering the rate of its body processes, the groundhog greatly reduces the rate at which it burns up its stored fat. Even so, the groundhog loses a third or even half its body weight by the time spring arrives.

The winter survival of groundhogs is remarkable enough, but the fact they manage to wake up at all is even more amazing. We suspect that we are not alone in finding that no amount of coffee, cold water in the face, or anything else can ease the misery of getting up at four or five in the morning for an early start on our spring fishing trips. And yet, every Algonquin groundhog puts us to shame each spring by making an almost unbelievable return from five or six months of near death to full wakefulness in just a few hours.

If you share our envy of this miraculous ability, you will be interested to know that scientists have learned the groundhog's secret. Before you get your hopes up, however, we hasten to add that although we will now reveal the secret, we humans will never be able to master the technique.

How does the "lowly" groundhog succeed where we groggy fishermen fail? The key is that the groundhog has large deposits of brown fat — as well as the white fat we

possess. The difference is that the brown fat, when burned by the body, can produce 20 times as much heat as white fat. In fact, at peak efficiency, the brown fat of a groundhog generates as much as 800 calories per minute. It is almost as if the groundhog's layer of fat were a built-in "electric blanket" that is switched on automatically when the first warmth seeps into the frigid burrow and signals that winter has gone. As the brown fat "turns on," the groundhog's temperature, breathing rate, heart beat, and blood pressure start to rise and the half-frozen muscles shiver fitfully.

Before long, the recovery is complete, and the groundhog emerges into the sunny world above. As babies, we humans also have brown fat (around the neck and between the shoulder blades), but as adults we have long since lost our brown fat and with it our capacity for the prodigious production of heat. About all we can do is enviously acknowledge the groundhog's superiority in the matter of waking up and welcome it back as an especially miraculous sign of spring. ❧

May 11, 1977, Vol. 18, No. 1 (D.S.)

"It Revealed Itself Wonderfully to Him ..."

This week marks the 60th anniversary of the death in Algonquin Park, on July 8, 1917, of a tall, quiet man named Tom Thomson. Very few of our readers need an introduction to Thomson, since few painters have had such a profound influence on art in this country and few paintings are more familiar to Canadians than his famous canvasses "West Wind," "Jack Pine," and "Northern River." Today, these and other Thomson paintings are universally recognized as classic portrayals of Canada's north country, and we can only guess what new heights of artistic expression he might have achieved had death not taken him so early in his career as a serious painter.

Thomson is of even more interest to us in Algonquin because it was here that he found his real inspiration and did almost all of his now priceless work. Looking around today at the same scenery he sketched in the Park's early days, we know that Tom Thomson uncannily captured the true essence or "feel" of Algonquin. Even knowing this as we do, however, we suspect that we are far from alone in being unable to fathom the idea of creating a great painting. We appreciate the results, but it is difficult for us to imagine ourselves doing the same thing.

There is one limited sense, nevertheless, in which we can understand what went on in Tom Thomson's mind because we can see many people today doing what he did 60 years ago — getting Algonquin slowly but thoroughly into the bloodstream. Only the particular form of his involvement and its lasting results mark Thomson as different from many thousands of other Park visitors.

The truth is that when Tom Thomson came to Algonquin for the first time in 1912, he was much like anybody else. He was 34, made a reasonably good living in Toronto (as a commercial artist), and there was no hint in his mind or anybody else's of the latent genius that was to express itself in the next five years. True, he did do a little "Sunday painting" in the countryside around Toronto, but he came to the Park not out of a burning drive to find suitable subjects for his art but, rather, because he had heard about Algonquin from friends and thought he would see it for himself. It was not as if he had

The Tom Thomson cairn at Hayhurst Point, Canoe Lake.

a sudden revelation either, when he did come. He camped at the Tea Lake dam, went fishing a lot, and did a bit of sketching — but nothing that really amounted to anything.

Still, whether it was the prospect of more good fishing, the chance to do some serious sketching, or the peace of wild surroundings, something caused Thomson to return to Algonquin in 1913, this time for the whole summer. It was that year the Park consolidated its hold on him. He perfected his canoeing skills and slowly became more and more aware of the Park's subtle moods and beauty. When he returned to Toronto that fall he brought sketches that greatly interested other artists such as A.Y. Jackson, J.E.H. MacDonald, and J.W. Beatty. These men, especially Jackson, generously gave Thomson the benefit of their much greater artistic training and experience while they, inspired by Thomson's visionary renditions of the north country (generally believed at the time to be not worth painting), were so eager to try themselves that they headed up to Algonquin in February. Thomson himself went up for the summer in May in company with Arthur Lismer. In the fall of 1914, Thomson, Jackson, Lismer, and Fred Varley sketched in the Park on their small birch panels, each exploring what at the time were revolutionary techniques and subject matter. Jackson dubbed the little group "The Algonquin Park School of Art," and although its members were soon scattered by the First World War, those who survived joined forces again in 1920, in the Group of Seven, and went on to paint all of Canada. There is no doubt that this major school of Canadian art and the rich cultural legacy it left to Canada were originally inspired by Algonquin and the visions it stirred in their missing comrade.

Thomson spent 1915 based at Mowat Lodge at the north end of Canoe Lake, did a bit of guiding and fire-ranging, and did the sketches for his canvasses "Tea Lake Dam" and "Spring Ice." The following year he spent on the east side of Algonquin working full-time as a fire ranger — although he did find the time to do the sketches for some of his most well-known works, including "West Wind," "The Drive," "The Pointers," and "Jack Pine" (the subject of which, though dead for many years, did not fall until this past winter).

After working on these masterpieces in his "shack" in Toronto during the winter of 1916–17, Thomson returned to Algonquin for the last time in late March. He recorded the unfolding of spring 1917 on Canoe Lake with a sketch every day for two months and only laid aside his paints when the greens of summer put Algonquin into its least colourful season of the year.

Tragically, Tom Thomson did not return from a fishing expedition on July 8, and his death was confirmed eight days later when his body surfaced on Canoe Lake. Endless discussions, books, magazine articles, and television series have suggested that foul play may have been involved, but this is of little consequence.

The only important thing is that Tom Thomson, although he began like any other casual Park visitor, eventually began to see the endlessly beautiful secrets of Algonquin, and he gave us all the priceless gift of that vision. No one said it better than J.E.H. MacDonald on the cairn erected up on Hayhurst Point overlooking the north end of Canoe Lake.

"He lived humbly but passionately with the wild. It made him brother to all untamed things of nature. It drew him apart and revealed itself wonderfully to him. It sent him out from the woods only to show these revelations through his art. And it took him to itself at last."

To commemorate the 60th anniversary of Tom Thomson's death, the National Historic Sites and Monuments Board of Canada, in co-operation with the Ontario Ministry of Natural Resources, will unveil a plaque at the foot of Canoe Lake at 10:00 a.m. on Friday, July 8. That evening, a special program on Tom Thomson will be held at the Pog Lake Outdoor Theatre beginning at 9:15 p.m., and during the week of July 6 to July 13, several Tom Thomson paintings will be on display in the lobby of the Park Museum.

July 6, 1977, Vol. 18, No. 3 (D.S.)

Secret Signals in the Dark

Almost all of us who have camped in Algonquin have experienced the feeling of being totally absorbed by our campfire. In fact, it is so easy to let the flames hypnotize us that often even the distant wail of a loon or the fleeting glimpse of a deer mouse fails to make us aware that thousands of living creatures are going about their lives just beyond the flickering circle of light cast by our fire.

Our unawareness of the life surrounding us is even more understandable in view of the fact that we can neither see nor hear the vast majority of our night-time neighbours — making it all the easier for us to yield ourselves totally to the fire's captivating glow and warmth.

There are a few creatures out there, however, that betray their presence and give us a hint of the complex comings and goings that we normally never know about. One good example that any of us can see at this time of year, particularly near lakes and creeks, is the flashing of fireflies.

We confess to more than a little interest in fireflies, not only because they give dramatically visible proof of the presence of abundant life in the darkness but also because they have to be among the most amazing creatures on Earth. After all, how can mere

insects light up so brilliantly, and what do they accomplish by doing so?

The answers to such questions may not seem important to people who say, quite accurately, that humans have been enjoying the spectacle of fireflies for thousands of years without knowing how or why the light is produced. We think, however, that the truth about fireflies, uncovered by patient research, is far more amazing than anyone could ever have expected — and well worth a brief look.

To be sure, the basic life history of fireflies is not very unusual. They are beetles (not flies), which begin life as flat larvae in damp earth and leaves, preying on slugs, snails, and insects. As adults, some species do not feed at all, others eat nectar and pollen, while still others continue to eat insects. In some cases, adult females are wingless (in which case they are known as glow worms), but in many species both the males and females can fly.

Now all this is straightforward enough; where the fireflies part company with other insects is in the method they use to find each other. In most insects, males find females through a highly developed sense of smell, which in some cases will permit males to

Male and female fireflies communicate through coded light flashes.

locate a single female many miles away. Male and female fireflies, on the other hand, find each other through light signals, and each sex accordingly has a special light-producing organ on the underside of its abdomen. The chemistry of firefly light production is now fairly well understood and is particularly remarkable because it is 100 per cent efficient. That is to say, all the energy used by the firefly is transformed into light, with no production of heat. This is something humans have been unable to accomplish with even the best light bulbs or electronic flashes.

Of course, fireflies did not develop their light organs to teach wasteful humans about energy conservation but rather to ensure that males find and mate with females, in spite of darkness and thick vegetation. It is not enough, however, for a firefly merely to send out light. It must also be able to recognize signals from the opposite sex and to distinguish them from those of other species. It has, in fact, been found that the males of each species of firefly have a distinctive flash and that only females of the same species will respond — by flashing back after a definite interval. For example, the male of one species flies near the ground in strong, regular undulations. As he approaches the bottom of an undulation every six seconds, the male starts a flash that ends when he is well up on his next upward swing. The result is that he makes regular "J's" of yellow-green light every six seconds. If he comes within a few feet of a female, she will respond with a flash of her own, but the male will fly towards her only if her flash follows his by almost exactly two seconds.

With such a marvellous system of "coded" light signals, each species of firefly seemingly has a foolproof way of eliminating confusion and making sure that males mate only with females of the same species. By and large this is true, but codes are made to be broken as much in the world of fireflies as in our own. It seems that the females of some of the larger fireflies recognize the male signals of smaller species, respond with exact imitations of the appropriate female signals, and … in this manner lure the unsuspecting males to their waiting jaws. …

This has to be a particularly ingenious (and nasty) trick to play, but we suspect it is really not too different from countless similar dramas that take place each night totally unseen in the darkness beyond our campfires. ∞

July 13, 1977, Vol. 18, No. 4 (D.S.)

The Lilies and the Lily-Eaters

Long-time readers of *The Raven* will know that we have a special interest in the orchids of Algonquin. This interest stems not only from their extreme beauty but also from the fact that most of our orchids are rather rare. This adds a special challenge to orchid-hunting and makes us much more inclined to stop and admire them when we are lucky enough to find one.

It also means that orchids have what is perhaps an unfair advantage in the popularity contest with other, much more common flowers that we tend to take for granted. The fact is that many flowers we see each day are every bit as beautiful as our orchids, are just as fascinating in the ways they have adapted to live in the Park environment, and — simply because they are so common — are far more important to wildlife than all of our 35 species of orchids put together.

You don't have far to look these days to see a perfect example of what we mean. In fact, all you have to do is go for a short paddle in a sheltered bay or a meandering stream, and the chances are excellent that you will soon see dozens, if not hundreds, of water-lilies. Basically, we have two kinds — those with white blossoms and those with yellow. The white ones are at their peak right now (although you should keep in mind that the flowers are closed up by mid-afternoon), and the yellow ones will be coming into full bloom a bit later on. In either case, the flowers are, if anything, even more spectacular than our Park orchids, and for this reason alone are well worth a close look.

But water-lilies have much more than their blossoms to attract our interest. To begin with, they have evolved unique features that enable them to prosper in what, to most plants, are totally formidable conditions. Since water-lilies grow in moderately deep water, they don't have to contend with shade from overhead trees. However, the waters they grow in are often so heavily stained that little sunlight reaches the bottom, and there is usually so little oxygen that life would be difficult in any case. The obvious solution to both problems is to send leaves up into the air from the bottom of the pond, but this would mean investing a lot of energy in the growth of strong supporting stems. Water-lilies have achieved the most economical possible way of getting their leaves to the bright sunlight and rich oxygen of the air by having leaves that float on the surface. This sounds simpler than it is because the leaves of most plants breathe through pores on their lower surfaces. Perhaps not surprisingly, the pores of water-lily leaves are found exclusively on the upper surface — so they can get oxygen directly from the air after all. Water-lilies do have other, rather special problems, such as getting air down to their roots (solved by special tubes in the leaf stems) and having to store enough energy in their rootstocks every summer so they will be able to send new leaves all the way up to the surface the following spring to replace the ones destroyed by winter ice. In spite of all these obstacles, and as anyone who has done any canoe-tripping in the Park can tell you, water-lilies are spectacularly successful — being found just about everywhere.

As a consequence of their abundance and obvious prosperity, it is only normal that water-lilies are important

to wildlife. Of course, it is almost a cliché that frogs use lily pads as hunting platforms, and every fisherman knows that bass like to lurk under their protective cover, but even more important is the use of water-lilies by a whole host of lily-eaters. The fact that lily pads almost always show signs of being chewed on by small insects gives us a hint of the high nutritional value of water-lilies. This suspicion is confirmed by the fact that Indians used the seeds and rootstocks as food and that moose spend much of the summer browsing on lily pads, their flowers, and stems. Also, moose have even been reported to dive as deep as 18 feet to get at the rootstocks.

The most interesting of all the lily-eaters, however, is the beaver. Now, as everyone knows, the popular image of a beaver is one of an animal that cuts down trees and eats bark. Well, this picture is accurate in the fall, but at this time of year and throughout the summer generally, beavers in Algonquin hardly ever go near trees, let alone cut them down. Instead, they stay in their ponds and live almost entirely on aquatic vegetation — of which by far the most important item is water-lilies (flowers and all). The relationship between the beaver and water-lilies is particularly interesting because in many cases it is the beaver that creates suitable habitat for water-lilies in the first place (by damming up a pond for itself). It is almost as if the beaver were an unintentional farmer. What's more, beavers often spread water-lilies in their ponds by accidentally dropping or discarding pieces of rootstock they have dug up elsewhere in the pond. All this has considerable, if unintended, importance to the beaver because it means the beaver can spend the entire summer eating nutritious, easily obtainable food right within the safe confines of its pond, and it does not have to risk the danger of wolves by going out on land to cut down trees. Also, we have never yet heard of a beaver that was squashed by a falling lily pad.

Humans may not benefit from water-lilies as much as beavers do, but this is no reason to take them for granted. They may be common and they may happen not to be orchids, but they have to be among Algonquin's most fascinating flowers all the same.

July 20, 1977, Vol. 18, No. 5 (D.S.)

Beavers love to eat the water-lilies that abound in the beaver pond environment.

Night-time Entertainers

Just about every regular Algonquin camper has, at one time or another, been woken up, or possibly been scared out of his wits, by explosive hoots, shrieks, and cacklings suddenly turning the night-time silence outside his tent into a madhouse. If you have not yet experienced this yourself, it's just a question of time before you do because the creature responsible for all this bedlam, the Barred Owl, is a common, year-'round Park resident.

When one of these owls finally does choose a perch near your campsite, you may not get much sleep but you may also be treated to some real entertainment — especially if you can see the performer. One fairly typical incident was described over 50 years ago by an early naturalist:

"At one of my lonely wilderness camps in the month of March a pair of Barred Owls came to the trees over my campfire and took up the night with their grotesque courting antics. As imperfectly seen by moonlight and firelight, they nodded and bowed with half-spread wings, and wobbled and twisted their heads from side to side, meantime uttering the most weird and uncouth sounds imaginable; some like maniacal laughter and others like mere chuckles interspersed here and there between loud 'wha whas' and 'hoo-hoo-aws'."

Unfortunately, these occasional night-time visits are all we normally see of the Barred Owl. True, many people have had good success in bringing them in by imitating their most common call — an emphatic, rhythmic "Who cooks for you? Who cooks for you all?", but most of the time we just hear the distant, crazy hoots coming from black hills silhouetted against starry skies, and we can only guess at what the owls are up to.

Personally, we find this a little frustrating, if for no other reason than that we share the common human curiosity about the lives of entertainers. Learning about the Barred Owl's world is doubly difficult, and doubly fascinating, because it is one in which humans are almost totally helpless. In fact, when you stop and think about it, the ability of our Barred Owls to navigate among the branches of a pitch-black forest and to successfully locate and capture prey is nothing short of astounding.

Barred Owls can put on a real show!

Of course, everyone knows that owls have superb night vision; the eyes of the Barred Owl in particular are about 100 times more sensitive to light than our eyes, which means the owl can see in what to us appears to be total darkness. But even this is only half the story. Experiments have shown that even in the complete absence of all light, when even an owl can't see a thing, the Barred Owl can still capture mice using its hearing alone. The secret of this uncanny ability is that the owl's ears, hidden under the feathers behind its face, have a different shape and location on either side of the head. A given sound therefore arrives at the owl's brain slightly faster through one ear than through the other, and the owl can interpret the difference so as to exactly pinpoint from where the sound is coming. At first glance, it may seem odd the Barred Owl should have this ability. After all, it is probably rarely or never so dark that a Barred Owl cannot see, and hearing alone is of little use in avoiding such obstacles as trees. However, when you remember that Algonquin Barred Owls stay here all winter, the importance of keen hearing becomes obvious. Night or day, the mice the Barred Owl hunts are almost always hidden beneath the snow. If you can imagine sitting for hours 30 feet up in a tree on a cold winter night, waiting to hear the sound of a mouse running along a tunnel under a deep blanket of snow and then dropping down feet first to grab the unseen victim, then you will have some idea of what every Barred Owl can, must, and does do to survive.

However impressive this capacity to find invisible prey may be, the Barred Owl is not guaranteed to "live happily ever after." For one thing, it is a virtual prisoner of the night, not because it can't see in the daytime but because it has achieved completely silent flight at the expense of speed and manoeuverability. This works well at night when the owl can strike its prey unseen and unheard, but in the daytime most intended prey could see the owl coming and get out of the way with no difficulty.

An even bigger problem is that the supply of mice is highly variable — even in a typical Barred Owl territory of about one square mile. Often mice are so scarce, in fact, that Barred Owls are hard-pressed just to keep themselves alive, and raising young is out of the question. When they do breed, a pair of owls have to feed their one to three young long after they leave the hollow tree nest in early June. At that time, the baby owls still can't fly, and their one talent is climbing tree trunks by using their bill and claws. Even now, in the middle of the summer and with the ability to fly, the youngsters are still totally dependent on their parents for food. They fly after the old birds uttering a hoarse, whistled "sheeeeip," which lets the adults know where they are and that they want more mice — fast. The hard-working parents have to put up with this constant harassment right into October or November because it is only then that the instinct and finely-tuned skills necessary for hunting begin to appear in the young.

With the extreme demands placed on them by the young owls, it is a wonder the adults find the time and energy to indulge in their marathon hooting sessions. May we suggest that if they wake you up, you enjoy the entertainment provided by such truly remarkable birds. You can, after all, sleep in the next morning. You can be sure the owls will. ∞

July 27, 1977, Vol. 18, No. 6 (D.S.)

Ancient Leftovers

Although we make no claim to having an Algonquin version of the mythical Loch Ness Monster, we know that many readers will be at least a little disappointed in this because almost all of us are intrigued by the thought of strange, primeval beasts surviving to this day in the murky depths of large lakes. How else can you explain the persistent reports (with a total lack of any real supporting evidence) that such creatures exist, not only in Loch Ness but in many other large lakes of the world as well?

Actually, here in Algonquin, we don't have to make extravagant claims about the survival of some ancient, relict life-form deep down in remote Park lakes. The fact is, we have proof of such survival — and not for just one kind of animal but for five.

Now it is true that none of these survivors is very big and they hardly qualify as "monsters," but you would be hard-pressed to find another five animals that can tell us such an interesting story about the history of Algonquin.

Four of the five animals are tiny crustaceans, less than a quarter of an inch long, which feed on even smaller animals and on algae. None has a common name, but the scientific term for the one pictured here, *Mysis relicta*,

The Deepwater Sculpin lives on in the depths of Cedar Lake.

refers to the fact that it is a relict, or survivor, from the last Ice Age, which ended in Algonquin 11,000 years ago.

The fifth relict is a very strange-looking fish, the Deepwater Sculpin, only two or three inches long, that preys on the relict crustaceans. All five of these animals live in very cold water, often over 100 feet below the surface.

The really odd thing about these dwellers of the deep is their distribution. Although the Park has plenty of cold, deep water, the four crustaceans live only in the chain of lakes beginning with Manitou and Kioshkokwi in the far northwest corner of the Park and extending down the Petawawa drainage — including Cedar, Radiant, Travers, Grand, and a few nearby lakes as well. The Deepwater Sculpin has an even more restricted range, having been found only in Cedar Lake (and only once at that), although it is such a difficult fish to catch it seems very likely it occurs in some of the other lakes as well.

There are two puzzling questions about this distribution. One is the matter of how the sculpin and the crustaceans ever got into the Park in the first place since they are normally found in the cold, brackish waters of Arctic regions. Since these animals obviously did get into Algonquin, the second question is why are they found only in parts of two major watersheds stretching across the north side of the Park?

These questions might still be unanswered except for other investigations carried out independently by geologists. It may seem hard to believe today, but 11,000 years ago Algonquin was being uncovered by the slow,

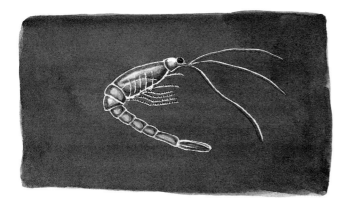

***Mysis relicta**, one of four ancient crustaceans stranded in the deep water of several lakes in the north part of Algonquin.*

northward melting of the last glacier. To the west of the Park area and occupying the present-day basins of Lakes Huron and Michigan (plus much surrounding land) was a huge body of water, called Lake Algonquin, formed by the melting glacier. As more and more land was freed from the ice, Lake Algonquin had a succession of outlets, but the one of most interest here was uncovered when the ice melted north of Fossmill, a now-abandoned station on the CN track just beyond the Park's northwest boundary. When this happened, Lake Algonquin suddenly had a new outlet, some 160 feet lower than the old one, and for two or three centuries the forerunner of the upper Great Lakes drained east across what is now Algonquin Park to the Champlain Sea, an inland arm of the Atlantic occupying the modern Ottawa and St. Lawrence valleys.

There can be little doubt that Lake Algonquin, formed from icy meltwater, was ideal habitat for our four crustaceans and the sculpin, and it seems reasonable they would also have lived in the mighty river that drained the lake. Eventually, however, the Fossmill Outlet came to an end when the retreating glacier exposed an even lower outlet for Lake Algonquin at what is now North Bay. With the termination of the river across Algonquin, the only places where the sculpin and crustaceans could survive

would be in any deeper lakes that happened to be left in the abandoned river channel.

By a not so strange coincidence, the lakes where biologists have in fact found the five relict species surviving today lie within what geologists had earlier deduced was the Fossmill Channel. Indeed, the presence of the relicts in those lakes, and their absence from similar lakes elsewhere in the Park, is strong evidence that the geologists were absolutely correct in their theory about the existence and location of the channel. By the same token, the Fossmill drainage provides a neat explanation of how the relicts got into Algonquin in the first place and of why they are found only in the lakes stretching between the northwest and southeast corners of the Park.

Our strange little sculpin and crustaceans have been living mostly unnoticed in the depths of those northern lakes for the last 11,000 years — ancient leftovers from a long dead river that once drained the biggest lake in the world. Our relicts may not get the headlines that the Loch Ness Monster does, but we think they are a lot more interesting. After all, nobody had to make them up.⁓

August 10, 1977, Vol. 18, No. 8 (D.S.)

How It's Done

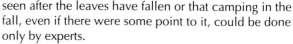

Fall has come to Algonquin and with it have arrived clear, silent days and frozen, starlit nights. The campgrounds are largely empty now, and most visitors drive in just for a few hours to admire the fall colours along the highway.

Even such short autumn visits to Algonquin can be interesting, but we admit to a little sadness when we see, even on busy weekends, that the Park is almost completely deserted by six o'clock each evening. We know that our departed daytime visitors have only had the briefest glimpse of Algonquin from their cars. In many cases, furthermore, they have left with the impressions that there is not much to be

seen after the leaves have fallen or that camping in the fall, even if there were some point to it, could be done only by experts.

The truth is that daytime visitors are missing a great deal because camping and taking the time to really explore the Park during this season can be extremely rewarding.

Now, it is all very well, you may say, for those of us who work here to express such an opinion because, after all, we have years of experience and know "the places to find wildlife." This reaction is reasonable enough, so rather than support the argument ourselves, we will present excerpts from an account sent to us by two ladies from England, Eileen Alleyne and her sister Rosemary Perry, after their camping visit to the Park last October. In reading their story, it is well to keep in mind our two English visitors were far from being rugged, outdoor types to whom camping in the snow and walking miles each day in search of wildlife are normal holiday pastimes. They had camped only twice before, were using a borrowed tent, and were quite incapable of chopping firewood. In fact, with their "very British" accents and almost total lack of experience, they seemed wildly out of place in Algonquin — but read the excerpts that follow.

"Two and a half years ago, during September, my sister, Rosemary and I spent a wonderful two weeks camping in Algonquin Provincial Park, Ontario. We were delighted with the bears and watching for moose, beaver, otter, Pine Marten, etc., and by the wild, hauntingly beautiful cries of the loon; not to

Rosemary and Eileen meet a wolf.

mention the overall indescribable 'experience of wilderness,' which can only be fully appreciated by camping in it. Our one disappointment was that we found no trace of wolves.

However, we recently camped there again for two weeks during the cold second half of October. The Great Wolf Spirit must have divined that the two ladies were again flying all the way from England, longing to meet wolves and hear them sing; for to make amends for their non-appearance during our previous holiday, we were treated to a whole series of fascinating encounters — far more than we could ever possibly have hoped for.

On our first day, after it had rained on our tent most of the night and was now dry and very cold, we walked for about seven miles down the familiar logging trail, which we knew from the previous holiday. It was much used by all the animals, large and small — in fact, the only animal that never used it during our holiday was Homo sapiens, except for our two selves! There were many different scats and tracks, including moose, and amongst them many wolf scats strewn along its sandy surface, so we knew there was a pack in the area.

During the last night before the snow came, beautiful, ice-cold, still and starlit, one of our neighbours was talking with us by our campfire when he stopped short in the middle of a word, spellbound by the howl of a wolf across the lake, who was immediately joined by more in a crescendo of wild, tuneful harmony, each joining on a different note and all melding; the pups, too young to sing, accompanying their elders with excited yelps. The song was taken up and joined by even more wolves, and the whole sky and forest seemed filled with ethereal floating music. Then, as suddenly as they had begun, both wolf choirs ceased simultaneously.

Several days later, after the snow had come, making it so easy to follow tracks, we walked to our favourite lookout place, three miles along the snow-covered trail. There were continuous flurries of snow, so we both wore our macs and hoods all in one over our heads, but the wretched macs were totally un-snow proof, so underneath them we wore black plastic rubbish bags. We also wore our mackintosh trousers over our other ones, so that we looked very bulky, like bear cubs or giant beaver!

We had not been long standing at our separate lookouts when I heard Rosemary call in a carefully modulated but quite clear voice, 'Wolf.' I immediately crept up the bank as stealthily as possible, but before I reached the top she called again, much louder, 'WOLF, WOLF' — I softly, but

with extreme irritation, called back 'Don't, you'll frighten him.' Then, I saw him, an enormous silver grey wolf, with a beautiful, broad-browed, fur-haloed head, trotting straight towards Rosemary with his head up, his ears pricked, intensely curious. As swift as a dream, the thought flashed through my mind, 'I must have died and be in Heaven, how else can this big, wild wolf be trotting towards us, totally unafraid?' When he was some 12 feet only from Rosemary, he took his gaze off her and watched me walking slowly towards him. He then slowed, and after another second or two he pulled up and leisurely turned away from us back onto the trail — then again he stopped and turned around to stare at us for another minute or so and we on our side gazed admiringly back at him, appreciating his splendid physique and fascinating wolf face. A few yards further down the trail, he stepped aside to leave his 'card' in the snow by a tuft of grass. Perhaps our meeting had excited him too, and he wanted to let us know that it was his territory as well as ours.

As you can imagine, never will the inexpressible pleasure leave us of meeting such a big, completely wild wolf and being treated by him as his interesting equals. A little later we walked back along the trail, following his track, his footsteps imprinted in our opposite-facing bootprints — easier walking for him; his track led down the trail, straight across Hwy. 60, across the snowy picnic ground where our car was, and into the forest beyond — by then it was 4:30 p.m., still broad daylight.

Back at our camp our two neighbours had gone, leaving us in sole occupation, humanly speaking, for our last two nights. Much as we missed them, it was a fascinating experience to feel ourselves alone, surrounded by the forest, a part of the life around us. On the last night we built up a large fire from the wood left by our neighbours. The heat was dispersed by the cold wind, but it added to the magic of the evening, lighting up the tall tree trunks and the small scattered flakes of snow that softly drifted down."

Eileen and Rosemary had many other fascinating experiences with wolves, otters, and other wildlife when they were in the Park last fall, but we are sure that even the few we have cited here would be greatly envied by the vast majority of our visitors. In fact, you might even suspect, given the highly unlikely backgrounds of Eileen and Rosemary, that they were just plain lucky. True up to a point, but the really essential ingredient in the success of our English visitors was that they took the time to explore, to look, and to listen. That's how it's done — and Eileen and Rosemary took away priceless experiences as proof.⚭

September 7, 1977, Vol. 18, No. 12 (D.S)

Close Encounters of the Worst Kind

Just about everyone, we imagine, is familiar with the recurring science fiction theme of a devastating attack on our planet by some alien life-form. The attackers possess such formidable weapons that their victory over the human race seems totally inescapable. Only the last-minute detection of a fatal weakness in the attackers enables the desperate human defenders to save the day.

Now we may be exaggerating a little, but we maintain that distinct similarities exist between this scenario and the attack we have been undergoing for the last several weeks. We are referring, of course, to the annual onslaught of mosquitoes. Some proud survivors of previous attacks belittle the seriousness of the current one by pointing out that of the world's 3,000 kinds of mosquitoes, only about 25 ever attack humans, that even then just the females bite, and that they only take two or three milligrams of blood — hardly a great quantity.

We concede the truth of these statements but, frankly, are not impressed by them. The individuals that bite may be a small minority of all mosquitoes, but it really doesn't matter; they are still so numerous that they constitute a definite threat, if not to our lives, then certainly to our enjoyment of the outdoors.

To those of you who share our view about the gravity of the present situation, we submit that our only hope lies in following the strategy employed in all the science fiction stories: we must carefully study the pesky aliens in an effort to find some weakness we can exploit. The rallying cry must be "Know thine enemy!"

The first step is to watch a mosquito stick it to you. (It may go against the grain but, let's face it, lots are going to get you no matter what you do, so you may as well watch one.) You have to admit, however grudgingly, that mosquitoes are marvellously well adapted for their way of life. In most cases they land so lightly that you don't even know it, and within seconds they are penetrating your skin. If you look closely, you will see two parts to the feeding apparatus. The larger, outer sheath is not inserted in your skin but is bent back like a hairpin during feeding, and a more slender tube is inserted straight down for about half its length into your skin. Actually, this feeding tube consists of six separate parts. These include a large

tube for drawing your blood up, a much smaller tube for sending saliva down (to prevent your blood from coagulating), and two structures with fine teeth on their edges, which the mosquito uses to literally saw its way down into your skin. For even the most thick-skinned human, a mosquito takes no more than 50 seconds to insert its feeding tube, another two and one-half minutes to "fill er up," and a mere five seconds to withdraw the tube and make its getaway.

If you always terminate your observations at this point by obliterating the mosquito, you get no marks for scientific detachment and you will have to settle for the smug satisfaction stemming from the act of paying one back. It must be admitted also that there isn't much to be gained by watching a mosquito taking your blood with impunity because no one has yet found an exploitable weakness in this part of the mosquito's behaviour.

For example, mosquito repellents do not work by giving you a bad taste or smell that dissuades a mosquito from inserting its feeding tube into your skin. Rather, they work by jamming the mosquito's detection system and deflecting the potential attacker before it lands in the first place. To understand how this happens, we must first understand how mosquitoes find us and, thanks to many years of research, we now know the basic sequence of events.

More often than not, even a hungry female mosquito rests on vegetation and does not fly very often. Even a small local increase in carbon dioxide, however, such as one caused by a passing animal, causes the mosquito to take flight and fly about more or less randomly. If she encounters a warm, moist convection current — given off by all warm-blooded animals — the mosquito will quickly fly "upwind" and perhaps encounter the source. Of course, a mosquito can't see a convection current any better than we can, and she may very well fly out of the current by mistake and lose the trail. When this happens, however, the sudden decrease in air moisture is detected by special sensors on the mosquito's antennae, and this causes the mosquito to turn. The chances are reasonably good that she will then fly into the same or another moist convection current, and she will once again be on the right track.

When the potential victim is one of us (the good guys), liberally doused with repellent, the sequence is altered. At first, things are not too encouraging because repellents actually cause resting mosquitoes to take flight, just the way carbon dioxide does. In other words, the repellent actually helps alert mosquitoes to our presence and makes it more likely they will find our convection current trail. As they make their final approach, however, the moisture sensors are jammed by the repellent vapour coming off our skin. What this means is that, even if the air moisture is increasing (as it does close to our skin), the sensors detect less moisture, just as they would if the mosquito had flown out of a moist convection current.

Thus, the repellent "fools" the mosquito into "thinking" that she has flown off-track, and she turns. Normally, this would give her a chance to relocate the trail, but in this case she will be "automatically" turned away each time she approaches the source of the repellent vapour.

So do not despair fellow mosquito fighters; the enemy may assault us in countless bloodthirsty hordes and rend the night-time silence with their fearful whines. But stand firm, praise the Lord, pass the diethyl toluamide, and watch them turn harmlessly aside. The day is saved!⌒

July 5, 1978, Vol. 19, No. 3 (D.S.)

Acid, Acid, Go Away*

As we write this, a soft rain is falling. A few years ago we would have been quite happy to hear it pattering on the leaves outside and watch it dancing on the gray lake. Not anymore.

The problem, you see, is that normal rain hardly ever falls on Algonquin Park anymore; what we get instead is acid.

Now, you may be forgiven if you find this statement a little hard to believe, for it does indeed seem preposterous that it could "rain acid" in a place such as Algonquin, and, very definitely, it is a matter that requires some explanation.

To begin with, when we say that the rain is acid we do not mean that it will burn your skin or eat holes in your car. To be sure, very strong, concentrated acids can do this, but they are exceptional. Most acids are far less dangerous and, in fact, we actually eat some kinds. Vinegar is one good example, and grapefruit juice is another. We can usually tell an acid by its sour taste, but the fundamental characteristic that sets acids apart from other liquids is less obvious. Everyone knows that the smallest particles of water (molecules) are themselves made of two atoms of hydrogen and one of oxygen (hence, the formula H_2O). However, even in pure water, there is always a small percentage of molecules that break up and give rise to one negatively charged particle designated "OH" and one positively charged hydrogen particle or "ion" designated H+. Normally, the number of these hydrogen ions is very small, but certain substances, when dissolved in water, can react with the water molecules in such a way as to increase the number of hydrogen ions. Whenever this happens, we call the resulting solution an "acid."

The trouble is that two of these substances having the ability to turn water into acid are being released into the atmosphere in enormous quantities through the burning of coal and oil and the smelting of metal ores. The two substances are sulphur dioxide (SO_2) and nitrogen dioxide (NO_2), and when they are washed out of the air by rain, they dissolve in the rain and turn it into acid.

This process is happening throughout the world but is particularly serious in heavily populated and industrialized areas, such as western Europe and northeastern North America. We know that to many visitors, Algonquin may seem to be remote or "way up north," but we really aren't all that far from much of our continent's heaviest industry. In fact, the greatest single-point source of sulphur dioxide in the world, emitting 1.3 million tons every year, is located at Sudbury, just 100 miles northwest of the Park.

Although the acid rain falling on Algonquin is not dangerously corrosive, we would not like to leave you with the opposite and equally false idea that the acid falling from the sky is inconsequentially weak. Scientists measure the strength of acids on a scale called "pH," giving progressively lower values for stronger and stronger acids. Distilled water has a pH of 7.0, normal rain used to be slightly acid at pH 5.6, but the rain (and snow) that now falls on Algonquin has pH values that normally range from 4.38 to 3.95 or even, on one occasion two winters ago, as low as 2.97.

Although these values are very acidic, the results might still be tolerable if the lakes and streams of Algonquin had the ability to "buffer" the effect of the acid rain. In many areas of the world, lakes contain substances that can remove or "soak up" any excess hydrogen ions delivered

---

** This article appeared before the existence and threat of acid rain were generally known or appreciated by the public. As such, it caused some alarm and was picked up by Canadian Press, **The Globe and Mail**, and numerous radio and TV stations across Canada. Later work in the Park failed to establish any positive evidence of acid rain damage, and in at least some cases, it appeared that high acidity actually had benefits (see "Life in the Acid Vat," June 27, 1991, page 186).*

by acid rain. In Algonquin, however, the lakes lie on very hard, granitic bedrock that yields very few of these buffering substances. The result is that Park lakes have a limited ability to receive repeated doses of acid rain without themselves slowly becoming acidic.

We have not yet had any obvious disasters in Algonquin — but such strongly acid rain is apparently relatively recent in our part of Ontario. We cannot be very optimistic, however, when we look at areas with similar lake chemistry but which have been exposed to acid rain (even weaker than what we are getting) for longer times. In southern Norway and Sweden, for example, quite literally thousands of once prime trout and salmon lakes have been transformed during the last two decades into fishless, and often almost entirely lifeless, vats of mild acid. Closer to home, in Killarney Provincial Park southwest of Sudbury, several poorly buffered lakes have become quite acidic and lost all, or virtually all, their fish. It seems that Smallmouth Bass are particularly susceptible to acidity, followed by trout, burbot, and walleye, and finally by more resistant species, such as perch and suckers.

Even when the acidity has not yet reached the point where fish populations are lost (apparently because eggs and fry do not survive), the fish may become dangerous to eat. There is some evidence that the increased levels of mercury that have made some fish (especially large ones) in some Algonquin and other Ontario lakes unfit for human consumption may be linked to the increased acidity of the affected lakes.

What happens when acid rain falls into lakes such as ours is ugly enough — but at least we know (more or less) what is going to happen. We do not know, unfortunately, what the long-term effects will be of acid rain falling on roots and leaves up on land. It is difficult to believe, given the sensitivity of these organs, that there would be no effect, and indeed there is some evidence that the growth of trees and other plants is reduced when they are subjected to acid rain.

But even if we were to suppose that the eventual damage caused by the acid rain and snow will be confined entirely to our lakes and rivers, there can be no doubt that Algonquin (and many other parts of central Ontario) is approaching an ecological disaster of catastrophic proportions. Sadly, there is little evidence that society is ready to pay the price of cutting back on emissions of sulphur and nitrogen dioxides. Even if we were, and started to clean up our act right away, it might already be too late in many cases. …

No, we are not very happy about the drops falling outside. We fear for the future of the loon calling across the lake and, something like a child repeating the old rhyme on a wet day, we fervently wish we could make the acid rain go away.∞

August 9, 1978, Vol. 19, No. 8 (D.S.)

Park boundaries mean nothing to airborne pollution, which often originates many hundreds of kilometres away from Algonquin.

Walking (and Talking) on Water

We think we are on safe ground in stating that everybody enjoys sitting at the water's edge and

Water striders communicate by making, and detecting, vibrations on the water surface.

admiring the surroundings. This being the case, everyone has noticed, at one time or another, the long-legged insects called water striders skating over the surface of some quiet pond or river.

Water striders happen to be a special favourite of ours. Perhaps this is because we, like most humans, are just plain impressed by the ability to "walk on water." Beyond this, however, we find that the structures and behaviour that go with the water strider's unique lifestyle are particularly fascinating.

You see, water striders owe their "Biblical" powers to much more than their small size. What they stand on is a thin surface film of slightly denser than normal water, which forms on calm surfaces. But even a water strider would eventually sink except for certain life-saving anatomical features. The most obvious of these is the considerable support provided by the long legs, but even more important is the presence on the feet of stiff, water-repellent hairs. These hairs have the effect of depressing (rather than penetrating) the skin-like surface film. Yet another feature is that the sharp claws on the water strider's feet are situated well back from the tips and therefore away from the surface film that they might otherwise puncture.

Movement on the slippery film is accomplished by rowing with the long, middle legs while the hind legs and short, front legs are held on the surface for support. Zipping around on the surface of a pond sounds like fun, but water striders usually give the appearance of moving quite erratically and may well leave you wondering why they have taken up such a strange mode of existence.

Well, you will have to observe closely to see it, but the rewards of living on the water surface are considerable. One important food source that is opened up is smaller insects that live below the surface but come up to breathe, and a second is flying insects that fall on the surface and are unable to escape. A water strider attacks such a floundering insect in the twinkling of an eye, driving its mouthparts into the victim, pumping in a digestive saliva, and, several minutes later when the insides of the prey have turned into a nutritious "soup," sucking out the conveniently liquefied contents, then discarding the victim's empty shell.

What we find especially amazing in all this is that the water strider is alerted to the victim's presence, even in total darkness, by the tiny waves created by the struggles of the prey insect. In fact, there is a startling similarity to the detection by a spider of a victim struggling in its web. So sensitive are water striders to surface ripples, they can actually detect waves only a thousandth of a millimetre high and instantly pivot to face the precise direction from which they are coming.

Even less apparent to the casual, pond-side observer of water striders is the fact that these remarkable insects make use of their keen wave detection sense to communicate with each other. For example, a male who has found a suitable site for mating advertises the fact to passing females by moving his rowing legs up and down and thereby shaking the surface film. The waves he generates in this manner are not random, however. Each "call" begins at a high frequency (23 to 29 waves per second), shifts to a lower frequency (18 to 20 waves per second), and ends with one or two low-frequency waves (10 to 17 waves per second). If a female responds to such an interesting (for a water strider) proposition, she does so by gently beating her forelegs on the water to send out waves at a frequency of 22 to 25 per second. The male switches to a similar call, and the female approaches. Later, while the female is laying her eggs, the male warns off any other males by sending out very high or very low frequency calls.

It is extraordinary to realize that the surface film on which water striders glide about and find their food also serves them as a sort of watery tom-tom. Perhaps you may wish to think twice the next time you are sitting at the edge of a pond and are tempted to let your toes dangle in the water. After all, the ripples you create will drown out any being broadcast by the local striders — and nobody likes a person who interrupts important conversations.❧

August 23, 1978, Vol. 19, No. 10 (D.S.)

Hoodies and Woodies

A female Wood Duck making an unwelcome visit to the nest of a Hooded Merganser.

Autumns in Algonquin have an almost dream-like quality. The hard, bright sunlight somehow fails to warm the crystal clear air, and everywhere there is a complete, uncanny silence. Even the blaze of fall colours often seems unreal, and it is easy for the trail user or canoeist to slip into an absent-minded reverie.

We couldn't even guess how many times we have drifted off into one of these fall daydreams as we have lazily paddled up some glass-calm river, lost in the perfect reflections of stream-side asters and goldenrods. We do know, however, that what usually "wakes" us up (sometimes with quite a start) is the sudden rising of small ducks from some quiet hiding place up ahead. Often we have hardly recovered from the initial surprise before the ducks have sped away on faintly whistling wings, high over the treetops, and we are left wishing we had been alert enough to notice them on the water before they had taken off.

Sooner or later, of course, we all do manage to get a good look at these ducks, which are so typical of the Park's ponds and small lakes at this time of year. A good look is very much worth trying for because the two species you are most likely to see (or the males at any rate) are among the world's most beautiful waterfowl. One is the Wood Duck, and the other is the Hooded Merganser. The former bird is a true duck with a flat bill and a diet that is over 90 per cent vegetarian, and the latter has a thin bill with teeth-like serrations and preys almost exclusively on minnows, crayfish, and other animal food.

The only trouble with a good look at these birds at this time of year is that you will get no clue whatsoever as to the really interesting aspects of these two species. For, in spite of their dependence on entirely dissimilar food resources, "Hoodies" and "Woodies" (as they are often called for short) have many far-reaching and in some ways bizarre similarities in nesting behaviour.

We would like to at least touch on some of these features here because, unfortunately, both species are so secretive during the breeding season that you have almost no chance of observing them at that time of year.

The most fundamental fact in the nesting behaviour of Hoodies and Woodies (and to many people the most surprising) is that both these ducks lay their eggs in tree cavities (including the old nests of the large Pileated Woodpecker) and often as much as 30 or 40 feet above the ground. Tree cavities are obviously safer places to lay eggs than the conventional ground nests of most ducks, but they do have the very serious drawback of almost always being in short supply. This means that many female Wood Ducks and Hooded Mergansers are unable to find unclaimed nesting holes and are therefore unable to raise their own broods. The prospects are not entirely hopeless for these females, however, because they have the option of cheating. That is to say, if they can't find a cavity of their own,

they can dump some or all of their eggs in the nest of another bird.

In our human system of values, leaving some other female to incubate a double set of eggs and to raise all those extra young would be judged as very immoral behaviour. In nature, however, such terms have no meaning, and all that really counts is success in producing surviving young. Any strain of any species that is even marginally more efficient in producing descendants has (almost by definition) long since come to be the dominant or only surviving strain of that species. In the case of the female Wood Ducks and Hooded Mergansers without nests, it makes a lot of sense to dump the eggs in somebody else's nest. After all, there is no chance of producing a descendant if the eggs are "thrown away," but they have a good chance of being hatched by some unwitting foster mother. After that, there should be no problem because the young ducklings pick up all their own food and will not have to rely on the foster mother (who might be hopelessly over-burdened if she had to forage for both her own young and the ones that were dumped on her).

In fact, the unconscious "strategy" of laying eggs in another duck's nest is so successful (in producing a good return in the form of surviving young for very little initial investment in the form of eggs) that it is sometimes resorted to even by females who do have nests of their own. For them, slipping a few eggs into a neighbour's nest is a simple form of unintentional, but still effective, "insurance" against the possible loss of their own nests to, say, a marauding raccoon.

The result of all this is that Wood Duck or Hooded Merganser nests are often found containing eggs (sometimes over 40) contributed by two or more females. Even more interesting is the frequent presence of Wood Duck eggs in Hooded Merganser nests (and vice-versa). Such mixed clutches seem weird until you remember that female Hoodies and Woodies both breed in the same wooded swampy areas, both have the same egg-dumping behaviour, and, most important of all, both are competing for the same very limited tree cavities. We think it would be especially interesting to know how well baby, fish-eating Mergansers survive when they are raised by a plant-eating Wood Duck (or the other way 'round).

Another question that occurs to many people and was the subject of sometimes heated debate for over a century is the matter of how the young, flightless ducklings get from the often very high nest down to the ground. Although many early observers swore up and down that they saw female Hoodies and Woodies diligently transporting their young one at a time in their bills or on their backs down from the nest, modern observers (and

cameras) leave no doubt that the newly hatched ducklings, in response to a call from the female, unhesitatingly fling themselves out of the nest entrance and fall to earth. When they hit, they often bounce and are occasionally stunned, but only very rarely are they killed.

In most cases the female quickly leads the ducklings to water, tends them for the next five weeks, and then abandons them. They do not acquire the ability to fly for another month, at which point they start to leave their birthplaces and congregate (along with the newly moulted adults) in other favourable feeding places. Along Highway 60, a traditional fall location for Wood Ducks is Ring-neck Pond, just east of the Rock Lake turn, and Mew Lake is an excellent place to see Hooded Mergansers.

Woodies are with us until mid-October, and a few Hoodies linger on until the ice forces them south in late November. Until then, they feed quietly in thousands of silent, hidden beaver ponds and occasionally startle the odd, day-dreaming human who happens to intrude. ∞

September 6, 1978 ,Vol. 19, No. 12 (D.S.)

Exclusive! The Truth About Frogs!

In a wistful moment over two thousand years ago, the Greek philosopher Theocritus wrote those immortal lines, "Oh to be a frog, my lads, and live aloof from care."

Today, even if living one's life as a frog may not be everybody's first choice, we still think most people can see considerable merit in the idea. After all, you could do a lot worse than soaking up the sun all day while stretched out on a nice smooth lily pad, and we are sure just about every Algonquin camper associates the droning rumble of a Bullfrog chorus with pleasant memories of drifting off to sleep on warm summer nights in years gone by.

Now, this ancient and idyllic picture of froggish life is all very well, but on the undoubtedly correct assumption that readers of *The Raven* are noble seekers after truth, we will relate the quite different (and much more interesting) picture of our common Bullfrog, as revealed by recent studies.

Although it is the largest of the Park's six species of true frogs and is a formidable predator in its own right — not hesitating to attack and eat smaller frogs or even birds and small mammals on occasion — the Bullfrog must nevertheless contend with a long list of deadly perils.

The first is a tiny leech that attacks the eggs, sometimes even before the female has finished laying them. Although the jelly-like layer around each egg partly frustrates and slows down the attacks, an average of 50 per cent of all eggs in each egg mass are eaten before

they can hatch. Incidentally, while it is true that all eggs are equally defenceless before the onslaught of the leeches, the eggs laid by large females and fertilized by large males have much better chances of surviving. Large females confer an advantage to their eggs simply because they lay so many more of them (as many as 20,000, or three times the number laid by small females) that each individual egg has less chance of being found and eaten by a leech. Large males improve the chances of the eggs they fertilize because, being large and therefore strong, they control the most favourable mating and egg-laying territories. What makes a territory particularly favourable is warm water temperatures that speed up development within the eggs, reduce the time required for hatching, and, as a result, lessen the time available to leeches for finding and destroying the eggs.

However, even if they get past the leeches and make it to the tadpole stage, the success of the would-be Bullfrogs is far from assured. Their careers may be abruptly terminated by a fish or a dragonfly nymph, or there just may not be enough food, sunning places, or cover to accommodate all of the growing tadpoles and some will lose out in the competition for limited resources.

When winter closes in, the survivors are exposed to yet another grim reaper — mass suffocation resulting from the exhaustion of the oxygen supply in the water beneath the ice. If this happens, there will be thousands of dead tadpoles floating on the pond when the ice finally does go out in the spring.

Even when the tadpoles change into adult, air-breathing frogs in their second or third summer, they are far from being out of danger. Up on land, raccoons, herons, and many other predators are totally ready to put a casual, quite unemotional end to what has been until

also the most likely to attract the attention of and be slowly stalked by the almost imperceptible menace. And then, at the very pinnacle of Bullfrog success, he may be seized from below by guillotine jaws, dragged underwater, dismembered, and gulped down by the unseen Snapping Turtle. In a few seconds, all trace of the "successful" Bullfrog has disappeared forever.

No, a frog's life is not all it may seem. So the next time a Greek philosopher suggests you

then the frog's miraculous survival against enormous odds. In fact, the chances of a Bullfrog egg becoming a sexually mature adult are about one in 10,000. Such odds may be about a hundred times better than your chances of buying a winning lottery ticket but, even so, no one would dream of calling them good.

And so, what are the rewards for the tiny handful of survivors in these unforgiving sweepstakes? Although young females cannot produce as many eggs as older and larger ones, they are not otherwise held back from assuming full, adult behaviour and attempting to produce at least some young before fate catches up with them also — as it has long since done with most of their brothers and sisters. Young males, however, find themselves totally outclassed by older, larger males in the intense competition for good mating territories. About all the young males can do is lurk quietly near territory-holding males and attempt to intercept and seize a female that has been attracted by the roaring calls of the territory owner.

You might assume that if the young male manages to survive another two or three years and becomes a truly large frog, his "worries" would be over. He would be able to seize and hold a good territory, and he would be able to attract many females. This is all true, but one final "horror" lurks in the ooze of just about every Bullfrog pond. In fact, the ultimate irony in the Bullfrog's long battle against overwhelming odds is that the biggest, strongest, loudest, and seemingly most successful male is

couldn't lead a more carefree existence, you just tell him to read this issue of *The Raven*. We'll straighten him out.⌒

June 27, 1979 ,Vol. 20, No. 2 (D.S.)

Songs of the Seventies

We have no doubt that many people returning to Algonquin after an absence of one or two years get quiet enjoyment from renewing contact with familiar Park features. The slap of a beaver's tail on calm evening water, an old White Pine clinging to the brow of an ancient cliff, or the call of a loon — all are examples of those seemingly timeless values that visitors count on finding in the Park, year after year.

Far be it from us to take anything away from this enjoyment, but many of these sights and sounds are not quite as ageless as you might think.

Take, for example, the song of the White-throated Sparrow. There are probably not too many campers who know this bird by name, but just about everyone has stopped, at one time or another, to listen to its very sad, very clear whistles, "Sweet Canada, Sweet Canada, Sweet Canada, Canada, Canada … ." As one early writer put it,

"The White-throated Sparrow is one of the sweetest of singers, and for its full effect it should be heard on its northern breeding grounds at evening. When all else is silent save the occasional melancholy notes of the Whip-poorwill or the distant hoot of some owl, the effect produced by this incomparable song is surpassingly beautiful."

White-throats are abundant here in Algonquin, and there can be no doubt that their songs are very closely associated with the Park (consciously or subconsciously) in the minds of most visitors.

With a little persistence, incidentally, you can track down and get a good look at one of the singing males. Unique among Algonquin birds, White-throats come in two distinct colour phases independent of sex or age. The "white-striped" birds have a bold head pattern of bright white and dark black stripes, and "tan-striped" birds have a much duller pattern of tan and chocolate-brown stripes. No one really knows why the two colour phases exist in the same population or why white-striped males almost always mate with tan-striped females, and vice-versa.

There is, however, no difference between the songs of white- and tan-striped males; both types sing equally beautiful songs. But this is not to say that all White-throats sing alike. In fact, there are at least 15 different basic song patterns (involving different types of notes and changes in pitch) and usually additional peculiarities that make it possible for humans to distinguish one individual bird from another.

Not surprisingly, the White-throats can also tell each other apart, as shown by studies carried out here in the Park. As in other songbirds, male White-throats use song to proclaim their territories (usually about two acres in size) and to warn other males that they must leave or be attacked. But individual territory owners get to know the songs of their neighbours and more or less accept their presence. If a tape recording of a neighbour's song is played to a territory owner, the reaction is usually quite mild, but if the song of another strange bird is played from the same spot, the tape recorder will be furiously sung at or even physically attacked by the territory owner. Interestingly enough, if a neighbour's song is played from the wrong place — as, for example, the opposite side of the territory — the territory owner will attack just as he would if the song were completely new to him. It is only if a neighbour stays "in his place" that he will be accorded any tolerance.

It is an obvious advantage for male White-throats to be able to recognize their neighbours and to avoid wasting energy attacking them when they aren't really a threat. The full wrath of a

Two White-throated Sparrows singing it out at their territorial boundary.

territory owner should be, and is, reserved for any newcomers or neighbours who get out of line. Without differences in songs and the ability to recognize them, this economy of effort would not be possible.

How White-throats get their individual songs in the first place is another question, but there is reason to believe that "impressionable" young birds just out of the nest are permanently influenced by, and later imitate, the songs of their fathers or other nearby males. Nestlings raised artificially, away from adults, do eventually sing, but quite unlike wild birds.

There is also evidence that certain song patterns become more or less popular as the years go by. For example, the writings of several early naturalists leave little doubt that the most common pattern 50 years ago was one that could be written as "Oh Sweet Canada, Canada, Canada … ." But now this pattern is quite rare, and the most common one (accounting for over half of all songs) is "Sweet Canada, Sweet Canada, Canada, Canada, Canada … ." Several other trends have been detected as well, not to mention distinct regional "preferences" for one song pattern or another.

You would do well to keep this White-throatian fickleness in mind as you listen to the different songs of the individual birds around your campsite. After all, the song you like the most may have fallen from favour by the time you come back next year — it might not even make the Park's top 40.⌐

July 25, 1979, Vol. 20, No. 6 (D.S.)

Captain John and the Bear

Today, we can zoom up to Algonquin Park from urban southern Ontario in a few hours. Once here, we can camp in a manner that is only slightly less comfortable than the lifestyle theoretically left behind in the city. And even on a canoe trip far off in the Park interior, we know that in the event of some accident it would normally take just a few hours for a Ministry plane to be notified and rush us to a modern, nearby hospital. In short, it is very difficult for us to imagine what real hardship and isolation are like and very easy to forget that most people had a full measure of both just two or three generations ago.

In Algonquin Park we have no better illustration of this than the story of Captain John Dennison's family, who hacked a farm out of the Algonquin wilderness over a century ago and lived on it for almost 20 years. The farm (clearly indicated on the canoe route map) was located on Lake Opeongo just past the narrows connecting the South and East Arms of the lake. We recently had the opportunity to revisit the site with Captain John's great-granddaughter, Mrs. Berniece Lisk of Ottawa and Aylen Lake, and to learn a little of her family's remarkable and profoundly moving experiences here back in the days before Algonquin became a park.

Captain John was born in England, in 1799, and chose a career in the military. We do not know exactly when he came to Canada, but he did serve with distinction during the Lower Canada (Quebec) Rebellion of 1837. He was eventually demobilized in the early 1850s. Ten years later, at close to what we nowadays consider to be retirement age, he packed up his family and left the comforts of Bytown (Ottawa) to take up a Crown land grant at what is now the village of Combermere, southeast of the Park area. If that weren't enough, his two sons, John and Harry, decided in the late 1860s to start new farms on Lake Opeongo, and they somehow moved their wives, small children, farm animals, and their father,

Marker of the grave of Captain John Dennison.

Captain John, as well, some 60 miles farther into the roadless wilderness to start all over again.

Just why they went to so much trouble is not entirely clear. Mrs. Lisk feels that it was because of the excellent bear-trapping possibilities afforded by the Opeongo country. Others have suggested that the family was anticipating the extension of the Opeongo Line (a colonization road which — as it turned out — never did get that far), or that the attraction may have been the guaranteed supply of easily caught Lake Trout moving through the narrows.

Whatever the reason, they did come, and they did clear several hundred acres of land (perhaps as much as 600 acres in all). In fact, they were sufficiently prosperous that they managed not only to feed themselves but also to produce a surplus they could sell to logging camps. But the prosperity of the Dennisons, such as it was, was achieved at a high price. There was the back-breaking labour required to clear and run a farm on the stingy soil, and there was the unimaginable isolation.

One year, Harry Dennison left his wife and five small children alone on the farm with the austere Captain John, then in his seventies, while he went west to Manitoba, unsuccessfully looking for new land. We can perhaps accept that Mrs. Dennison was able to live those long months without television, without neighbours, and without any of the diversions we take for granted a hundred years later. The deaths of two children is another matter altogether; how she was able to stand the pain, without her husband and utterly isolated in the bleak, snowy wilderness, is almost beyond comprehension.

The last straw came a few years later. One day in 1881, Captain John (by then 82 years of age) and one of his grandsons (Jack, aged eight) decided to check a bear trap at the portage leading to the lake we now know as Happy Isle. Leaving Jack at the lakeshore, Captain John approached the trap but failed to realize that it had been sprung and that a bear lay hidden behind a huge log anchoring the trap. Apparently Captain John almost fell on the bear, was seized, and only had time to yell to Jack that he should go for help. The terrified youngster paddled the approximately eight miles back to the farm as fast as he could, but by the time Harry could get there Captain John was dead. The family buried the old man back at the farm, but they couldn't go on; within a year they abandoned the fields and farm buildings they had put so much into and moved back to Combermere.

When we visited the old farm, we found very little sign of any buildings, but the clearings were still very obvious (and somewhat ironically contained abundant bear sign). South of the farm we saw the two white birches, now grown to truly enormous size and between which apparently lie the unmarked graves of the two children who died on the farm. As for Captain John, his gravesite is still clearly visible. It is surrounded by a low, cedar-rail fence, and a weathered copper plaque reads "At Rest."

We found it just a little sad, when we got back to the lake, to see a powerful fibreglass and plastic boat go roaring by. We ourselves returned by motorboat to the bottom of Opeongo and were soon driving home listening to the car radio. Already, we were starting to forget that, not so very long ago, life was very, very different.∞

August 1, 1979, Vol. 20, No. 7 (D.S.)

Weapons and Counter-Weapons

At this time of year, when you huddle closer to your campfire and warm your hands around a cup of steaming hot chocolate, the dark Algonquin night seems to be completely at peace. All is quiet except for the distant wails of a loon or the sporadic rustlings of a nearby mouse, and it really does seem that the Park is fast asleep.

In fact, the night-time air is filled with machine gun-like bursts of sound that result from deadly and very wide-awake battles of incredible sophistication taking place all around us. The only trouble is that our human senses are so dull we never even suspect what is going on.

The one, slight hint we get of the excitement is when a moth lands on our sweater or we glimpse a bat swooping through the outer reaches of our campfire's glow. Even then, no one will fault you if you fail to recognize the moth and the bat as principal actors in the aerial drama going on above us. The connection between the two is not immediately obvious, and it may seem a bit far-fetched that either moths or bats could be capable of anything that is truly "sophisticated."

But let us consider them — starting with the bats. We have at least three kinds in Algonquin (and quite possibly another five as yet unrecorded kinds as well). All of them feed on insects (and very often large ones, such as moths), which they scoop out of the air using the membrane that

Tiger Moths can "jam" the echolocation system of bats and thus escape capture.

stretches between their two hind legs. This sounds simple enough until you remember that bats, though certainly not blind, have small, weak eyes that would be of limited use in spotting flying insects even in daylight, let alone on a pitch-black night.

Just how bats locate their prey and navigate between obstacles was a major scientific mystery as recently as 40 years ago. At that time, it was observed that blind-folded bats could manoeuvre perfectly well whereas bats whose mouths were gagged or whose ears were plugged were in serious trouble. If forced to fly, such bats did so hesitantly and frequently crashed into quite visible objects. Further work soon established that bats emit extremely high-pitched clicks (far above the upper limit of human hearing) and use the echoes returning from nearby objects to determine the location of those objects — almost a kind of radar.

But what bats do is much more sophisticated than merely determining locations. By emitting fairly long bursts of sound (one hundredth of a second or longer) on one pitch, bats hear echoes whose pitch is slightly altered if the object returning the echo is moving. (Up to a point, humans can do the same thing — for example, when the horn of a car or train seems to suddenly drop in pitch when it passes us at high speed.) Bats, however, can interpret the pitch change so accurately that they can tell exactly how fast and in what direction the object (a moth, for example) is moving and can alter their own course to intercept it.

In order to get a good picture of what the object actually is, bats emit a different sort of sound pattern — bursts of sound that are extremely short in duration but that contain a broad range of frequencies. The resultant echoes are complicated, but a bat's brain can unscramble them so well that it gets a very accurate picture of the object. This ability is so refined that bats can even detect immobile moths resting on rough surfaces such as tree trunks. (The old Second World War submarine trick of lying on the ocean bottom to avoid enemy sonar wouldn't work if the enemy were a bat.)

Typically, however, bats go after flying insects, and the sequence is almost invariable. In little more than one second the bat detects the victim's presence, alters course, steps up the intensity of the sound bursts to get a high-resolution image of the prey, scoops it up, and then bends its head down, while still airborne, to seize and devour the juicy morsel. Game over for the bug.

It might appear, in fact, that no insect could possibly foil a weapon so devastatingly sophisticated as bat "radar," and it is probably true that most victims never know what hits them. Nevertheless, in nature's struggles, as in our own, no weapon is unbeatable, and several groups of moths have achieved varying degrees of success against bats. An obvious first step is to be able to hear the ultrasonic bat sounds. Some moths having this ability fly away when they hear a bat coming, take evasive action if the bat comes closer, and, if the bat starts emitting the extremely intense bursts of ultrasound that signify the final attack phase, the moth dives into whatever vegetation lies below.

However impressive this ability may seem, it is crude in comparison to the defence mechanism evolved by the brightly coloured moths known as Tiger Moths. Not only can Tiger Moths hear bats, they can also imitate them so well that they actually succeed in "jamming" the bat brain's information-processing circuits. We don't know if you can really "blow the mind" of a bat, but every time a bat tries to attack a Tiger Moth, it ends up veering sharply away at the last minute — somehow baffled by the echo-like clicks sent out by the intended victim. Modern strategic bombers carry a great deal of super-sophisticated electronic equipment designed to jam the radar and other detection systems of incoming enemy missiles, or fool them into "thinking" the bomber is somewhere else. It is astounding to realize that a little moth can do the same thing to a bat.

We also find it a little frustrating that our own human hearing is so woefully inadequate. We sit by our campfire naively thinking that all is peaceful out there in the Algonquin night, and we never hear the slightest sound from the sophisticated war of ultrasonic weapons and counter-weapons being waged just above our heads.∞

August 22, 1979, Vol. 20, No. 10 (D.S.)

Minay-Goba-You to the Rescue

One of the most serious of modern man's conceits is that we invented sophisticated technology. Well, it may be true that we have brought things to an unprecedented level of complexity, but so-called primitive man had many devices and techniques that were every bit as ingenious as the gadgets we are so proud of today.

This was brought home to us in rather dramatic fashion a few weeks ago while on a rough, seldom-used canoe route on the north side of the Park. Having paddled far later into the evening than one should, we had a sudden, unscheduled encounter with a particularly nasty submerged rock. It left us with a dime-sized hole near the keel and a canoe that strongly resembled our spirits (both sinking fast). In fact, by the time we got to shore, only 10 feet away, there was already two inches of water in the bottom of the canoe and, with no repair kit and little remaining daylight, there was nothing to do but make camp and turn in right where we were.

The next morning, contemplating our pretty fix, we remembered that the Algonquin Indians used spruce gum, or "minay-goba-you" as they called it, to caulk birch bark canoes. We couldn't recall exactly how it was prepared but decided to give it a try. First, we put a hard, fist-sized lump of White Spruce gum and about one tenth as much White Pine pitch in a pot of boiling water. Then, because the Indians used to add animal tallow to keep the final product from becoming brittle on cooling, we put in a teaspoon of butter (the quantity was a pure guess). Soon, at the surface of the boiling water, was a golden-brown scum that we skimmed off and applied directly to the hole in the canoe. It cooled so quickly that we hardly had time to shape its contours with our fingers. Within seconds it had hardened to an amazingly tough, lacquer-hard consistency.

We could hardly believe that the minay-goba-you had worked so well. In fact, we continued on with our trip as planned for another two days and didn't take a single drop of water.

The modern, technological counterpart to spruce gum is fibreglass but, having now tried them both, we wouldn't hesitate to recommend minay-goba-you. It's absolutely free, you don't have to carry it with you (since it's always close by), and it hardens much faster than fibreglass — thereby getting you back en route much more quickly.

As far as we know, minay-goba-you is presently available in only one colour but, since it happened to match our canoe almost perfectly, we didn't argue the point.↝

August 29, 1979, Vol. 20, No. 11 (D.S.)

Spruce gum was of crucial importance in making birch-bark canoes watertight, and it can still be used today.

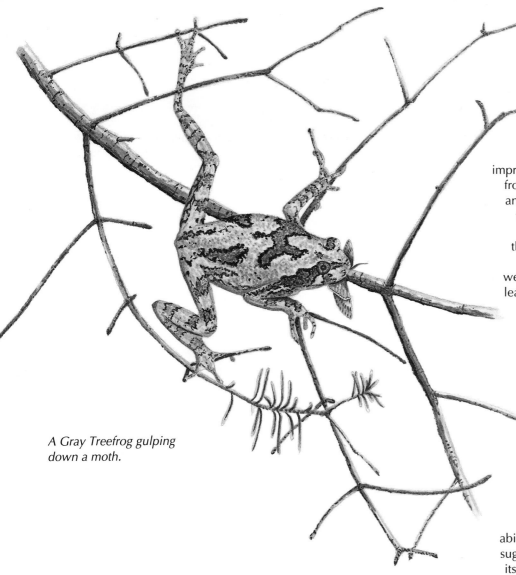

A Gray Treefrog gulping down a moth.

Superfrog

We have to admit that this title conjures up the image of Kermit, a stern look on his face and outfitted with a cape, flying around the world performing marvellous, superhuman feats. Now as we all know, such a notion is quite absurd because there is nothing superhuman about a frog. Real frogs just sit around in swamps, croaking and leading dull, quite unremarkable lives. Right?

Well, we beg to differ. If we (or Kermit) could do half the things that real frogs do, people would not be merely impressed; they would be awestruck. A particularly good example of what we mean is afforded by the common Algonquin frog that has somehow been saddled with the unprepossessing name of Eastern Gray Treefrog.

Treefrogs begin life as gelatinous eggs laid in beaver ponds and other similar bodies of water, about the middle of June. In a very few days they hatch out into golden tadpoles. After a summer of grazing on tiny algae, they transform into little frogs and leave the water. Everybody knows that tadpoles turn into little frogs, and we tend to take the process for granted. We really shouldn't. After all, if you want to impress your friends, just try changing from a golden, plant-eating "fish" to an insect-eating frog in the space of three months.*

Following that little number, the young treefrogs go on to their next trick. At the onset of cold weather they bury themselves under leaf litter in the forest and spend the winter beneath the snow in suspended animation close to the freezing point. We aren't sure which is the more difficult part of this feat — staying alive or waking up — but the frogs routinely do both each year.

Actually, what we have described so far is performed, with minor variations, not just by treefrogs but by the other eight Algonquin frogs and toads as well. The treefrog, however, has two additional abilities that really set it apart. One, suggested by the treefrog's name, is its ability to climb. If you hear the loud, musical trills of a treefrog and follow them to their source, you will see that the treefrog has swollen, sticky discs (not "suction cups") on the ends of its toes. These enable the treefrog to cling quite comfortably to vertical tree trunks or slender branches high above the ground.

And, if you are really lucky, you will see how efficient those sticky toes can be. As you watch the treefrog, entirely motionless except for the barely perceptible breathing movements of its throat, you begin to think that the animal is sound asleep. Suddenly, it is on another branch three or four feet away, dangling by one hind leg and busily stuffing a helpless moth into its mouth. Just remember, Tarzan had to use a vine!

Even these treetop acrobatics, however, are nothing compared to the treefrog's astounding ability to change colour. Many frogs change the tone of their skin from light to dark depending on such factors as temperature

---

* If you prefer, you may do the reverse transformation. Our experience indicates that observers are no less impressed.

and humidity, but treefrogs actually match their surroundings. One individual may be a bright, honest-to-goodness green, perfectly blending in with nearby foliage. But, if it takes up a new position on a lichen-encrusted tree trunk, it may change in an hour or so to a new, perfect camouflage consisting of an appropriately mottled pattern of gray and black, without the slightest hint of green. Or, down on the dead leaves of the forest floor, it will take on brownish hues, once again making the frog all but invisible against its background of the moment.

The advantages to the frog of being able to do this sort of thing are clear, but the limits of the frog's ability are not. In one experiment a treefrog was placed against a black and white checkerboard pattern, and it actually came up with an imperfect, but nonetheless creditable approximation of its totally artificial surroundings.

Now, any creature that can imitate a checkerboard, leap through the treetops, achieve suspended animation, and rapidly change from a water-dwelling herbivore to a completely different land- and tree-dwelling carnivore cannot be accused of leading a dull, unremarkable life. Sorry Kermit, we don't need you. Superfrog is alive and well and living in Algonquin Park.☞

June 26, 1980, Vol. 21, No. 2 (D.S.)

Treetop Eggonomics

Everyone knows that early summer is the time of year when birds and animals are raising their young. We suspect, however, that even our visitors who are parents themselves probably fail to realize just how hard those birds and animals are working. The fact is they are usually operating so close to their limits of physical endurance that any increase of effort would almost certainly bring about their complete exhaustion.

An excellent case in point came to mind 10 days ago when one of our museum staff discovered the nest of a Golden-crowned Kinglet near Tanamakoon Lake. As we shall see a bit later, kinglet nests are very special in their own right, but first a word about the birds that make them.

There are two kinds in Canada, the Golden-crowned and the Ruby-crowned, and both are common in Algonquin. Next to the hummingbird, they are the smallest birds in the Park, measuring a mere three and a half inches from the tip of the bill to the tip of the tail. They are whitish below, greenish above, and the males have brilliant crown patches that give the birds their names. Both are active little inhabitants of coniferous treetops, and both specialize in tiny insects.

The Golden-crowned Kinglet is a tiny bird that makes big nests and big families.

Now, we hardly have to point out that from late May to mid-July at least, Algonquin Park is an excellent place to find lots of insects. Kinglet food is so abundant, in fact, that the females of each species, when laying their eggs, regularly succeed in manufacturing one egg every day up to a total of nine or 10. The complete clutch weighs about eight or nine grams — which may not seem particularly impressive until you realize that the female who lays those eggs herself weighs only five or six grams. In human terms, it is roughly the same as if a woman had a 15-pound baby every day for 10 days in a row. (Good grief!)

And that is only the beginning. Eggs, after all, have to be incubated. In the case of a kinglet, one calculation suggests that the incubating female would have to supply 2,800 calories to her 10 eggs every day to assure their proper development (at an average air temperature of 60°F or 16°C). We tend to think of an incubating bird as just sitting on her eggs, whiling away the days until they hatch and the real work begins. In fact, the energy demands of incubation are quite appreciable — especially for a tiny little bird like a kinglet perched on her big pile of eggs.

Obviously, every calorie counts, and it is here that the kinglet's nest takes on special importance. Instead of being a mere cup or platform the way most bird nests are, serving only to support eggs and nestlings, a kinglet nest is the avian equivalent of a well-designed, well-insulated house — it makes the most of whatever heat is supplied to it. The nest is almost perfectly spherical, about six inches in diameter, with close to one-inch-thick walls of moss, lichens, and cobwebs, and lined on the inside with feathers. At the top is a small entrance hole and, most intriguing of all, large feathers are often arranged around this entrance with their tips all pointing towards the centre. This amounts to a sort of "revolving door," permitting the adults to come and go and yet significantly reducing the escape of heated air from the nest chamber. All in all, a minor engineering marvel.*

---

* If you would like to examine a kinglet nest for yourself, we now have the one from Tanamakoon at the Museum. We believe it is only the sixth Golden-crowned Kinglet nest to be found in Ontario — a result of the fact that they are extremely well hidden in thick spruce foliage.

Having got through the incubation period, the adult kinglets, especially the male, must then contend with the task of finding enough food to feed the 10 or so little ones. How they meet this challenge is little short of incredible. Thanks to a feeding schedule that rapidly increases to over 20 feeding visits to the nest per hour for each 16-hour day, the nestlings reach full adult weight in 10 or 11 days. To take up our human analogy once again, it is as if the parents of those 10 mythical 15-pound babies found enough food in just 10 days to get each one of them up to 150 pounds. … Baby kinglets actually stay in the nest for another nine or 10 days, during which their food intake is directed toward the development of feathers and the powers of flight and co-ordination they will need when they leave the nest.

The male continues to feed the young for a few days after that, but soon they are finding food for themselves. Two weeks following their departure from the nest, they leave the parental territory altogether and strike out on their own.

Now, you would naturally suppose that by this time the frazzled adults would be ready to take a richly deserved rest. It might appear that way indeed, but we forgot to mention one little "detail." Back when the female is incubating it seems that the male doesn't have much to do, and so (you'll never guess) he builds another nest! And, as soon as the young are big enough not to need their mother to warm them — a week or 10 days before they leave the (first) nest — she has completed a new clutch in the second nest and has started to incubate there, leaving the first brood largely in the care of her mate. It usually works out (about the time the male has finished up with the fledglings from the first nest) that the eggs in the second nest start to hatch and he must turn his attention almost immediately to feeding the second lot of youngsters.

Really, the whole business just boggles the mind. Certainly, we can't think of any better example to illustrate how utterly enslaved the birds and animals are at this season to maximizing their production of young. We humans sometimes don't realize how lucky we are to be able to sit back and enjoy the summer world around us.↵

July 3, 1980 ,Vol. 21, No. 3 (D.S.)

The Mouse That Does Push-ups

Some individuals just don't get the recognition they deserve. In spite of their considerable accomplishments they are condemned to living on the fringes of public esteem. Other people treat them with plain indifference or even (oh, the injustice of it all!) barely concealed condescension.

This same, unfortunate situation also exists with animals, and no better example could be found than the muskrat. See what we mean? Right away, you are probably thinking to yourself that the muskrat is a less than inspiring subject for contemplation but, please, do not fall into this error. Hear us out instead. You see, the poor old muskrat suffers from at least two serious disadvantages. First is the existence of its rather distant relative, the beaver. Although the two animals have many similarities in abilities and lifestyles, the beaver is bigger, has a few more attention-grabbing gimmicks (such as dam-building), and ends up getting all the glory — leaving the muskrat to appear as some sort of insignificant second-rater (quite unfair, really). The muskrat's second problem is its name. No matter how you slice it, the first part of the name makes you think of "smelly" and, as for the second part, let's face it, a rat is a rat. We could try using the Latin name, *Ondatra zibethica*, but somehow we don't think it would catch on. Of course, it isn't the muskrat's fault that it has grand-standing relatives or that English-speaking humans persist in calling it a "smelly rat," so the least we can do is make amends by considering this animal's special qualities.

To begin with, we should get it straight that the muskrat is not really a rat but a mouse. To be sure, it's a very large one, weighing between one and two kilograms, but technically that's what it is. It also departs from other mice in its adaptations for life in the water. Except for the tail and feet, the whole body is covered with a thick, buoyant coat of waterproof guard hairs and below that a dense underfur, the two combining to keep the muskrat's body warm and dry even in freezing cold water. A muskrat swims with alternate strokes of its hind feet. They are not webbed like a beaver's feet, but there are stiff fringes of hair along the sides of the toes that make for efficient paddling. The naked, scaly, vertically-flattened tail serves as a sort of keel to keep the animal on a straight course when it is swimming on the surface. But underwater, the tail is actively sculled back and forth, providing significant propulsive power. A muskrat can stay under for up to 15 minutes thanks to a high tolerance for carbon dioxide in the blood and the ability to reduce the heart rate and to relax the muscles during a dive. This capacity is very important in permitting the muskrat to escape from predators and to swim long distances under the ice in the winter.

During the summer we usually see muskrats in the evening, swimming across some boggy pond or creek. At a distance, it is sometimes hard to tell a swimming muskrat from a beaver, but if you look closely you will see that with a beaver it is usually just the tip of the head that is visible above the water whereas with the muskrat both the head and back can be seen. Of course, if you see the tail when the animal dives, there won't be any more doubt about the animal's identity.

A common sign of muskrats in Algonquin is a pile of clam shells in shallow water (they apparently pry open the shells with their teeth somehow), but most of the diet consists of water plants, of which cat-tails are by far the most important. In fact, because cat-tails are not particularly common in the Park, our local muskrat populations are nowhere near as large as in other areas, south of here, for example, where there are large cat-tail marshes. Apart from their relatively low numbers, there is another reason why the presence of muskrats is not all that obvious in Algonquin. Most of them tend to make burrows from under the water's surface up into pond- or stream-side banks. The classic muskrat lodge of heaped-up mud and cat-tail stalks is a relatively unusual sight in the Park. They are built away out in large marshes where there are no other possible havens from predators and bad weather. Also, since lodges are built mostly of plant materials, they can — up to a point — serve as a handy food supply. If a muskrat can't leave its lodge for some reason, it can stave off hunger simply by eating part of the bedroom wall. Of course, this is only an emergency measure, and most food must be sought outside the lodge.

In the summer, this is a relatively easy matter, and muskrats build scattered feeding platforms and sometimes floating rafts to which they can retire and eat food obtained nearby. In winter, however, a serious obstacle is posed by the ice. Muskrats do not store food close to their lodges the way beavers do. Even if they can stay underwater a long time, it would seem each animal would sooner or later use up all the naturally occurring supply of aquatic plants near its lodge and thus face starvation. In fact, this does not happen because soon after the ice freezes, muskrats chew holes in the ice at various locations around their lodges. They then bring up mud and vegetation to make mound-like roofs (which quickly freeze) over the holes. The little structures, just big enough to hold one muskrat, are called "push-ups," and they are of fundamental importance to their builders

because, as satellite-feeding, -resting, and -breathing stations, they vastly increase the area each muskrat can exploit during the winter. This behaviour is even more remarkable when you realize that each muskrat is apparently capable, in the total darkness that exists in the frigid water beneath the ice and snow covering the winter marsh, of routinely finding food and then the nearest push-up, and eventually going back to the lodge or burrow. They seem to know something about navigation that we don't!

There: we have a condensed account of an animal that obviously deserves more recognition than it normally gets. We think everybody should turn over a new leaf and let the muskrat share a little of the limelight we normally reserve for the beaver. And, if you have trouble getting enthusiastic about a "rat," just forget that dumb name and think of it as a "talented mouse that does push-ups." It's closer to the mark and certainly sounds a lot better.

July 17, 1980, Vol. 21, No. 5 (D.S.)

A Tale of Two Fishes

If you are a regular visitor to Algonquin, you are probably well aware of the Park's long-standing tradition as a centre of scientific research. As a matter of fact, over 600 scholarly papers have been based on work done here, chiefly at our three biological research stations, by our own government personnel and by university scientists from across Canada.

One very nice example of such work has been carried out by our Ministry of Natural Resources Brook Trout specialist, Jim Fraser. The results were published in 1978 in the *Transactions of the American Fisheries Society* under the title "The Effect of Competition with Yellow Perch on the Survival and Growth of Planted Brook Trout, Splake and Rainbow Trout in a Small Ontario Lake." It is especially fitting that we describe this investigation because the Society judged it the best paper of the year — no mean accomplishment when you consider the importance and scale of fisheries research in North America.

Jim did his work in Little Minnow Lake, a typical, small Algonquin lake at the end of a 1,490-metre portage leading east off Sproule Bay at the south end of Opeongo Lake. Little Minnow has an area of only 8.9 hectares (22 acres, if you prefer), is only moderately deep (14.3 metres), and originally its only fish were sticklebacks and four species of minnows.

Beginning in 1962, however, the lake was stocked each year with various combinations of Brook Trout, Splake (an artificial hybrid between Brook and Lake Trout), and Rainbow Trout (a western North American species not naturally found in Algonquin). Because fishermen returning from Little Minnow had to pass by the

Opeongo creel-checking station, it was possible to get a good idea of the returns resulting from the trout plantings. For about six years, both anglers and researchers had ample reason to be pleased but then, in 1968, Yellow Perch were discovered in the lake.

This meant the end of Little Minnow as a good trout lake because, as everybody knew, planted trout do very poorly in lakes containing perch. The exact reasons for this poor performance were unclear, however, and Jim realized that Little Minnow Lake might be an especially interesting "before and after" situation and a good place to shed light on the problem. For this reason, he continued to plant trout over the next six years and to closely monitor the survival, growth, and food habits of the trout and the perch.

One of Jim's most significant findings was that, with the partial exception of Brook Trout, there was no particular decline in trout survival. What did occur, however, was a drastic reduction in the growth rate of the planted trout. For example, Splake planted in 1963 (before the perch) reached an average weight of 673 grams two years later, whereas Splake planted in 1973 (after perch were well established) on the average weighed only 243 grams after the same length of time. Or, as another way of expressing the same thing, before the perch, fishermen caught about 4.1 kilograms of trout for every kilogram of trout planted; after the perch, they caught an average of only 0.6 kilograms of trout for every kilogram planted. In other words, less trout flesh was coming out of the lake than had been planted in the first place. As for the perch, they grew extremely well (24 centimetres in two years) immediately after their appearance in the lake, but much less rapidly several years later. By that time, however, the little lake had several thousand perch weighing a total of 180 to 270 kilograms (400 to 600 pounds).

These observations strongly suggested that the perch were beating the trout to the best food, growing very rapidly as a result, and then, when they reached high numbers, growing more slowly because they were competing among themselves for the lake's limited food supplies. Sure enough, an analysis of stomach contents showed that the trout originally ate many large food items, such as minnows, leeches, dragonfly nymphs, and crayfish, but that these kinds of food were largely taken over by perch when they appeared in the lake, and the trout ended up eating many more small items, such as caddisfly and midge larvae.

A second question coming out of Jim's work concerns the very nature of the planted fish. Obviously, they are quite inept at competing with perch for the best food. And when you stop to think about it, hatchery trout lead a pretty spoiled existence. There is always plenty of food in the form of liver pellets — which never try to get away. Food in a lake is seldom so predictable and never so co-operative. Perhaps the hatchery trout have had their original competitive qualities unwittingly bred out of them and find themselves with an unnatural disadvantage when humans force them to earn their own living out in the real world.

Perch usually out-compete planted Brook Trout in the struggle for food.

All this was an elegant demonstration that perch do well at the expense of planted trout, not because they eat the trout, infect them with parasites, or any other similar possibility but because they completely outclass the trout in the hunt for food. But Jim's work was more than an important contribution to theoretical biology; it also points out some serious considerations.

First of all, it emphasizes why it is forbidden to use live bait fish in Algonquin. Too often, fishermen have dumped the contents of their minnow pails into good trout lakes, and perch or other effective trout competitors have got established as a result.

If this is the case, it follows that we would get much better results, perhaps even in lakes that have no perch at all, if we raised and then planted young trout originating from eggs collected in the wild rather than from eggs produced by traditional hatchery stock.

Jim has been conducting research in several Park lakes into this very possibility, using various combinations of wild and traditional hatchery trout, and he tells us that his early results are very encouraging. Perhaps in a few years we will be able to report that Jim has solved the problem of perch competition, which he demonstrated so nicely in Little Minnow Lake.

July 24, 1980, Vol. 21, No. 6 (D.S.)

Everybody, at one time or another, has sat back and admired the sheer beauty of butterflies as they flit from blossom to blossom or soak up the summer sun. But there is another much less frequently appreciated reason for pausing to contemplate such lovely insects. Their very existence is a remarkable fact when you consider what they have just been through. However "carefree" grown-up butterflies may seem, they have lived most of their lives as caterpillars — and caterpillars do not have an easy time. Far too many things like to eat them. Even if we forget about mites, spiders, wasps, and other insects, birds alone account for astronomical numbers of caterpillars each year. Just watch a bird's nest for a while and you'll soon realize that the prodigious growth of nestling birds is fuelled by equally prodigious amounts of food — and very often that food is caterpillars. So relentless is the pressure from birds that they can often wipe out over 50 per cent or more of all caterpillars present in an area in just a few weeks.

Now, if you were a caterpillar, you would probably be less than thrilled with the prospect of being shoved down a baby bird's throat, and you might want to consider ways of avoiding such a mishap. Just for fun, why don't you stop and figure out what, in fact, you could reasonably do as a caterpillar to escape being eaten. Then we'll go on to see what real caterpillars do. No cheating now. ... Got your answers? Okay, read on.

Well, one fairly obvious thing you could try would be to be as inconspicuous as possible. You might do this by being green to match the leaves on which you were feeding, or you might have colours and markings to make you look like a twig or blend in with the bark of a tree. In fact, many real caterpillars are superbly camouflaged as twigs, bark, foliage, or even (bet you didn't think of this idea) bird droppings.

Another thing you might do would be to always feed on the underside of leaves so as to avoid being spotted from above. And you could be active only at night because insect-eating birds hunt mostly by day. Once again, we find that many caterpillars do both of these things. (A price is paid, incidentally, for not feeding by day. Less food means slower growth.)

Well, how did you do? Did you figure out these general strategies? Fine if you did, but don't feel too smug about it because if that's all you came up with, you would be a flop as a caterpillar (sorry about that). What you probably forgot is that caterpillars eat green foliage, and in so doing they leave holes and ragged edges on the leaves. It doesn't take much for birds to learn to associate such visible signs with the presence of fat, juicy caterpillars. Even immobility and good camouflage may not be enough to save a caterpillar from a sharp-eyed bird that has been alerted by obviously chewed-upon leaves nearby.

Don't feel bad if you slipped up on this. We'll give you another chance. This time, take a minute or two and

How Smart Are Baby Butterflies?

Anyone visiting Algonquin in early August has come at a particularly enjoyable time of year. The days are warm and sunny, the new crop of birds and animals is out exploring the world, and the annual show of roadside wildflowers is well under way. To top it all off, we have those ultimate symbols of carefree summer days — the butterflies.

figure out what you could do as a caterpillar to avoid or lessen the danger of tipping off birds to your presence by the tell-tale signs of leaf munching.

Okay, here we go again. The most obvious thing you could do would be to hide by day but at a long distance from your feeding leaf. That way, a bird might see signs of your presence but fail to find you nearby. In fact, many caterpillars do just that. One observer described a caterpillar that bypassed 113 perfectly good leaves and travelled over six feet every evening as it moved from its hiding place to its chosen feeding leaf.

A second tactic would be to stay on your leaf day and night but to feed evenly around the whole edge of the leaf rather than making holes or jagged edges. Night-time kitchen raiders will recognize this as a variation on the time-honoured ploy of taking a thin slice from the entire cut edge of a cake so that no one will notice anything missing (*The Raven* was a kid once too, you know).

Another devious strategy you might use would be to eat one small hole from each of many leaves. This is obviously not the most efficient way to feed, but it means you would flood the environment with false clues. Birds would have no idea where you really were. Sure enough, some caterpillars actually do this.

Perhaps the most ingenious trick employed by caterpillars, however, is the "destroy-the-evidence" routine. Especially in species that feed on leaves too big to finish in one night, some caterpillars will, when dawn arrives, actually back off the leaf, bite through and sever the leaf stem, and only then turn around and crawl away

to their daytime hiding places. In other words, instead of leaving a ragged half-eaten leaf that would alert hungry birds, the caterpillar leaves no leaf at all!

In our title we asked how smart baby butterflies are, and by now you may be shaking your head and concluding that they are a bunch of little green Einsteins. But actually, caterpillars have no "intelligence" at all. The reason they have such apparently ingenious strategies is simply that the "ordinary" varieties of caterpillar without such tricks were eliminated long ago, leaving only the kinds whose ancestors were lucky enough to have the chance mutations responsible for the appropriate but quite unconscious behaviour we see today. In fact, there is no more reason to think modern caterpillars are smart than there is to imagine that big grains of sand are smart for being held in a sieve while small grains fall through the holes. In the case of caterpillars, the "sieve" is the relentless pressure from hungry birds — which naturally prey most heavily on the caterpillars that are easiest to find.

Baby butterflies may not be smart but, personally, we find their intricate survival coloration and behaviour no less awe-inspiring for being developed instead by an age-old "natural-selection" exercised by birds. … Something to think about the next time you see a "carefree" butterfly flitting about in the summer sunshine.↩

August 7, 1980, Vol. 21, No. 8 (D.S.)

A Salty Story

Spring is returning to Algonquin and, with it, our first spring fishermen and campers. Warm, spring days — this is the time to catch a trout, to wander through sunflooded hardwoods with their carpets of wildflowers, and to listen to the ringing laughter of loons out on a blue, faraway lake.

Spring is known for all of these things in Algonquin, but, unless you regularly visit the Park throughout the year, you may not realize that spring is also the outstanding time of the year to see moose. Moose have been increasing in Algonquin over the last 10 years, and this past winter our aerial census indicated there were about 2,800 in the Park, or almost one per square mile. This is a very dense population for such a large animal. Even so, at most times of the year, it is not every day that you can see one.

Then, at the end of April, they suddenly become visible. As soon as the snow melts, they are everywhere along the highway. It is as dramatic as the first flights of migrating geese or the leafing out of the trees. Normally, the excellent moose-viewing lasts all May and does not really diminish until late June.

Now, the moose are there all along, of course, and many people have wondered why they are so much more

obvious in spring. Numerous theories have been proposed, but the mystery was recently cleared up by Dave Fraser, one of the scientists from our Ministry of Natural Resources Wildlife Research Branch. Dave did his work in Sibley Provincial Park on the north shore of Lake Superior, but the phenomena he studied and the conclusions he reached seem to apply equally well here in Algonquin.

The key to understanding the May moose-viewing explosion is realizing that all winter long, moose are forced to subsist on woody twigs — about 25 kilograms of the stuff every day. This may sound like a lot, but such food is extremely poor in the minerals needed by all animals, including us humans, for a healthy, balanced diet. One of the minerals that moose are starved for all winter is sodium, and we shouldn't be too surprised that moose will go well out of their way to get this nutrient when and if it becomes available. In some areas there are naturally-occurring sources of sodium in the form of mineral springs or seepage areas. As soon as the snow melts in the spring, the seepage areas are exposed, the sodium becomes available and the local moose start making regular visits to drink the precious water.

In most of the rocky Canadian Shield, however, and including Algonquin Park, there are no mineral springs and the moose would be out of luck — except for one thing. Humans keep Highway 60 open all winter by, among other things, putting sand on it when conditions are icy. Mixed in with the sand to keep it from freezing into big, unmanageable chunks is a small amount of salt (that is, sodium chloride).

By now, you have probably guessed the rest of the story. When the snow and ice melt in the spring, the salt dissolves in the water and, where the drainage conditions are suitable, it accumulates in roadside ditches. These salty puddles are discovered by moose the same way a natural mineral spring would be, and the big animals keep returning again and again to drink the water, not for itself but for the sodium it contains. And this is the reason why, in a sudden explosion following the spring thaw, moose become so visible along Highway 60 and along many other roads in moose country farther north. Needless to say, the phenomenon is even more striking in areas where pure salt is put on the roads during the winter because there, the spring roadside puddles end up with even greater salt concentrations.

Incidentally, even in such relatively extreme cases, the salt solution is far too dilute to be tasted by humans, although the moose don't have any trouble. It is of interest, also, that the moose are definitely after the sodium, not the chloride. Dave Fraser conducted a series of preference tests with various kinds of salts and found that moose only went for the ones containing sodium.

You may be wondering, if sodium is so vitally necessary for moose and if there are no natural mineral springs here, how did Algonquin moose get sodium before we unwittingly started creating artificial mineral springs along the highway. Well, there really is a rich, natural source of sodium in moose country. The aquatic plants, such as water-lilies, that grow so commonly in shallow, boggy areas and beaver ponds have it in quite high concentrations. Conventional wisdom always said that the reason moose spend so much time in June and early July feeding on aquatic plants was to escape all the biting insects. But this may be just a secondary benefit. The real motivation may be so that they can feast on all that delicious sodium. The only trouble is that the water doesn't warm up and aquatic plants do not really put on any new growth before June. Until then, those salt-hungry moose must do without — unless, or course, they happen to discover one of those salty puddles so graciously provided earlier in the spring by the Ministry of Transportation and Communications.

For our part, we are delighted that so many people get to see moose that would otherwise be out of sight back in the bush somewhere. But, unfortunately, there is a dark side to this story as well. Moose attracted to the highway seem inevitably to lead to moose-vehicle collisions, almost always involving drivers who do not take the danger seriously. Believe us, those big yellow and black moose-warning signs along the highway are there for a reason. Last year there were 14 collisions, resulting in as many dead moose, thousands of dollars worth of vehicle damage, and one human fatality. As we go to press, there have already been two collisions this year — fortunately with no one being killed.

Some people manage to crash into stationary moose in broad daylight, but the real danger occurs at night. Because they are so dark and often do not turn to face oncoming vehicles (which would permit the driver to see the reflected eyeshine), moose are extremely difficult to see after dark. Experienced drivers realize this and accordingly drive slowly and with extreme alertness. It is especially wise to travel at less than the posted limit at night at this time of year. If you go faster than 80 kilometres per hour, it is doubtful that you will be able to see a moose on the road soon enough for you to react and stop in time.

So please, enjoy the spectacle of those magnificent (if salt-starved) moose attracted to the roadside — but also recognize the danger. Otherwise, our story about winter salt might turn out to be a story about spring tragedy.⤳

April 29, 1981, Vol. 22, No. 1 (D.S.)

Dragons and Dragon-Slayers

Humans have always been fascinated by stories of supernatural beasts. In fact, almost every culture in the world has tales of one terrifying monster or another, and some stories have been popular for hundreds or even thousands of years. One good example is the Greek legend of Perseus, which was recently highlighted in the motion picture version "Clash of the Titans."

In contrast to such tales, real life and real animals may seem rather routine and unspectacular. We contend, however, that this impression is due to our failure to really look at what we see around us — especially when it comes to smaller animals.

We would certainly learn to pay attention in a hurry if we woke up one day to find ourselves reduced to the size of an insect. For example, there are "monsters" in the tea-coloured lagoons (beaver ponds) of Algonquin, which we could continue to ignore only at our extreme peril. Specifically, we have in mind the "nymphs" or immature forms of dragonflies that are so common in Algonquin. Allowing for scale, these creatures are as fearsome and bizarre as any lurking in the ancient legends or dreamed up by the movie industry's special-effects men.

Dragonfly nymphs don't have gills. Instead they can extract oxygen from water drawn into their lower intestine. By forcibly expelling that water, they can rapidly "jet propel" themselves many feet away from any danger. (In human terms this would be like jumping several hundred yards.) Most of the time, though, dragonfly nymphs creep about very slowly in shallow water until they come within range of prey — a mosquito larva, another nymph, or sometimes even a minnow. Then, in a movement so fast that it can be seen only on slowed-down movie film, the extendable lower lip darts out, grabs the prey with sharp teeth, and instantly snaps it back to the nymph's jaws. These immediately start to devour the still living victim.

Living nymphs are well camouflaged and hard to see, but at this time of year you can easily find the cast-off skins of nymphs that have left the water to begin their adult life. And, if you are really lucky, you may find one actually making the transition. From the time the nymph's skin starts splitting down the back, about three hours are needed for the adult to fully emerge, expand its crumpled wings, and allow them to harden for the first flight. What human legend relates anything more fantastic than this? Before your eyes the underwater monster is transformed into one of the most graceful creatures of the air.

It is well worthwhile to watch adult dragonflies. Not only can they hover in one spot like a helicopter, they are

The last millisecond in the life of an Algonquin dragonfly.

also able to fly backwards and sideways. These remarkable powers permit the precision dartings and manoeuverings by which dragonflies routinely capture flying insects. The victims are caught and held in the dragonfly's basket-like assemblage of legs, eaten in the air, and, when the nourishing insides have been consumed, the lifeless skeletons are discarded. (You will be happy to know that many of the insects getting this treatment are mosquitoes and deerflies.)

Dragonflies are also interesting to watch for their territorial and mating behaviour. The males of many species defend territories and aggressively expel other males. They immediately seize females, however, holding them behing the head with claspers on the end of their abdomen. Mating is then achieved, in flight, when the female bends the tip of her abdomen forward to the male's second abdominal segment and accepts the package of sperm stored there. After mating, the male may continue to hold the female behind the head and drag her to a suitable egg-laying area, or he may release her but continue to guard her until she has finished laying. Either way, his behaviour seeks to ensure that no other male will mate with her and that he will indeed be the "father" of the eggs she lays.

Dragonflies have been on earth essentially unchanged since long before the dinosaurs appeared. While they are highly perfected flying machines, if you watch them much you will see that even they are no match at all for a devastatingly effective "super predator" that lives here in Algonquin. That predator is the Eastern Kingbird, a common member of the flycatcher family that specializes in large insects like dragonflies found around boggy ponds and streams.

Many predators, such as hawks or wolves, rarely catch more than 10 per cent of the prey animals they go after, but we have yet to see a kingbird miss its intended meal. Sometimes they seem to loaf along, "sculling" as it were with vibrating wingtips; at other times they streak out to the doomed dragonfly with deep, powerful wingbeats. Sometimes the victim doesn't see the end coming; at other times it tries to take evasive action. But a kingbird can twist and turn with astonishing dexterity, and the result is always the same — a loud snap as the kingbird crushes the dragonfly's body into immobility and then an unhurried return to a suitable feeding perch. Considering the skills of the victims, such performances are awesomely impressive.

Dragonflies and kingbirds do not usually compel our attention the way larger animals do, but that's our problem. And happily, it's a problem we can correct simply by really looking at our surroundings. Who needs a made-up "Clash of the Titans" when all of July we can see "Dragons and Dragon-Slayers" in real life. Don't miss it. Now showing at a beaver pond near you.☜

July 9, 1981, Vol. 22, No. 3 (D.S.)

A Canine Copycat?

Sooner or later, every visitor to Algonquin sees a Red Fox trotting along in the evening beside a roadside ditch or its eyes momentarily reflecting our headlights after dark.

To most of us, foxes are pretty familiar animals, and we are sure no one has any trouble recognizing them as members of the dog family. Granted, a fox is much smaller than a timber wolf (Algonquin's only other member of the family), but the similarities between the two still seem so obvious that they hardly deserve comment.

Well, as a matter of fact, a Red Fox may look like a "dog" alright, but it sure doesn't behave like one. Instead, and in almost every detail of its lifestyle, it functions as (of all things!) a perfectly good cat!

Now, a statement like this seems to contradict everyone's sense of order — cats and dogs, after all, have the reputation of being total opposites — and it certainly calls for some supporting evidence. But all you have to do, really, to actually see how a fox is catlike is to watch one hunt. For one thing, foxes do not travel in packs or go after dangerous prey larger than themselves as do other members of the dog family. Instead, just like cats, they hunt small animals off by themselves. Such prey may not be particularly dangerous, but they do present major problems. The chief one is that, if warned, they can escape very quickly, either up into trees, as with squirrels and birds, or down into burrows, as with mice and chipmunks. Foxes are therefore obliged to use a very undoglike, but eminently catlike, technique of stealthily approaching the prey and pouncing before the danger is realized.

In the case of rodents that can be heard or scented but not seen in thick vegetation, a fox moves very slowly, putting each front foot down ever so carefully — and sometimes lifting it up and trying in a different place. The hind feet, furthermore, are placed exactly where the front feet have been so as to minimize the chances of snapping an unseen twig or otherwise warning the prey. When it is within striking distance, the fox crouches deeply and then jumps in a high, arching leap towards the intended meal. The idea is to land right on the invisible prey and pin it to the ground with the forepaws. Such leaps usually cover six feet or less, but foxes have been seen to catapult (from a standing start) for as much as 15 feet on the flat and for as much as 25 feet downhill. The precise launch trajectory is determined by the fox's uncannily acute hearing, which can detect the faintest rustling of a mouse and pinpoint its source to within one degree. Should the mouse move while the ballistic fox is on its way, small mid-course manoeuvres can be accomplished by violently manipulating the tail. (This, of course, is highly reminiscent of a cat's ability to right itself during a fall.)

When a fox is after squirrels or birds, it uses a very different, though still very catlike hunting technique. Such animals are less likely to be hidden by vegetation and depend on sight much more than hearing to detect danger. To hunt them successfully, a fox must be much more careful about being seen, and so, when a hunt begins, it immediately crouches, belly almost touching the ground, and remains absolutely motionless, staring intently at the prey. Whenever the prey is looking the other way, the fox slinks forward in its crouching position, only to freeze into rock-like immobility the instant the victim turns its head again. If it gets close enough, the fox streaks forward, still low to the ground, and attempts to grap the prey with its mouth at the end of a headlong, horizontal leap.

Having caught the prey, a Red Fox continues to behave like a cat by occasionally "playing" with its victim, by killing it with a squeezing bite of needle-like teeth, and sometimes by temporarily caching it for later use.

Because they use catlike techniques to hunt catlike prey, we should not be surprised that foxes have evolved certain catlike anatomical features as well. For example, a fox's eye has a vertically split pupil, just like a cat's, and also a glistening layer of connective tissue behind the retina. This increases the fox's powers of night vision by reflecting light back over the retina a second time and causes the eye to glow a dull green colour. In addition, the fox has semi-retractile claws (for use in capturing mice and chipmunks) and sensitive "whiskers" on its muzzle along with similar bristles on its wrist joints. The latter enable a fox (or a cat) to determine its foot placement with the extreme sensitivity required for an absolutely silent stalk.

All these features make sense given the fox's catlike existence, but we are at a bit of a loss to explain why foxes should threaten each other by standing broadside, arching their backs and raising their fur. And why do young foxes hiss and spit at danger and adults give distinctly catlike meows and high-pitched screams?

Readers whose sense of order is violated by all this catlike behaviour from a supposedly respectable member of the dog family can take heart that the Red Fox is not a complete sell-out to the ways of its fellow canines. Foxes may have eyes like cats, may hunt like cats, may kill prey like cats, may display like cats, and may even sound like cats but, by all that is holy, we haven't yet had a report of a Red Fox up a tree.

It's really quite reassuring. After all, cats are cats and dogs are dogs. … Aren't they?⌒

August 13, 1981, Vol. 22, No. 8 (D.S.)

Before the Main Event

Unless you happened to be in the Park 450 million years ago, you probably don't know too much about what was the most spectacular event by far in Algonquin's history.

Mind you, all is not lost. Even if you missed it, you can still see evidence of the big event by taking the very rough gravel road leading from Deux Rivières, up on the Ottawa River, south into the Park. Before you arrive at the canoe route access point at Brent on Cedar Lake, you will pass an observation tower perched on the rim of the enormous and ancient Brent Crater.

We must caution that, even from the top of the tower, you have to know what to look for (craters age over the years, like the rest of us), but from the air, you would have no problem at all recognizing the distinctly circular shape. The crater floor is almost two miles wide and is partly covered by Gilmour and Tecumseh Lakes. Diamond drilling investigations conducted after the crater was discovered in 1951 showed that younger limestone now fills all but 500 feet of the crater's 1,400-foot depth and that, below the limestone, the original granites and gneisses are highly shattered for another 2,000 feet. The evidence indicates that this enormous hole in the ground was blasted out when a meteorite, perhaps only 500 or 600 feet in diameter, struck the earth at about 10 miles per second. Such a collision would release the same energy as 250 million tons of TNT and, if it were to happen again today, be quite sufficient to flatten every tree in and well beyond Algonquin Park — and even to blow out windows in Toronto. … All things considered, it's just as well you weren't here 450 million years ago.

Personally, we had always thought of the Brent Crater as a cataclysmic, but still freakish, event of nature, having no lasting significance. However, we now know of at least 100 giant meteorite craters around the world (24 in

Canada). Evidence has also been gathered to suggest that one ancient collision may have been a key event in the history of life — including our own — on this planet.

This came out in dramatic fashion last winter at an international conference held in Ottawa to consider a new theory to explain the extinction of the dinosaurs. As most everybody knows, dinosaurs dominated the Earth for about 220 million years until, about 70 million years ago,

The day the Brent Crater was created was not a good time to visit Algonquin Park.

they abruptly disappeared — along with about three-quarters of all other then-living animals and plants. Many ideas have been advanced to account for the mysterious mass extinctions, but the one most favoured now is that a huge meteorite (probably a stray asteroid from the asteroid belt between Mars and Jupiter) was responsible. Calculations show that an asteroid six miles across could do the job if it hit the Earth at the same speed as the Brent meteorite — 10 miles per second (that's three seconds to go from the West Gate to the East Gate).

The resulting explosion, by far the largest in Earth's history, would have instantaneously created a crater 25 miles deep and 150 miles wide. The stupendous shock wave itself would have wiped out untold numbers of animals nearby, but the real killer would have been the millions of tons of dust blasted up into the sky. Soon carried around the globe by the jet stream, the dust would have enshrouded our planet and blocked out the sun for three to five years.* During that time, the earth's surface would be cold and dark, plant growth would cease, and the dinosaurs and most other animals would freeze or

---

* On a much smaller scale, the same effect is created by modern-day volcanoes. The volcanic explosion of Tambora in Indonesia, for example, threw so much sun-blocking dust into the high atmosphere that the following summer (1816) saw snowstorms and killing frosts in June, July, and August in both Europe and North America. Crops failed and many people came perilously close to starvation the next winter.

starve to death. Some plants would survive as dormant seeds or spores, but the only animals that could make it would be those that ate seeds or dead plants and animals.

Scientists cannot point to a 70-million-year-old crater of the appropriate size to back up the new theory, but the impact might well have occurred in the sea or some other place where all traces could have been destroyed since the explosion.* Besides, there is another kind of evidence that gives powerful support to the asteroid idea. In sedimentary rocks in many places around the world, there is a thin layer of clay at the 70-million-year level, precisely where the fossils of dinosaurs and other animals of the day abruptly disappear. This clay layer is extremely rich in an element called irridium, an element that is very rare on earth but that happens to be found in high concentrations in meteorites from outer space.

When the dust from the giant meteorite collision finally settled (and formed the clay layer), the few surviving plants and animals found a world that would never be the same. The dinosaurs and other dominants were gone forever, and the way was open for the survivors to evolve into new forms that could take their

---

* Since this article was written, scientists believe they may have found the correct crater, a huge 150-kilometre-diameter structure along the coast of Mexico's Yucatan Peninsula.

places. The mammals were the most successful in filling the biological voids, and many new types did indeed appear. Among the new lines was the one that eventually gave rise to the primates, including us, the human being.

The really interesting and important point is that if the dinosaurs had not been destroyed — if the slate had not been wiped clean, so to speak — it is very doubtful that we and other modern mammals ever would have evolved. The dinosaurs would still be here, barring the door.

Something to contemplate if you climb the observation tower up on the Brent Road and gaze out over the now peaceful and wooded crater. The explosion that blasted it out of solid granite so many millions of years ago was far more devastating than the biggest thermonuclear bomb ever conceived by man. In fact, if we could go back in a time machine to watch the formation of the Brent Crater, we wouldn't dare go any closer to it than several hundred miles.

And yet, compared to the explosion caused by the asteroid slamming into the Earth 70 million years ago — the incredible, planet-shaking explosion that blocked out the sun, killed the dinosaurs, and changed the course of biological history — the Brent Crater was nothing at all. A mere "piffle" before the main event.∽

September 2, 1981, Vol. 22, No. 11 (D.S.)

Algonquin in Autumn — Behind the Signs

Another summer has slipped by. Most of the campgrounds are closed and empty now, and already we see signs of the approaching winter. Small bands of migrating warblers forage in otherwise silent woods, asters and goldenrods adorn the roadsides, and squirrels are putting in long hours harvesting the cones that will be their food supply during the months ahead.

Everyone enjoys observing the sights of an Algonquin autumn, and a trip to the Park at this time of year is an old tradition in Ontario. Still, we think it fair to say that most visitors are content to do one or two trails — to lose themselves for a day in the Park's quiet mood — and very often fail to realize how many intriguing stories there are behind the outward signs of fall surrounding us.

Take, for example, the most spectacular of all the fall sights in Algonquin — the turning of the leaves. As we go to press, some trees have started to change already, and when the colours reach their peak in the last week of September or the first week in October, thousands of visitors will marvel at the sea of blazing reds and golds. In fact, we are usually so entranced by the show, we seldom stop to wonder why the leaves change colour in the first place. If we do, we generally assume we are merely

seeing the cold-induced death of the leaves and leave it at that. But the truth is far more subtle and, if better known, would make fall colours even more impressive than they already are.

Simply put, the colour change is just one stage (which happens to be visible to us humans) of an orderly, programmed process by which trees shut down their summer activity and prepare for winter. The process actually begins way back in July and is so vital that, without it, our broad-leaved trees would all die.

To appreciate what is going on here, you have to recall the fundamental importance of green leaves. What gives them their colour is chlorophyll, the amazing chemical that captures the sun's energy and which is then used to combine water and carbon dioxide to make sugars and, from them, starch, cellulose, and all the other complex substances that make up a tree. It

is one of the basic miracles of life on this planet that the forests and all other plants around us have been created from water and an invisible, odourless gas. (And, on top of all that, the same process gives off the oxygen to which we and all other animals owe our lives.)

Leaves are indeed the most marvellous chemical factories ever known, but there are limits to what they can do. Those of deciduous trees, for example, are much too thin and delicate to survive an Algonquin winter. It is obvious they must die, but if they merely froze in place and then broke off during winter, the results would be disastrous.

The reason for this is that, in addition to the complex chemicals made by the leaves themselves, plants contain minute but precious quantities of simpler substances originally obtained through their roots from the soil. These substances, often called "minerals" or "nutrients," include magnesium (an essential component of chlorophyll), nitrogen (a part of all proteins), and others such as calcium, phosphorus, and potassium. All living things (including humans) need and have nutrients, but in a tree, a very high proportion is contained in the leaves (because that is where most of the tree's chemical activity takes place). The point is, a tree cannot afford to lose most of its nutrients each fall when its leaves die, or else it would be in an impossible situation the next spring when it went to manufacture a whole new set of leaves. It could never absorb enough replacement nutrients through its half-frozen roots to do the job in time.

It is therefore very much in the interests of deciduous trees to salvage as many as possible of their leaves' nutrients and store them away in woody tissues before the leaves are killed and lost. In fact, trees "hedge their bets," as it were, by starting to remove nitrogen and other nutrients from the leaves almost as soon as the long prime growing days of June and early July are over. This continues until, sometime in September usually, the leaf finally loses its ability to manufacture chlorophyll and we humans notice for the first time that something is going on — because the leaf then changes colour. By this time, half of the leaf's nutrients have already been removed for "safe-keeping," and the question then is how many of those still in the leaf can be salvaged before the leaf is finally killed. An early frost, for example, could inactivate the enzymes that remove the nutrients or could clog the transportation routes with ice crystals. Either way, remaining nutrients would be trapped inside the leaf and be lost to the tree.

It is here that the brilliant fall colours may play a subtle role. In many trees, including birches and aspens, the disappearance of the green chlorophyll merely unmasks yellow pigments that were there all the time. However, in the two trees that put on Algonquin's best show, the Sugar

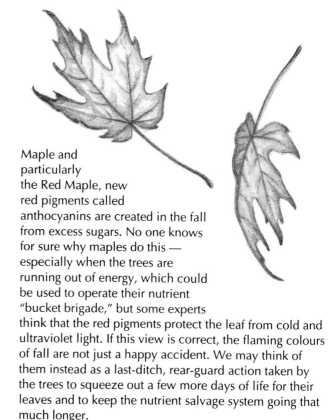

Maple and particularly the Red Maple, new red pigments called anthocyanins are created in the fall from excess sugars. No one knows for sure why maples do this — especially when the trees are running out of energy, which could be used to operate their nutrient "bucket brigade," but some experts think that the red pigments protect the leaf from cold and ultraviolet light. If this view is correct, the flaming colours of fall are not just a happy accident. We may think of them instead as a last-ditch, rear-guard action taken by the trees to squeeze out a few more days of life for their leaves and to keep the nutrient salvage system going that much longer.

The magnificent colours of our autumn hardwoods are beloved by everyone. But although the spectacle dazzles us every year, we usually fail to realize its full significance. What we are seeing is not so much the death of this year's leaves as the final transfer of precious nutrients from the leaves back to the parent trees.

It is astonishing to realize that life simply could not go on from one year to the next in our Algonquin forest without this sophisticated nutrient recycling system, which culminates each year in the glorious display of fall colours. Who ever would have guessed that so much was going on behind just this one old and familiar sign of winter's approach?☜

September 10, 1981, Vol. 22, No. 12 (D.S.)

Blackbird Jungle

Spring in Algonquin is a time of returning life and, for humans, a time for long-honoured rites. We may go on a fishing trip to some remote lake in the Park interior, or we may simply marvel at the hillsides awash with pastel greens, yellows, and pinks. Perhaps we will just relax in the warm sunshine but, one way or another, we will rejoice in the beauty of spring. This is only normal and natural, but sometimes our sunny dispositions at this time of year cause us to look at nature through rose-tinted glasses and to miss the true significance of what we see.

A very good example of what we mean is given by Red-winged Blackbirds. Red-wings are a common sight along every boggy river and in every marshy bay in the Park these days, and they too seem to be celebrating spring. Everywhere we look, the males are perched on cat-tails and alders, giving gorgeous displays with brilliant red, raised shoulder patches and loudly calling their characteristic "konkaree." But, however joyful the blackbirds appear to be, their displays — or their lives in general — are not celebrations at all. In fact, put in human terms, the Red-winged Blackbird society is a violent, brutal system where rival males are in a constant state of war with each other and with landless challengers who will take over a territory at the slightest lapse of the owner. It is also a society where the females are forced to subsist in quarrelsome harems and are severely punished if they try to leave.

You may find this a little surprising because, observed casually, Red-winged Blackbirds seem to be rather aimless in their movements and not organized in any obvious way. Nevertheless, you can easily see for yourself the true nature of Redwing society because so much of their lives takes place right out in the open. It is, in fact, a very interesting pastime to watch Red-winged Blackbirds. In order to help your personal observations, we offer the following abbreviated guide to Redwing behaviour.

Male Redwings return to the Park a month or more before the females do. This year, for example, the first female was seen on April 26, but some males had been here as early as March 24. It must be difficult to find food at that time of year with everything covered by ice and snow, but the males have to come back early if they are going to compete successfully for territories. The typical means of staking and maintaining a claim is by directing two kinds of displays toward neighbouring males.

In the "song-spread," a male Red-wing thrusts his head forward, lowers and spreads his tail, spreads his wings, raises his red epaulets, and sings loudly. In the bill-tilting display, he stretches his head skyward at his territorial boundary, compresses his body feathers, and exposes his epaulets.* The message conveyed by these displays is roughly the same — "Look at my shoulder patches, ye mighty, and despair!"

Eventually, neighbours work out mutually acceptable boundaries but, even then, they must contend with landless drifters, who persistently test the territory-owners by slowly flying overhead trying to find one they can dominate. The reaction of a territory-owner to such an incursion is to fly above the invader, force it down into the cat-tails, and attack it. If the invader tries to escape, he does so by flying upwards, and it is a common sight to see a male Redwing climbing higher and higher above a bog with another male diving and pecking at him all the way.

---

* There is no doubt that the function of the red epaulets is to enhance the threatening nature of these displays toward other males, not to impress females. Males whose epaulets have been experimentally painted black have great difficulty in hanging on to their territories, but if they succeed, they have no problem acquiring females.

When the brown-streaked, almost sparrow-patterned females arrive, they choose the best-looking territories (on the basis of good nest sites and food supplies) and move in. The formation of a pair bond with the local "warlord" male is instantaneous as far as the male is concerned. Unless he already has a harem of two or three, he automatically regards any female entering the territory as his property. To be sure, he will court her by leading her through bog vegetation, with his wings raised over his back, to a potential nest site, bowing to her and even going through the motions of building a nest. But it's not as if he is actually going to build the nest for her (that's

"women's" work) or in any way take no for an answer. If she tries to leave, he will pursue her, even well outside his territory, and peck her unmercifully until she returns to where she "belongs."

The female must then put up with the male's constant demands for sex. These often lead to headlong chases, with the desperate female sometimes crashing into obstructions or flying right into the water. What's more, she is confined to only a part of the male's territory since he allows it to be subdivided (conveniently enough for him) by two or more females. Should one female attempt to evict another, the scarlet-shouldered tyrant will punish her severely and immediately.

All the work of nest-building, incubation, and feeding the three or four nestlings is left to the female. Only when the young have fledged does the mate contribute a bit to the on-going task of feeding them.

The initiation of baby Red-winged Blackbirds into the realities of their world starts very early. Redwing society includes nonbreeding one-year-old males, which are the blackbird equivalent of "young hoodlums." When they encounter a fledgling just out of the nest innocently begging for food, they certainly won't feed it but they may very well attempt to mate with it.

We hope this guide to the way things are done in Redwing society hasn't shocked or dismayed you. In fairness, we should also point out that the males are fearless defenders of their mates and young, not hesitating to attack predators many times their size. In any case, we really have no business judging nature by human values, and, besides, you can't argue with success. Redwing behaviour may conform more to the "law of the jungle" than to our own, but their design for living has helped make these birds the most common on the continent. Wintering flocks in Tennessee often number in the millions, and major control programs hardly seem to make any difference.

Next year you will once again find Redwings along every boggy river and in every marshy bay in Algonquin. Let's accept them on their own terms. They do not live by our rules or emotions, but this should not prevent us from enjoying one of the Park's most magnificent spring spectacles — a marsh dotted with resplendent Redwings defiantly proclaiming their territories to the world and meting out terrible vengeance to all who dare to defy them.∽

May 6, 1982, Vol. 23, No. 1 (D.S.)

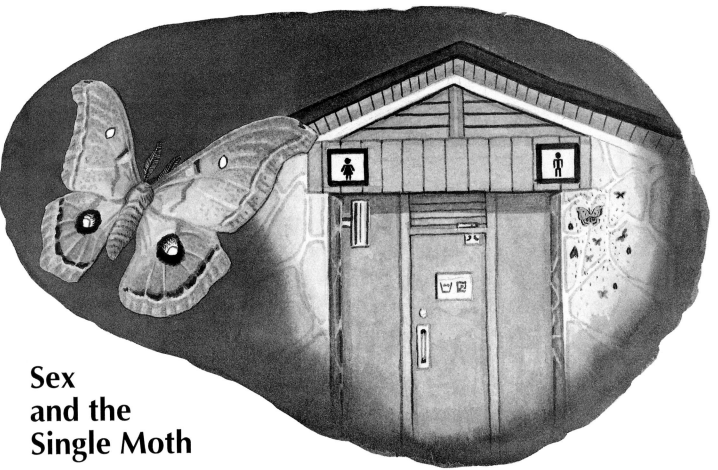

Sex
and the
Single Moth

As everyone knows, this is the time of year
when plants are flowering and animals are raising
their families. Indeed, the annual early summer flush of
new life is such a well-known phenomenon that we take
many aspects of the process for granted.

For example, one obvious and seemingly simple
requirement we hardly ever think about is that males and
females of each species must find each other in the first
place. Now, this may not seem to be much of a hurdle,
but it can be more difficult than you might imagine,
especially for animals that are scarce or rather immobile.
It may also be a very tall order for animals whose senses
are considered primitive (which really means "different
from ours").

One such group of animals is the moths, which we see
these mornings resting around lights at our campground
washrooms and offices. Most Algonquin campers have
stopped at one time or another to examine these silent
creatures of the night and to admire their tremendous
variety of form, colour, and pattern. There are hundreds
of different kinds, but those that people notice most often
are the white ones with the pink legs and antennae,
known as Rosy Maple Moths and the pink and gray,
long-winged, nectar-eating Sphinx Moths, which are the
night-time counterpart of hummingbirds. Most striking of
all are the giant silkworm moths, which include the pale
green Luna Moth, the giant Cecropia Moth, and the
Polyphemus with its beautiful colouration and eye-like
transparent spots in the four wings.

Can you see where this male Polyphemus is going?

The latter species, because it attracts so much
attention, is a good example to illustrate just how
different the life of a moth is from that of most animals
and to show what they are up against when they try to
find a mate.

Any Polyphemus you see this year started its life last
year as an egg laid in 1981. The resultant larva was very
tiny at first but, after a summer of almost non-stop leaf
consumption, had become an enormous, juicy green
caterpillar. With the approach of cooler weather last fall,
it spun a silken cocoon wrapped in the still green leaves
of the host tree. When the leaves turned colour and fell,
so did the cocoon, and it spent the winter on the forest
floor beneath the insulating blanket of snow.

A few weeks ago the current batch of adult
Polyphemus Moths began emerging from their cocoons
and, for the first time in their lives, it became necessary
for them to seek out others of their own kind. As a matter
of fact, the sole function of the adult Polyphemus is to
mate and lay eggs. They have only rudimentary mouth
parts, do not feed, and live out their last days on fat stored
up the previous summer. Since they have only a short

time to live, it is all the more important that they lose no time in finding a mate.

But just how can a Polyphemus succeed in this? Being an insect, it has compound eyes, which do not have very good resolution. Besides, even keen eyesight would be of little help at night in the thickly forested environment of the Polyphemus. Sound might do the trick except that it would also betray the moth's location to bats, owls, or flying squirrels — against which a moth can do very little. About the only possibility left is odour, but there are real problems with this idea as well. While it may be plausible that a strong-scented female moth could attract males in her immediate vicinity, it seems quite ludicrous that she could effectively advertise her location over long distances. As the great French naturalist Jean Henri Fabre said, "One might as well expect to colour an entire lake with a single drop of carmine."

It sometimes turns out, however, that the truth is implausible. In the last few decades scientists have established that female moths do indeed communicate their presence to males even up to several kilometres away by releasing volatile sex attractants called "pheromones" (a different kind for each species of moth). Even more amazing, they don't succeed in transmitting the message (as you might expect) by flooding the environment with enormous quantities of pheromone. In fact, at a given moment, a female moth typically contains only one millionth of a gram of the male-exciting chemical. And, in one of the pioneering investigations into the subject, researchers needed 500,000 female gypsy moths to extract a mere 12 thousandths of a gram of pheromone.

The secret of the moth chemical communication system lies instead with the fantastic sensitivity of the male pheromone detectors. If you look at the antennae of a male Polyphemus, for example, you will see that they are intricate, feather-like structures, which have the effect of maximizing the surface area that can come into contact with pheromone molecules floating in the air. Furthermore, a male can detect the presence of pheromone when the concentration is only a few hundred molecules per cubic centimetre. Even then, the actual number making contact with the antennae and triggering a response may be only one or two molecules. In fact, the sensitivity threshold of male moths to female pheromones is so low that, theoretically, the one millionth of a gram in her body could, if it were all delivered to male antennae, excite over one billion eager suitors!

Under real-life conditions the pheromone system has its greatest efficiency when there is a slight breeze (say, three or four kilometres per hour). Under these conditions a male can detect a female almost five kilometres upwind. (Interestingly enough, when the breeze is stronger, the maximum detection distance is less, not greater, because the increased turbulence has the effect of diluting the pheromone more rapidly.) At great distances from the female the pheromone is distributed so uniformly that an excited male has no direct clue as to the whereabouts of the female. Instead, he flies upwind until, at the end of his long journey through the forest, he starts to detect the increasing pheromone concentrations, which are a sure sign that the female, invisible and silent though she may be in the summer night, lies just ahead … .

All in all, moths have a marvellous and unbelievably sensitive chemical communication system permitting the sexes to find each other under difficult circumstances. It is even more amazing when you think that it is all done unconsciously. Females are unaware of what they are doing by releasing pheromones, and males react in an equally unconscious manner. To paraphrase one manufacturer of those artificial human pheromones we call perfumes, moths "don't know what they want and don't have to ask for it," but boy meets girl just the same. For proof, you only have to look at all those beautiful moths resting outside our washrooms and offices each morning. After all, they didn't just happen. ∞

July 1, 1982, Vol. 23, No. 2 (D.S.)

Singing the Blues?

An Indigo Bunting proclaiming its territory along the Parkway.

In last week's *Raven* we ran a short piece about the unusual presence and nesting of a pair of Eastern Bluebirds near the Spruce Bog Boardwalk. Since then, one of our readers has pointed out that 1982 is also unusual for the large numbers of another "blue bird" present in the Park.

He had in mind the gorgeous all-blue finch known as the Indigo Bunting, a bird that likes to live at the edge of brushy clearings, including the artificial one created by Highway 60. We can only speculate on the reasons, but the Indigo Bunting, although often entirely absent from Algonquin, is indeed a common sight this year along the highway corridor. Our reader's point, therefore, was well taken except that he then had the effrontery to ask if "blue" birds sing sad songs.

Normally, of course, *The Raven* has no time for puns, but we are going to make an exception in this case if only because most people tend to think just the opposite — that bird song is an expression of happiness. To be sure, we almost always associate bird song with beautiful spring and summer mornings, but there is no convincing reason to suppose that the happiness we feel on such occasions (or any other human emotion) is shared by singing birds.

The truth, we think, is far more interesting, and Indigo Buntings are an excellent case in point. If you listen carefully to their pretty, canary-like songs, you will notice that while they are all recognizable as Indigo Bunting songs, they are by no means always identical. This immediately raises some intriguing possibilities. For example, do the birds themselves recognize these differences? Do different songs convey different messages? Are song differences hereditary, or are they learned and, if so, where and from whom? It might seem very difficult to shed light on these questions but, thanks to modern tape recording and sound analyzing equipment, it is possible to "preserve" songs and produce detailed graphic representations of every note within them. When this is done, it is seen that an Indigo Bunting song consists of distinct phrases, separated by silent periods lasting only a few hundredths of a second.

A look at the small sample of song phrases or "figures" reproduced here will show that Indigo Buntings can produce a tremendous variety of such figures. Nevertheless, when the songs of individual buntings are analyzed, each bird is found to repeat only one song (rarely two) consisting of the same three- to 10-song figures. Put in human terms, it is as if one person you knew repeatedly said "irt" to you, another one never said anything except "atalep," another one just "spleckor," and so on. Of course, the only information you would get from such repetitions would be that the speaker was human, his or her sex and whereabouts, and possibly some idea of the speaker's size and strength.

In much the same way, a male Indigo Bunting, regardless of his particular song's makeup, probably always transmits the same information, namely, "I am a magnificent male Indigo Bunting in breeding condition," with the implication that females are welcome, other males are not. One very strong indication in support of this idea is that an Indigo Bunting song played backwards (which necessarily contains a totally new set of song figures never heard in nature) gets just as strong a response from territorial male buntings as a normal song does. This is very much like our reaction to a movie sound track played in reverse; the words sound weird alright but they still sound human.

But if the basic message is always the same and any old Indigo Bunting song will do the trick, why do individual birds always stick to the same song? It is certainly not because of any lack of ability. Indigo Buntings that sing "spleckor" are not anatomically prevented from singing "atalep," but for some reason they never do. The advantage seems to be that neighbours get to know each other as individuals. This means that when an established bunting sings, he announces his presence to his neighbours but at the same time conveys the information that it is just the same familiar bird guarding his territory and posing no real threat. If he were to change his song, his neighbours would have no way of knowing that it wasn't a stranger seeking to set up a new territory and very likely to steal all or parts of their land. The neighbours would therefore have little choice but to attack, and the male who came up with the different song would have gotten himself into a lot of unnecessary trouble. By the same token, it would be no good if all birds sang identical songs because, once again, neighbours would be unable to identify each other.

There is thus a premium on males having their own individual songs and sticking to them, but with the added constraint that any individual song must still be recognized as being that of an Indigo Bunting. After all, if you are going to scream "atalep" at your neighbours all day long, you will want to be taken seriously. Variation is apparently kept within reasonable bounds by the way birds acquire their individual songs. This seems to take place when birds are one-year-old and attempting to set up a breeding territory for the first time. When they find themselves in competition with an older, more experienced bird, they quickly come up with an exact imitation of their rival's song and retain it for life. This explains why the number of song figures used by Indigo Buntings is great but not endless and why it is not unusual to find two neighbours singing identical songs. This latter point seems to contradict what we said earlier about the importance of neighbours singing different songs but, as long as only two birds are involved, the problem is probably not very serious. There may be some slight confusion for other neighbours, but of course there won't be any for the two birds themselves and they may not even realize their neighbour is singing a song identical to their own. Nor do we find that these song clusters persist, let alone grow, from year to year. Young males seldom return to their first-time territories but tend to look elsewhere for better land as they become more efficient competitors.

Thus, the pattern of Indigo Bunting communication is achieved. Through it, males are able to make themselves instantly recognized as prospective mates or competitors to all other Indigo Buntings. At the same time, by having their own "personal" songs, neighbours can learn each other's identity and achieve some sort of social stability with a minimum of territorial fighting during the breeding season.

All these are very practical considerations indeed, so there is no reason to think, as our reader proposed, that the songs of Indigo Buntings are sad. Nor is there any reason to believe, as many more people tend to, that the songs are an outpouring of happiness. It may not be very romantic but, to all those gorgeous Indigo Buntings along the highway this year, song is just another tool for survival. Any sadness, or any joy, is in the ear of the beholder.⤶

July 5, 1982 ,Vol. 23, No. 3 (D.S.)

Opeongo Chronicle

Anyone who ever gazes at a map of Algonquin Park and dreams of faraway places soon is drawn to Lake Opeongo. It is the largest lake in the Park by a good margin, and there is something about that twisty shoreline, the many secluded bays and islands, and even the name itself that appeals to the imagination. One can hardly help wondering what the great lake looks like and what its moods and secrets are.

Well, you don't have to go very far to learn about the moods of Lake Opeongo. Many people have been fishing and camping on Opeongo for decades, and they know it intimately. They have seen the lake when strong north winds send rolling white caps and flying spray crashing onto pebbly beaches. They have seen it on perfect summer mornings when the lake is a sheet of glass reflecting with breathtaking fidelity the forests crowding down to the shore and the cottony clouds suspended 20 feet above its surface. They know the excitement of hauling up a big Lake Trout from the depths of the East Arm, and they know how good a hot cup of tea can taste back in camp after a cold September day out on the lake.

Nevertheless, if it is one thing to know the moods of Lake Opeongo, it is quite another to know its secrets. We suspect, in fact, that even among very old Opeongo hands, a majority are unaware of just how many things have gone on over the years in and around their favourite lake. We don't pretend to have an exhaustive list ourselves, but we have been able to glean a fair bit of Lake Opeongo history from various sources.

For the benefit of all those who share our special interest in the Park's biggest lake, we would like to present the following abbreviated account of some of the historical highlights.

1826 — A Lieutenant Briscoe, looking for a new transportation route between the upper Great Lakes and the Ottawa Valley, became the first known European to visit Lake Opeongo.

1829 — Alexander Sherriff of Quebec City, exploring for new agricultural lands, visited the lake he called "Abeunga" (presumably a better rendition of Opeongo's original Indian name). Interestingly, he reported the presence of a small Hudson's Bay Company fur trading post at the entrance to the East Arm.

1847 — D. Macdonnell conducted a timber survey of the Opeongo watershed. At that time there were huge White Pine towering 130 feet high along the shoreline and scattered through the hardwoods back on the surrounding hills.

1860s — Logging for pine was under way, and great log booms were slowly winched by horse-powered capstans on specially constructed rafts towards Opeongo's outlet at the foot of Annie Bay (then called Graham Bay after a logger from Renfrew). A wooden dam with stop logs was built there, possibly as early as 1867, to help the loggers flush the great square timbers down the Opeongo River.

1870 — John and Harry Dennison of Combermere, their wives, infant children, and father, Captain John Dennison, then aged 71, moved 60 miles into the wilderness to start a new farm (which they called "Sunnyside") just inside the Narrows leading into the East Arm. Almost totally cut off from the outside world, they cleared 600 acres with back-breaking labour and managed to grow enough food for themselves and successive logging camps around the lake.

1881 — Old Captain Dennison was killed by a bear that he had caught in a trap set at the Happy Isle (then Green Lake) portage leading out of the North Arm. His grave, back at Sunnyside, is marked by a simple copper plaque that reads "At Rest."

1885 — The Dennisons abandoned their farm, but the Fraser Lumber Co. continued to work it.

1893 — Algonquin Park was established.

1902 — The St. Anthony Lumber Co. of Whitney built a spur line to the south end of Opeongo from the Ottawa, Arnprior, & Parry Sound Railroad (itself completed across the Park six years earlier). Today, the Opeongo Road and much of Highway 60 between the Opeongo Road turnoff and Whitney run on the old track (which was abandoned sometime between 1910 and 1916).

1916 — Jack Whitton, the butcher in Whitney, was given a commercial fishing licence to net Lake Trout and Whitefish in Opeongo. He only did this for two years, possibly because the one-way horse-drawn wagon trip bumping along over the ties of the abandoned railway took a full four hours (about what it now takes to drive from Toronto!).

1920s — Alexander (Sandy) Haggart of Whitney was taking tourists in to Opeongo by wagon and in 1928

acquired the right to operate one of the old lumber company buildings at the foot of the lake as "Opeongo Lodge." By 1929, the railroad bed had been sufficiently improved that it was being referred to as an "automobile road" — the first and only way cars could enter Algonquin until Highway 60 was built in 1936.

1928 — The first Smallmouth Bass (source unknown) appeared in Opeongo. Their subsequent success did not affect the Lake Trout fishery but probably doomed the native Brook Trout and greatly depressed the crayfish population.

1930 — John R. Bates, a Pennsylvania businessman, acquired a cottage lease (the only one ever granted on Opeongo) on what became known as Bates Island. Johnny had apparently come out on the right side of the 1929 market crash and spent the better part of the next 35 years doing what he loved best — fishing on the great lake and trying out a lot of "secret" ones in behind the surrounding hills. A person could do worse.

1936 — An eventful year. Sandy Haggart disposed of his interests in Opeongo Lodge to Joe Avery in whose family the lodge and the succeeding outfitting concession remained until 1977.

Highway 60 was also completed across the Park in 1936, and Superintendent Frank MacDougall, concerned about the inevitable increase in visitation and its impact on our fisheries, persuaded Dr. W.J.K. Harkness of the University of Toronto to establish a fisheries research station in Algonquin. At first, the researchers worked out of an abandoned highway construction camp at what is now the Costello Lake Picnic Ground, but by 1940 all staff were housed at the lab's present location on Lake Opeongo. Since then more than 400 people have done work at the "fish lab," and many have gone on to occupy senior university and government positions across Canada. Research has centred on studies of the basic physical and chemical characteristics of lakes (which determines their ability to produce fish) plus long-term studies on Algonquin's three main game fish (Lake Trout, Brook Trout, and Smallmouth Bass). Over 500 reports, theses, and scientific papers have been based on this work.

1948 — The Cisco or Lake Herring was deliberately introduced to Opeongo in an attempt to provide a suitable prey species for Lake Trout and improve their growth. Within a few years trout were indeed feeding mainly on Cisco, were heavier, faster-growing, and more fertile — although they also began maturing at a later age.

1968 — The old Opeongo Lodge building burned and was replaced by the present store.

1970 — Johnny Bates died, and his lease was disposed of by his widow a couple of years later.

… These are some of the known events and changes that have occurred on and around Lake Opeongo over the last 150 years. For the most part, they are the events that just happened to be recorded by historians or preserved in our own archives. No doubt, there are many others, long since forgotten, about which we will never know. In this respect, we can't help very much — you will just have to join us in exploring the great lake, getting to know its moods, and wondering about its secrets… .∽

July 15, 1982 , Vol. 23, No. 4 (D.S.)

Everybody's Favourite?

A year ago this week we were pleased to host two rangers from a national park in Australia on their first visit to North America. Everything was new to them, and we got a tremendous kick out of their enjoyment in seeing our flora and fauna for the first time. They were so keen, in fact, that they insisted we teach them how to handle a canoe so they could go off into the Park interior on a five-day canoe trip.

When they returned, they were bubbling with excitement over what they had seen — loons appearing magically out of the morning mist, a moose feeding only metres away from their canoe, and, in the light of a full moon, a beaver gliding across a remote, glass-calm lake.

We couldn't help sharing their delight and enthusiasm, but we certainly didn't find any of their reactions particularly surprising until, that is, they told us about what they considered to be the absolute highlight of their trip — the cute little striped animals that visited them at almost every campsite.

At first we could hardly believe that chipmunks had beaten out all the distinguished competition in an Algonquin wildlife popularity contest. But, since then, we

have come to the conclusion that this really shouldn't be so surprising. When you stop and think about it, the reason North Americans take chipmunks for granted is simply the animal's extreme abundance and familiarity. Our Australian friends didn't have this problem, of course, and so they were able to see chipmunks with completely fresh eyes.

One of the things that struck them right away was that the Eastern Chipmunk* is one of the most easily observed Park mammals. It is not only active by day but also so unconcerned with the presence of a discreet human observer that you can actually follow individual animals going about their business — a privilege accorded by very few wildlife species. For example, with a little patience, you will learn just how much time a wild animal spends looking for food and get a good picture of a chipmunk's diet — apart from human handouts, of course. In spring they spend a lot of time eating buds and digging up the bulbs of Trout Lilies; in midsummer, they turn to berries — Choke Cherries, Pin Cherries, raspberries, and others. Later on they consume hazel nuts, acorns, maple keys, and beechnuts, depending on the year's seed production, and, at all times, they eat a surprising amount of animal matter — slugs, snails, insects, frogs, and even snakes on occasion.

Another easily observable aspect of a chipmunk's life is the ground it covers. A typical home range, especially in the preferred hardwood forest habitat, is so small (a quarter or a third of an acre or so) that you can keep up with its owner and observe many of its social and food-gathering activities.

There is, however, a limit to what you can see because, as every chipmunk-watcher knows, much of their time is spent out of sight, in burrows. Each animal excavates its own underground home, taking great pains to scatter the earth inconspicuously on the forest floor after first removing it (in its cheek pouches) via a temporary "work hole" — which is usually some distance away from the one or two very well-hidden permanent entrances. The burrow may be up to 10 metres long and reach one metre below the surface.

By investing so much time and energy in constructing its burrow, the chipmunk gains a haven from many of its numerous predators, a place to raise its young, and — perhaps most important of all — a reasonably warm place to spend the winter. Very soon now, chipmunks will be starting to lay in their provisions for the coming cold season. Each animal makes countless trips with bulging cheek pouches (one was seen to carry 48 cherry pits in one load) down to its special food storage chambers. When winter arrives, most of the time is spent curled up asleep in a leafy bed but, every so often, the groggy little chipmunk staggers off to the "bathroom" (another chamber reserved for this one purpose), eats some food, and then collapses back into a deep sleep.

Chipmunks wake up for good in early April (well before the snow has gone here in the Park), and the males temporarily leave their home ranges in search of females. A month later the young are born, usually in litters of four to six. Although they are blind, naked, and helpless at birth and are raised by their mothers unaided, baby chipmunks grow up extremely rapidly. They have fur starting at the age of five days, stripes are visible as early as 10 days, and they emerge from their mother's burrow in June at about six weeks old. In another month they leave to seek a place of their own.

In spite of the hard work involved in raising youngsters, many of the mother chipmunks turn right around and have another litter in midsummer. Even more startling, some of the young females from the first litters also participate in this second breeding season when they are only two and one-half months old. The second wave of young chipmunks will not appear above ground until September, and we imagine that they must really have their work cut out for them if they are to dig a burrow and store enough food for the winter.

This brings up a dark side to chipmunk life, which most people probably do not suspect. Very few chipmunks — even the "experienced" adults — succeed in surviving for long. There are just too many animals out there that like to eat* chipmunks, and the crops of nuts and fruit they depend on are just too unpredictable. At the very most, only about half of all chipmunks survive from one year to the next, and a three-year-old is a very rare chipmunk indeed.

Even if the deaths of chipmunks are commonplace, the production of young is still so high that we are mostly unaware of the rapid population turnover. We also see them as a constant feature of the Park environment. Deep down inside we probably all have a soft spot for chipmunks. After all, who can resist such bright-eyed little charmers as they fearlessly inspect us, forepaws clasped to the breast, waiting for a handout? Their one problem in the popularity sweepstakes is they are just so common and familiar that, on this continent at least, we tend to take them for granted.

Personally, we are grateful to our Australian friends for jogging our dormant appreciation of chipmunks and helping us to rediscover what fascinating creatures they really are. We hope that you, too, will spend some enjoyable moments watching them lead their busy lives, but we suspect it will always be our visitors from overseas who best appreciate their qualities. In fact, didn't someone once say, "A chipmunk is not without honour save in his own land"?✎

July 29, 1982, Vol. 23, No. 6 (D.S.)

---

* The Eastern is by far the more common of Algonquin's two kinds of chipmunk. The rare Least Chipmunk is smaller and has stripes that go all the way down the back to the base of the tail.

* We once surprised a fox who dropped the nine chipmunks she was carrying back to her young. Baby foxes have to eat, too!

Design for Survival

We believe it is fair to say most people consider plants to be rather straightforward and simple. After all, they don't seem to do much. They have roots, leaves, and a stem — and sometimes pretty flowers — but basically they just sit there, day after day, leading uneventful lives as part of the background greenery.

This impression may be a normal one, but if truth be known, every plant species is subtly adapted to its particular environment and has many ingenious "design features" that are nothing short of astounding. The sad part is that, even though plants won't run away from us and their "secrets" are mostly right there in plain view, we continue to walk right by them, failing to realize what we are missing.

An excellent example of just how subtle and fascinating an "ordinary plant" can be is available to us now and for the rest of the season in the form of Jewelweed (also known as Spotted Touch-me-not or Snapweed). If you aren't familiar with any of these names, you may nevertheless know the plant itself. It usually grows waist-high in thick, rank patches in sunlit openings and almost always in wet, totally saturated soil (such as along stream edges or beside beaver ponds). The leaves are thin and rather pale green, with an attractive silvery appearance when wet with rain or dew (giving rise to yet another common name, "Silver-leaf"). The easiest way to recognize Jewelweed, however, is to spot the beautiful, orange-yellow flowers, specked with deep red and hanging from the branch tips. Each flower is open at one end and terminates at the other in a curved, nectar-filled spur — which explains why Jewelweed patches are very popular with bees and hummingbirds.*

Jewelweed is an annual. That is, it grows from seed every year — which is no mean feat when you consider that it often reaches well over a metre in height in the short Algonquin growing season. How it does this involves the first of

Jewelweed or Spotted Touch-me-not.

---

* We can recommend a couple of good places to see Jewelweed — just off the Beaver Pond Trail at the water's edge west of Post 2, and 30 metres east of the (old) Museum washrooms (follow signs to "The Jewelweed Patch").

Jewelweed's many "ingenious" features. Instead of slowly growing a "costly" wood or pithy stem for support the way most plants do, Jewelweed takes advantage of its water-logged habitat and grows a "cheap," hollow stem whose strength depends on high water pressure in the cylindrical cells of the stem wall. The cells are a bit like balloons, remaining "rigid" as long as they are fully inflated.

While Jewelweed can thus quickly outgrow any potential competitors in its preferred damp sites, this efficiency is of only marginal value. No individual plant or animal (much less an annual) lives forever, so the only meaningful way a living thing can "survive" is to reproduce. It must, furthermore, leave at least as many descendants as its neighbours or else its offspring will be increasingly outnumbered in future generations — and eventually disappear entirely. In the case of the Jewelweed, this means that each plant must produce as many seeds as possible every year, the seeds must be transported to favourable growing sites, and nothing must eat the seeds before they germinate the next year.

Total success in these areas is impossible but anyone who has ever touched a ripe seed pod knows that Jewelweed has a rather special way of getting its seeds launched in life. The seed pod explodes violently, scattering the seeds up to two metres away (and explaining the name "Touch-me-not"). An interesting secondary advantage of these booby-trapped seed pods is that they blow up in the faces of seed-eating birds who try to open them. If the seeds land in water, as they often must, they float and can thus be carried away to another (usually suitably damp) site elsewhere at the water's edge.

Of course, long before a seed gets dispersed, it must be produced in the first place, and this is the purpose of flowers. To us, Jewelweed flowers are merely beautiful adornments; to the plants, they are major, energy-demanding investments. Each one is a large structure endowed with special, bright pigments and a copious supply of nectar, the purpose of which is to "bribe" bumblebees, hawkmoths, and hummingbirds into paying repeated visits — and to inadvertently achieve cross-pollination by carrying pollen from one flower to another. Since Jewelweed flowers cannot produce and receive pollen at the same time in their development, it seems they really do need the services of outside agents to be fertilized and that the big investment in showy flowers is justified.

The only problem is that cross-fertilization is not a sure thing. Pollinators may be absent or, even worse, the flowers may be victimized by rip-off artists. Only recently, at one Jewelweed patch, we watched a bumblebee visit dozens of flowers but never saw it make the slightest effort to enter the open end (where it could have delivered or picked up pollen). Instead, it briefly inspected the nectar spur at the other end, then flew to the next flower. When we examined the flowers ourselves, we found that something (probably a bumblebee) had cut a hole in each spur, drained out the nectar, and defeated the whole purpose of the flower.

Being an annual and under the absolute necessity of producing seed in order to survive to the next season, a Jewelweed exploited in this way would seem to be doomed. All is not quite lost, however, because in addition to the showy flowers at the top of the plant, Jewelweed produces a second kind of "flower" — tiny, vaguely bud-like structures, one or two millimetres long — lower down on the plant. Called "cleistogamous" flowers (Greek for "hidden marriage"), they never open and they contain only a few grains of pollen. But even if they look insignificant, they have the virtue of being entirely self-contained and of never failing to produce seeds.*

For us, these tiny, self-fertilizing flowers have to be the ultimate of Jewelweed's sophisticated design features. After all, it is one thing to be able to shoot up a metre in a few weeks (thanks to the economical, light-weight stem design), and it is all very well to have exploding seed pods to scatter the seeds and foil seed-eating birds. Even the showy flowers with their elaborate enticements to trick insects into transporting pollen to and from other blossoms may be ingenious but still fall short of the exquisite subtlety of cleistogamous flowers. What they amount to is what we humans often call "hedging our bets." Just as a successful gambler holds back a little in reserve in case his calculated risks don't pan out, the Jewelweed employs a similar strategy of insuring against total (reproductive) ruin. Even if every one of the showy flowers fails to produce seeds, the cleistogamous flowers will still "save the day" and enable the Jewelweed to survive until the following season.

If you find it astounding that an "ordinary plant" can be capable of such refined gamesmanship, just remember that Jewelweed is only one of about 1,000 higher plants making up the background greenery of Algonquin, and there is no reason to think it is particularly special.

… Who ever started the idea that plants are simple and straightforward?◦

August 5, 1982 , Vol. 23, No. 7 (D.S.)

---

* You may wonder: if cleistogamous flowers are so economical and dependable, why does Jewelweed ever bother to produce the costly cross-pollinated flowers? The answer seems to be that cleistogamous (self-pollinating) flowers produce less vigorous and adaptable offspring. Unable to adjust to environmental changes, they lose out over the long term.

Move Over E.T.

By now, most Park visitors have probably seen "E.T.," the film that in a few short weeks broke all box office records. For anyone who doesn't know, E.T. is a weird-looking creature from outer space who gets stranded on Earth and survives only because some children put out candy and gradually befriend it.

If you sense a little pique in our attitude toward E.T., you are not mistaken. We admit (grumble, grumble) the space creature has a certain charm, but we also find it annoying that people will make so much fuss over an imaginary extra-terrestrial yet totally ignore real creatures of equal or greater interest here on Earth.

For example, we don't think E.T. can hold a candle to the common and fascinating little animals known as Harvestmen or Daddy Longlegs. Yet many people either fail to notice them or, if they do, pass them off as spiders. Daddy Longlegs have eight legs like spiders but otherwise are quite different. The body has a comical egg shape (never with a "waist" as in spiders), and the two eyes are back to back on a funny little turret on the animal's back. Another pair of short appendages, called "pedipalps," at the front of the body, are used to manipulate food, and there is also a pair of jaws, but the total effect is quite different from that created by a spider's appearance.

The most striking difference, of course, is that, proportionately, a Daddy Longlegs has much longer limbs than a spider. In fact, if a Daddy Longlegs had a body as big as ours, it would be carried along 20 or 30 feet above the ground by a forest of independently moving legs 40 to 50 feet long. The most important legs of all are the extra-long second pair. They touch the ground ahead of all the others and are equipped with special

sense organs enabling the Daddy Longlegs to get an advance taste and feel of the ground over which it is about to pass.

Daddy Longlegs can be found in many different habitats but almost always where it is somewhat damp. They must drink regularly — by going to the edge of a pool, resting one or more legs on the water's surface, and lowering the body to immerse the jaws. Unlike spiders, Daddy Longlegs do not spin webs or have poison, and they are not really capable of immobilizing live prey. Instead, they feed mostly upon dead insects or the eggs of insects and spiders. They readily accept bread or animal fat and do quite well in a home terrarium.

In such a situation you can watch them and see aspects of their behaviour you might otherwise miss. For example, every Daddy Longlegs keeps itself scrupulously clean. After eating, it washes its jaws and then cleans each one of its legs by drawing the leg slowly through its jaws.

Another interesting piece of behaviour is the moult. As with insects and spiders, Daddy Longlegs have hard, outer skeletons, which must be shed at regular intervals if the animal is to grow. Given its extraordinary shape, it seems scarcely possible that a Daddy Longlegs could withdraw itself from its old skeleton, but this actually happens. First the skeleton splits at the front end of the animal and the body partly emerges through the gap. The pedipalps then bundle the bases of the legs together and force them towards the jaws, which in turn slowly drag each leg, one after the other, out of the old skeleton. The new skeleton is soft at first and expands somewhat before hardening, thus accommodating the new growth.

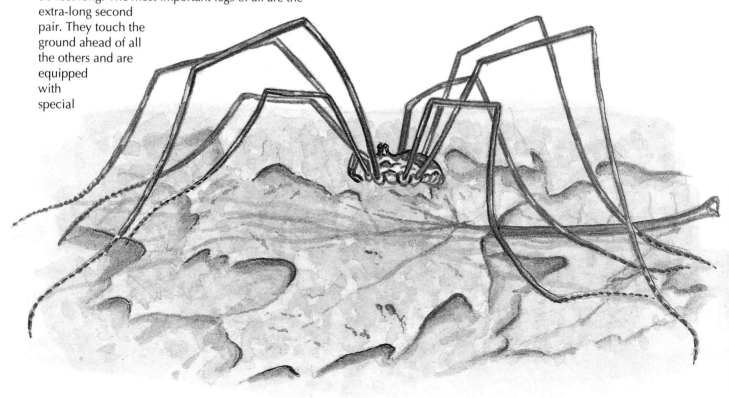

Daddy Longlegs in captivity get along very well together. So well, in fact, that males and females have no courtship — they mate as soon as they meet. The tiny eggs, less than half a millimetre across, are laid in moist sand and hatch out into tiny versions of the adults. The young take about two and one-half months to reach maturity, moulting about once every 10 days.

Most aspects of Daddy Longlegs' biology with animals encountered in the wild are rather difficult to observe, but at least one is easy to see. Daddy Longlegs possessing all eight legs are often in a minority, especially late in the season, and it is obvious they have many predators. Strange to say, although they have the ability to part with a leg on short notice, they don't have the power to replace the missing part the way many other "lower" animals do. Still, they can survive with one or several missing appendages, and there is even a record of a Daddy Longlegs somehow managing to get along with only two left. About the only real defence they have against predators is the ability to release a bad-smelling odour from two glands on their sides.

We are quite sure that no special-effects man will ever dream up a make-believe creature more bizarre or appealing than a real Daddy Longlegs. What could be crazier than a little oval creature with turret eyes bouncing along high above the ground, occasionally releasing puffs of skunk-like vapour and, when necessary, dropping an enormous leg or two to appease some fearsome predator? We can also state with some confidence that Daddy Longlegs will be doing their thing long after the E.T. craze is well and truly forgotten.

And, for any kids out there who insist, in spite of everything, on remaining loyal to that little upstart from outer space, we have the final, crushing argument. Take it from us: no Daddy Longlegs will ever sneak into your house at night and try to steal your Smarties. So there.∾

August 12, 1982 ,Vol. 23, No. 8 (D.S.)

Who Invited the Greedies?

A common perception among Park visitors is that humans have developed a thorough understanding of the natural world and no questions remain unanswered. Scientists are presumed to have investigated the ecology and life history of every living thing, and all that is required to learn about such matters is to consult the appropriate authority.

This is a rather unfortunate impression because, in fact, there are mysteries everywhere around us in the natural world, and it is a highly enjoyable and fascinating pursuit to delve into them. By way of example, we would like to share some thoughts with you this week about the great Evening Grosbeak mystery.

Everyone who has visited the Park in August has seen Evening Grosbeaks or, if you have just arrived, you soon will. They are the spectacular black, white, and yellow birds that travel in big flocks and, especially in the morning, can often be seen right on the shoulder of Highway 60. They seem to have favourite places (such as just east of the Information Centre) for picking up the pieces of grit that aid in the digestion of hard seeds. They are also very noisy and quarrelsome, and it will come as no surprise to anyone who has ever watched them at a winter bird feeder that some people call them "the greedies."

So, what is mysterious about this familiar and abundant bird? Simply this: 60 years ago, there were no Evening Grosbeaks at all in Algonquin Park. Amazingly, it was only in the 1920s that they started extending their breeding range from their original stronghold west into Ontario. The first nests, including two here in Algonquin, weren't found until the 1940s. By any standard there was an explosive change in their status, from total absence as a breeding bird to high, though still variable, abundance.

The obvious question, of course, is how to account for such a development. At the time it occurred, one authority came up with — and many others have since repeated — the guess that Evening Grosbeaks expanded their range because of widespread plantings of Manitoba Maples in eastern towns and cities. Upon serious examination, however, this idea doesn't seem to stand up. There is no doubt that Evening Grosbeaks like to eat Manitoba Maple keys during their winter wanderings down south, but this fact hardly explains their summer breeding success up here in Algonquin and other places where there are no Manitoba Maples at all.

How, then, might the mystery be explained? Well, we believe a clue was provided back in 1946 when the stomach of a nestling from one of the Algonquin nests was examined and found to contain fragments of cherry seed. Now, this was a very strange discovery. Most small birds, even those that eat seeds as adults, use protein-rich insects to feed their growing young. Also, it seems impossible that Evening Grosbeaks could use cherry seeds to feed nestlings because, as everyone knows, each seed is enclosed in an extremely hard pit or "stone."

But, rather than just idly theorizing, we ordered our *Raven* research department into action. With our most sophisticated scientific equipment (bathroom scales and a hammer), we determined, using samples of seven pits each, that the average pressure required to crush a cherry stone is considerable indeed — 23.4 pounds for Pin Cherry and 26.4 pounds for Choke Cherry.

This seems like an extraordinary degree of pressure to be developed by a bird that weighs a mere two ounces, but Evening Grosbeaks don't have enormous bills for nothing. As a matter of fact, they differ from other finches in having four special knobs inside the bill, two above and two below, which serve to wedge a slippery cherry stone securely into the best spot (near the back of the bill) as the powerful jaw muscles apply their stone-shattering strength.

Still, there is no evidence like direct evidence, and, although we have never actually seen grosbeaks crack a cherry stone, we have certainly heard them do it. Others, too, have stood quietly near a stand of Pin Cherries full of quarreling greedies and listened to the unmistakable sound of cherry stones being broken. Those who have watched the process say that the birds always discard the actual fruit and are interested only in the stone. They swallow a certain amount of shell fragments along with the kernel, presumably because they help digestion in the same way that little pieces of gravel do. There also seems to be little doubt that crushed cherry pits are one of the chief foods used by adult grosbeaks to nourish young birds in the nest, and this explains why good grosbeak years seem to coincide with excellent Pin and Choke Cherry years (like this one).

It is intriguing to think that Evening Grosbeaks are adapted to eating cherry stones of all things and that they are probably dependent on them for successful breeding. But what bearing could this have on the question we originally raised — that is, what can account for the invasion of Evening Grosbeaks 60 years ago? After all, no one seriously thinks that the birds came up with their stone-eating adaptations one fine day back in the 1920s and cherry trees didn't suddenly appear back then either. What connection could there possibly be?

Frankly, we didn't see any link between cherries and the grosbeak invasion ourselves until someone pointed out what should have been obvious all along. Both the Pin Cherry and the Choke Cherry are short-lived pioneer species that grow only in open, sunny areas such as those that result from fires and clear-cuts. And, as anyone familiar with the story of man in Ontario will know, large areas of the north, including Algonquin, were logged and burned in the late 1800s and early years of this century.

… This is the insight that we believe finally clears up the great Evening Grosbeak mystery. Following early logging and fires, Pin and Choke Cherries must have prospered as never before, and this can only have helped make the northern forests of Ontario much more attractive to Evening Grosbeaks. In fact, if our reasoning is correct, Algonquin was transformed from a place where grosbeaks couldn't live to one where they do very well. Albeit unintentionally, humans put on an enormous cherry feast, and we shouldn't be surprised that the birds adapted to eating cherry stones soon showed up to reap the harvest.

Who invited the greedies to Algonquin? … Probably us! ∞

August 26, 1982, Vol. 23, No. 10 (D.S.)

Evening Grosbeaks discard the flesh of Pin Cherries and Choke Cherries but crush and eat the cherry stones!

Another Century, Another World

Algonquin Park is often spoken of as a "timeless" place, and it's easy to see why. Whether we stay along Highway 60 or go off on a real canoe trip in the Park interior, we almost always see the Park as a huge, wild country with thousands of square miles of remote forests, lakes, and streams. This wilderness stands in such marked contrast to the fast-paced, always-changing urban settings where most people live that we tend to think Algonquin has always been, more or less, the way it is now. We also tend to think that the way we experience the Park has a timeless nature as well — an escape for generations of North Americans back to a simpler lifestyle, back to the way things used to be.

To be sure, almost everyone who has spent much time here knows there were other chapters in Algonquin's human history before ours. The trouble is, we know well only what we have experienced ourselves. To take one good example, the life and times of the pioneer loggers in Algonquin Park 100 years ago seem rather vague and far away. We realize they were here but, deep down inside, we don't really believe they were much more than a minor, passing phenomenon in the "timeless" Algonquin Park we see today.

Every once in a while, however, we come across something that forces us to realize just how enormous an impact the pioneer loggers had on Algonquin. An excellent case in point is the fascinating research being carried out by Dr. Grant Head of Wilfrid Laurier University in Waterloo, Ontario. Dr. Head has painstakingly gone through "tons" of archival records to assemble maps showing the quantities and locations of the timber cut by the pioneer loggers in the Ottawa Valley.

We have reproduced part of one such map showing the square timber* production for the Park area for the single winter of 1866–67. Each dot on the map represents 400 "pieces" of square timber (each piece being on the average 50 feet long and 30 inches across each side). If you count up the dots, you will see that the pioneer loggers of 115 years ago made the astounding total of almost 30,000 pieces of square timber (cut from the same number of giant White Pine trees) having a volume of about 1,500,000 cubic feet — all in just one unexceptional winter.

These numbers are impressive, to say the least, and help bring into much clearer focus the historical reality of pioneer logging. Nevertheless, the figures in themselves don't even begin to describe the life of the old Algonquin lumberjacks off in the winter woods or to convey how profoundly different this life was from our own.

Square timbers were the trunks of huge pine trees, felled and squared off on all four sides to a "table-top" finish by skilled men using only axes.

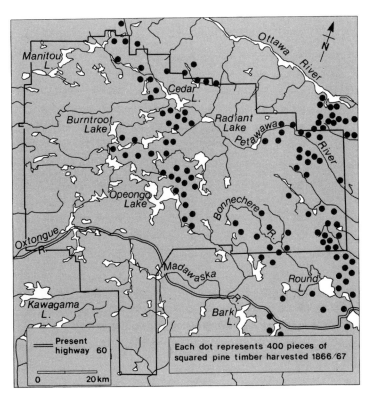

The cutting of pine for square timber in the Algonquin Park area, winter of 1866–67 (map prepared by Dept. of Geography, Wilfrid Laurier University).

"Off in the woods" is no idle phrase. From the time they left their rough farms in the Ottawa and St. Lawrence valleys to go to the shanties in late fall, the loggers would spend five or six months, toiling six days a week, in the then-remote Algonquin highlands. We know from other accounts of the square timber trade that the 1866–67 production would have been accounted for by about eight camps of 50 men each, or a total of 400 men (plus about 200 horses).

A camp typically included at least one stable and at least one "camboose" shanty to house the men. Built entirely of logs cut on the spot, a camboose might measure 40 by 35 feet, but its walls were only six feet high. There was only one door and, if there was any window at all, it was only a small one for the benefit of the clerk. The rest of the men had to make do with the light coming in the large central chimney or from the fire itself. All along two opposite walls were "muzzle-loading" bunks where the men slept, two to a bed, fully clothed except for their boots and with only two blankets over top. The "mattress" consisted of another blanket spread over balsam boughs laid on poles.

We might not find the bedding arrangements very appealing, but in those days that was the norm. As far as we know, no one ever complained about them — any more than they did about the food. The latter consisted of salt pork, tea, blackstrap molasses, beans, and bread — and that was it. Breakfast was at 5 a.m. so that the men didn't waste precious daylight hours walking to work. Lunch would be eaten in the bush, and supper, back at the camboose, was at 6 p.m. The exhausted men didn't even get to eat at a table. Instead, they had to manage by sitting on benches and supporting their tin plates on their knees. They had no forks and used only knives.

When spring finally came, most of the men went back to their farms and families, but others signed on for the drive. In the spring of 1867, the 30,000 square timbers were sent down the Petawawa, Barron, Bonnechère, and Opeongo Rivers to the Ottawa. There they were assembled into great rafts, perhaps 200 in all, and, together with many hundreds of others cut elsewhere in the upper Ottawa Valley that year, were guided down to the St. Lawrence and on to Quebec City for shipment to England. We do not know how many young men lost their lives in the drive of 1867, but there were probably a few at least, for it was cold and dangerous work.

It really is difficult to realize how different the life of the lumberjacks was from our experience of the same place today. We come here to relax in beautiful surroundings; they came to work like dogs with only dim, lice-infested hovels for shelter. We come to escape, however briefly; they came for six months of unrelieved winter isolation. We come to enjoy a fragment of our (altered) natural heritage; they came to scratch out a living without the least comprehension or concern that they would remove almost all of the Ottawa Valley's original big pine in just a few decades. ... No, it really is difficult to imagine how different things were just three or four generations ago, even in a "timeless" place like Algonquin. It was another century and another world ... .∞

September 2, 1982, Vol. 23, No. 11 (D.S.)

To Sleep the Impossible Sleep

The Park is quiet and still now. The busy summer season is behind us, most of the campgrounds are closed, and many interior portages have seen their last canoeists for 1982. To be sure, a few visitors come to enjoy the clear, silent beauty of autumn in Algonquin, but, after the best colour at the end of the month and the Thanksgiving weekend in October, they too will be gone for another year.

What we are seeing, of course, is the approach of winter — a season many of our visitors would rather forget about but whose importance to Algonquin can scarcely be exaggerated. There is simply no escaping the fact that deep snow and intense cold will grip the Park for six long months, from November until the end of April. Getting through this period is by far the greatest and deadliest challenge facing our wildlife.

Of all the possible ways to cope with this reality, we suppose that the most attractive (short of flying south) is hibernation. The idea of avoiding all the unpleasantness of winter by sleeping through it has an undeniable appeal. It also has an undeniable efficiency when it involves the virtual complete shutdown of energy-demanding body processes. A hibernating groundhog, for example, doesn't eat a thing all winter long, surviving on nothing but body fat for six long months by reducing its body temperature to just above

Imagine nursing one or two babies for three months while sound asleep, and all the while not drinking or eating a thing!

freezing, its heart beat to three or four a minute, and its breathing rate to once every five minutes.

That animals get through the winter this way is well known, of course, and most readers will accept hibernation to be perfectly reasonable. Nevertheless, there is one Algonquin animal whose winter-long sleep seems to defy all logic, and that animal is the Black Bear.

You may be a little surprised at such a statement because the idea of an old bruin snoozing away the winter in a nice warm cave somewhere is so familiar that it stands almost as the accepted symbol of hibernation.

Well, the fact is bears do a great many "crazy" things while hibernating, and first on the list is their choice of den sites. Some bears actually do spend the winter in a "nice warm cave," but many more simply crawl under a brush pile, fallen tree trunk, or overhanging rock. Bears prepare bedding by raking in leaves and clubmosses, or by piling up coniferous branches (bitten from living trees) and bark stripped from cedars. Otherwise, their dens have no insulative value at all. They probably serve as windbreaks, and snow may eventually drift over the bear and "den." More often, however, the sleeping animal remains exposed to the often bitterly cold outside air.

Even this might be somewhat understandable if bears were true hibernators that shut down their metabolism to the absolute minimum to sustain life (the way a groundhog does). At least that way, bears might reduce some of the energy losses they needlessly incur through choosing poor-quality dens. But, with typical disregard for the laws of physics, bears lower their body temperature only a few degrees (to about 88°F) and continue to burn up energy at fully half the summer rate. Their heart rate drops irregularly to as low as eight beats a minute, but they can always wake up in just a few minutes.*

It would be remarkable enough if bears were content merely to survive winter in their seemingly illogical way, but that is only part of the story. Every second year, female bears give birth to two or three cubs in January and then resume their deep sleep. The cubs are very small at birth (less than a pound) and hairless, but they survive by snuggling up against the sparsely furred underside of their mother. In the three months leading up to their emergence from the den, their weights will increase to the four- to eight-pound range, thanks to the rich milk provided by a mother who, you will remember, is almost always asleep and who hasn't eaten or drunk anything since the previous October.

The whole business is quite amazing, and, to us, it seems impossible somehow that a bear should be able to sleep through a cold Algonquin winter in a makeshift den

on only a summer's worth of stored fat — let alone simultaneously bring two or three cubs into the world and nourish them for three months. The experts point out that a bear is probably a more efficient hibernator than most animals simply because it is so large. They also draw attention to the superb insulating winter pelt of a bear (especially on the back and sides) and to the bear's energy-conserving sleeping position (upright but curled up in a ball with the top of the head on the ground, tucked in between its forepaws).

The experts may be right, but we still have the impression that what bears do during the winter must require far more energy than what they can store up the previous summer. We find it extremely interesting, moreover, that many early peoples around the world apparently shared our difficulty. They attempted to "balance the equation," as it were, by supposing that hibernating bears gain extra sustenance by sucking their paws. One ingenious variation on this idea held that bears deliberately walk on berries all summer long so that they can lick up the juice the following winter. Oddly, there actually is a basis for these ideas; bears do lick their feet during hibernation because they slough off their old foot and toe pads while in the winter den and the new ones are quite tender!

However bizarre this behaviour might be in itself, it is really just one more crazy thing — and a minor one at that — bears do during their winter sleep. Almost everything about bear hibernation seems to fly in the face of our conventional ideas about survival and energy conservation.

We can only marvel at how they manage to get away with it all — at how they "sleep the impossible sleep" through the long, cold Algonquin winter.∾

September 9, 1982, Vol. 23, No. 12 (D.S.)

---

* One researcher in Minnesota described the time he tried to hear the heartbeat of a hibernating female bear by pressing his ear against her chest. For two minutes he heard nothing, but then the beat began strongly and rapidly. As the waking bear lifted her head, the researcher squeezed backwards out of the den as quickly as he could. Outside, he could still hear the heartbeat and timed it at about 175 per minute. (He assures us that he first checked to make sure the heart he was hearing wasn't his own.)

Bear Biochemistry

Bears don't go into an almost death-like state the way many other hibernators do, but they aren't merely "asleep" either. For example, they do not urinate at all during the winter (whereas other so-called true hibernators have to wake up every few days to relieve themselves). Bears avoid poisoning themselves, however, because they are somehow able to break down their waste products and recycle the nitrogen to repair body proteins. The result is that bears only use up fat in their winter sleep. They have very high cholesterol levels but no known problems with hardening of the arteries or gallstones, apparently because they produce a special bile juice called "ursodeoxycholic acid." When given to humans, this same acid dissolves gallstones, and medical researchers are very interested indeed.

The Birds That Did the Singing

The idea of singing about an Algonquin winter may seem a trifle far-fetched, but anyone who visited the Park this past winter season quickly discovered there was song just about everywhere.

Pouring down from the tips of tall spruce in the west and from lofty pine boughs in the east came the beautiful, canary-like trills and chattery warbles of Red and White-winged Crossbills. And, it was a simple matter to see the birds themselves. Abundant and conspicuous, they were noticed by just about everyone. The male Red Crossbill is somewhat larger than a sparrow and brick-red except for a dark tail and wings. The male White-wing is pink instead of red and, in addition, has two flashy white wing bars. Females have grayish-green replacing the pink or red, but both sexes of both species share the characteristic that gives them their name: the tips of the bill are quite definitely crossed.

You may be wondering why these exotic-looking finches should have arrived in such numbers and why they were actually singing even back in January and February. Normally we associate bird song with the breeding season, which, especially in the North, is in the spring when food supplies to feed ravenously hungry babies are at their annual maximum.

Algonquin winters are not exactly noted for their abundance of food, so what could account for the crossbill behaviour last winter? Were they fooled by the warm weather into starting their breeding cycle several months too early?

The answer is, not at all. The warm weather had nothing whatsoever to do with the winter crossbill show. Instead, the birds really were nesting — in the middle of the winter — and their food supplies actually were at a maximum!

Crossbills specialize in the extraction of seeds from the cones of spruce, pine, and larch. They are nomads, roaming the coniferous forests of the northern hemisphere and settling whenever and wherever they chance on forests with good seed crops. In the best situations they are stimulated into singing, pairing off, building a nest, and raising young — whatever the time of year.

If you were in the Park last August, you may have noted that many of our coniferous trees were heavily laden with cones. You might have predicted then that the coming winter would be excellent for crossbills. In fact, it was not until just before Christmas that their numbers really started to build up and the air started to fill with song. The highlight came in late January when a nest of the Red Crossbill (the first ever for the Park) and two of the White-winged Crossbill were found near the Achray turn-off on the Park's east side. There is no doubt in anyone's mind that both species nest here quite regularly in good seed years, but it took the sharp eyes of an American graduate student Craig Benkman to actually prove it.

Craig came here especially to study the ecology of crossbills and, thanks to him, we now have a much clearer understanding of how crossbills manage the trick of getting the seeds out of those hard, woody, and often tightly closed cones. The birds are so good at it that it is rather difficult for a human to see exactly what is going on, even when very close, but Craig has made careful observations on captive birds. A crossbill first clips off a cone, holds it at a comfortable angle under its left or right foot (depending on which way the individual bird's bill is crossed), and then inserts the crossed tips of the bill under one of the cone scales. It opens its bill sideways (see diagram) in such a way that the scale is pried away from the cone. When the seed within is thus exposed, the crossbill pulls it out with its tongue. The bird then allows its bill to return to the normal position and goes on to the next scale.

This amazing adaptation is, of course, the key to the crossbill's ability to exploit and prosper on a food supply no other birds can even get at. It is actually even more subtle than that. The heavier, more robust bill of the Red Crossbill suits it better for working on the bigger cones of pine whereas the more slender-billed White-winged Crossbill is more efficient with larch and spruce.

None of this mattered in the winter of 1982–83. All our major conifers had excellent seed crops, so both kinds of crossbills hit the jackpot. It was a winter they could, and did, sing about for months on end.⏎

April 28, 1983, Vol. 24, No. 1 (D.S.)

Sex in the Pulpit

As every visitor to Algonquin knows, now is the time of year when the Park's plants and animals are at their busiest in the annual job of reproducing their own kind. There is no doubt that the long days and warm temperatures of early summer make for the best possible conditions for raising babies or producing seeds. But sometimes we make the mistake of thinking that the task is actually easy.

The truth is that the production of surviving offspring is a very energy-demanding task and can easily push parents to the brink of their capabilities. This being the case, we should not be too surprised that some plants and animals have evolved ingenious, even bizarre, ways to increase their chances of success.

A good example of this is one of the Park's less common flowering plants (but one you may well know already from back home) — Jack-in-the-pulpit. The peculiar "behaviour" of Jack-in-the-pulpit is not immediately apparent even though the plant is undeniably interesting to look at. A perennial that grows in rich hardwoods, it consists of one or two big, three-parted leaves plus the flower, or pulpit, on a separate stalk. A close look at the pulpit will show it to be a graceful, modified leaf that ranges in colour from solid green to green with white or purplish-brown stripes. The pulpit encloses and shelters a fleshy spike whose base is covered with dozens of tiny flowers. In a given pulpit these flowers are either all male (they produce pollen only) or all female (they produce only ovules or potential seeds).

Because the sexes are separated this way, an individual female Jack-in-the-pulpit must be pollinated by pollen from a separate (male) plant. The transfer is accomplished by fungal gnats, insects that normally lay their eggs on mushrooms but are somehow seduced by the odour or colour of Jack-in-the-pulpits. The deceived gnats fly right into the pulpit and then tumble down the slippery walls to the base of the spike where the flowers are.

In male Jack-in-the-pulpits the pulpit chamber is not completely enclosed. There is a small gap through which the gnats can escape, usually with a few grains of pollen adhering to their bodies.

In female pulpits, however, there is no gap at all — and no escape for any gnat that enters. The advantage of this to the plant is that a trapped gnat will vainly thrash around at the bottom of the pulpit until it dies and, in the process, be more likely to transfer any pollen grains it is carrying to the female flowers. It cannot be said that the system is particularly efficient — each female pulpit usually ends up producing only about five seeds out of the hundreds possible — but it does work.

Apart from the details of its pollination, there is nothing particularly unusual, so far, about the sex life of Jack-in-the-pulpits. For example, many other plant species have male and female flowers borne on separate plants. The special thing in this case is that individual Jack-in-the-pulpits regularly change sex from one year to the next. This year's female may well be next year's male, or vice-versa! Obviously, this is more than just a little bit kinky, and you may legitimately want to know what has been going on all these years in our Algonquin Park pulpits.

A few clues are given by the places where Jack-in-the-pulpits live and by the seeds they produce. First of all, because they grow in heavily shaded forests where little or no direct sunlight reaches down to the ground, Jack-in-the-pulpits have a very low energy intake. Compounding the problem, they are perennials and, each spring, must start from scratch, putting up new leaves and a pulpit using underground energy reserves stored up the previous summer. Under these conditions it takes years and years for a Jack-in-the-pulpit to reach large size, and a knee-high plant may well be 20 years old.

Second, Jack-in-the-pulpit seeds are very large, and producing them (not to mention the bright red berries that enclose them) represents a major energy drain on the plant. Even the very largest Jack-in-the-pulpit will have to spend 10 per cent of its summer energy intake to produce just five seeds, and more often the figure is closer to 20 per cent. Smaller plants would have to spend an even greater proportion of their available energy on seed production, and this would probably mean they wouldn't have sufficient reserves to produce new leaves and a flower the next spring — assuming they even got through the winter.

If producing female flowers borders on suicide for a small Jack-in-the-pulpit, producing male flowers is much less risky. The pollen they produce is required for only a short time at the beginning of the season and then the flower can be allowed to wither away, with no on-going energy demands as with seed-producing female flowers. In other words, a male Jack-in-the-pulpit can afford to start flowering when it is quite small, whereas a strictly female plant would have to wait so long before it could afford the luxury of flowering that it might well be stepped on by a moose or attacked by a fungus first.

With this background, it makes sense for Jack-in-the-pulpits to be able to change their sex. When small, they can produce male flowers and still have enough energy left over to increase their stored energy reserves each year. When these reserves have

Jack-in-the-pulpit plants change sex from male to female and sometimes back again.

reached some critical value that will permit the plant to put up really big leaves, it can switch over to being a female. Even then, however, the energy drain may be so costly that the plant may revert back to being a smaller male for a year or two. How soon it will be big enough to take on the crushing burden of motherhood once again will depend on how lucky it is in avoiding injury and how warm and sunny the summers are. We suspect that, here in Algonquin with our poor soils and short growing season, very few of our Jack-in-the-pulpits, even the old ones, are big and strong enough to be females two years in a row.

The beauty of the Jack-in-the-pulpit's sex-changing system is that it allows individual plants to reproduce earlier and more often. They can be fathers whenever they are too small to be mothers! As one wag put it, it's really a case of Jack and Jill in the pulpit (although not both at the same time, tsk tsk).

And just how, you may wonder, does one tell a "Jill-in-the-pulpit" from a "Jack-in-the-pulpit" if you should spot one or the other along a trail or portage? You'll be sorry you asked … . Female Jack-in-the-pulpits, you see, really are … big mothers.↩

June 30, 1983, Vol. 24, No. 2 (D.S.)

Trouble and Bass

It is probably fair — and reasonable — to say that most Park visitors view the summer as a very easy season for Algonquin's permanent residents. Temperatures are high, food is abundant, and there are long hours of daylight to be devoted to foraging and the raising of young.

And yet, the truth is that life can be very difficult in the warm season and some animals are pushed to the limits of their tolerance by adverse summer conditions. A good example of this is the Smallmouth Bass.

You may find it rather odd that we would point to a fish, and particularly to the Smallmouth Bass, as a summer hardship case. If anything, fish would appear to be better protected against the extremes of the outside world than most animals, and the Smallmouth Bass is usually cited as an especially noteworthy success story here in the Park. Smallmouths, not originally found in Algonquin, were introduced to many of the lakes along what is now Highway 60 in the early years of this century. In contrast to most attempts to establish alien animals outside their normal range, the introductions of Smallmouth Bass were quite successful. Today, decades later, many lakes such as Smoke, Cache, and Opeongo have very significant Smallmouth populations, and angling for these fish is an important summer pastime for many people.

So in what sense, then, can we say the Smallmouth Bass is being pushed to the limits of its tolerance by summer conditions in Algonquin? Well, if you are a bass fisherman, you will know that the quality of Smallmouth fishing can vary tremendously. Some years it could hardly be better and then, just a summer later, it can collapse almost completely. Generally speaking, such collapses occur when all the three-year-old fish (which often constitute the bulk of the catchable fish — at least in heavily fished lakes) are "missing" from the lake. This means, of course, that something either prevented the bass from reproducing three years earlier or wiped out the fish produced that year before they got big enough to be caught. This is rather mysterious because what that "something" might be is not immediately obvious.

In fact, if you look at the life cycle of the Smallmouth Bass, it seems that they should do rather well. Unlike trout, which spawn in the fall and then require all winter for the eggs to develop, Smallmouth Bass spawn in June. The warm water means that the eggs develop much faster and are therefore exposed to predators for a much shorter time. In fact, bass eggs hatch in only four to 10 days, and, what's more, they are fiercely guarded by their fathers during all this time. The paternal care also continues after the young emerge (about 2,000 per nest) and only breaks down when the young disperse from the shallow spawning shoals about three weeks later. The young spend the rest of their first summer feeding on their own in deeper water. When cold temperatures arrive, they retreat to rock crevices and spend the winter hidden from predators in an inactive, non-feeding state.

Where is the weakness in this seemingly excellent system for getting young Smallmouth Bass started in life? Research carried out at several places in Ontario, including our own Harkness Laboratory on Lake Opeongo, has shown that, of all things, it has to do with the weather. When young-of-the-year Smallmouth Bass are in their winter hiding places, they don't eat anything at all and depend for survival on the food reserves they have built up during the summer. The bigger they are in the fall, the more food reserves they will have and the better their chances of making it through until spring. The catch is that in a warm summer the young bass are more active, feed more, and attain a greater size than in a cool summer — to the point where summer weather is a major factor in determining whether the young bass of a given year will survive their first winter.

There is another weather-related problem as well. Bass start to spawn when the water temperature climbs above 15°C (or 60°F).

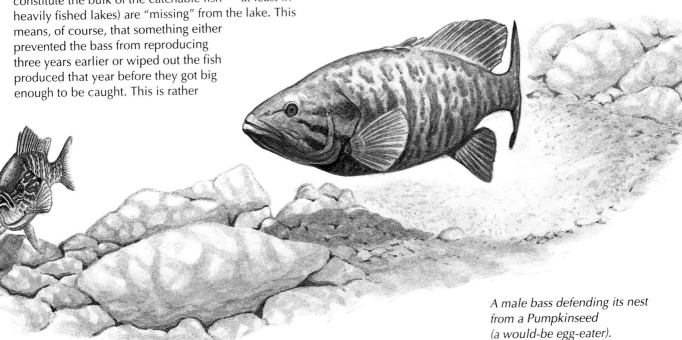

A male bass defending its nest from a Pumpkinseed (a would-be egg-eater).

Unfortunately, there is no guarantee that the temperature will stay above that mark. Short as the bass incubation period may be, there is always a chance that it will turn cold again or that a storm will push cold water into the newly warmed spawning shallows. Even if the cold doesn't kill all the eggs, the turbulence will and, in just a few hours, all the bass nests in the lake may be wrecked.

To be sure, the adults can spawn again, and many do nest again after such calamities. Nevertheless, the delay makes it correspondingly less likely that the young from the second nestings will have enough time, in what is left of the summer, to grow big enough to last through the following winter.

Clearly, the reproductive fortunes of Smallmouth Bass are in a real squeeze between late spring storms and cool summer weather, and it gets worse and worse the farther north you go. Eventually, a point is reached beyond which the summers when bass can reproduce are so unusual that the fish just can't sustain themselves.

Although Algonquin summers are not that cool, we aren't really far south of the line, and we shouldn't be surprised that, from time to time, all or most of a year's bass production is completely wiped out. As long as this doesn't happen too often, our bass will be able, in their good summers, to add big batches of young bass to their population and they won't die out. If our climate were ever to turn a few degrees colder, however, Park bass would fail to reproduce more often than they succeeded, and the brief era of Smallmouth Bass in Algonquin would come to an end.

The suggestion was made earlier that most people imagine summer as a time of year when bass must be in idyllic harmony with the Park environment. Well, not to sound too sour a note — even under the water, bass do have their troubles with wind and cold weather, and the reality of their situation here is completely bass awkward.∞

July 7, 1983, Vol. 24, No. 3 (D.S.)

Who Is Subtle and Sophisticated?

Humans tend to think of subtlety and sophistication as their exclusive attributes. We confidently assume that animals, however beautiful they may be, lead rather simple and straightforward lives in comparison.

As with most forms of snobbery, the truth is that this human-centred sort blinds us to the real qualities of the supposedly lowly victims of our condescension. We hardly give a second glance, for example, to the moths we see resting around campground office and washroom lights these mornings, and yet their lives are almost unbelievably intricate.

One group to whom we might pay particular attention is the underwing moths. These are the medium-sized moths with rather dull, mottled forewings and strikingly patterned, often brilliantly coloured hindwings. There are many different species, each with its own distinct variation on this basic theme. Often they have colourful names dating back to a more whimsical era of biology. Thus, we have the Serene Underwing, the Beloved Underwing, the Betrothed Underwing, and even the Wayward Nymph. On the darker side, there are the Tearful Underwing, the Dejected Underwing, and the Inconsolable Underwing, such names apparently stemming from the old superstition that moths represent the souls of the dead, flying in darkness and ever seeking light.

Notwithstanding their fanciful names, all the underwings have in common a constraint in their lives that very definitely comes from the real world. They all rest with the dull forewings covering the spectacular hindwings, and it is evident that the sombre markings are camouflage to reduce the danger from predators — insect-eating birds, in particular — as the moths rest on tree trunks during the day. The camouflage system is quite subtle: darker species, when given the choice, will choose to rest on dark-coloured trunks, and the opposite is true with light species. They also have an uncanny ability to align the markings on their wings with similar markings on the bark in such a way that the outline of the wings is broken up and obscured as much as possible.

This is very subtle to be sure, but it's far from the whole story. If the underwings have been able to evolve such sophisticated disguises, one must then ask why they have not all come up with the same one. Surely one design must be best of all, and it should "pay" every species to evolve toward it.

To understand why this has not actually happened, you have to know something about how a predator's brain operates. Most predators, including birds, are surprisingly conservative and unadventurous. They tend to learn from a few good experiences with one or two particular types of food and then continue to look for these types, ignoring or refusing to experiment with novel types of prey.*

Knowing this, try putting yourself in a moth's situation for a moment. Your best strategy would be to look different enough from other species that predators, even if they did see through your tree trunk disguise, would not confuse you with some other moth they had already learned to like. You would then have a chance of being

---

* If this tends to confirm your ideas about animals being simple and unsophisticated, you might reflect on the success of fast food chains with humans. Isn't the prosperity of hamburger outlets built on the fact that we would rather stick with the familiar most of the time?

104   *The Best of The Raven*

passed over by your dangerous but conservative enemy, and you would live to see another day.

In fact, it really does seem, in underwing evolutionary history, that look-alikes have attracted far too much attention from predators, and the survivors have been those that looked distinctly different from each other. Not only do all present-day species at a given locality have distinct patterns, but also among the common species are usually two or three quite definite forms that look as different from each other as true species do.

The result is that even abundant species escape having to pay the normal penalty for being common — high exposure and, consequently, high risk that predators will get to know and specialize in eating them.

It must be recognized, however, that not even this subtle refinement in disguises can be entirely foolproof. Predators are very sharp-eyed and, especially when driven by extreme hunger, will occasionally try the unfamiliar. It is then, when the camouflage of the forewings has failed, that the flamboyance of the hindwings comes into play. When seized by the wings on one side, an underwing moth flips open its free wings and exposes the striking pattern and colours of the other hindwing. The sudden, totally unexpected appearance of a dazzling pattern where before there was only a dull, tree trunk disguise is apparently enough to make many birds release their grip long enough for the moth to escape. (You can sometimes see the proof of this for yourself, incidentally. Many moths have distinct beak imprints on their wings, indicating they have been seized by a bird and then released.)

Once again you may think that moth predators must be pretty simple if they fall for such an unsophisticated trick. But is it really so unsophisticated? We venture to say that none of us would do much better if, for example, a hamburger we were about to bite into suddenly flipped open and revealed pulsating red and black innards. Those of us who didn't die on the spot from a heart attack might reasonably be expected to at least drop the hamburger.

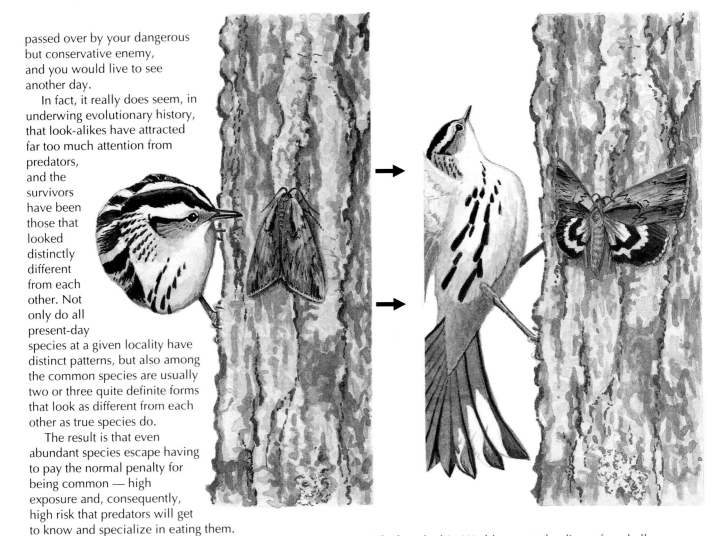

Black-and-white Warbler meets the dinner from hell.

Of course, with time and if you had no other choice, you might convince yourself to eat the thing anyway. It might not be so easy, however, if you were up against underwings. As with their camouflaged forewings, each species has its own unique hindwing colours and pattern, no doubt making it correspondingly difficult for predators to get used to, and overcome their fear of, those suddenly exposed hindwings.

It is scarcely credible to most of us that lowly moths, to whom we scarcely give a thought, have such astonishingly subtle defences against those animals who would eat them. Perhaps humans should come down a peg or two and realize what amazing features these "simple" creatures really possess.

And, oh yes, let's be thankful that eating a hamburger isn't nearly so complicated as devouring an Inconsolable Underwing. We "sophisticates" might not fare too well!☞

July 14, 1983, Vol. 24, No. 4 (D.S.)

Some Like It Hot

July is Algonquin's most summery month, and we are sure that many Park visitors like nothing better than to stretch out and soak up the sunshine. This just has to be one of life's most enjoyable luxuries.

The surprising thing is that humans aren't the only creatures that like to indulge in serious basking. Many others, from turtles to butterflies, also like to sunbathe and, at first glance, this is rather curious. After all, humans are on vacation but animals aren't so lucky. They have to work hard to survive and can't afford any wasted moments.

A basker upon a basker.

than the same species do in the southern United States — even though Algonquin turtles have a much shorter summer and seemingly that much less time to waste on "idle pleasures."

The answer to the paradox is that turtles are said to be "cold-blooded," which means that, by themselves, they can't generate a constant, high body temperature the way humans can. Instead, they can only get warm by absorbing heat from their surroundings. As a consequence, when the weather is cold, turtles become colder and more numb, less and less able to move or carry on their body processes. There is one way, however, that turtles can extract a little more heat from their surroundings — and that is through basking. By crawling out of the water, stretching out its legs, and spreading out its toes, a turtle presents a maximum surface

Take the example of turtles. They only have the May through September period in which they can be active. In these five months they must do a year's worth of finding food, eating, and growing, not to mention mating and laying eggs and then storing up enough fat reserves to get them through the following seven months of winter.

Under these circumstances it seems odd that turtles spend long periods basking. Stranger still is the fact that some Algonquin turtles spend far more time basking here

area to the sun and, in fact, can often achieve an internal body temperature that is eight to 10 degrees warmer than the surrounding air. Because a basking, extra-warm turtle has its body chemistry speeded up, it can, for example, digest its food much more quickly than if it hadn't taken the time to bask. Furthermore, when it does go back into the water, it probably can hunt more vigorously and effectively — at least until it cools off again.

Another benefit of basking has to do with egg production. Female turtles are especially fond of sunning themselves in May and June, and it may well be that they do so to speed up the development of their eggs so they can be laid earlier and given a head-start in life.

Seen in this light, basking may be of crucial importance to turtles that have to contend with the short Algonquin summer. It has been suggested, for example, that Snapping Turtles — which aren't found much farther north than the Park — might not be able to survive here if they didn't spend so much time warming themselves in the sun.

For other animals, basking may be important not so much for long-term survival as for day-to-day existence. You don't have far to look for such animals because the butterflies, so conspicuous at this time of year, are prime examples.

Now, it is quite apparent that butterflies, if they are to be successful in life, must fly around, find food, avoid predators, and find mates. The catch is that butterflies can't generate enough muscular power to get airborne unless their body temperature is at least 81°F — and more typically around 95°F. And, as everyone will realize, butterflies in Algonquin might have to wait a long time indeed for temperatures that warm. Even on our rare, really hot days, it would be unusual for the temperature to get as high as 80° or 90°F before late morning. The fact that butterflies are on the wing in much cooler conditions means they must have some trick to raise their temperature.

Some butterflies, especially those that fly early in the year, have the ability to create their own internal heat by rapidly contracting their wing muscles (a sort of shivering) until they are hot enough to take off. Such a procedure is energetically very expensive, however, so many more butterflies rely on basking.

By spreading its wings and orienting its body to catch the sun, a butterfly can often raise its body temperature as much as 30 degrees Fahrenheit above air temperature in a relatively few minutes. For a while people thought that such impressive increases were achieved by the butterfly's blood being warmed as it circulated through the veins in the wings (along the idea of solar heating panels). Recently, however, it has been found that a dead butterfly's body warms up just as fast as a live one under the same conditions. The heating effect, therefore, must be caused simply by the physical presence of the wings close to the body. Further research has shown that it is the scaly or hairy (and often dark-coloured) bases of the wings that quickly absorb the sun's energy and then warm up the adjacent body where the wing muscles are. The wings also trap warm air between the butterfly and the basking surface and create the effect well known to any camper who has left his tent in direct sunlight for the day.

These physical properties of the wings allow basking butterflies to warm up and get going far earlier in the morning than would otherwise be true. And, because a flying butterfly actually cools down (by moving through cooler air and, in effect, fanning itself with its wings), short basking sessions between flights permit a butterfly to quickly get its temperature back up into operating range and resume activity. Such ability obviously makes the difference between being able to operate in the Algonquin environment and not being able to live here at all.

Turtles and butterflies are just two examples of the many groups of animals for which basking is almost a way of life. Personally, we find it fascinating that "catching a few rays" — an idle luxury for us humans — is a crucial survival strategy for other animals. It's something to contemplate the next time you see a turtle or a butterfly soaking up the sunshine. … We all like it hot, but some actually need it that way.∞

July 28, 1983, Vol. 24, No. 6 (D.S.)

Hearing Is Believing?

The Marsh Hawk (now officially called the Northern Harrier) hunts by sound as well as sight.

We humans pride ourselves on our ability to look at the world around us and figure out how it works. Yet the truth is very often we do just the opposite. Instead of really looking, we accept what people tell us, even when such conventional wisdom doesn't make much sense. To give just two examples: people believed for centuries that swallows hibernated in the mud of river bottoms and that beavers used their flat tails as trowels. There wasn't the slightest bit of real evidence for either idea, of course, but they were repeated so often that everybody took them to be facts and accepted them without question.

Today, we may at times smile at these myths, but we really have no right to do so. Modern research is still finding plenty of cases where our beliefs turn out to be based not on real observations but on "something we have heard" instead.

A minor but interesting example of this is afforded by one of the Park's birds of prey, the Marsh Hawk.* Marsh Hawks are uncommon in Algonquin but, where they do occur, are easy to spot. Their preferred habitat is open, treeless bogs, and they can be seen flapping along or gliding close to the ground on long wings held up in a shallow "V." Males are a silvery gray colour with black wing tips, while females are brown above with cream, brown-streaked bellies. Both sexes have a conspicuous

---

* The best place to see Marsh Hawks along Highway 60 is in the big bog at the Spruce Bog Boardwalk stretching south along Sunday Creek down to Norway Lake. As a matter of fact, the Park's only two known Marsh Hawk nests were both found here (on the ground) in 1975 and 1981. This bog is now most easily seen from the deck of the Algonquin Park Visitor Centre.

white patch on the rump, and the presence of this mark should remove all doubt about the bird's identity.

Now, when we see a Marsh Hawk sweeping along over a wild Algonquin bog or suddenly dipping down into the vegetation and then emerging with a mouse in its talons, we admire the spectacle, but that's about as far as it goes. We have all heard about the keen eyesight of hawks, and most people (ourselves included) always uncritically accepted the notion that the hunting successes of the Marsh Hawk (as with all the other species) were due to their incredibly sharp eyes.

In fact, if we had really stopped to observe and think about it carefully, we might have suspected that something more subtle was going on. After all, is it really possible for a Marsh Hawk to spot rodents scurrying along under a metre or more of thick bog vegetation? We might also have wondered about the Marsh Hawk's face. Unlike other hawks, the Marsh Hawk has peculiar "facial discs" surrounding each eye, giving the bird a vaguely owl-like appearance. But although these clues were always present, no one ever picked up on them until a few years ago when an American researcher, Dr. William Rice, finally took the time to look at what was actually going on instead of just repeating the old assumptions.

Dr. Rice knew that some owls have a hunting pattern similar to the Marsh Hawk's (low, over open areas). He also knew that owl facial discs are an anatomical feature permitting the birds to locate the source of any sound so precisely that they can capture mice, even in total darkness, by sound alone. Could it be that Marsh Hawks also use sound rather than sight to find their prey?

Dr. Rice first tested this idea in his laboratory. He presented captive Marsh Hawks with two movable speaker platforms at a fixed distance from their perch and taught them to expect a food reward if they flew to the correct platform after a mouse squeak was broadcast over one of the speakers. The Marsh Hawks soon showed that they could identify the correct speaker platform even when they were only two degrees apart horizontally. That's almost as good as some owls and far better than other day-flying hawks.

This performance indicated that a Marsh Hawk, with a 10 centimetres talon spread, might be able to hit a completely hidden mouse (about five centimetres across), provided the mouse squeaked when the hawk was no more than three or four metres away (10 to 15 feet).

There was still room for doubt, however, because the captive hawks failed to demonstrate conclusively that they could pinpoint sound sources as well vertically as they did horizontally. They would need the ability to do both, of course, if they were going to zero in on a tiny, invisible mouse. The ear openings of a Marsh Hawk, furthermore, are situated perfectly symmetrically on the bird's head. (In owls, the ear opening on one side is higher than on the other, and it is believed that the consequent slight difference in arrival time of a given sound at each ear is what permits owls to locate sound sources vertically.)

To settle the question, Dr. Rice chose an old field frequented by Marsh Hawks and installed a network of 10 miniature speakers just below the soil surface. By broadcasting mouse squeaks, he was able to attract passing Marsh Hawks. There was no doubt that wild

hawks used sound, at least in the initial phase of a hunt. Then, instead of letting the birds zero all the way in to the broadcasting speaker, he stopped the squeaks when the hawks were three or four metres away. Although this meant that the hawks were receiving no clues as to the location of the "invisible mice" from then on, it was obvious the hawks had already precisely pinpointed the origin of the squeaks. It was routine to find talon puncture marks in the speaker housings. On one occasion, a Marsh Hawk swooped down, ripped the speaker right out of the ground, and kept on going with the wires dangling behind it.

This episode rather dramatically established that Marsh Hawks can, and probably usually do, hunt by sound alone. And, with the benefit of hindsight, it really makes sense. No eyes are keen enough to see right through the thick ground vegetation growing in the places where Marsh Hawks hunt. Hearing would be much more useful under such circumstances.

But, however obvious this may now seem, even the best "authorities" went along for years saying that Marsh Hawks hunted by sight, never questioning the idea for a moment. Now, thanks to the experiments of Dr. Rice, we have learned that the conventional wisdom everyone has been repeating was incorrect.

It just goes to show: hearing is not always believing. It may be alright for those fascinating Marsh Hawks, but not for us humans. ✑

August 11, 1983, Vol. 24, No. 8 (D.S.)

Pity the Poor Fagus

It is probably fair to say that most people take trees for granted. True, trees seem to "just stand there" most of the time, and they certainly don't lead lives like those of animals. But it's a pity all the same that so few people realize how difficult and complex a tree's existence can be.

Take, for example, our common Beech tree. This is the handsome, broad-leaved species that grows here and there in our hardwood forests and is immediately recognizable by its beautiful, smooth, gray bark. The bark is so invitingly smooth, in fact, that many a tree (not here in the Park, we are happy to say) has been chosen to record such immortal messages as "John loves Marcia" or "Tom adores Sally."

We think this is rather sad because, even if Beech trees have no feelings, they are still very thin-skinned, and being disfigured in this way doesn't do them any good at all — especially in a life beset by other serious challenges and obstacles. Perhaps if we all understood just what Beeches are up against, Tom and John would give them the respect they truly deserve and find some other place to swear their devotion to Sally and Marcia.

Now, the notion of Beech trees having a difficult life may seem hard to believe. A gnarled old Beech way back

in the Algonquin forest might seem to be the very picture of timelessness and, indeed, some Beech trees apparently live as long as four centuries. Even the more typical 250 years is still more than twice as old as any of humans will live, so it may seem that Beech trees, in fact, do very well.

To begin appreciating the truth of the matter, you have to realize that every big Beech tree is a "one in a million" survivor from a vast number of potential trees that started out in life at the same time. For each seed that lands in a good site, many more have the misfortune of germinating in places that are too wet, or too dry, or too shady, or too sunny — or have something else that isn't right for young Beech seedlings. The great majority of Beech seeds, in fact, barely get started before they come to grief. The situation is slightly better with suckers, erect shoots growing up around an established tree from its shallow root system. Because they are still connected to, and nourished by, the parent tree, the suckers can often withstand more severe conditions than true seedlings, and sometimes they form dense thickets of potential new trees.*

---

* We must resist the temptation to call these young trees "sons of beeches." The truth is that they are just as much daughters as they are sons. All individual Beech trees, when they are mature, produce not only male flowers (which produce pollen) but also separate female flowers. The latter, of course, produce the seeds (called beechnuts).

No matter how a Beech tree gets established, its future is far from guaranteed. Its chief problem will be the shade of the forest canopy above, and, even if it can live for a long time in deep shade, it won't grow and has no chance of long-term success unless one of the big trees shading it falls down and lets in the sun. Even then, there won't be room for all the contenders, and competition among all the available young Beech trees will be severe. Worse, Beech trees are not alone in the race to fill the vacant hole in the canopy. A young Sugar Maple may well be the eventual winner.

Assuming a Beech tree does make it up into the canopy, however, it still isn't home-free. The thin skin of Beech trees is highly susceptible to injury. Through the smallest wound, spores of wood-rotting fungi may enter and sap the vigour of the struggling tree. There is even a parasitic flower called Beechdrops whose roots attach themselves to the roots of Beech trees and siphon off the tree's energy. (These strange little plants — which have no need for chlorophyll the way normal plants do — will appear above ground and briefly flower later in September. They stand about a foot high and are reddish-brown in colour.)

If all this wasn't enough, there is one more obstacle to Beech tree prosperity, and it is a real heart-breaker. When Beeches are between 40 to 60 years old they start to produce, at irregular intervals of a few years, large crops of beechnuts. Beechnuts are big, edible, and nutritious, and, in fact, the scientific name of our Beech tree, *Fagus grandifolia*, comes from a Greek word, phago, meaning "to eat." To the tree, the advantage of a big seed is that the resulting seedling will be big and vigorous and have a good chance of getting its root down through the thick layer of dead leaves on the forest floor. (This is a much bigger problem than you might think, and some other trees — Yellow Birch, for example — whose seeds are very tiny, only get started when the seeds happen to fall on exposed mineral soil or perhaps a rotting log or stump.)

There is, however, a very heavy price that Beech trees must pay for producing big, nutritious seeds. Good food attracts hungry mouths, and big crops of ripening beechnuts are highly popular with Black Bears. The bears do not wait for the nuts to fall, however; they go right up the trees after them (often leaving characteristic claw scars on the trunks). The loss of the beechnuts would be bad enough, but the bears, being so heavy, cannot directly reach the beechnuts out at the ends of the branches. Instead, they install themselves in some convenient crotch in the tree and bend the branches so as to bring the tips within reach. Usually the branches break off, and, if they don't fall to the ground when the bear is finished with them, they end up lodged in the tree crotch where the bear was sitting. Sometimes really big accumulations of branches (locally called "bear's nests") result, and when the leaves are off the trees they are highly conspicuous.

Needless to say, it is a bad day for a Beech tree when a bear pays a visit like this. Not only does the tree lose most of its beechnut production, but it also gets severely

Dinner for the bear, big trouble for the Beech.

damaged in the process, and its eventual death through fungal infection is greatly hastened. It is, in effect, adding injury to insult — neither of which is particularly needed by the tree.

No, we weren't exaggerating when we said a Beech tree's life is beset with serious trials and obstacles. Surely everyone can see that these beautiful old trees have quite enough to put up with in life without being carved up by some callow youth trying to impress his lady friend of the moment.

But, if the ardent swains among you are unmoved by this argument, perhaps we can appeal to your own self-interest. Let's face it, Tom and John, thoughts of Sally and Marcia may be uppermost in your minds right now, but what about next year? Do you really want to leave a permanent record of your previous "commitments?" Take our suggestion and write your messages in the sand at one of our picnic grounds instead. It's a lot faster and easier to erase if you have to. … Or, putting it another way, why fib on a Fagus when you can lie on a beach? ∾

September 1, 1983, Vol. 24, No. 11 (D.S.)

The Rites (and Risks) of Spring

Few things are more marvellous than the return of spring to Algonquin Park. Hillsides take on pink and green pastel hues as the trees flower and the buds swell. Moose come to the edge of the highway to drink their fill of salty water. Spring Beauties carpet the forest floor, and fishermen head out for the year's best Brook and Lake Trout fishing.

There is such a sense of renewal and return of good times, in fact, that sometimes too simple a picture is painted of the natural world and we miss some of its underlying subtlety. For example, one of the most characteristic sounds of spring in Algonquin is the drumming of male Ruffed Grouse, and, on the face of it, hardly anything could better symbolize the confident welcoming back of springtime's warm weather and prosperity. If you carefully edge closer to a drumming male grouse, after all, you will see a handsome bird drawn up to its full height, surveying the scene from its display log. The neck ruffs are erect, the tail is fanned out magnificently, and then, with calm, almost disdainful dignity, he begins to drum. Half-open wings powerfully beat the air — "thump" — and then again, and again and again and again, faster and faster until the wings are lost in an invisible blur and the sounds merge into a frenzied, muffled drum-roll, "thump … thump, thump thump thump thump thump whirrr!"

Anyone watching such a spectacular outpouring might reasonably assume that it is an exuberant, spring-induced call to females and an aggressive warning to other males. There would be little evidence to suggest something else that is also true about drumming grouse — namely, that they are indulging in a very risky business where they quite literally put their lives on the line.

This may be a bit of a shock. Most people can accept that over half of all young grouse chicks fail to make it through their first summer, and everyone knows that winter takes a heavy toll of young and old birds alike. Nevertheless, we all assume that in spring, things must be easy. It would be nice for grouse if they were, but, if you stop to think about it, these birds quite obviously have a serious problem that won't go away just because the weather turns nice. The camouflage, careful movements, and explosive flight of Ruffed Grouse are sure indicators that they must be highly prized by predators. Any grouse that stood out in appearance or behaviour were eliminated long ago, leaving the secretive, hard-to-find strain of birds we know today.

There is just one problem with developing a highly perfected means of staying out of sight. If mating is to occur, the birds must overcome their own excellent camouflage, and that means some sort of deliberate self-advertising display. The more spectacular and far-reaching the display, in fact, the more successful will be the advertisers (males in the case of grouse and most other birds) in attracting potential mates. The catch is, of course, a display that can pull in females from far and wide can also pull in predators.

A male grouse can reduce this risk by choosing a big display log with good visibility and yet with enough surrounding cover to impede attack from the air. Nevertheless, the predators of Ruffed Grouse have had their skills sharpened by hundreds of thousands of years of coping with their prey's defences. A Goshawk may patiently manoeuver itself closer and closer to a drumming grouse. Then, with powerful wing beats, it rapidly accelerates into its final attack, a devastating streak through the trees with incredible, precision rotations of its body and wings to avoid hitting trunks and branches. The strutting grouse sees nothing — or sees everything too late. In the twinkling of an eye, only a couple of feathers drifting down beside the log remain to show that a grouse had ever been there … .

Nearby, a busy bumblebee buzzes from one sunlit Trout Lily flower to the next and a Winter Wren sings from the tangled roots of a wind-thrown spruce.

A few hours later, another male Ruffed Grouse, intimidated until then by the drumming of his rival, works up enough courage to take over the vacant log. Perhaps he will succeed where his predecessor failed. Before fate catches up with him as well, he may father one or two broods and pass on his genes to future generations.

Thump … thump … thump, thump thump thump thump thump whirrr!

Spring is here!✑

April 26, 1984, Vol. 25, No. 1 (D.S.)

Real Magic

It is a common childhood fantasy to imagine oneself endowed with magical powers. Who among us did not dream in our younger days of being able to become invisible or sprout wings so as to escape the clutches of some unsavoury monster? As adults, of course, we realize that such flights of fancy have no reality beyond the fairy tales and dreams that spawn them. Then again, perhaps we should not be so hasty.

happen more or less as you would expect for one of these animals. Eggs are laid in the water and hatch out into small larvae or "tadpoles." Like frog tadpoles, they have tiny mouths with which they eat microscopic plant matter in their shallow pond habitat. These larval newts have an appearance that differs considerably from regular tadpoles, however, because, instead of internal gills, they have exotic-looking, many-branched, external gills sticking out from the back of the head on each side.

The life of a newt tadpole is as brief as it is bizarre. After three months the larva transforms into a completely

A male Red-spotted Newt (left) courts a female by rubbing the side of his head on her nose and fanning her with his extra large tail.

After all, any young pollywog or caterpillar collector can tell you there really are creatures in this world that are capable of astonishing transformations, and who are we adults to say that the birth of a butterfly or a toad is not in the realm of magic? We think the younger set deserves full marks for the wonder they feel before natural phenomena, and we would like to relate the story of another truly "magical" creature they and their perhaps skeptical elders may be unaware of.

We have in mind one of the Park's five salamanders, the Red-spotted Newt, an animal that has a life history of which any sorcerer's apprentice could be proud. To appreciate why the newt is so special, the best course is to follow the successive stages it undergoes through life. Newts are amphibians, and in the beginning things

different land creature called an "eft." Instead of gills it now has lungs, and it moves about on four legs stalking and pouncing on live prey. Along with the radical change in diet, it has a wide mouth suitable for seizing and swallowing its victims.

More striking than the eft's new lifestyle is its colour: a flaming reddish-orange all over except for two rows of round red spots bordered with black down the back. Being such a conspicuous colour does not seem to make much sense for a two-inch-long "defenceless" little salamander, especially for one that often ventures out into the open. As with many other brightly coloured animals, however, the eft is highly poisonous. Snakes have been observed to spit out efts they have attempted to swallow and then frantically wipe their mouths as if to get rid of the taste. Probably one such experience suffices to teach most predators that the bright colour is a warning, not an invitation.*

The strangest thing of all, however, about the eft stage is that it is not the newt's adult form — far from it. After living completely on land for a period lasting one to three years, the eft transforms into yet another creature, as different from the eft as the eft was from the tadpole. The third adult form is a water-dweller, inhabiting quiet ponds and weedy bays of larger lakes. It has a long, finned tail, is about four inches long, and is coloured yellow below and olive green above. The poisonous properties of the eft are retained (adult newts are shunned by leeches, for example), but otherwise there is hardly a hint of any relationship with the eft stage. About the only visible clue is the presence down the back of the same red spots bordered with black that the eft had. Even then, no one would ever find serious fault with you if you presumed the eft and the adult were two separate species.

Adult newts have to come to the surface to breathe, and in the fall they actually leave the water to hibernate on land. Otherwise, they are completely aquatic. We suspect that newts are locally common in suitable habitat here in Algonquin, although it's hard to be sure because they are so well camouflaged in the thickly vegetated waters they prefer and they are often most active at night.

The only practical way to observe them is in an aquarium, and when we are lucky enough to capture some they have made highly interesting displays at the Park Museum. They hunt small aquatic animals by sight and swim after them with powerful strokes of the tail.

---

* These creatures are obviously better eft alone.

A Mite Peculiar

Humans have a common tendency to dismiss "low" forms of life as uninteresting. The truth is, however, that many small and supposedly primitive creatures have lives every bit as fascinating as the bigger, more familiar animals that normally get all our attention. We don't suppose, for example, that you could come up with a better example of apparent lowliness than the tiny mites that parasitize the ears of the common Armyworm Moths here in Algonquin. Mites are small, segmented creatures related to insects and, in this case, make a living by forcing their way into the moths' ears and sucking their blood.

It is possible that moth ear mites would be excellent candidates for dead last in any contest for a human's affection, but in the categories of fascinating and sophisticated behaviour, these creatures are real

The male's tail, incidentally, has a much deeper fin than the female's, apparently because of the special role it plays in courtship. The male grasps the female's neck with his hind legs, rubs her nose with the side of his face, and fans her with that special tail. This serves to transport chemicals secreted by glands at the base of his tail to the nostrils of the female. She will be won over by his perfume's strength, so the more efficient his tail, the more successful he is likely to be.

Assuming she does accept him, the male will deposit a package of sperm nearby on the bottom of the pond and the female will pick it up into her body, thus assuring fertilization. Soon she will attach up to 400 eggs here and there on pond vegetation, and, a week or two after that, the next batch of newt larvae will emerge and start the cycle all over again.

It is interesting to reflect that even the "simplest" frog or salamander achieves something astounding by changing almost overnight from an aquatic creature to a completely different inhabitant of the land above. But the Red-spotted Newt goes far beyond this! It transforms itself from a water creature to a land creature and then returns to the water as yet another, totally new incarnation. Each of the stages is barely or not at all recognizable as having any connection with the others, and each has its own almost supernatural properties.

Perhaps we should not be so quick to dismiss childhood dreams and fairy tales when, with our own eyes, we can see a tadpole change into a miniature red dragon and then into a dancing underwater suitor who showers his mate with aqueous perfume. It may be magic, but it's also real.☞

The Raven's competitor in New York will notice that, in this issue, we have printed all the newts that's fit to print.

June 28, 1984, Vol. 25, No. 2 (D.S.)

contenders. The observation was made a few decades ago that either the right or the left ear of an Armyworm Moth may be infested — even overflowing — with ear mites, but it is always just one ear, never both. The ears of an Armyworm Moth are located on its back, very close to each other on either side of the midline, just ahead of the abdomen. It is impossible to believe that all the mites on a moth are somehow forced into going into one ear only by the position of the ears or by some phenomenon of blind chance. For some reason the mites all "deliberately" choose the same ear even at the expense of overcrowding and heightened competition. The question is why?

To answer this problem we have to know what a moth uses its ears for in the first place. Regular readers of *The Raven* will know that moths are a favourite food of bats and that they can be located, even in total darkness, by the bats' high-pitched ultrasonic calls. The bats listen for the echoes of these sounds and are able to translate them into useful information about the nature and exact whereabouts of nearby objects — including food items. Armyworm and some other moths are not completely defenceless, however, because their ears are tuned in to the frequencies used by bats, and they can hear them coming in time to drop to the ground or take other evasive action.

No one seriously imagines that the ear mites have consciously realized the folly of deafening both ears of their host and have therefore voluntarily restricted their activities to just one ear. Everything we know about mites suggests they are little automatons, acting out their lives according to unalterable programs "wired into" their unthinking brains. So, how then, did moth ear mites acquire their startlingly appropriate behaviour patterns? It seems most likely that ear mites did not originally restrict themselves to just one ear, and they no doubt paid a high price as they unwittingly made their hosts into highly vulnerable targets for foraging bats.

Then, somewhere way back when, a mite suffered a mutation that made it and its descendants refrain from entering a moth ear that wasn't already parasitized. The new strain of mites would have had an enormous advantage because they would be unconsciously preserving the ability of their hosts to hear and avoid bats. This, of course, amounts to self-preservation of the mites.

Today, thousands of years later, we see only the "new" strain of one-ear-only ear mites. Just as big grains of sand are held back by a sieve, so too have the old style of nondiscriminating ear mites been screened out by the relentless pressure from bats.

This still doesn't explain the mechanism by which mites actually end up in one ear only. How do such tiny, blind specks avoid the fatal mistake of entering an unoccupied ear when the moth's other ear has already been colonized? To answer this question we have to follow a mite as it leaves one moth and infects another. Young female mites hatched in a moth ear are impregnated by waiting males even before they have struggled free of their larval skin, and soon thereafter they make their way to the moth's proboscis. From there they hop onto a flower visited by the feeding moth and then later transfer to a different moth visiting the same flower. Once on her new host, the female mite begins to push her way through the forest of hairs covering the moth's body until she reaches the exact midpoint between the moth's left and right ears.

After pausing for a few minutes, she goes to one of the ears but soon returns to the midpoint. Only after travelling back and forth between the ear and the midpoint some eight or 10 times in the next hour, does the colonizing mite settle for good in the chosen ear.

Subsequent mites arriving on the same moth may follow different routes to the midpoint but they always get there one way or another. They will even go right past an ear to reach the midpoint and then unhesitatingly follow the path taken by the first mite and enter the occupied ear. The original mite, in going back and forth over the same route, has probably laid down some sort of chemical trail for other mites to follow, thereby assuring that only one ear will be colonized.

The later arrivals are at first resisted by the first colonists — which makes it even more astounding that the second, uninfected ear, just a short distance away, is never colonized. It would be so much easier to go to the unoccupied ear — except, of course, that this would deafen the moth and almost guarantee that a bat would eat the moth and the mites along with it.

Moth ear mites are animals none of us will ever see unless we make a very special effort to do so. But, just because they are almost invisible to our usually uncomprehending senses, it does not automatically follow that these tiny creatures are therefore insignificant or unworthy of our attention. The fact that their sophisticated behaviour is so finely adjusted to take advantage of their host but, at the same time, to preserve it from destruction, is nothing short of astounding. These supposedly lowly animals are more than a mite peculiar; they are mity amazing.⌁

July 5, 1984, Vol. 25, No. 3 (D.S.)

Doing Our Part

This is one of several articles on Algonquin's Peregrine Falcon reintroduction program, which ran from 1977 to 1986. In all, 64 young falcons were raised to independence. None of the Algonquin birds is known to have returned to the Park, or elsewhere, as a breeding bird, but overall the continent-wide program has been a success. Peregrines now breed at numerous locations in eastern North America and may someday re-establish themselves in Algonquin.

Ten days ago, gazing up at the huge granite cliff east of Whitefish Lake, we saw something very special. Four young Peregrine Falcons stood exercising their wings on a wooden platform beside a specially constructed "hack box" fastened to the side of the cliff.

Old Algonquin hands can probably guess how the birds came to be there. They had actually spent the previous two weeks inside the box being fed every day through a plastic pipe leading down to the box from the top of the cliff. During that time they had transformed from the downy Alberta-hatched babies we had picked up at the Toronto International Airport back in June to well-feathered young falcons that were now ready to take a major step towards eventual independence. At dawn of the sixteenth day the hack box door was slowly raised, until nothing more remained between the four birds and the wild Algonquin landscape stretching out to the horizon before them.

Briefly, that is how the falcons came to be standing on the Whitefish cliff that day, but of course there is much more to the story than that. Why would we go to so much trouble for just four birds, and what is so special about the Peregrine Falcon anyway?

Very simply, the Peregrine is one of the world's most magnificent birds. Only now, however, is it beginning to recover from a tragedy that all but destroyed it here in North America and in Europe as well.

Although it weighs less than one kilogram and is only slightly larger than a Crow, the Peregrine can reach over 200 kilometres an hour in its awesomely devastating attacks on other birds from high in the sky. It was this unparalleled mastery of the air that made the Peregrine so highly prized by royal falconers. Fearing nothing, it reigned supreme as one of nature's most successful predators, and it nested on suitable cliffs virtually worldwide.

Then in the 1950s something went terribly wrong. In Europe and then in North America, adult falcons began laying thin-shelled eggs that cracked under the weight of the incubating birds or otherwise failed to hatch. With no

Young Peregrine Falcons at their cliffside hack box.

young birds to replace the old birds when they died, the Peregrine began to disappear from cliff after cliff. Research soon showed that the trouble was caused by DDT picked up in the falcon's diet of smaller birds. Unfortunately, DDT is very long-lasting poison, and, when eaten by an animal, it tends to stay in that animal's body for good. What was especially disastrous in the

Peregrine's case was that, with each prey item it consumed, the Peregrine got, and therefore kept, the entire load of DDT the prey had taken a whole lifetime to accumulate. Thus, in very little time, the level of DDT (or its breakdown products) in a falcon's body could build up to the 10 to 20 parts per million that is sufficient to interfere with normal egg shell production.

Even more frightening was the realization that Peregrines couldn't find safety in parks and other wilderness areas. In Algonquin, for example, it did not matter that very little DDT was ever used. Not only did the falcons have to leave the Park every winter for areas where DDT was used extensively, but also, even back in the Park during summer, falcons were unknowingly eating birds that also had picked up DDT outside Algonquin during the winter. As large and as wild as it is, the Park offered no refuge at all for the falcons. In fact, the last known Peregrine nesting in Algonquin was in 1962 — about the same time as the last nestings everywhere else in eastern North America.

The prospects of ever again seeing eastern Peregrines were very remote — and still would be — except for two things. First was that Cornell University in the United States and the Canadian Wildlife Service in this country obtained young birds of our race of Peregrines from its last remaining population in the Rockies in the early 1970s and undertook to keep the race alive by raising and breeding the young birds in captivity. Second was the drastic curtailment of DDT in 1969 and the consequent, though still slow, decline of DDT levels in many of the prey species traditionally taken by Peregrines.

Thus, re-introduction of the Peregrine to its former range became conceivable, and several agencies all over Canada and the United States pitched in. The idea was to take young falcons hatched in captivity, raise them at suitable places in the wild, and hope that they would learn to hunt, go off into the world as wild birds, and eventually pair up and nest. After that, the Peregrines would be raising young on their own, and there would be no further need for human involvement.

Because it was widely believed at the time that any young falcons that survived to breed would almost certainly make the attempt at the very same places where they had been raised, the Ontario Ministry of Natural Resources chose, for its contribution to the project, two traditional Peregrine nesting cliffs here in Algonquin. It was expensive because all supplies had to be flown in, but we wanted to give the young birds every possible advantage by encouraging attachment to sites we knew wild Peregrines had successfully used in the past. That was how the Algonquin Peregrine project began, and from 1977 through 1982, our teams of dedicated falcon foster parents raised a total of 52 young Peregrines to the

point, in August, where they could go off on their own, able to fend for themselves and begin their fall migration.

Although we knew, as with many birds, that only 20 per cent of young falcons normally reach one year of age, we still had high hopes that the survivors among our birds would return to their release sites and set up housekeeping.

That this has not yet happened is certainly a disappointment but not the calamity you might imagine. It has turned out we were quite wrong about how faithful young falcons are to the cliffs on which they are raised. Elsewhere, young birds have been observed to return to where they were raised and then move on after a few hours or days. This could easily have been happening here in Algonquin as well, but without the complete springtime surveillance that exists at some other sites, we would have to have been extraordinarily lucky to see even one brief reappearance by any of our birds.

Most important of all, there have now been well over two dozen successful nestings in Canada and the United States by falcons released into the wild by the same technique used here in Algonquin. Often these nestings have occurred far from where the birds were raised. A pair that nested on an Edmonton office building, for example, included a bird that had been raised in the Rocky Mountains. The female of another pair that nested in 1983 in Arnprior, east of Algonquin, had been released in Hull, Quebec.

The strong possibility exists, therefore, that some of our Algonquin birds really have survived but are breeding in places where they have escaped detection. By the same token, because we now know that success does not depend on using traditional Peregrine nesting cliffs, we don't have to continue with our original two cliffs in the Park interior. Budget restrictions had, in fact, forced us to abandon our Peregrine work in 1983, but this year, with the probability that an inexpensive site close to Highway 60 would work just as well, we are back in business again — this time at the cliff overlooking Whitefish.

We don't know, of course, how successful this year's foursome will be, but we have every reason to believe that sooner or later some of our birds will become, here or elsewhere, part of a fully restored Peregrine population in North America.

Humans came perilously close to destroying one of this continent's most priceless wildlife assets. Now, in an effort involving many governments, universities, and individuals across North America, that asset, the magnificent Peregrine Falcon, is being brought back to its rightful place. We are happy to once again be doing our part. ∞

July 26, 1984, Vol. 25, No. 6 (D.S.)

Subtle Tree Subtlety

Leaves being attacked by caterpillars release volatile chemicals that trigger the production of defensive chemicals in neighbouring trees.

enemies will produce hundreds of new generations in the same period and have a correspondingly good chance of (inadvertently) coming up with a new strain that can counter the tree's defences. The fact remains, however, that trees are usually one step ahead of their leaf-eaters, and so there must be another factor that enters into play. Recent research has shown that trees do not merely try to hide behind a chemical wall but, in fact, use their defences in sophisticated ways so as to keep their insect attackers "off balance."

For one thing, not every leaf on the same tree has the same chemical content. The leaves of our familiar Sugar Maple, for example, contain large amounts of tannins (the chemicals that give tea its astringent taste), but adjacent leaves may differ in their tannin content by up to 200 or 300 per cent. The consequence of this variablitiy is that a leaf-eating caterpillar is forced to travel widely, tasting many leaves along the way, before it finds one or two that are relatively palatable. In these travels the caterpillar will necessarily spend significant time in exposed places (on stems, for example) and run a higher risk of being spotted and eaten by a bird than if it were able to stay on leaves (where most caterpillars are almost invisible). In addition, the travelling caterpillar is forced to expend time and energy that otherwise could have gone into eating and growing. This may mean that the caterpillar stage will have to be prolonged, and this, also, will increase the chances of being eaten by a bird or attacked by a parasite or a disease. Another possibility is that, even if the caterpillar does change into a pupa at the regular time, it will be in poor condition and give rise to a smaller adult that will lay fewer eggs.

A second general way that trees make life difficult for leaf-eating insects is by changing the array of poisons present in the leaves as the season progresses. Most trees, in fact, have a definite succession of insect enemies chewing on them, which implies that each insect species can tolerate only one narrow range of the changing leaf quality. Under these circumstances it is very difficult for any insect to build up to epidemic proportions.

There is one time that trees leave their leaves relatively unprotected — in the spring at and immediately following leaf-out. Many insects have eggs that are timed to hatch out and cash in on the first flush of tender, nutritious, and, for once, tasty leaves. Even then, however, success is not guaranteed. Trees can afford to let their chemical guard down in early spring because late frosts will often kill off the newly emerged caterpillars "for free."

This is not to say that a tree attacked by caterpillars must rely on the weather or its pre-programmed changes of leaf chemicals for salvation. In fact, when leaves on a

Compared to animals, plants seem to be very simple and unsophisticated. They are quite unconscious, they can't move, they have no muscles or nervous system, and they seem totally at the mercy of anything that attacks them.

Still, if you stop and think about it, plants do remarkably well. Take trees, for example. Although whole forests are devastated by the Spruce Budworm and other leaf-eaters from time to time, such events are by and large much rarer than you would expect. And, in normal years, between the unusual major outbreaks of leaf-eating insects, only about seven per cent of a forest's leaf surface is consumed. This low attack rate is rather curious in view of the tremendous reproductive rates and variety of insects on the one hand and the apparent helplessness of trees on the other. Obviously, there must be something that operates to keep leaf-eating insects in check, but what could that something be?

One particularly good way to approach the problem is to try tasting a few tree leaves yourself. The chances are you will find them uninspiring or downright disagreeable. If this suggests to you that leaves produce noxious chemicals that might help to dissuade would-be leaf-eaters, you will have come very close to the answer. As a matter of fact, leaves are the origin of many quite powerful insecticides, poisons, and drugs (we said taste those leaves, by the way — not eat!). Nevertheless, this doesn't explain everything. Insects are famous for their ability to evolve immunities against poisons and should be able, given enough time, to handle any new chemical insecticide produced by trees. Insects have the advantage, in fact, because they have a very rapid turnover of individuals — as contrasted with a tree that may live for centuries. During its long lifetime the tree must make do with the abilities it was "born" with, whereas its insect tree are damaged, nearby leaves have the ability to greatly increase their content of insect repellents. The tannin content of Sugar Maple leaves may go up by 50 per cent in three days, and poplars under attack can double the content of phenols in still undamaged leaves in even less time. The heightened chemical defences may last for two or three years, helping to slow down and sicken the attacking caterpillars.

Most amazing of all, it is not just leaves on attacked trees that step up their poison content, but also leaves on neighbouring trees not yet reached by the caterpillars. Laboratory experiments suggest that when a leaf is damaged, it releases a volatile chemical that spreads through the air to nearby leaves, stimulating them into increased production of defensive chemicals. It is almost as if stricken leaves warn their neighbours of approaching trouble.

If the remarkable abilities of trees to detect, deter, and confound their insect enemies surprise you, you may still be wondering why trees really need to be so sophisticated. If you are a tree, why not just pack your leaves with poison and leave it at that? In fact, there really are good reasons for the flexible defence posture of trees. In addition to making it difficult for insects to evolve countermeasures, the variable chemistry of tree foliage makes good "economic" sense. Poison molecules are made from sugar and other chemicals that would otherwise be used for the tree's growth and reproduction. In other words, poison manufacture is achieved only at the expense of other important tree activities and should not be entered into lightly. The best compromise, therefore, is to divert as little energy as possible into chemical defences unless a real attack is imminent. Under these circumstances, of course, it is best to drop everything else and "man the chemical barricades" against the advancing hordes — which is exactly what trees really do.

Trees may seem simple and unsophisticated at first glance, but appearances can be deceiving. The truth, as one observer noted, is that they have a lot of very subtle tricks up their leaves.⤸

August 2, 1984 ,Vol. 25, No. 7 (D.S.)

What's in a Name?

We think that just about everybody, at one time or another, has spent an hour or two gazing at a globe or map, dreaming of faraway places and savouring their exotic names. With over 1,500 named lakes and rivers, the map of Algonquin is fine material for such rainy day musing. A great many of the Park's features — its human personalities, trees, and wildlife — have given their names to Algonquin lakes, which is why the names alone capture something of the flavour and atmosphere of our wild landscape and its history. Of course, it always helps if you know the stories behind the names. While space does not permit us to delve deeply into the subject, *The Raven* is pleased to provide the following tidbits for our fellow Algonquin map-gazers.

Spreading the map out on a picnic table or on the living room floor back home, we naturally first notice the larger lakes and rivers. Many of these have names of Indian or French origin that go back a long time. The biggest lake in the park, Opeongo, was referred to as early as 1837 as "Abeunga," an Algonquian word meaning "place where there are sand beaches." The name "Petawawa" is also of Indian origin and means "a noise is heard far away" — probably a reference to the roaring stretches of white water on the Petawawa River.

The Bonnechère River (pronounced "bunshare") has been called that way since away back in the early 1700s, but no one knows today who gave it such a pretty name. We can only speculate that some early fur traders or missionaries stuffed themselves with wild game on the river bank because in French "faire bonne chère" roughly means to have a first-rate meal. As for the old woman referred to in the name "Lake Lavieille," this was how the old voyageurs referred to the wind — the fickle wind that, on a whim, could speed them on their way or bring them to a standstill.

Returning to the subject of Indian names, we find that not many remain today. No doubt, early loggers and surveyors found many of the old names too much to cope with, or they may simply not have had the opportunity to find out what the old names were. This is a pity because many of the Indian names are a fascinating mix of real and magical forest beings. For example, between the South River and Butt Lake on the west side of the Park we have Mujekiwis, ruler of the winds of heaven; Kwonishi, the dragonfly; Chibiabos, the musician; Shawshaw, the swallow; Mama, the woodpecker; Papukiwis, the storm fool; Pezheki, the bison; Pugawagun, the war club; and Mubwayaka, the sound of waves on the shore. Of supreme importance in the life of the Indians was Manitou, the Beneficent Spirit, so it is only natural that his name was given to one of the largest lakes in Algonquin (in the Park's northwest corner).

Be that as it may, for many years Manitou Lake appeared on Park maps as Wilkes Lake. This name was never accepted by local residents, however, and with all due respect to the late Mr. Wilkes (a law partner of a long dead premier of Ontario), we always thought Manitou had a lot more to do with Algonquin Park than Mr. Wilkes did. That is why we reinstated Manitou 10 years ago when the first edition of the current canoe route map was printed.

We made many changes on that occasion, and our purpose (apart from getting into Manitou's good books, of course) was to clear up previously existing confusion. For

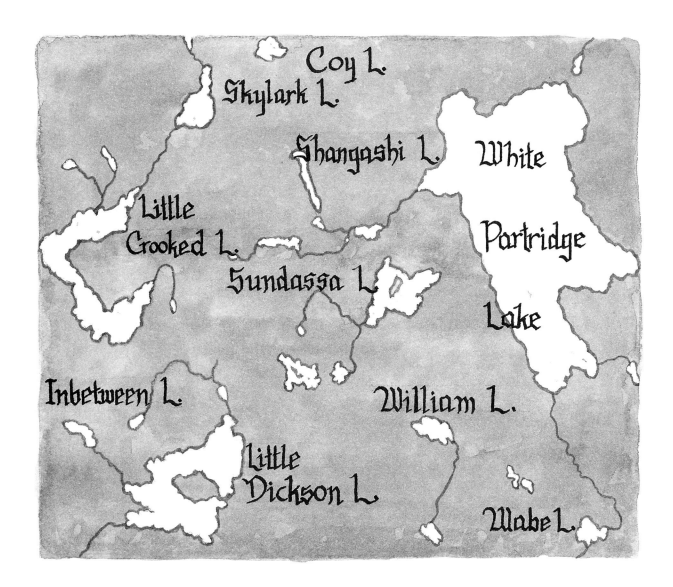

example, there were no fewer than 13 pairs of lakes in the Park with the same name. There were two Raven Lakes, two Sylvia Lakes, two Boot Lakes, and even two Otterpaw Lakes. Working with the Ontario Geographic Names Board, the agency of the Ministry of Natural Resources that keeps order in the province's bewildering maze of place names, we cleared up this problem by adding another word to one of the names. For example, we now have one Raven Lake and one North Raven Lake.

Another somewhat different sort of confusion we wanted to eliminate 10 years ago was that resulting from the presence of dozens and dozens of unnamed lakes. All told, we named 119 lakes and ponds on the 1974 map for the first time ever. Some names had been in local use for many years, but most were entirely new. We attempted to honour Park explorers, early rangers, members of The Group of Seven artists, and men who

were instrumental in the creation of the Park (Hawkins, Balfour, Lawren Harris, and Kirkwood, to name a few). We also used trees, flowers, and birds that are typical of the Park (for example, Ironwood, Lady-slipper, and White-throat Lakes).

There are many more of these relatively new names, but, frankly, we can't help our fellow map-gazers with the old names that we find most fascinating. We would love to know, for example, if Carcajou Lake got its (French) name because someone saw a wolverine there — an animal that certainly does not occur in Algonquin. And wouldn't it be interesting to know the story behind Lost Coin Lake, or what stupidity was committed on Folly Creek, or if Shall and Shallnot Lakes have anything to do with the ponds named He and She.◌

August 9, 1984, Vol. 25, No. 8 (D.S.)

The Case of the Sneaky Mushroom

The Raven takes special pleasure in reporting on this unexpected new finding about mushroom ecology because the discovery was made by Greg Thorn, a summer naturalist at the Park Museum from 1975 to 1980. It was here in Algonquin, as a matter of fact, that Greg developed his interest in mushrooms, an interest that quickly led to an unrivalled knowledge of Park fungi, the publication of the Algonquin mushroom checklist in 1981, and his current work on a Master's thesis under Dr. George Barron at the University of Guelph. Many readers will remember the excellent mushroom hikes and talks given by Greg during his Algonquin years, and join with us in congratulating him on his important contribution to biology, as well as wishing him every success in the future.

Many visitors to the Park enjoy wild mushrooms as food. The flavours can be subtle and excellent and, provided the collector can positively identify any species eaten, collecting wild mushrooms is an activity we wholeheartedly encourage.

Personally, we have been keen on wild fungi ever since friends served us steak with pearly white Oyster Mushrooms over 20 years ago. Although we have learned to identify and prepare many other kinds since then, the memory of that first meal remains vivid, and the Oyster Mushroom continues to be a favourite. In some ways, it can be viewed as the model edible wild mushroom — good tasting, easy to identify, and abundant.

Yet, as far as the basic biology of the Oyster (and others) Mushroom is concerned, we naively thought all those years we had a pretty good picture of how things worked. The structure we ate was just the reproductive part or "fruit" of the mushroom plant — in the same sense that a blueberry is the reproductive part of a blueberry plant. The only difference, really, was that you can easily see the non-berry part of a blueberry plant whereas, with a mushroom, the non-reproductive part is much less visible. For one thing, it consists of very tiny thread-like structures called hyphae (singular hypha). Second, the hyphae are out of sight in dead leaves on the forest floor or inside dead wood.

Oyster Mushrooms growing on dead wood are a familiar sight, but the parts we see serve only to produce millions of spores that assure reproduction. The really important part of the mushroom is invisible, consisting of microscopic, thread-like structures growing through and digesting the wood itself. In the case of the Oyster Mushroom, as shown here, these threads are capable of immobilizing and digesting tiny nematode worms that also live in the wood.

The visible, reproductive part of a mushroom doesn't contain seeds the way a blueberry does. Instead, it produces millions of microscopic spores, each capable of starting a new mushroom plant. The spores* float through the air and, although chances are slight, some of them happen to land on surfaces suitable for the particular species of mushroom in question. In the case of an Oyster Mushroom spore, this is the exposed, dead wood of a hardwood tree, such as a Sugar Maple.

The spore gives rise to a hypha that grows into the wood, branching again and again until it forms an enormously complicated network of threads that digest the wood and break it down — rot it, in other words — into simpler chemicals. When conditions are warm and moist enough and if the thread network is healthy enough, some of the threads will come together and produce one or more of the visible, spore-producing structures we call mushrooms.

These were the basics — or so we thought — of an Oyster Mushroom's life, and it all seemed quite simple. With the benefit of hindsight we might have suspected that reality would be a bit more complicated.

At first glance, the hyphae of an Oyster Mushroom would seem to be in an especially favourable spot. A lot of energy is locked up in the cellulose (food) surrounding an Oyster Mushroom growing inside a dead tree. To actually use this food, however, the mushroom must break the cellulose down, and this requires the action of enzymes. Enzymes are proteins, and all proteins contain nitrogen. The problem for an Oyster Mushroom is that dead wood contains very little of this vital commodity. And, unless the Oyster Mushroom can get past this problem, it will be unable to manufacture the enzymes and other proteins it needs to feast on the bountiful supply of cellulose all around it.

To make matters worse, the Oyster Mushroom has to compete with bacteria, some of which can take nitrogen right out of the air and make their needed proteins that way. The Oyster Mushroom, unable to perform this difficult chemical trick, might seem to be left at the starting gate in the race to exploit the rich bounty (in other words, the dead wood) left when an old tree dies.

Old Algonquin hands will recognize that this situation is quite similar to that found in bogs — which are also notoriously poor in nitrogen. The fact that several bog plants (Sundews and Pitcher-plants, for example) get

around the problem by trapping protein- (nitrogen)-rich insects suggests a possible solution for the Oyster Mushroom as well.

To be sure, insects are far too big and powerful to be captured by mushroom hyphae, but other, more suitably sized nitrogen sources are available. The woody environment of the Oyster Mushroom is shared by tiny worms (less than one millimetre long) called nematodes. They make a living by preying on the bacteria that digest the same wood attacked by the Oyster Mushroom. Because they have fed on the nitrogen-rich bacteria, the nematodes are themselves a rich source of nitrogen.

In hindsight it makes excellent sense that mushrooms would be able to tap this source of nitrogen but, until last year, no one realized that they actually do. The Oyster Mushroom and 10 other species of wood-rotting fungi have now been shown to be carnivorous nematode-eaters and thus to have solved their nitrogen-deficiency problem. Whenever a nematode approaches an Oyster Mushroom hypha too closely, it is stunned by a chemical given off by the mushroom. Over the next hour new threads from the mushroom converge on the immobilized (but still living) nematode, enter its mouth, grow through its body, and digest it from the inside out. Within 24 hours the drama is over, and the Oyster Mushroom is making new proteins of its own from those taken from the nematode.

Although it may seem gruesome to us, the fact that the nematode is only paralyzed — rather than being killed outright — before the Oyster Mushroom begins to feed on it, is actually a very subtle feature. If it were dead, the nematode would be quickly attacked and at least partly consumed by bacteria before the mushroom threads could make physical contact with the victim. By keeping the nematode immobile but alive, the Oyster Mushrooom can avoid the bacteria problem and keep all the nematode's precious nitrogen for itself.

At the start of this article, we confessed to having a naive belief in the essential vegetarian simplicity of mushrooms. For years, in fact, we have enjoyed delicious snacks of fried-up Oyster Mushrooms without suspecting that what we were doing to them they had already done to tiny animals inside old tree trunks. The amazing discovery that the Oyster Mushroom and its relatives are "meat-eaters" brings up once again the thought expressed first and best by Shakespeare: "There are more things on heaven and earth than are dreamed of in your philosophy." ... Of course, for any nematodes reading this, the message is somewhat less elegant: "If you don't want to be paralyzed and devoured alive, beware of the fungi among ye!" ⸙

August 30, 1984, Vol. 25, No. 11 (D.S.)

---

* *Since you began reading this article, you have breathed in hundreds — if not thousands — of mushroom spores. Most got breathed right back out again, but many landed on the internal surfaces of your lungs and windpipe. Tiny, hair-like projections lining those surfaces are now slowly beating so as to move the spore-laden mucous out of your lungs and up to your throat, where it can then be swallowed.*

Gawunk, Gawunk!

Summer is ending in Algonquin. The days are getting shorter, the nights are nippier, and most of our campgrounds are closed for another year. Many of our 1984 visitors have returned to work or school, and thoughts of the Park will be fading into the background.

This is all perfectly normal, of course, but, just the same, we think it's a little unfortunate. The fact is Algonquin will be offering its two greatest spectacles of the year in the next few weeks, and, of the two, only one (the fall colours) will be seen by a relative handful of late-season visitors. The other spectacle, sad to say, is not even known about, let alone observed, by the vast majority of people passing through the Park — even though it coincides with the peak of the colours and in spite of the fact that Algonquin is one of the very best places in North America to see it.

Not to prolong the mystery, the spectacle we are referring to is the "rut," or mating season, of the moose. It is no secret, of course, that moose have become abundant in Algonquin Park over the last few years, and thousands of people have thrilled to the sight of a huge bull moose feeding out in some shallow lake in late spring or early summer (the time when moose are easiest to see). But, however impressive such a sight may be, it barely hints at the spectacle the same bull will provide in late September at the peak of the rut.

Imagine yourself out at dawn on a frosty morning later this month, looking out over a boggy meadow. You can't see her, but you know there is a cow moose on one of the surrounding hills because, every so often, you hear her nasal, moaning bawl, at times remarkably like that of a domestic cow. The minutes pass, you drink coffee, and you run on the spot to keep warm. Then, suddenly, from the woods behind you comes a blood-chilling roar followed by the unmistakable clatter of antlers being violently thrashed against small trees. Soon you become aware of a strange, deeply resonant "hiccough" coming at intervals of 10 seconds or so — "gawunk … gawunk … gawunk." The noise gets louder and louder until, at last, the bull emerges from the trees at the edge of the meadow. His body is surprisingly difficult to pick out in the gray light of dawn, but the great orange-tan antlers (from which the nourishing layer of skin has been shed only a week before) almost gleam. Slowly and deliberately, the bull walks along the edge of the trees "gawunking" and licking his lips with his big, pink tongue.

He pauses to sniff the ground and then starts to dig, first with one front hoof and then the other. Clots of earth fly out behind until the "rut pit" (a shallow hole about one metre in diameter) is finished. The bull urinates in the pit and then gets down to wallow in the reeking puddle, waving his head and antlers about — apparently to pick up as much "perfume" as possible and to render himself even more sexually attractive.

Across the bog another "gawunking" bull appears, but the first animal merely turns and slowly lowers his head. The newcomer watches this presentation of antlers, recognizes the superiority of the first bull, and signals its submission by whining and averting its gaze. The first animal continues majestically on its way, "gawunking" and licking his lips, towards the waiting cow … .

Impressive as such vocalizations and rituals may be, a brief observation such as this one barely begins to tell the story of what is really happening during the rut. If we could follow a prime bull throughout these crucial two or three weeks, we would be astounded by the prodigious expenditure of energy such an animal makes. Because the cows remain in relatively small "patrol areas," 500 to 1,000 metres in diameter, the bulls do the travelling. In fact, each bull is in a race with other bulls to find as many receptive cows as possible in the short time available. If a bull is going to be a winner in this race and leave more descendants than his competitors, he can hardly afford to spend time on anything else. Some studies have indeed shown that a bull in the rut may spend as little as two per cent of his time eating, he may burn off as much as 150 pounds (12 per cent) of his weight, and he may wear off over half an inch from his front hooves during his travels.

Of course, the biggest of all energy drains will occur if he gets into a real altercation with another bull. This is actually a rather rare occurrence because, except for young bulls, most moose apparently have a realistic appreciation of their own abilities. As in the incident described earlier, two bulls confronting each other usually size each other up and the issue is quickly resolved without an actual fight. Only if the two bulls are very evenly matched do things get serious. Even then, the term "fight" is misleading because there is no attempt to injure or kill. Instead, each bull carefully lowers his antlers and engages them with those of his opponent. Then the heaving and shoving starts, with each bull straining his utmost to push the other backwards and force it to yield. Although such contests are conducted according to strict, surprisingly "sportsmanlike" rules,

they can go on for hours and utterly exhaust both participants.*

It is perhaps worthwhile to reflect on why such fantastic amounts of energy are expended by bull moose. There are, after all, not only the activities of the rut, but also, in the preceding summer, each bull grows a new, enormous set of antlers. These may weigh up to 60 pounds, but they have only one, very specialized use — to intimidate or vanquish rival bulls during the rut. You might imagine that a "no-frills" bull that didn't waste so much energy growing antlers would be healthier and live longer than our current model. As a matter of fact, it probably would — but it would also fail to leave any (antlerless) descendants. Even an unhealthy moose with antlers could always push an antlerless rival out of the way and proceed to the waiting cow. That is why the theoretical superiority of a "sensible" moose without antlers would be meaningless. The fact is that, no matter how costly antlers may be, it is vital for a bull moose to have them.

But far be it for us to complain about the strange tangents taken by evolution. On the contrary, we are extremely grateful. After all, Algonquin Park offers no finer spectacle than a huge bull moose, his polished antlers gleaming in the gray light of a September dawn, purposefully striding on to his next conquest. Gawunk, gawunk!↝

September 6, 1984 , Vol. 25, No. 12 (D.S.)

---

* Such struggles are also awesomely spectacular to a human observer. We remember one sparring match between two big bulls beside the highway at Brewer Lake early one December. This is long after the rut when anything serious would be at stake, and, in fact, they would have lost their antlers shortly afterwards. But even if it was a minor joust, the two great animals went at each other before our eyes, and the Brewer Lake basin literally echoed with the smashing, crashing, and clattering of their antlers for a quarter of an hour. Then, suddenly, the contest ended, and the two bulls resumed browsing side by side as if nothing had happened.

Those Magnificent Moose and Their Flying Machines

This is our first *Raven* for 1985, but we feel safe in betting that you have already read or heard about at least one Algonquin news item elsewhere this year. Back in January the press and all the Canadian and United States television networks carried prominent, coast-to-coast coverage of the spectacular transfer of moose from the Park to the State of Michigan. Interest in the project was so high that for days on end two Park employees did nothing but answer enquiries and do interviews over the phone. And, even though it was the dead of winter, we actually had to erect barricades to keep the public from crowding in too close on the operation down at our Mew Lake base camp.

Without a doubt, the moose transfer was the biggest and most important event involving Algonquin wildlife in years. Although the news is now several months old, we still think it worthwhile to devote a whole issue to the subject. Many readers may have caught only fleeting coverage earlier on, and, besides, we now have the opportunity to bring everybody up to date on how our moose are doing in their new home.

Before doing that, however, we need to explain why the project was undertaken in the first place. To understand that, you have to know how remarkably similar the release site of the transferred moose, in the Upper Peninsula of Michigan, is to Algonquin Park. Not only do the Upper Peninsula's forests look like ours, but also many details of their history closely parallel events that took place here. Both areas were originally populated by moose, but that changed in the late 1800s and early years of this century when logging and severe forest fires destroyed many of the original forests. In both areas these changes favoured the temporary prosperity of White-tailed Deer, a southern animal not really at home in the "north woods" but certainly capable of capitalizing on the second growth that followed the destruction of the first forests. The problem, as far as moose were concerned, is that deer carry a parasitic brainworm which, although apparently harmless to deer, is fatal to moose. When deer are numerous, any local moose almost inevitably contract the parasite and die. Thus, although no one knew why at the time,* the moose populations of the Upper Peninsula and of the Park dwindled as deer numbers increased. By the early 1900s, moose had disappeared altogether in the Upper Peninsula, and here in Algonquin they were certainly extremely scarce, if not altogether absent. Not very far

---

* The brainworm and its effects on moose were discovered here in Algonquin back in the 1960s.

north of Algonquin, however, was good moose country that the deer had never invaded in any great numbers. This meant a source of moose close at hand to repopulate the Park or augment any that were left if conditions ever changed. And, as every regular visitor to Algonquin knows, conditions have changed dramatically. The fires that created good deer habitat are a thing of the past, the numbers of deer have gone down, the risk of a moose being infected with brainworm has correspondingly fallen, and now, in the last 10 years, moose numbers have "exploded." We believe the Park population numbers about 4,000, and it may still be growing.

The same repossession by moose almost certainly would have occurred in the Upper Peninsula as well, except that Lake Superior, lying between it and moose country to the north, barred the way. It is true that some moose cross over at Sault Ste. Marie at the east end of the Peninsula, but they are few in number. In any case, they have a long way to go through hostile, worm-infested deer country before they reach the suitable areas of the Upper Peninsula farther west.

Nevertheless, the fact that those newly suitable but mooseless areas existed led Michigan wildlife officials to reason that a moose re-introduction would now work. All they had to do was "inoculate" the suitable areas with the nucleus of a new moose population, and nature would do the rest.

That is the background for the "great moose transfer of 1985." Rest assured, there was a tremendous amount of planning and consultation back and forth between Michigan and Ontario before all the details were worked out and work got started on January 21. The basic idea sounds simple. A small chase helicopter went out in search of moose, preferably out on a frozen lake, came in close for a shot from a tranquilizing gun, and then hovered nearby to prevent the moose from going back into the bush during the five minutes or so required for the drug to take effect and the moose to go down.

At that point a second larger helicopter came in with a crew of men, who fitted a special sling around the moose so that the helicopter could lift it back to our base camp at Mew Lake. We shall never forget the scarcely believable sight of moose after moose being ferried in over miles of frozen lakes and forests. At first we would see just a tiny speck dangling below the distant helicopter until, as it came closer and closer, the "speck" resolved itself into half a ton of blindfolded, ear-plugged moose. Back then, however, there was little time to marvel. As soon as a moose was lowered to earth, another team of men (about half from Michigan and the rest from Ontario) went to work. Within 10 minutes of its arrival, the moose was weighed, measured, checked for pregnancy, given antibiotics, fitted with ear tags and radio-collar, relieved of a blood sample, tested for brucellosis and tuberculosis, and lifted by a crane into a special 1,000-pound crate to await shipment to Michigan. During all this time the animal's temperature was constantly monitored, and a veterinarian was ready to take remedial action should the temperature climb or fall from the normal range. Just before the crate was shut, an antidote was administered to reverse the effects of the tranquilizing drug and restore the moose to full consciousness — which usually happened in two to five minutes.

Whatever the number of animals caught in a day — it varied from one to four — they were all driven on the same truck nonstop through the night on the 14- to 24-hour trip (depending on the weather) to the release site in Michigan.

All this sounds straight-forward enough, but the use of drugs is a tricky business at the best of times, and no operation of this magnitude had ever been attemped before. The project planners believed that 10 to 20 per cent of the animals would be lost due to drug- and handling-related stress and that it would take two years to transfer the desired 30 or so moose. In fact, 29 animals (10 bulls, 19 cows — of which 18 at least were pregnant) were transferred in just two weeks, far surpassing the most optimistic predictions and making it unnecessary to stage a repeat program next winter. Another five animals, unfortunately, were lost (three in the Park and two shortly after arriving in the Upper Peninsula), but four of the deaths were of moose handled in the first two days of the project (when drug dosages were still being adjusted), and only one animal was lost after that.

A drugged and blindfolded moose being transported to Mew Lake for later shipment by truck to Michigan.

The really important result is that the nucleus of a new moose herd has been established in Michigan, and, if expectations are borne out, the population will reach 1,000 by the year 2000 — all thanks to the 29 moose transferred this winter. As we go to press, all 29 are doing well and still live within 20 miles of the release site. Soon the cows will be having their calves, and the population expansion will begin. The effect for Michigan of this handful of moose will be enormous.

For Algonquin, also, the transfer was very important — not financially (the people of Michigan paid all the bills) or even ecologically (the temporary loss of less than one per cent of our moose is insignificant) — but rather in terms of our mission and tradition. The Park has a long history of helping less fortunate jurisdictions with wildlife restocking projects. Today, the descendants of Algonquin beaver, marten, fisher, otter, and even deer are all alive in various parts of North America. Being able to add the restored moose population of Michigan to that list is a privilege of which we are very, very proud. ∽

A similar transfer of moose to Michigan was repeated in 1987. The two shipments established a core breeding population that by 1992 had grown to approximately 220 animals.

April 25, 1985, Vol. 26, No. 1 (D.S.)

Food for Sky Whales

This is the time of year when nature is at her most bountiful. Everyone knows that our woods and waters are full of living plants and animals, and we all sense that life in these places is extraordinarily rich and complicated.

This being so, it is rather remarkable that our perception of the third possible area where life can exist is entirely different. The air above our heads is a realm that one basically thinks of as empty. Its only users — and then only at low levels — seem to be transient birds flying by from A to B and somewhat more numerous and purposeful* mosquitoes.

The truth is, however, that the early summer skies above Algonquin are occupied by literally hundreds of millions of tiny creatures suspended high in the air, each for as long as several days at a time. We almost never see these animals, and even just 60 years ago their very existence was only guessed at. But they really are up there. As a matter of fact, it took the invention of the airplane and deliberate attempts to sample the sky for living organisms by towing specially constructed nets before the question was settled.

Within a few years, the early researchers had collected tens of thousands of insects, spiders, and other creatures. Most were found at heights of between 60 and 600 metres, but some were collected as high as four and one-half kilometres above the ground. Some of the collections were accounted for by strong insects, such as large moths and dragonflies, but many more were very small and weak fliers, such as aphids, midges, and tiny beetles or wasps.

Even more amazing was the presence of animals that have no wings at all. Among these were tiny spiders and caterpillars (wafted aloft on strands of silk spun by the animals themselves), but also thrips, mites, book-lice, and springtails, most of which have no obvious means of getting, or staying, airborne.**

At first it was thought that many of the high-altitude insects must have been dead even before they hit the plane-mounted collecting screens. Gradually, however, it became apparent that most were alive and that females could lay fertile eggs upon returning to earth.

Here was a clue as to why so many tiny animals deliberately flew high up into the sky or otherwise allowed themselves to be helplessly carried by the wind hundreds or even thousands of kilometres away from their birthplace. Many tiny animals build up in numbers in local areas so rapidly that they can quickly outstrip their food supply. Since they have no way of knowing where food might be plentiful and no way of getting there under

---

* These all fly from thee to me—ed.

** These animals are so tiny they can easily be captured by a gust of wind, and then they fall so slowly that even a gentle breeze can make them gain altitude.

A Common Nighthawk scooping almost invisible food out of the sky.

their own power in any case, perhaps their best — or only — chance is to get high enough that the wind can take over and blow them away to some new favourable area.

Some insects, it has been learned, have a definite pattern of leaving the ground at a set time of day, flying higher and higher over the next several hours and then, perhaps at nightfall, gradually starting to descend. They may repeat this for several days until finally their efforts are rewarded — they encounter strong winds that sweep the tiny gamblers away, perhaps to a prosperous new life. Of course, they may just as easily end up in a lake or an ocean and die as a result, but even a small chance is better than no chance, and that is probably what they would have had if they had stayed at home.

Whatever the fate of the individual animals, so many of them are aloft at any one time during June and July that one pioneering biologist was reminded of the millions of small floating animals in the ocean known as plankton. He coined the term "aerial plankton" to designate the huge and hitherto unsuspected populations of airborne animals, and the name has stuck to this day. It is true that the animals making up the aerial plankton are not permanent residents of the sky the way that oceanic plankton inhabits the water, but there are still many strong similarities between the two.

One of these concerns their predators. Plankton in the ocean is eaten by whales which, indeed, are mostly just huge plankton-eating machines. They merely swim along with their mouths open, filtering out the tiny plankton with their specially adapted, food-straining mouthparts. It

may not sound particularly efficient, but you can't argue with results as big as whales.

The skies over Algonquin aren't noted for whales, but they do have seven different kinds of birds that make their living in a distinctly whale-like manner. Just like whales, they scoop up plankton with their (for them) large mouths as they buoyantly move along through the nutritious soup in which they live — in this case, the warm summer air.

Swallows, of which we have five resident species, specialize in flying insects found close to the ground or water, and they often stop to perch and rest before resuming their hunt.

The other two eaters of aerial plankton, however, are real "ocean-goers." Chimney Swifts stay in the air all day, often at heights and speeds so great that we scarcely realize they are up there. Only when they give their rapid, "chippering" calls do we look up and see their tiny, cigar-shaped silhouettes rocketing by on twinkling wings.

The last and largest of Algonquin's airborne plankton-eaters is the Common Nighthawk, a bird that leaves its daytime hiding places on the ground late in the day and rises to truly prodigious heights in the darkening sky. It apparently specializes in aerial plankton that also rises late in the day, and we earth-bound humans would hardly ever be aware of its presence were it not for the sounds it makes. These include vocalizations best described as "nasal beeps" and other "booming" noises made by the Nighthawk's wings as it dives in its sky-high courtship display.

The most remarkable thing of all about the high-altitude plankton-feeders, however, is that they exist at all. The season for airborne insects, mites, and spiders in Algonquin is scarcely two and a half months long, and yet there are so many of them that no fewer than seven species of birds make special trips up from the tropics to live, and raise their young, on the aerial food.

Who would have thought that nature's early summer bounty could extend so richly even into the "empty" sky? It's food for sky whales, and it's food for thought.✐

June 27, 1985, Vol. 26, No. 2 (D.S.)

Three Chimney Swifts on twinkling wings.

The Island-Hopper-Killers

To us earthbound humans, the powers of flight enjoyed by insects and birds are profoundly impressive. The idea of being able to spread a pair of wings and effortlessly zoom far away seems almost magical and leaves us feeling more than a touch of envy.

What we tend to forget in such moments is that no creature can live independent from the world around it. Every living thing needs certain ingredients for success, and this holds true, sometimes in very surprising ways, for even the most accomplished "masters of the air."

In Algonquin, no better example of this can be found than the Merlin, a small member of the falcon family. Merlins are not particularly striking in appearance (both sexes have streaked bellies, and the back is bluish-gray in the males and dark brown in females and the young), but they are devastatingly fast aerial hunters. They seldom fail to impress us with their speed and agility. Even the name, recalling as it does the unpredictable magician, Merlin, of King Arthur's court, suggests total, unforgiving command of the environment. Although they are only about 30 centimetres long and lack the heft of their more powerful relative, the Peregrine Falcon, hunting Merlins are so fast that they have always attracted attention. In medieval Europe, trained Merlins were often flown from the hand, particularly by ladies, to hunt small birds.

Tame or wild, Merlins do not resort to stealth, concealment, or surprise to get within striking range of their food the way other birds do. They merely launch themselves from a perch and go after their intended victim. They can reach speeds in excess of 80 kilometres per hour, even in level flight, and there is apparently no bird — even swifts and swallows — that they can't overtake. They may either snatch the prey out of the air as they dart past or kill it first with a blow from the feet and then circle back to retrieve it. A pursued bird may temporarily avoid death by a last-second twisting or turning, but the Merlin will quickly return for as many tries as it takes. The only real hope of escape is for the intended prey to reach cover. A Merlin will not pursue anything into a forest or other vegetation.

Some Merlins have such easy lives that they apparently have plenty of time and energy to spare on such unproductive activities as pursuing and harassing much larger birds. The idea of a Merlin killing and eating a gull, a Raven, or a Peregrine is obviously ridiculous, but Merlins occasionally "amuse themselves" by flying circles around and sometimes actually striking such non-prey.

Now, none of this contradicts the common impression we have of birds, especially birds of prey, being effortlessly at home in their environment. And yet, although Merlins have hardly any rivals as masters of the air, the fact remains that they are very rare in Algonquin. Why, if they are so competent, haven't they been able to do better?

A possible answer to this question has recently been suggested by information coming out of the Ontario

Out in the open, this Yellow-rumped Warbler has almost

Breeding Bird Atlas, a five-year project (finishing this year) to document the precise distribution and breeding status of birds in Ontario. We now have breeding records for Merlin from several locations in the Park, and there is a striking similarity about all of them. In every case the nests have been on islands in large lakes — Hogan, Lavieille, and all three arms of Opeongo. There is also a record from Aylen Lake, just outside the Park, where the birds nested on a peninsula jutting out into the lake.

The forests on these islands are in no way different from those found on the mainland, so at first there seems to be no obvious reason why nesting Merlins should be confined, as they apparently are, to this one, very specialized type of situation.

When you remember, however, that Merlins never chase prey into forests and must have lots of open space for a successful hunt, it may make sense for Merlins to hunt and nest near lakeshores. Given how thick our forests are, birds out over the open water may, in fact, be the only prey that is really available to Merlins in Algonquin.

Of course, this still does not explain why Merlins choose islands (or peninsulas) instead of the much more common mainland shores of lakes. We think, though, that there is a plausible reason for the preference. In most cases there is probably little reason or incentive for small forest birds to leave cover and head out across a lake and unwittingly make themselves vulnerable to a waiting Merlin. When there is a nearby island out in the lake, however, the temptation to go out and harvest its food

resources is likely much greater, and the small bird traffic to and from islands may accordingly be much busier than across lakes. If this reasoning is correct, the best of all situations for a nesting pair of Merlins with many mouths to feed may be a whole group of islands all separated from each other or the mainland by distances small enough to tempt crossings by small birds but large enough for Merlins to operate effectively. The channels in such an "archipelago" would be highly productive feeding grounds for Merlins.

In this regard it may be no coincidence that the best place for Merlins in Algonquin Park appears to be the group of islands at the top end of Lake Opeongo's South Arm. Possibly the same pair of Merlins has bred there for the last three years at least and are there now, accompanied by three young from this year's nesting.

If you go up to the islands to see the Merlins, you may be lucky enough to see one single out a small bird, turn on the after-burners, and pluck it out of the air. It is an awesomely impressive performance, but the fact still remains that Merlins aren't quite the masters of their world that they at first seem to be. In fact, they can apparently make a living here only as highly specialized "island-hopper-killers." Merlins may be wizards in the air, but, as with all magicians, the ingredients still have to be just right.✐

August 8, 1985, Vol. 26, No. 8 (D.S.)

no chance against the Merlin overtaking it from behind.

Everything You Wanted to Know About Dragonfly Sex but Were Afraid to Ask

Okay, okay, we give up. For 25 years a small but brazen and vocal minority of our readers has been clamouring for an exposé on dragonfly sex. "No," we said, "a thousand times 'no.' *The Raven* is a reputable journal dedicated to the serious discussion of important social issues."

Well, times change, and if you turn to this week's centrefold you'll see what all the fuss is about. This is the so-called "wheel positon" of dragonflies. It is a common sight at this time of year around our beaver ponds and along our rivers. And, we have to admit, anyone seeing it for the first time can't help but ask themselves, "What ARE they doing?" or "Do dragonflies know something I don't?"

Not to worry. We aim to clear up these questions and, what's more, to introduce you to the really interesting part of dragonfly sexual behaviour — the part that occurs after mating.

Dragonflies in the wheel position are indeed in the act of mating — a process that begins when the male uses special claspers at the end of his abdomen to seize the female just behind her head. Whether this occurs when the dragonflies are in the air or perched, the male, still holding on to the female, bends his abdomen forward so that his ninth abdominal segment comes into contact with his second abdominal segment. This permits the transfer of sperm (produced in the ninth segment) to a special holding chamber in the second segment.

Having made this initial transfer, the male then straightens out his abdomen (more or less). The female in turn brings her abdomen forward in such a way that her ninth abdominal segment (containing her sex organs) makes contact with his second abdominal segment (where the sperm is). This, then, is the wheel position illustrated here, and it, of course, leads to the second and final transfer of sperm, this time from the male's body to the female's.

Now, if this were all that were involved in the dragonfly mating game, we might mark it down as nature's most remarkable case of sexual athleticism but otherwise just another variant on the theme "boy gets girl." In fact, the truth is much more complicated.

After the male dragonfly has transferred sperm to the female, he does not fly away as you might expect. Indeed, the males of many species do not even release their grip but instead continue to grasp their females behind the head as they fly along laying their eggs. Some

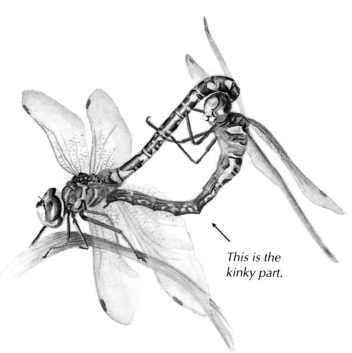

This is the kinky part.

The "wheel" position of mating dragonflies (the male is on the left).

other dragonfly males do release their grip, but they don't go far away. They hover just above and behind the female and follow along during the egg-laying process. If you watch this behaviour, you will soon see that the males doing this are quite visibly guarding the females from other males. Rivals attempt to seize and mate with an egg-laying female, and the guarding male just as determinedly attempts to drive them away and let the female continue uninterrupted.

Whether a male indulges in "contact" or "non-contact" guarding behaviour, the question is why he bothers at all. If he has already mated with the female, surely he has won out in the unconscious competition with other males to pass on his genes to the next generation. Indeed, would he not be better off to abandon the female immediately and go off in search of other conquests? That way he could fertilize even more eggs and leave even more descendants than rival males who persisted in "uselessly" guarding their mates.

The key to understanding why male dragonflies behave as they do lies with the fact that merely mating with a female dragonfly does not guarantee fertilization of her eggs. Sperm injected into a female's body during mating is only stored there and is not used to fertilize the eggs until the moment they are actually laid. This means that, no matter how many males have already mated with a female, none of her unlaid eggs has been fertilized. A late-arriving male therefore has a real chance of being the one who becomes the "father" of the eggs when they finally are laid.

All he has to do is mate with her in such a way that his sperm, and not that of any previous males, is in the best position to fertilize the eggs. In some dragonfly species the males actually scoop out and discard any sperm already in the female's body before they inject their own. In other species the males push previous sperm packages farther into the female so that they are much less likely to be in the optimum fertilizing location.

The upshot of this extraordinary "sperm competition" is that the winning male (the one who actually fertilizes the eggs) is the last one to mate. That is why male dragonflies go to such lengths to guard their mates from other males until egg-laying is completed.

There is, of course, the further complication having to do with the two types of guarding behaviour, contact and non-contact. Studies have shown that males who guard their females by maintaining their grip behind the female's head during the egg-laying process are guaranteed of not being displaced — so contact guarding might seem to be the best method. Non-contact guarding does have advantages under some circumstances, however. It can allow a male to quickly seize and inseminate any new female who happens by while he is guarding the first. In fact, if he is really lucky, he may end up guarding two females that he was last to mate with and even try for a third.

Perhaps the most important thing of all in the sexual behaviour of dragonflies is the light it sheds on the way evolution works and the help it gives us humans in comprehending the world around us. Dragonflies are mere insects, incapable of understanding the implications of their own behaviour, and yet they act in ways that are astonishingly sophisticated and appropriate for their own reproductive success. The explanation for this paradox lies with the "natural selection" that operates in favour of any strain of any plant or animal that leaves more descendants than other strains. Dragonflies that guard their mates have left numerous offspring (who also guard their mates). Any dragonflies whose genetic makeup did not include guarding behaviour left fewer descendants than their rivals with each generation and eventually became such a tiny fraction of the population that, for all practical purposes, they disappeared. Something like the way small grains of sand are the only ones to pass through the "selection" exercised by a sieve, so, too, mate-guarding dragonflies are the only ones that have passed the test of natural selection as the most effective reproducers.

So you see, notwithstanding anything we implied earlier, we have not totally abandoned our dedication to the serious discussion of important ideas. But, if any customs official objects to the explicit nature of the illustration contained in this issue, by all means cut it out. We can survive because, no matter what you may have heard, people don't buy *The Raven* for its racy pictures. (It's the interviews.)⌁

July 4, 1985, Vol. 26, No. 3 (D.S.)

A Different Point of Smell

Humans have a natural, probably inescapable, tendency to assume that all creatures perceive the world the way we do. For us, seeing and hearing are so overwhelmingly important among the possible ways of detecting what is happening around us that it is difficult to imagine any other way of operating.

Nevertheless, it is a fact that many animals use their eyes and ears very little — or even not at all — relying instead on what we consider to be the "minor" senses of touch, taste, and smell.

Given our human limitations, we can never completely successfully get inside the skin of such animals to gain a convincing feel for how they monitor the world around them. But perhaps we can make a good try.

One creature that we could choose — although it might seem a surprising choice to some — is Algonquin's

The Brown Bullhead perceives the world through its barbels.

common Brown Bullhead or "catfish." We say surprising because, even if bullheads look a trifle strange with their big "whiskers," wide mouths, and smooth, scaleless skin, they do have eyes, they are still quite evidently fish, and there is no obvious feature about their appearance that would compel us to think they might operate in radically different ways from us.*

Still, when you stop and consider their behaviour, bullheads must possess some special abilities. They are chiefly active at night, they often inhabit quite muddy water (hence, another common name, mudpout), and much of their food is somehow detected hidden in the ooze of lake and creek bottoms. Neither sight nor hearing can be of much use in these circumstances. Indeed, some local populations of bullheads are actually blind and still do very well.

The only really visible features about these fish that even hint at an ability to operate in dark, murky waters are the eight robust whiskers, more properly called "barbels," located under the chin, at the corners of the mouth, and beside the eyes. Most of the barbels are directed downwards, and it does not require a great leap of imagination to think that they could be very useful in detecting by touch any prey animals buried in oozy bottom sediments. That is, in fact, the purpose of the barbels. When they make contact with suitable food, the bullhead instantly engulfs the victim with its cavernous maw and swallows it, all in one incredibly rapid, convulsive movement.

Bullheads detect and approach food that is far beyond the reach of their barbels, however, and something other than the sense of touch must be involved. That something else is the bullhead's sense of taste operating in several hundred thousand (!) tastebuds all over the skin. It is almost as if each bullhead were a big swimming "tongue" capable of tasting all the subtle flavours diffusing through the water and even determining the direction of each flavour's source.

This is impressive enough, but there is far more to bullhead life than feeling and tasting a path through dark water to the next meal. These fish have a complex social behaviour which, depending on poorly understood circumstances, may range from possession and recognition of stable territories by individual neighbouring fish to the opposite extreme of many fish living together in crowded but peaceful clans. Either way, it is obvious that bullheads must have the ability to remember and recognize each other as individuals.

Theoretically, their sensitive tastebuds might permit bullheads to do this, but, in fact, it is all done through their sense of smell. The exclusive function of a bullhead's nose is the identification of other fish and the reading of their moods and intentions. This has been dramatically shown by experiments involving two fish that have shared the same tank, fought with each other, and then been separated and housed in different tanks. Even months later, if a bit of water is transferred from one of the tanks to the other, the bullhead in the receiving tank will "go crazy" in its attempt to attack, or flee from, the old enemy it apparently believes has invaded its tank. As no comparable reaction is observed when water is transferred from a total stranger's tank, it is apparent that bullheads have the ability to detect the presence of another bullhead from some chemical in the water and also to recognize the particular individual fish that gave off the offending "eau de bullhead."

Humans might be able to remember and recognize the scent of a rival after many months but would never take any kind of action unless they could see the other person as well. With bullheads it's the other way 'round. In their world, vision is such a subtle and undependable sense that failure to actually see a nearby rival is of no consequence if that rival can be clearly and unequivocally smelled in the same tank. That is all the proof any reasonable bullhead could ever need! By the same token, a bullhead with a damaged, non-functioning nose is a social misfit, quite incapable of distinguishing one individual bullhead from another — and constantly gets into trouble.

We said at the outset that it is very hard to get inside another creature's skin. If we were inside that of a bullhead, we would see and hear very dimly or not at all. Instead, we would taste faraway food with our skin, pinpoint it with our whiskers, and determine the identities and moods of our neighbours with our nose. This may not seem like a very appealing existence, but that impression is just another reflection of how imprisoned we are by our own particular range of senses.

Or, to put it another way, beauty lies in the barbels of the beholder. ❧

July 11, 1985, Vol. 26, No. 4 (D.S.)

---

* As a matter of fact, in some ways, bullheads show rather striking similarities to us. For fish, bullheads have a highly developed parental behaviour beginning when both the male and female excavate a nest about a foot wide and six inches deep. The several thousand eggs are guarded by the parents during the 10-day incubation period, and this continues for several weeks after they have hatched. The babies very much resemble tadpoles, and they keep together in a tight, spherical mass that is herded about by the adults.

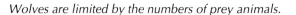

Wolves are limited by the numbers of prey animals.

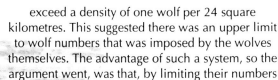

No Wolf Is an Island

Of all the wild animals that visitors to Algonquin Park hope to see, there cannot be much doubt the wolf is the one that best embodies the idea of wild independence. After all, here is a creature famous in fact and legend for its intelligence and strength, its complex social system, and the exemplary extended care it gives to its young. It has no natural enemies, can travel tirelessly day and night, and is a feared hunter whose mournful howls still send shivers down our spines. When all is said and done, no other animal comes close in our human perception to matching the wolf's mastery of its rugged wilderness environment.

And yet, something isn't quite right. If wolves are so totally in command of their own destiny, why are they so rare? Here in Algonquin few campers ever get to see a wolf, and even hearing one is always an unusual and memorable event. We believe, in fact, there are only 100 to 200 wolves in all of the 7,600 square kilometres of Algonquin, and the reason is not at all obvious. With so much going for the wolf, especially in a protected area like the Park, you would think wolves would be more successful.

Now, we are far from the first to wonder about the scarcity of wolves. Early researchers, including those who studied Algonquin's wolves 25 years ago, spent a lot of time wrestling with this fundamental question. And an even more puzzling problem they had to face was that after 1958, when the rangers stopped killing 50 to 60 wolves in the Park every year, the population did not go up. It stayed the same!

A possible explanation for these mysteries came when the researchers examined the limited information then available and discovered that wolves never seemed to

exceed a density of one wolf per 24 square kilometres. This suggested there was an upper limit to wolf numbers that was imposed by the wolves themselves. The advantage of such a system, so the argument went, was that, by limiting their numbers to a level below that which the environment would support, wolves would never run the risk of eating themselves out of house and home. This idea of voluntary population control in wolves became quite popular, partly because of the evidence but also, we suspect, because it fitted in quite nicely with the widespread picture of the wolf as a truly independent wild spirit in full control of its own fate.

As often happens in science, however, the first attempt at explaining a difficult problem doesn't work out — and so it was in this case. For one thing, it is difficult to see how reproductive restraint could ever evolve in wolves or any other animal. Cheaters (who left as many young as they possibly could) would always be rewarded by leaving more descendants than would be left by individuals who "played by the rules." More importantly, as more information was gathered from different wolf studies across North America, it began to become clear that the idea of a special upper limit on wolf numbers was a myth. As a matter of fact, even among stable wolf populations free from hunting and trapping, the differences were enormous. Some areas had densities almost 20 times as great as others. (One stable population had one wolf per 24 square kilometres; another had one for every 375 square kilometres.) Obviously, the idea of wolf numbers being limited by voluntary restraint is difficult to reconcile with such enormous differences. This was especially so when the researchers discovered that the areas with 20 times more wolves also had 20 times more available prey.

It seemed, therefore that, however low the wolf numbers might be, the limits were not adhered to out of enlightened self-interest on the part of the wolves but were imposed on the wolves by the local food resources after all.

Further support for this idea came from an examination of wolf populations that were not stable but were actually increasing. Where there were many prey individuals (deer, moose, or caribou) for every wolf present, the wolves increased rapidly. It didn't matter at all if the wolves were already abundant. If there was lots to eat, they would still increase — and keep on increasing — but at a slower and slower rate until their numbers reached a level where they were in balance with the prey available to support them.

This seems straightforward enough, but it still doesn't answer the second question faced by the researchers — namely, why there was no increase in the Algonquin wolf population after 1958, the year in which Park wolves were finally given protection. Up until then, rangers had, on average, removed 20 per cent of the population every fall and winter. It was only common sense to think that this kind of pressure must have been controlling wolf numbers and that when the pressure was taken off, the wolves would increase.

The explanation for their actual failure to increase lies with the production of pups. When wolves are in balance with their prey, the number of pups is rather low — only 15 to 30 per cent of the fall population. This is much less than you would expect since a typical pack of five to seven wolves can potentially double in size when it produces a litter of about the same number of pups each spring. The reason pups don't survive very well over the summer in a stable wolf population is that the adults, who are in balance with their prey, are hard-pressed to find enough food for their young.

This all changes, however, when man steps in and removes part of the wolf population. Then there is more prey available for each surviving wolf, they have less difficulty finding food, and they can produce more surviving pups. In fact, the best information available now indicates that a wolf population can sustain a kill of up to about 40 per cent every year and still not decrease.

To give a concrete example of what we mean here: suppose there were 100 wolves in an area one fall and that rangers killed 40 of them. The 60 remaining wolves would find food conditions so good the following summer that they would be able to produce 40 surviving pups, and we would be back up to the same number (100) we started with when the "control program" began a year earlier. When you remember that Park rangers in the old days managed to kill only about 20 per cent of the wolves in Algonquin every year (not 40 per cent), it is obvious the wolves were having no trouble at all in

keeping up. All the rangers were doing was stimulating a higher production of pups and killing a lot of wolves that were going to die soon anyway. To have had any real effect on the Park wolf population, they would have had to more than double their efforts.

And when the killing of wolves was stopped, all it meant was that the 100 wolves of our previous example would have dropped back to 80 or so during the hard times of winter (instead of 60) and then given birth to a more normal number of surviving pups (about 20) the following summer, to once again produce the same fall population of 100 wolves.

This explains why neither the killing of wolves in Algonquin nor its cessation in 1958 had any significant effect on Park wolf numbers. It should not be inferred, however, that an untouched wolf population will always stay at the same level. In fact, the recent history of Algonquin's wolves is a good demonstration of the contrary. Although our figures are not precise, no one has any doubt that the Park has many fewer wolves now than it did 25 years ago. That is, wolves are rarer in 1985, after a quarter-century of protection, than they were in the days when rangers were doing their best to get rid of them!

In view of all the new evidence that wolf numbers are controlled by the food supply, it is reasonable to suspect that the prey available to our wolves must have decreased since 1958. Back then, in fact, the Park abounded with deer and had few moose. Now it has the highest moose population in Ontario and deer are quite scarce.

It could be that Park wolves have declined simply because the total amount of moose flesh out there is less than the amount of deer flesh available in the old days. Or it could very well be that our rather small race of wolves is less able to tackle moose than deer.

Whatever the exact reason, the decline of our wolves in the face of a changing prey base once again points out the startling fact that the wolf is far from the free spirit we often imagine. In reality, its fortunes are controlled in an uncannily precise, mathematical way by the food supply. The wolf may be Algonquin's supreme predator, but it is no more free of ecological chains than the lowliest mouse or flower.↩

August 29, 1985, Vol. 26, No. 11 (D.S.)

Neat but not Gaudy

We hardly need to point out that those of you who come to Algonquin in the fall, especially in the last week of September, are seeing the Park at its most magnificent. New visitors quickly find out, and old Park hands already know, that the dazzling reds and golds of maples, aspens, and tamaracks combine with the greens of lakeshore conifers to produce spectacles unmatched at any other time of year.

We wouldn't dispute for a minute the unanimous admiration for this aspect of Algonquin. All the same, we often think it a little unfair that almost no one ever pays any attention to the other, opposite side of Algonquin, namely, the trees that happen not to contribute very much to the fall colour extravaganza.

One tree that particularly comes to mind is the Speckled Alder although, even now, we confess to feeling a little defensive about mentioning it on the same page as the other more famous trees. We are very conscious that the attitudes of most people toward the Speckled Alder usually range from outright condescension at worst to complete indifference at best. And it must be admitted that, at first sight, there is very little about alders to attract our attention or admiration.

In case you are not already familiar with the Speckled Alder, this is the small, deciduous tree that grows in great, dull-green profusion in creek bottoms, around lakes, beaver ponds, bogs or, it seems, in any other place imaginable with moist soil. It has no commercial value and seldom gets to be more than 25 feet tall — in fact, some authorities think of it as a big shrub and not a tree at all. The smooth-barked, horizontally-streaked trunks rarely exceed six inches in diameter, and they sprawl all over the place so that an alder swamp is very difficult to walk through. Even worse, they grow like weeds and are the absolute bane of our portage maintenance crews.

As for colour, it is almost embarassing to bring up the subject. The undistinguished, rough leaves just seem to slowly wither up into grayish-brown curls and fall off to reveal the equally unaesthetic trunks and branches.

All in all, the Speckled Alder might seem to be an eminently forgettable tree — and indeed it would be, if

A Speckled Alder visited on a winter's day by a flock of Common Redpolls in search of the tiny seeds contained in the "cones."

intrinsic value were determined by outward appearances alone. Fortunately, the good readers of *The Raven*, being a cut above the common rabble and generous to a fault, will want to hear our case for the despised alder before reaching their own conclusions.

To begin with (albeit on a minor point), the Speckled Alder, while basically plain in appearance, is not totally without anatomical distinction. Alders belong to the birch family and, as such, produce pollen and seeds on the same tree in separate male and female catkins. The latter, as they mature over summer, turn into hard, woody structures strongly resembling the cones of evergreen trees and serving the same purpose — the protection of the developing seeds (technically called nutlets) held between the cone scales. The cones persist on the tree several years after the seeds have been released, and this makes identification of alders very easy. They are our only broad-leaved trees with cones.

A second, though still modest virtue of the Speckled Alder you might wish to consider is the fleeting, but nonetheless real, beauty it exhibits at certain times of the year. On mild, rainy days in winter the wet trunks become a rich, chocolate-brown, adding a welcome depth of colour to the whites and gray-greens of the snowy landscape. Later, on warm, sunny days in April, the male catkins swell dramatically into yellow, russet, and purple garlands festooning the alder swamps and releasing golden puffs of pollen when jostled by passing animals or skiers. It is one of the first and most subtly beautiful signs of spring in Algonquin.

We have to concede, however, that these are rather fine arguments and perhaps irrelevant to the majority of our visitors who never see the Park in winter or early spring. The real reason the poor Speckled Alder should be given its due is that this lowly tree is really an ecological giant!

We say this because the alder's rootlets have tiny swellings containing bacteria, which have the ability to take nitrogen out of the air and incorporate it into chemical substances useful to plants. Every living thing needs nitrogen to make the proteins that, among other things, serve as the chemical machinery of all life processes. Animals get their supply by eating other animals or from plants. Most plants, in turn, get their nitrogen not from the air but from scarce compounds in the soil. Often the soil is so poor in these compounds that the growth of plants is severely limited. That is why any plant (such as the Speckled Alder) has a tremendous competitive advantage if it has some unusual means of tapping the abundant supply of nitrogen gas in the air instead. This explains the notoriously rapid growth of alders, even in sandy, sterile soils. But there are far-reaching beneficial consequences for other plants and animals as well.

For example, alder leaves are four times richer in nitrogen than the leaves of other plants. When they fall into our creeks and rivers each autumn, as billions upon billions of them do, those drab, seemingly inconsequential alder leaves bring a vitally important contribution of nitrogen that will make itself felt throughout the aquatic food chain. Insect larvae graze upon the nutritious leaves, and they in turn support larger, predatory insects and minnows, which form the food base of Algonquin's prized Brook Trout.

The same sort of thing holds true when alder leaves — or the dead trees themselves — fall on land. They fertilize the soil and make subsequent plant and animal growth far more luxuriant than it would otherwise be.

This is basically why the Speckled Alder is so tremendously important in the ecology of Algonquin Park, but there are other impacts as well. If you come to the Park in October when beavers are completing their winter food piles, you will see that the majority comprise mostly or even entirely Speckled Alder. Alder is not the preferred winter food of beavers, but, being so abundant and fast-growing, it is by far the most important here in Algonquin and without a doubt responsible for the beaver's local prosperity.

Another impact stems from the fact that alders cover big tracts of land and constitute a definite habitat. As with maple forests, spruce bogs, and other Park habitats, alder swamps have their own complement of smaller plants, insects, and animals that never or seldom live anywhere else. There is, for example, the Alder Flycatcher, which lives exclusively in alder creek bottoms. The gorgeous Golden-winged Warbler, which has invaded the Park from the south in recent years, very often has the same preference.

Even in winter, alders play a role in the lives of other animals. Most alder seeds are shed in the fall, but some stay in the cones all winter, and these sometimes serve as a secondary food source for wandering winter finches, such as Tree Sparrows and Redpolls. Some individual birds have learned how to land on nearby branches and shake the seeds loose from the cones with their feet.

If you add up all the positive attributes of the Speckled Alder, there is no escaping the conclusion that this unassuming little tree is actually more important in the life of Algonquin than many of the gaudy species that attract all our attention in the fall fashion show.

Perhaps, as we admire the colours later this month, we should remember that the Park has another, less spectacular side to it, which is exemplified by such trees as the Speckled Alder. This would give us a more profound and less superficial appreciation for the inner workings of Algonquin. There is one more fairly obvious benefit to be gained from such an attitude as well — it does wonders for the Park's alder ego.❧

September 5, 1985, Vol. 26, No. 12 (D.S.)

To Keep a Good Thing Going

As any fisherman can tell you, nothing can compare to heading off into Algonquin Park in the spring to go trout fishing. What indeed can surpass the pleasure of being outdoors in wild surroundings, glimpsing a moose around a bend in the river, the beauty of spring wildflowers along the portage, good times with good friends, and, above all, the excitement of catching a beautiful Lake Trout and then eating it by a crackling fire on the shore of a lonely Park lake?

A beautiful Lake Trout.

We don't need to describe the rewards of fishing in Algonquin to the people who come back for more year after year, but we do think it appropriate to reflect on them — especially this year.

In 1986 the Park, along with all other Ministry of Natural Resources districts, is presenting a draft Fisheries Management Plan for public review and input. Open houses were held in Huntsville, Whitney, and Pembroke in late May, and there was an exhibit on the subject all summer long at the Park Museum. At all of these locations a free background document was made available, as well as questionnaires to be filled out. The questionnaires will be used to help the Park make a final choice among the various possible tactics that have been arrived at to tackle the Park's several fisheries problems.

When we talk about "problems" with Algonquin's fisheries, some people may well raise their eyebrows. After all, the Park is famous for providing some of the best Lake and Brook Trout fishing in southern Ontario, and there are few areas anywhere that have such a high concentration of relatively pristine trout waters. This is true and all very well, but important lessons are to be learned from such excellence. It may not be realized, even by many seasoned Park fishermen, that Algonquin was not always such a standout in Ontario's fishing scene. In fact, originally, there is every reason to believe that in many ways the Park area was probably poorer than the rest of southern Ontario. This would be a simple consequence of the fact that Algonquin Park is a highland area with a short growing season and very poor, shallow soils. Such conditions make for low production of aquatic algae and other plants, and therefore low production of all the creatures, including fish, that ultimately depend on those plants.

How then, has it come about that the Park area, if it was originally one of the poorest fish-producing areas in the province, is now one of the best? Well, it's not that Algonquin has actually got any better; it's just that the rest of southern Ontario's trout fisheries have deteriorated so badly that the Park has been left the winner "by default," so to speak. There are three main reasons why Algonquin has been spared from the same fate suffered elsewhere (or an even worse one, considering the Park's greater initial fragility).

One reason is that, since Algonquin is a headwater area with virtually no development, local or upstream pollution does not affect the Park's water quality. A second reason is that winter fishing is not permitted within Algonquin. But the most important factor of all is that so much of the Park is difficult to reach and consequently receives tolerable fishing pressure.

Fishing in Algonquin is excellent, therefore, not because the Park is intrinsically so special but because we humans haven't been able to get our hands on the fish. If we had been able to, the fishing would have gone down the tubes a lot more completely here than it has elsewhere. We can't emphasize this too much because it has enormous and fundamental implications when one considers season length, types of permissible gear, use of motors, number of people allowed into the Park, or anything else that permits fishermen to be more numerous or efficient at killing fish.

But why, you may legitimately ask, do we place so much emphasis on this idea if fishing is so good in Algonquin Park? In fact, why do we even need a plan? This is a fair question, but the answer is simple. Fishing is good in the Park, but we still do have serious local problems that must be tackled immediately.

Let us consider the most important problem taken up by the Plan, that is, what we now know to be a serious problem of over-fishing for Lake Trout in the large lakes along Highway 60. We don't have precise, scientific data for all the lakes, but where we do — in Smoke Lake and Opeongo — the picture is not bright. And we have no reason to think the other lakes are any better off. Unlike most Park lakes, these ones can be reached very easily, and, as the data for Smoke Lake clearly show, the Lake Trout are being hammered far too hard. Many fewer fish are being caught (in spite of increased effort), and those that are being taken are much smaller.* Things simply cannot continue that way.

* This fact shows, incidentally, that the decline of the Lake Trout fishery in Smoke Lake is being caused by over-fishing, not by acid rain. Acid rain stops reproduction so that the ensuing collapse is characterized by fewer and larger fish (not fewer and smaller fish).

Theoretically, one might solve the overexploitation problem by stocking the lakes with however many hatchery-reared Lake Trout it would take to keep good fishing. The trouble is that it is always expensive and inefficient, and often a total failure as well. For example, between 1948 and 1964 over 200,000 Lake Trout were planted in Lake Opeongo. Only 25 (about 0.01 per cent) were ever caught. At today's prices the Opeongo plantings would cost more than $30,000 — or over $1,000 for each recovered fish. But even if the stocking had worked, we might have achieved a very undesirable result.

Instead of merely supplementing the native Opeongo Lake Trout stocks, we might very well have swamped and diluted them to the point where the natural strain no longer really existed. We would have destroyed a wild strain of Lake Trout finely adapted to Opeongo conditions and replaced it with a domestic, hatchery-reared variety much less able to get along without our help than the original victim of our good but misguided intentions. It would be as if we decided to play God: wipe out the natives of the Amazon jungle and then stock Eskimos there. Would we then wonder why our stocked people didn't do as well as the original natives? If we are serious about having people in Amazonia or trout in Opeongo, it makes much better sense (biologically and economically) to conserve the native stocks.

In the case of trout in Highway 60 lakes, that necessarily means reducing the pressure humans are now exerting on those fish. We could conceivably use a number of tactics to do this, and it is in this area that we want your opinions before we choose some or all of the possibilities. We could, for example, reduce the creel limit (although very few people get their limit even now). We could ban downriggers, fish-finders, and the use of lake herring as bait, but how effective this would be is uncertain. We could also reduce the season length on Highway 60 Lake Trout lakes or ban fishing from motorized boats (to lower fishing efficiency and bring the impact of fishermen more into line with that seen in the Park interior, where fishing continues to be excellent). Some of these possible tactics are bound to be unpopular with some people, but we just can't get away from the fact that something meaningful must be done to reduce exploitation if these fisheries are to survive. We can't have it both ways.

The Lake Trout over-fishing problem is serious, but things aren't all bad by any means. As a matter of fact, the Plan outlines several ways we think fishing opportunities in the heavily used Highway 60 Corridor can actually be increased (by establishing new Brook Trout or artificial Splake fisheries in small lakes that presently have no fishing). And, of course, the fundamental truth about fishing in Algonquin Park is that it continues to provide terrific trout fishing experiences in a magnificent environment.

In this we are so much more fortunate than many other areas. Our Fisheries Management Plan does not attempt to do the impossible. It merely seeks to keep a good thing going — and with your help, input, and understanding, it will succeed.⤸

April 24, 1986, Vol. 27, No. 1 (D.S.)

Eternal Life — Here and Now

At one time or another we have probably all fantasized about living forever, or perhaps returning to Earth to live other lives in different forms. Of course, no one takes these musings very seriously. Everybody "knows" that immortality and reincarnation may be recurring themes in daydreams but have nothing to do with reality. Such idle imaginings are better left — if we accept the conventional wisdom — to small children or science fiction writers.

Well, as often happens when humans are "sure" about something, it turns out there really are many living things that apparently do succeed in living forever. And, just for good measure, these life forms are simultaneously capable of a kind of limited reincarnation as well.

We are not talking about some exotic, rare, or mysterious group of animals either. Rather, the organisms we refer to are very common and familiar to us all. To see good examples of the living things that have unlocked the secrets of eternal life, you need look no further than the ferns growing at your feet. Here in Algonquin Park we have 41 kinds of ferns, not counting another 21 so-called "fern allies" — the club mosses and horsetails. They grow in just about every imaginable habitat, and they are all capable of what, for us, are some extraordinary feats of living.

Typical ferns seem to consist just of big, leafy fronds growing out of the ground. If anything, their fine, graceful patterns make them appear on the delicate side and anything but immortal. Besides, haven't we all seen the fronds of at least some kinds of ferns killed by the first frosts in early September? It is in fact true that individual fronds of many fern species are killed each fall (although other kinds have evergreen fronds that last all winter under the snow). Nevertheless, the fronds of a fern are only the above-ground, visible part of the fern plant, and just because the fronds (sometimes) die in the fall, we have no real reason to say the whole plant is dead. After all, no one would say that a maple tree dies just because its leaves turn colour and fall off each autumn. The only real difference in this regard between a maple tree and a fern is that the parts of a fern that live on through the winter are hidden from our view underground. These parts are called rhizomes or rootstocks, and they grow along parallel to the surface and just a few centimetres down. They send out small roots along their length to draw water and nutrients from the soil, and, in spring and summer, they send leafy fronds into the air above. The amazing thing about the rootstocks is that, although the oldest sections may be dying, new sections are growing at the same time, invading new territory. As far as anyone knows, this process can continue indefinitely. As long as there is suitable habitat for the fern rootstock to invade, there is no evidence it will ever die. It is even possible the rootstock could keep "chasing itself around in circles" forever, growing at its "head" and dying at its "tail." This may not be exactly what you had in mind when you dreamed of immortality as a child, but it still remains that such a tail-chasing fern would have a continuous existence over hundreds or thousands of years (or more) and remain genetically exactly the same. It would never die and never change. For all practical purposes it would be immortal.

As if that weren't enough, ferns have a second, more delicate way of perpetuating themselves, which involves floating off into thin air, reincarnation as a completely different plant, and then reappearance as a fern. If you look at the undersides of the fronds of most fern species, you will soon discover that some of them have distinct, usually dot-like structures arranged in definite patterns. These "fruit-dots" contain spore cases, which produce thousands of microscopic, single-celled spores. Spores are a bit like seeds of flowering plants in the sense that they are reproductive "packages." They can be transported away from the parent plant and, if they reach favourable locations, can grow into new plants.

The startling difference is that, whereas a maple seed grows up to become a maple tree, a fern spore does not grow up to become a fern. Instead, it produces a distinctly different, very small plant technically known as a "gametophyte." It is only a few millimetres across and grows flat on the ground. Often thousands of them are crowded together in a small area, and they are frequently passed off as moss. Although they contain chlorophyll

Humans dream of immortality, but ferns may achieve it.

like other green plants, their real purpose is not to manufacture sugar but to produce sperm and eggs. These develop in separate structures on the underside of the gametophyte. Gametophytes grow in damp places because the moisture provides a medium through which the sperm can swim to an egg and fertilize it. The fertilized gametophyte egg grows up to become not another tiny gametophyte but a big frond-bearing fern instead. The fern will eventually produce spores, which will produce more gametophytes and continue the cycle, alternating each generation between entirely different-looking plants.

When sperm fertilize an egg from the same gametophyte, the result is a fern that is genetically identical to the previous "fern incarnation" (that is, two generations back). In human terms, the process is almost as if you were to scrape some skin cells off your arm and watch them float off to some suitable place for development. There, your genetic package would grow up not into a human being but into something entirely different — a toad maybe?, or perhaps a mouse or an orchid. Take your pick, but, whatever it was, the creature that came from your skin cell would then mate with itself and produce not another toad or mouse or orchid but an exact copy of you instead. If this sounds totally bizarre, just remember that for ferns it is entirely normal, and the result is yet another route to possible immortality.

Of course, it can also happen that an egg may be fertilized by a sperm from an entirely different gametophyte. In this case, the new fern plant will not be an exact copy of its maternal "grandparent" but a truly new fern instead, with its own unique genetic blending contributed by two different parents, just the way human children are, for example.

If this last possibility has a much more comforting and reassuring ring of familiarity to it, bear in mind that the fertilizing sperm could also come from a gametophyte of an entirely different fern species. When this happens, the fertilized egg grows up into a hybrid, or cross, between two species. Many such hybrids are known, particularly among the group known as Wood Ferns. Most are sterile, but occasionally fertile hybrids* arise as well. Experts

* The End of One Eternity

*Three hybrid ferns are known from Algonquin Park, of which the most famous, a single plant resulting from the crossing of a Marginal Shield Fern and a Fragrant Cliff Fern, was discovered on the shore of Greenleaf Lake in 1973. This was the first (and still only) time this particular combination had been found, and it was named the Algonquin Wood Fern (**Dryopteris algonquinensis**) in honour of the Park by the investigating scientists (see **The Raven** of July 17, 1974, for full details or page 23 of this collection of essays).*

We are sorry to report, however, that sometime between 1976 and 1979 the plant disappeared. Judging by remaining evidence, there is a strong possibility that it was actually dug up and removed. Although Greenleaf Lake is quite remote and the exact location of the plant never revealed, there apparently are collectors determined and selfish enough to do such an inexcusable thing.

believe that some familiar fern species may have sprung into existence quite suddenly as a result of the chance wandering of a single fern sperm onto the wrong gametophyte! It gives one pause to think that such "lowly" life forms as ferns are capable of such incredible feats. For us humans, even with all our modern technology, thoughts of immortality, reincarnation, or the creation of new species are never seriously considered. They are merely dismissed as idle, futuristic daydreams. Ferns, on the other hand, don't give them a second thought. These beautiful green plants demonstrate the secrets of eternal life here and now.∞

July 24, 1986, Vol. 27, No. 6 (D.S.)

A Purpose Within a Purpose

The natural world has more than once been compared to one of those intricate dolls: just when you think you understand it, it turns out to be hiding another doll inside and, within that, another and another and another.

As with such dolls — only more so — nature leaves us time and again amazed at its intricacy and what other subtleties might still lie undiscovered beneath its simple outward appearance.

One excellent example of what we mean is afforded in great profusion these days by the spires of bright pink flowers growing along sunny roadsides and portages. As most people know, the plant is called Fireweed, and it is one of Canada's most characteristic and beautiful native wildflower species. We personally always make a point of going over to a patch of Fireweed at some time each summer just to soak up the fragrance, the sun, and the dazzling colour one finds in such places. A few nectar-collecting bumblebees lurching buzzily about among the flowers complete the picture of hot, lazy days that seem to last forever.

Now, on the face of it, there is nothing at all here to suggest anything more complicated than what we have just described. But, as with those dolls, perhaps we are missing a whole new dimension that lies hidden beneath the scene's outward appearance. Let's take a closer look.

Bumbling with a Purpose

Bumblebees seem to zoom around crazily, as if they were drunk and anything but purposeful. If you watch them carefully, however, you will see they really do follow a pattern. When they arrive at a Fireweed plant,

they almost always first visit an individual flower near the bottom of the spire, then move upwards, visiting other flowers as they go. They always miss more flowers on a spire than they visit, however, and they consistently leave spires before they have reached the uppermost flower.

Does this make any sense, or does it just confirm our original impression about the simplicity of bumblebees foraging in a Fireweed patch? After all, if bumblebees were really serious about collecting nectar, they would surely do better to start at the top of a spire and work down (easier than flying straight up, as they are actually observed to do). It should also be better, you would think, to visit every flower on each spire (rather than just a few) so as to avoid long, energy-demanding flights between spires.

Is the bumblebee using the Fireweed, or is the Fireweed using the bumblebee?

Well, someone has gone to the trouble of measuring nectar volumes contained in individual fireweed flowers, and it turns out that the lowest flowers on the spire have the most nectar. It really does make sense, therefore, for a bumblebee to start at the bottom of a spire and to abandon it for another before reaching the top. As for the habit of visiting only a few individual flowers on the way up, what bumblebees are actually doing is to always fly to the closest, vertically higher flower on the spire. This indeed results in many flowers being missed, but it also minimizes the chances of a bumblebee inadvertently revisiting a flower already emptied of its nectar seconds earlier.

Thus, whatever our first impression may be, bumblebees do not "bumble" around erratically. By adhering to three simple rules (1. Start at the bottom; 2. Move up to the nearest flower above; 3. Leave when the nectar volume in higher flowers falls below a certain level), they achieve an impressively high efficiency in nectar collection. Even if it is all done through instinct, the fact remains that bumblebees behave with a fine-tuned purposefulness few of us would ever have suspected.

But is that really all there is to it? Could it be that the surprising sophistication we have just seen in bumblebee behaviour conceals yet another hidden "purpose?" Read on.

Seducing with a Purpose

Flowers exist to produce seeds. In the case of Fireweed, a typical plant will produce about 45,000 from the 100 or so individual flowers that open on each spire over the course of the summer. The best seeds are produced when a flower is fertilized by pollen from another, unrelated plant. The Fireweed's showy flowers are elaborate structures whose purpose is to seduce bumblebees into making such pollen transfers. The bright colour gets the attention of the bees, and the nectar provides a reason for an actual visit — during which the bumblebee unintentionally picks up pollen that may then be transported to another flower. So far, so good, but the system as described here really seems much too crude to work very well. After all, the best results can only be expected when bumblebees collect pollen from flowers on one Fireweed spire and take it to flowers on another, separate spire. But what is there to prevent bumblebees from merely moving pollen from one flower to another on the same spire? The flowers might end up being fertilized alright, but it would be a kind of incestuous self-pollination that would result in poor-quality offspring.

It might seem hopeless for a brainless, immobile Fireweed plant to make bumblebees take its pollen to appropriate "foreign" flowers, but, in fact, they have subtle features that accomplish this. To begin with, each flower on a Fireweed spire lasts for only two days (they open from the bottom of the spire to the top over the summer season). During the first day of its life, a flower produces pollen but cannot be fertilized itself. During the second day it is fertile but produces no pollen. This feature prevents individual flowers from fertilizing themselves, but, of course it does nothing to prevent the equally undesirable possibility of pollen from an upper (male) flower pollinating a lower (female) flower on the same spire.

We have already seen, however, that the lowermost (female-stage) flowers are the ones with the most nectar and are preferentially visited first by bumblebees. The higher male (that is, pollen-shedding) flowers have less nectar and are visited afterward. Following that, the bumblebees move on to other plants. The result, then, is that visits to pollen-shedding flowers on one plant are immediately followed by visits to pollen-receptive, female flowers on another plant. In other words, bumblebees move precisely the way Fireweed plants should "want" them to.

This is amazing enough, but the "control" exercised by Fireweed over the movements of bumblebees goes even further. A bumblebee can carry only so much pollen, and, if a bumblebee were to visit every single female-stage flower on a fireweed spire, it would run out of pollen long before it visited the last one. Many female flowers would therefore be drained of their nectar but remain unfertilized, which is obviously an undesirable waste from the Fireweed's point of view. Other things being equal, bumblebees should be "persuaded" to visit only a few female flowers on a spire so that all will be assured of receiving pollen. After that, they should move into the upper, pollen-bearing flowers on the spire to have their pollen load replenished (for transport to the lower, female flowers of the next spire to be visited). But that, as you will remember, is exactly what bumblebees actually do — not, of course, because the bumblebees have any sympathy for the needs of Fireweed but because the distribution of nectar-bearing flowers on each spire makes it more efficient for bumblebees to move quickly up each spire and to miss many flowers on the way.

The startling reality is that the passive and "powerless" Fireweed plants are controlling the bumblebees and bending them to their purpose, almost as surely as if they were leading them around on leashes.

What at first seemed so simple is far more subtle than we could ever have imagined. First, we learn that the "bumbling" bees move according to their own precise purpose, and then that their sophisticated behaviour exactly serves the purpose of the Fireweeds. Who is using whom?

It is truly astonishing to realize how scenes in the natural world can hide layer upon layer of unsuspected, intricate purpose beneath apparently simple external appearances. And, for all we know, there may be even more hidden purposes buried deeper than the ones touched on here. ... Something to think about the next time you sit down on a warm summer afternoon to enjoy a simple scene of bumblebees buzzing "aimlessly" among the graceful spires of a Fireweed patch.⌘

August 7, 1986, Vol. 27, No. 8 (D.S.)

Appearances Can Be Deceiving

There can be no doubt that humans consider autumn the most tranquil and beautiful season in Algonquin. Everything about the Park in fall supports this impression. The campgrounds are mostly empty, the woods are silent, and morning lakes are calm as glass.

Among wildlife, we often encounter dozing mergansers soaking up the sun on bleached logs at the water's edge, or chipmunks with bulging cheeks scuttling back to their burrows through dry leaves on the forest floor. Or, if we are really lucky, we may glimpse a sleek, antlered buck standing in golden hardwoods before it bounds away with high, graceful leaps.

All these images reinforce the picture we have of nature being at its most peaceful and bountiful this time of year. But in the natural world, reality is often very different from the way we perceive it, and these examples are good cases in point. The beautiful buck in the hardwoods may seem to be the epitome of grace and harmony, but we would have a very different impression if we were able to see how a buck really lives in the fall. This is the time of year leading up to the rut, or mating season, of the deer. In Algonquin the rut peaks in November, but even in September the lives of our deer have started to be anything but tranquil. Antler growth, begun last May, is now finished, and the nourishing layer of skin called velvet, which covered the antlers all this time, has been shed.

If they haven't already started, bucks will soon be using their newly exposed antlers in sparring contests with other males. Rival bucks lower their heads, casually engage their antlers, and start pushing with all their strength. Usually one animal is bested in less than a minute and withdraws. Nevertheless, at the beginning of the season, very young males often persistently challenge older bucks, even if they are invariably forced back immediately. Eventually, even such inexperienced youngsters learn from these contests how they stack up against other males, and a dominance hierarchy among bucks is established. The value of this is that, when things get really serious later on, rival deer can almost always size each other up quite realistically without having to waste energy or risk injury in an actual fight.

After a month or more of preliminary sparring contests, the mood of the bucks becomes much more intense, not to say downright ugly. They lose all tolerance for other bucks and begin to chase does. At first they merely trot along, their tails raised high and their noses to the ground, following the doe's scent. As they close in, they adopt a "courtship posture" with the neck extended and lowered and the chin slightly raised. But, at this stage, does almost

A buck leaving a scent on a debarked sapling by rubbing it with his forehead.

invariably want nothing to do with the males. Sometimes a trailing buck gets the message when the doe stops to urinate. The buck sniffs the urine and then raises his head while curling back his upper lip for about five seconds. It is believed this manoeuver helps to concentrate the urine vapour in the buck's nostrils and permits him to evaluate where the doe is in her reproductive cycle, and therefore how long it will be before she is ready to mate. If the doe's receptive period is a long way off, the buck may leave in search of another doe. Sometimes, however, he charges after the doe anyway. The doe will run hard and may leave her fawn far behind in an effort to get away from one of these aggressive bucks — and with good reason. In captivity, bucks have been known to kill unreceptive does that couldn't get away.

Normally, however, tension and violence are far more likely to come to the fore between rival bucks than between a male and a female. If two bucks chase the same doe, the dominant buck lays back his ears and stares directly at his adversary. A subordinate male usually signals submission by turning away, but if he doesn't, the dominant animal bristles his hair, lowers his antlers, and stiffly walks towards him. This almost always suffices to make the inferior animal turn. Only rarely are two bucks so evenly matched that their confrontation escalates into a real battle.

In these cases the two rivals may slowly circle each other at a distance of only one or two metres, grunting all the while before suddenly smashing their antlers together in an incredibly violent, instantaneous mutual charge. There follows an intense bout of shoving and neck-twisting until one buck is forced to retreat.

"Rub-urination" in which a buck rubs his hindlegs together while urinating on them at the same time.

The chasing of does and the competition between bucks is relatively easy to understand, but the rutting season in deer is accompanied by other, quite bizarre forms of behaviour that are much less comprehensible. All through the rut, for example, bucks thrash saplings and shrubbery with their antlers. They then rub their foreheads on the debarked "buck rub," apparently leaving a scent produced by glands in the skin, but no one really knows what purpose is served.

Bucks also leave other, more complicated signposts in the form of "scrapes." First the buck reaches up into a tree — sometimes standing on his hind legs — mouths a branch, pulls it down (often breaking it), and then releases it in such a way that it springs across his forehead. Then, below the marked branch, he scrapes a shallow, circular depression with his forefeet, clearing it of leaves and other debris. As a final touch he urinates into the depression. It is suspected that does may visit such scrapes and leave scent messages of their own, but, again, no one knows for sure why deer do these things.

A third peculiar behaviour exhibited by bucks during the rut is "rub-urination" in which a buck squeezes and rubs his hindlegs together while urinating on them at the same time. The urine reacts with secretions produced by glands on the inside surface of the buck's legs to produce a powerful, far-reaching odour that even humans can smell quite easily.

Any or all of these behaviours* might serve to intimidate other bucks — or perhaps attract does when they finally do become ready for mating. Finding a buck might not seem to be a problem for a doe (given how eager the males are), but maybe it was in the past. Before European man arrived on the scene and greatly improved deer habitat through logging and forest fires, deer were almost certainly rarer than they are now. It may be that deer evolved their present signpost behaviours back in a time when does could not be guaranteed of finding a buck when they needed one unless they had a few smelly clues to guide them.

Does are fertile and will mate only for a period of 24 hours. During that time they are jealously guarded by a dominant buck. Mating itself is simple, quick, and violent — often the doe is knocked off her feet.

With the end of the rut, aggression subsides, the swollen necks of the bucks recede, and eventually the antlers are dropped. The exhausted bucks turn their attention to eating, for they have lost as much as 30 per cent of their weight during the rut and need to replenish their reserves if they are going to make it through the approaching winter.

It is difficult for humans to imagine what the deer have been through because we see so little of their lives. About all we can hope for is to catch a glimpse of a beautiful buck in golden fall hardwoods. When we do, we marvel at the animal's grace and beauty, and quite naturally assume that a buck's life is as tranquil as it seems. … Appearances can be deceiving.☞

September 4, 1986, Vol. 27, No. 12 (D.S.)

---

* Some authorities maintain that, among bucks and does, rubbing trees with your forehead, curling your lips, grunting, and peeing on your legs are terms of endeerment.

Career Paths for Sunfish

Of all the blessings enjoyed by humans nowadays, one of the most precious is the tremendous range of careers and lifestyles available to us. Just stop and look through the job ads in any newspaper, for example, and it is immediately obvious how much more varied and interesting our human possibilities are compared with those open to other creatures. A moose may be "lord of the forest," but it actually leads a quite rigidly defined existence, in a rather small area usually and with a monotonous, hardly changing diet. Even something supposedly as "free as a bird" lives in a largely pre-programmed manner and moves back and forth each year between the same wintering and summering areas.

This sort of thing being almost universally true, it is interesting to note that the animal world does have a few exceptions — cases where individuals of certain species

The "sneaker" male at left is looking for a chance to dash in and fertilize some of the eggs that the "honest" male (upper right) would otherwise take care of exclusively.

actually branch off at an early age and pursue very different lifestyles. One very timely and close-at-hand example is the Park's common member of the sunfish family — the Pumpkinseed. Pumpkinseeds are the gorgeous, little, shallow water fish covered with beautiful rainbow-hued iridescent scales and which so many youngsters have enjoyed catching when they first tried their hand at fishing. In early July, Pumpkinseeds are especially conspicuous because this is the nesting season. Many shallow shoreline areas have obvious, "cleaned-off" patches, five to 10 inches in diameter, and, if you look closely, you can see the male fish in or near the nests, guarding them against intruders. It is the males, in fact, that have constructed the nests by vigorously fanning the bottom with their tails and clearing off the debris so as to expose the hard, clean sand or gravel below.

After that it is a matter of waiting for, or persuading, a female to visit the nest and release her eggs. Courtship consists of displays and swimming in a circular path just above the nest, and culminates in egg-laying. At this point, the male is oriented straight up and the female, her lower surface touching his, is at a 45-degree angle. The female releases her eggs, the male expels small quantities of sperm, and the fertilized eggs settle down into the nest. Eventually, thanks to the contributions of several females, there may be from 2,000 to 15,000 tiny eggs in a nest. Females leave after egg-laying, but males continue to hover nearby, guarding the eggs against predators and fanning them so as to improve the oxygen supply. Hatching follows in a few days, but the males continue to guard the minute youngsters in the nest for as long as 11 days after that. They chase away predators and retrieve any babies that stray from the nest by bringing them back in their mouths. This care by the male is absolutely essential if the young are to survive, and the Pumpkinseed is often cited as a good example of a fish with highly developed parental behaviour.

Be that as it may, there is nothing in what we have described so far that even hints at some sort of alternate lifestyle that might be adopted by sunfish. The fact is, however, that, even if male Pumpkinseeds are often thought of as model fathers, most of them are anything but. Far more males adopt a radically different way of life, called "sneaking." Sneaker males do not build nests, and they do not guard eggs or young fish. What they do instead is lurk close by a nest being guarded by an "honest" parental male Pumpkinseed and wait for chances to dash in and add their sperm when the nest owner is spawning with a female. They may get chased away, but when the owner is thus distracted, another sneaker may well dash in and capitalize on the situation. The result is that many — often a majority — of the eggs being cared for by honest, nest-building males have, in fact, been fertilized by sneakers.

One of the most remarkable things about all this is that the two behaviours ("honesty" and "sneakery") are under genetic control, the same way eye colour, for example, is in humans. In other words, a young male Pumpkinseed is

born either a parental or a sneaker and does not change from one to the other during his lifetime.

Parental-type males refrain from sex in their early years no matter what opportunities present themselves and only start to build nests and mate with females when they are about six or seven years old. By that time they are quite large (seven or eight inches long) and relatively strong and formidable.

Sneakers, on the other hand, begin to show their distinctive sexual behaviour when they are only one year (rarely) or two years old. Because they put so much energy into sneaking, they grow less quickly than young, still-celibate parentals, and by the time a sneaker is four or five years old, it is noticeably smaller than a parental of the same age. The youthful philandering of the sneakers exacts such a toll, in fact, that they rarely live beyond the age of five years — even though that is before parentals even start to breed, let alone wear out and die of old age themselves.

In the natural world the only behaviours that last any appreciable time are those that maximize an individual's chances of producing young. (Individuals possessing different kinds of behaviour leave no descendants at all or so few that they are swamped after a few generations by the descendants of the more prolific varieties.) Seen in this light, sneaking might be the more effective strategy for a young male Pumpkinseed. There is no guarantee you will escape the many predators that live in our lakes and live long enough to become a parental, so maybe it would pay to start fertilizing eggs (by sneaking) as early as possible. That way, even if you die early, you will have fathered at least some of the next Pumpkinseed generation. Probably some 80 per cent of male Pumpkinseeds are sneakers, but the minority, the honest parentals, can never completely die out in this species. This is because only parentals guard young, and survival is impossible for Pumpkinseed fry without such care. There comes a balance point (when there is about one parental for every four sneakers), therefore, at which the two behaviours are equally likely to leave descendants. (If there were fewer parentals, there wouldn't be enough for the sneakers to parasitize and trick into raising their young. Some sneakers would, therefore, start to fail to leave descendants, and parentals would increase until the balance was re-established.)

We think it truly remarkable that sunfish follow two so distinctly different lifestyles, but this is nothing compared to what humans have available. Of course, we should be thankful for having more choices than Pumpkinseeds do. It would be as if the only possibilities open to us were either being honest fathers who had to care for other unscrupulous males' kids or zooming around devoting almost all our energies to fathering children who would be raised by others. Who would want to be faced with such alternatives?

But then, on second thought, maybe you shouldn't answer that question.✆

July 3, 1987, Vol. 28, No. 3 (D.S.)

Quackery Revealed

Of all the sights of early summer in Algonquin Park, few are more appealing than a mother duck walking or swimming along with her brood of ducklings crowding close behind. Part of the appeal stems from the obvious mutual "affection" we see between such mothers and their offspring, but some of the appeal also comes from what humans perceive to be the comical side of the situation. The peeping, fluffy ducklings literally fall over themselves in their efforts to keep up with mom. She, for her part, waddles along with a slightly ridiculous demeanour and only makes matters worse when she utters a few loud, nasal quacks.

It is probably safe to say, in fact, that however endearing we may find a family of ducks to be, we would never credit them with much brains, subtlety, or sophistication. This is unfortunate. It may be that ducks don't have the kind of mental capabilities possessed by humans, but we would be missing the mark by a wide margin to dismiss them as just a few amusing clowns. Ducks accomplish quite major feats of survival in their difficult lives, and do so through some rather amazing and subtle communication systems that are worthy of our complete respect.

Take hatching, for example. In nature, clutches of duck eggs all hatch out in the space of about three to eight hours. This synchrony is important because it means all the ducklings have about the same time to dry out and develop some co-ordination before they leave the nest about a day later and together follow their mother out into the big, dangerous world. If a clutch of wild duck eggs is hatched in an incubator, however, the individual eggs hatch out, not in a matter of hours but over several days. Clearly, this would be a disaster if it happened in a natural situation because the resulting brood of ducklings would be of widely differing abilities. Some would be ready to leave the nest before others had even hatched, and a few young birds would almost inevitably be left behind. Why, then, does this sort of thing not happen in the wild?

Incredible as it seems, the ducklings actually co-ordinate the time of their hatching by communicating with each other while they are still in their eggshells. A day or two before a duckling actually starts to hatch, it penetrates the air pocket at the blunt end of the egg and begins to breathe. In so doing, it starts to make soft, clicking sounds that are quite audible if you put the egg up to your ear.

These sounds are also heard by the unhatched ducklings in adjacent eggs, and soon more and more eggs are clicking and being heard by their neighbours. No one knows exactly how it works, but this pre-hatching "egg talk" has definitely been shown to help get the clutch into hatching synchrony. Even a clutch whose eggs are segregated into different incubators in a lab can be made to hatch just as synchronously as a wild clutch merely by letting the eggs "talk" to each other through microphones and speakers.

The babbling of unhatched eggs has much more importance than just this, however. It also plays a major role in the "imprinting" of the ducklings on their mother. Many years ago the great Austrian biologist Konrad Lorenz showed that hatchling geese would follow the first moving thing they saw and regard it as their mother, no matter how inappropriate. Even if such deceived young birds were later exposed to their real mothers, they failed to switch back, instead remaining faithful to the human, the wagon, the cat, or whatever other object on which they had been "imprinted." These observations were real enough, but Lorenz was working with young birds that had been deprived not only of seeing their mothers but also of hearing them — including during the period just before hatching.

This is an important point because, in the real world, incubating ducks respond to the clicking of their eggs with soft clucks of their own, thereby exposing their imminent ducklings to the sound of mother's voice at least 24 hours before the young hatch out and actually see her. Even then, they may be under her body or, as with Wood Ducks, in a dark tree cavity where they can't really observe her before they leave the nest a day or so later. The possibility exists, therefore, that ducklings really imprint on the sound of their mother's voice, and that Lorenz obtained the results he did mainly because his birds had heard nothing before they hatched and had been forced into a "secondary" sort of visual imprinting on the objects or people Lorenz presented when they emerged from their eggshells.

In fact, this seems to be the case. Ducklings that have heard their mothers before hatching will afterwards follow any object that gives recorded maternal clucks and will ignore quite realistic duck decoys. On the other hand, if they have not heard their mothers before hatching, they will imprint just as readily on a decoy equipped with a speaker playing a human voice as they will on a decoy that plays their mother's clucks.

Even more subtle is the ability of ducklings in some species to remember and recognize the particular clucks of their own mother. Young Wood Ducks and Mallards, for example, will not follow just any old female of their species (or recording thereof) but only the individual female Wood Duck or Mallard heard while still in their eggs. And it is here that we come to the real advantage enjoyed by ducks and ducklings who start to communicate with and get to know each other even before the young birds break out of their eggshells. By establishing a firm bond well before the time of

nest-leaving, the mother and her offspring virtually eliminate the possibility that the young will imprint on the wrong object when the ducklings do leave the nest. And since the bond is based on the sound of mother's voice rather than on her appearance, the chances are much better that any duckling that does go astray will not be confused by another distant female's voice and will, in fact, home in on the right mother.

All this, we think you will agree, is astonishingly sophisticated for animals that, though enjoyable to watch, are often written off as feathered stumblebums or somewhat less than brilliant.

So let's look kindly upon our web-footed friends. After all, a duck may be somebody's Great Communicator. ∞

July 9, 1987, Vol. 28, No. 4 (D.S.)

Setting the Record Straight on Hummingbirds

With some justification we modern human beings pride ourselves on the knowledge we have accumulated about the world around us. Over the years we have probed more and more deeply into the inner workings of nature and have managed to considerably roll back our original total ignorance. Nowadays we can look back at the craziest ideas once held to be fact by the most eminent of scholars and smile at how far we have come in our understanding. For example, everyone at one time "knew" that swallows spent the winter in the mud of lake and river bottoms. Similarly, hummingbirds obviously had to migrate each spring and fall in the back feathers of geese or eagles because such small birds could not possibly travel to Central America on their own power.

The only problem with taking a condescending attitude toward such "silly" old notions is that we all too easily forget our ancestors didn't have the benefit of recently conducted research. Besides, even if our modern ideas are correct, they often sound as crazy as the ones they have replaced.

Take, for example, the case of hummingbirds. No one seriously believes any more that they hitchhike north and south each year, but modern work has shown that our hummers really do depend on other, totally unrelated birds for survival.

For anyone who has watched a hummingbird pugnaciously defending a patch of flowers these days or kept a hummingbird feeder back home, this idea may be a little difficult to swallow. After all, hummingbirds appear to detest even themselves, not to mention other bird species. In fact, they violently attack and harass almost any other creature, whether insect, mammal, larger bird, or different hummer that dares to encroach on their turf. Then, too, their well-known specialization on nectar-feeding (only occasionally supplemented with small insects) would seem to remove the need for any kind of relationship with, or dependence on, some other kind of bird.

In the northern part of their range, Ruby-throated Hummingbirds, such as this female, depend on the sap flowing from holes made by Yellow-bellied Sapsuckers.

In our part of the world, however, there is a problem with the standard, flower-feeding way of life for hummingbirds. The Park may have lots of nectar-rich Fireweed and Jewelweed available these days (and riverside stands of Cardinal-flower on the east side), but for much of the season, suitable flowers are scarce or altogether absent.

How does a hummingbird that arrives back in May survive, let alone raise young, before the appearance of usable flowers in July? There simply aren't any good sources of nectar out there until then. It turns out that what saves the day for hummingbirds in the critical, early part of the season is tree sap. It may not be nectar, technically-speaking, but sap has a sugar content (15 to 20 per cent) remarkably similar to that of the nectar secreted by typical hummingbird flowers. There is also incomparably more sap than flower nectar out in the Algonquin woods, even at the peak of the summer flowering season. The only problem, of course, is how a minuscule, fragile bundle of feathers like a hummingbird can gain access to the supply.

It does so by visiting holes drilled in tree trunks by the Yellow-bellied Sapsucker, the common local member of the woodpecker family that specializes in the practice of drinking tree sap. People have known for a long time that hummingbirds frequently visit active sapsucker trees, but only recently has it been learned just how close and important the relationship is for hummingbirds.

First came the realization that tree sap was indeed an excellent nutritional substitute for flower nectar. Then came a study of female hummingbirds which, in every case, built their nests within a few seconds' flight of a sapsucker tree and which, during incubation, apparently depended entirely on the sap they were able to obtain there. Added to these findings was the recognition that hummingbirds in North America are invariably found only as far north as sapsuckers and that hummers come back in the spring only three to four weeks after sapsuckers do. This happens to be the time it usually takes sapsuckers to stimulate a copious flow of sap from one or more trees in their territory. Finally, several observations have been made of hummingbirds closely following both foraging and flying sapsuckers for long periods, which strongly suggests that hummingbirds recognize their unintentional benefactors and follow them around to locate their feeding trees.

Most authorities now believe hummingbirds simply would not occur in Algonquin Park and other northern parts of their range if it weren't for sapsuckers. It may sound crazy that hummingbirds would depend on a kind of woodpecker for survival, but the facts strongly point to just that.

So the next time you hear someone repeating the old idea that hummingbirds hitch rides on the backs of larger birds, tell them that they just haven't been keeping up. Then proceed to reveal the depth of your ornithological understanding to your adoring friends and acquaintances, and set them on the path of true enlightenment. "Hummingbirds," you should declare solemnly, "hitchhike through life not with geese or eagles but with sapsuckers."

We're sure everyone will be impressed.✎

August 6, 1987, Vol. 28, No. 8 (D.S.)

A Time for Big and a Time for Small

Deep down inside, humans are very impressed by large sizes. The big fish or the big moose always command much more attention than the smaller ones, and we unfailingly assume just about that the large animals are successful and admirable while the small ones are paltry and insignificant.

Yet, when you stop to think about it, the world has infinitely more small creatures than big ones. For every lordly moose there are thousands of lowly mice; for every hawk there are literally millions of insects. Whatever our human preferences, small size must have some advantages, else the legions of small animals would not have triumphed — in numerical terms at least — over their supposedly better-off larger relatives.

There is, in fact, a balance between bigness and smallness that operates throughout evolutionary history to determine an animal's size. A particularly fine example of the conflicting pressures involved is afforded by the two weasels we have in Algonquin, the Short-tailed and the

Long-tailed. The Short-tailed Weasel, also called Ermine for its white winter fur, is the smaller species and the more common. While this is in keeping with the general rule about small species being more numerous than large ones, there is much more to the issue than that. In particular, the males of each species are almost twice as big as the females. For example, female Short-tails average about 55 grams, male Short-tails come in around 90 grams, followed by female and male Long-tails, which average 110 and 190 grams, respectively. In relative terms these are truly enormous differences (male Long-tails are almost four times as big as female Short-tails, for example), and they raise some fundamental questions. We know that both sexes of both species eat the same food (mainly Meadow Voles found in beaver meadows and other damp, low-lying shrubby areas), so how is it that the Park supports two species of weasels? Surely one or the other should be more efficient and have supplanted the other long ago? And then, within each species, why do such pronounced, twofold size differences persist between the sexes? Again, one size should be best for the weasel way of life, and one would expect it to be the norm for both males and females.

In particular, we have to wonder why both sexes of both species have not become larger, or at least as large as the male Long-tailed Weasels. Many observations indicate that male Long-tails dominate the smaller weasel size classes. They are the first to be caught in trapping programs (suggesting that they dominate the others and impose their own priority at new food sources), and they are the last to disappear from an area when there is a food shortage. Why then are female Long-tails so much smaller than males, and why do the even smaller Short-tailed Weasels not only persist in the presence of their larger relatives but also actually outnumber them?

Short-tailed Weasels (Ermines) and Long-tailed Weasels both turn white in winter, except for the black tip of the tail.

The explanation for the male-female size differences in both species apparently has to do with their different roles in reproduction. Males compete with each other for females, as well as food, so it really does pay them to be large. Small males don't get mates. Females, on the other hand, have to raise their young unassisted, and this means finding and killing all the mice necessary to feed both the growing young and themselves. Small size is an advantage in meeting this demand for two reasons. For one thing, being small means lower food requirements. One researcher has calculated that a female weasel needs to catch 20 per cent less food per day than would a hypothetical female the size of a male. This could amount to 50 fewer mice over the period of raising young, and if food is scarce, such a lowered requirement could make all the difference between success and failure in raising the young. The second advantage enjoyed by a small female is that she is more able to follow mice through tiny passages and has a correspondingly better chance of catching the large numbers she needs.

Turning to the question of how both Long-tailed and Short-tailed Weasels manage to co-exist in Algonquin, we find a clue to the puzzle in the ranges of the two animals. Long-tailed Weasels are very close to their northern limits here in the Park but are found right down into northern South America. Short-tailed Weasels, by contrast, range far up into the Arctic but go no farther south than the northern United States. On the face of it, this is the opposite of what you would expect. Generally, big animals do better in the north because it is easier for a large body to keep warm in cold weather. With weasels, nevertheless, it is the small Short-tail that lives in the north and the large Long-tail that lives in the south.

When you remember, however, that most mice live in tunnel networks under the snow all winter long, the advantage enjoyed by Short-tailed Weasels in the north is obvious. They, but not their big cousins, can effectively pursue mice through those tunnels no matter how deep the snow.

When snow is not a factor, it apparently pays a weasel to be big (like a Long-tail); when snow isolates the winter food supply from the outside world, it pays to be small (like a Short-tail). Here, in the mid-latitudes of North America, conditions are not clear-cut so we have a transition zone with both species present. Presumably Long-tails do quite poorly in years with lots of snow and Short-tails are out-competed in years of little snow and low food supplies — but neither species is ever completely eliminated.

One could scarcely imagine a better example of the "tension" that can exist between two or more forces shaping the lives of animals than that told by Algonquin's two weasels. Sometimes the large size so fancied by us humans can indeed be advantageous, but at other times the very key to survival may lie in being small. Bigger is not always better — and that, if you haven't already guessed, is the long and the short of this story.✑

August 13, 1987, Vol. 28, No. 9 (D.S.)

The Best of The Raven

A Glimpse of the Old Days

We believe it is a fair comment that most visitors to Algonquin value the Park for its sense of timelessness. Here, after all, only a few hours away from hundreds of modern industrialized towns and cities, is a vast, beautiful tract of land still covered by the forests and inhabited by the animals that were present centuries ago.

Also, it is quite probable that many of us assume the Park has seen little or no change at all and that time really does stand still here. However, if the truth were known, important people and ideas have come and gone in Algonquin just as they have elsewhere. Sometimes the effects were short-lived, but in other cases what we see now and regard as quite normal can be traced back to particular personalities or philosophies, which, themselves, are largely forgotten today.

This fact was brought home to us recently when someone drew our attention to the Superintendent's annual report for the year 1901. We hope you find the excerpts printed here interesting. In a few places we have added notes of explanation when we deemed them necessary or useful. Keep in mind that when Superintendent Bartlett wrote his report, there were no telephones, no radios, no highway, and no campgrounds and the handful of visitors who did come took the train to Park Headquarters, then at Cache Lake.

Jan. 13, 1902

To the Honourable
The Commissioner of Crown Lands

"Sir, — As is customary, I respectfully beg to hand you herewith report on the Algonquin National Park for the year 1901. (Although officially called a 'national' park up until 1913, Algonquin has always been under Ontario's jurisdiction. – ed.)

The Park staff is composed of eleven rangers besides the superintendent. The month of January, 1901, was mostly taken up getting wood at headquarters, making sleighs, snowshoes, etc. Then the rangers went out in pairs to their several sections, each man drawing a sled loaded with provisions. February, March and April were spent patrolling the Park. During the month of May the rangers returned to headquarters by canoe leaving sleds and snowshoes in the shelter houses for next winter. In the months of June and July the rangers were employed, except when prevented by fires, in improving grounds and buildings at headquarters, cutting out portages etc. August was principally devoted to building new shelter houses, repairing those already built, and cutting out portages. In September most of the rangers again took canoes, and those who have sections farthest removed from headquarters carried with them supplies sufficient to last until they came out at Christmas on snowshoes, bringing their sleds with them to take back supplies for the spring. (Of the Park's original

system of beautifully built 'shelter houses' or ranger cabins, only 20 remain today. Many were deliberately destroyed in the 1940s and '50s after the ranger cabin system was abandoned. – ed.)

We have built five large fishing boats which have been put on the following lakes: Cache, Cranberry (now Canisbay), Source, Head and Hilliard. We built two new bark canoes, made several sleds and snowshoes, erected two large wood-sheds, raised the partly fallen kitchen at the superintendent's house, dug cellar under it, dug drain from house to lake … built winter quarters for pheasants, Belgian hares, etc. My men have done good work and have succeeded wonderfully in keeping out trappers when you consider the large area they have to cover. Our deer, pheasants, etc., have done well. We raised two very fine fawns last summer.

There have been a large number of visitors to the Park, all of whom have expressed themselves delighted with the success that has attended the efforts of the Government to protect the game and fur-bearing animals. Deer are very numerous everywhere and can be seen at almost all times in large numbers from the train as you pass through. Beaver, mink, otter, etc., are also very plentiful, and have increased wonderfully. Wolves, I regret to say, are very bold and numerous this winter, and the rangers have put out a large quantity of poison to destroy them. Moose are plentiful, and are frequently seen by the rangers and tourists. (Bartlett's misguided, though for the time quite normal, efforts to poison wolves in Algonquin Park had almost no significant effects on wolf numbers but did kill many other animals and virtually wiped out the local Raven population. Today, of course, wolves are not only protected in Algonquin but are one of the reasons why the Park is world-famous. – ed.)

The Black Bass put into these lakes during the past two years have increased far beyond my most extreme hopes, and are very abundant. Young bass can be caught in any of the lakes in great numbers. (Of all Superintendent Bartlett's many attempts to establish new, non-native fish and wildlife species in Algonquin, only his Black (i.e., Smallmouth) Bass project was successful. We should never forget, however, that when Mr. Bartlett introduced bass to such lakes as Smoke, Cache, and Opeongo, he destroyed a much more important resource than he created. Those lakes originally had Brook Trout populations, which are extinct today because of the bass. – ed.)

Lumbering is going on in the Park at several points, but we never had less trouble with the employees of the lumber firms than we have had during the past year, and I feel that the different license holders are co-operating with us as they never did before. Smallpox has visited some of the camps in the Park this season and there are several cases reported at Lake of Two Rivers. I think some strong measures should be taken to stamp out the disease in these camps.

The St. Anthony Lumber Co. have surveyed a line from Whitney to Great Opeongo Lake with the intention of running a log road through to haul their timber out by rail. The line is graded to the Park boundary and the contract calls for the completion of the line to Opeongo Lake by August next. (This line was indeed built and used but was abandoned sometime before 1920. The present-day Opeongo Road and Highway 60 from there east to Whitney are largely built on the original roadbed of 1902. – ed.)

My staff have just finished cutting and hauling a large supply of firewood. They will now fill the ice house and then go out to their several sections until spring."

Your obedient servant,
G.W. Bartlett, Superintendent ∽

August 20, 1987, Vol. 28, No. 10 (D.S.)

Not a Care in the World?

One of our favourite sights at this time of year is two or three young foxes chasing each other through the long grass by the roadside. Indeed, what more entertaining and perfect picture of youthful innocence could there be than these red streaks in the lush growth of late summer. They are so tireless, exuberant, and carefree that they often remind us of some of our fellow fox watchers — school kids on their summer holidays.

Of course, even if there are certain resemblances, fox pups are "students" in a survival school very different from that attended by any of our children. This may seem like an obvious thing to say, but it bears repeating all the same because humans often lose sight of the realities of animal existence. Although none of us past the age of three actually believes that animals are people dressed up in funny costumes, our childhood fairy tales really do leave an impression, and, even as adults, we often persist in believing that animals and humans do, or should, share the same values.

Actually, the case of fox pups is a good illustration of just how far off the mark we can be when we fall into that sort of trap. A family of foxes is far from carefree and indeed has elements that, by our standards, could only be called brutally inhuman.

To begin with, using the word family is really stretching a point. Foxes are basically loners, and even if a male and female often share the same territory, they go their own separate ways for most of the year (because hunting alone is a more efficient way to catch small, elusive prey items such as mice and chipmunks). In late February or early March, however, when the Park is still deep in snow, the sexes seek each other out and

mating occurs. The female chooses and refurbishes one of several already existing dens on the territory and gives birth to her young in late April. Five or six is the average litter size, although there may be as many as 10. The pups are tiny and helpless at first and would quickly freeze if their mother did not constantly keep them warm during their first 10 to 14 days of life. Fortunately, the male brings food back to his nursing mate and makes such intensive care possible. Later, both parents and occasionally a daughter from the previous year are kept busy almost around the clock trying to keep the hungry mouths well fed after weaning.

So far, even if the fox family was put together in a bit of a hurry, nothing we have described sounds particularly inhuman. Indeed, both parents are models of devotion, and even "big sis" pitches in to help with the chores. But wait; things are about to change!

In fact, just after they get their teeth, at about three to four weeks of age, the pups start to fight each other viciously. Sometimes individual pups are actually killed in these struggles. But even if this doesn't happen, the contests establish, in a period of about 10 days, a strict and virtually permanent order of dominance among the pups. This means that the number one pup will always get, or be able to steal, any piece of food brought back to the den by the adults. By contrast, the lowest-ranking pup will never get or keep any food at all unless every higher-status pup has a full stomach. Since, in fact, there rarely is enough food to satisfy the demand, it is entirely normal for the weaker pups to starve to death while the others are well-fed. Even more ghastly to our human way of seeing things, the adults do absolutely nothing to prevent these "murders." They act for all the world as if the horrible deaths of their children didn't even matter.

Now, it is true that many of our human fairy tales relate some pretty unsavoury events, but we personally can't recall any as gruesome as those that occur in every fox den. The behaviour is even more perplexing because it is so contradictory. One minute the adults are perfect parents; the next they watch indifferently as their babies turn into murderous thugs. How can this possibly be justified or understood?

Although the behaviour of foxes can never be justified in human terms, it certainly can be understood. As a matter of fact, the family life of foxes contains some thought-provoking indications about how the real (non-fairy tale) world actually operates in general. It may well be true that adult foxes feel something like the affection we humans have for our babies, but the more fundamental reason why the foxes we see today actually care for their young is that they can't help it! In the past there may well have been mutant foxes that had no inclination to have young or care for them. Needless to say, such varieties would have died out quickly. The only strains of foxes that have survived to our day are those that were born with, and have passed on, the instinct to have babies and make sure they survive. Seen in this light, child-rearing in the society of foxes or other creatures is more inevitable than praiseworthy and, if anything, may be seen to be on the selfish side. After all, we know that no individual creature can live forever, but a second-best alternative available is to have your genes live on in your descendants. By reproducing itself, a living thing can perpetuate its genes — and that may be the fundamental thing that a fox does (as opposed to "loving its cute little puppies") when it gives birth to and cares for its young.

Even an apparently generous and loving daughter fox that stays with its parents and helps raise younger brothers and sisters may be doing so for very selfish reasons — albeit quite unconsciously. By raising siblings the daughter fox is raising babies that, on average, carry just as many of the daughter's genes as would its own babies. If the daughter can't find a territory and mate of her own, helping her parents raise more young is the most reproductively selfish thing she can do. She may also gain useful experience for her own breeding attempts. Either way, big sister is in it for herself.

But how then to explain the murderous behaviour of baby foxes towards each other and the indifference of the adults if the name of the game is survival of genes? In the case of the young, if there isn't enough food to go around, it's easy to see that each youngster should fight tooth and claw to avoid being at the bottom of the heap. After all, if you don't live, you can't pass on any of your genes. In these circumstances the tendency to attack your brothers and sisters is the only behaviour that can possibly last more than one generation. The alternative behaviour (being generous and letting the others have first crack at the food) inevitably means that you thereby starve — and therefore fail to reproduce and pass on your (suicidal) gene for generosity.

As for adults, why should they care which of their young are the ones that survive (given that some must die)? As a matter of fact, from their point of view (or that of their genes), the worst thing they could do would be to try to overrule their competitively superior offspring and try to enforce food-sharing. They might well prolong the lives of their weaker young, but only by weakening the stronger ones. The final result might be an intact litter of uniformly weak babies that are all doomed to die instead of a reduced number of potential winners. Playing referee might be "moral" by human standards, but it would be very "stupid" for any fox that was unknowingly attempting to maximize the survival of its genes to succeeding generations.

By now it should be apparent, if it wasn't already, that the real world of foxes playing in the long grass of summer is far removed from that experienced by our children. And the brutalities of the foxes' existence are far from over. Soon, unless food supplies happen to be exceptional, the surviving pups will be forced to disperse into totally unknown country far beyond their birthplaces in probably futile attempts to find territories of their own.

Only a few hard-bitten individuals ever make it to adulthood — so nothing in their lives could be called innocent or carefree the way we understand these terms. To compare them ever with our children is really to miss the fundamental nature of their lives.

You could even say that, if fox pups are like school kids, then they are very much students in the school of hard fox.❧

August 27, 1987, Vol. 28, No. 11 (D.S.)

Jockeying in the Halls of Chickadee Power

Summer is drawing to a close. The nights are nippy, and patches of red and yellow leaves are already apparent — even if the peak of colours won't be here for another three weeks. The Park's animal life shows important signs of change as well. Birds are migrating overhead every night, bears are fattening up, and red squirrels are busy clipping pine cones for their underground larders.

All these developments, of course, are preparations for the coming winter. And, as everyone familiar with the cold season in the Park realizes, hardly anything could be more important for all living things than to get ready for, or escape from, what is about to happen to Algonquin. The cold, the snow, the lack of food — all are going to impose the severest of tests, which most of the Park's inhabitants can ignore only at their certain peril.

One creature, however, is apparently immune to the crass considerations of winter survival and seems to just sail through the cold without a care in the world. Right now Black-capped Chickadees are abandoning their summer breeding territories and coalescing into little flocks that will spend the coming fall and winter patrolling their winter ranges in the woods. We don't have to tell regular winter visitors to Algonquin that these little bands of chickadees are among the very few — and the most welcome of all — signs and sounds of life in the otherwise lonely winter woods. No one who is greeted by a rollicking, inquisitive chickadee flock can fail to have a warm feeling for such tiny bundles of feathers and their confiding, seemingly so good-natured dispositions.

And yet, at the risk of shattering some long-held illusions about chickadees, we believe most people admire these tiny birds for all the wrong reasons. The truth is that chickadees don't just coast through the winter, and their flocks, far from being the "happy, little welcoming committees" we tend to imagine, are in reality the scenes of very serious, very real, power struggles.

If you watch a winter flock of chickadees closely, you will soon appreciate that their lives are not easy at all; they are constantly on the move, searching for food from dawn to dusk. As a species they are obviously successful in finding enough overwintering insects, insect eggs, and stored seeds from the previous summer to survive, but as individuals they often fail. Freezing to death, starving, or being so busy looking for food that they fail to see a predator in time are all quite normal fates for chickadees in winter. Indeed, these dangers are probably why chickadees form flocks in the first place. By travelling in a group, flock members have a better chance of detecting enemies. They can huddle together for warmth on cold nights, and they can each exploit food over a much larger area than if they were forced to stay in pairs or families on their summer territories.

This much is easy enough to appreciate, but there is more to winter chickadee flocks than mere survival. The problem is that when spring finally arrives, each chickadee flock will break up into individual pairs, each pair with its own exclusive breeding territory. This would be fine except that every winter flock has about 10 members but occupies a flock territory that can be split up into only two or three breeding territories. The extra birds (representing an excess still remaining from the previous year's nestings) must either die or be driven away.

The stage is set for a very serious contest, but few of us could imagine how complicated a game chickadees actually play. Studies of banded birds have shown that flock members adopt one of two main strategies in their efforts to achieve eventual breeding status. An individual chickadee may become either a "regular" or a "floater."

Regulars, which always stay in the same flock on the same territory, are invariably present as equal numbers of males and females. They are, in fact, pairs — either old, established pairs that have bred together before or new ones established at the time of flock formation.

There is a definite dominance hierarchy among these birds, and this is important in determining who eventually gets the all-important breeding positions. Since the average flock has five pairs of regulars but the flock territory has room for only

Regulars or floaters?

two or three pairs to breed, it is important for a regular flock member to be part of a high-ranked pair.

Floaters, the other category of bird in winter chickadee flocks, are individual, unpaired birds of either sex. As the name suggests, they move about among neighbouring flocks. Floaters also have a dominance hierarchy but always rank below all the regulars in whatever flock they are with.

Even if not all the regulars have a chance to breed, the chances for the lowly floaters to breed as well might seem especially hopeless. However, there is a way for them to get a breeding position. If a high-ranking regular dies, it is almost always replaced, not by the next-ranking regular but by the highest-ranking local floater of the same sex. The floater leapfrogs over all the low-ranking regulars and fills the slot opened up by the regular's death, pairing with its widow. It seems that the lower-ranked regulars are locked into position by virtue of being already mated, and they are not free to leave their slot the way an unmated floater can (sound familiar?). As a matter of fact, being a low-ranked regular is such an unattractive proposition that if one of them dies, their spot is not usually filled by a floater. Apparently it is more advantageous for a floater to wait and be ready for a chance at the slot of a high-ranked regular, should one open up (in any of the several flocks it regularly visits), than it would be to lock itself in as a low regular in a single flock.

This same order of relative likelihood to become a breeder is reflected in the way chickadee flocks form in the first place. The first birds to arrive are the high-ranked regulars, and they, of course, have it made if they survive the winter. The next birds to join the flock become floaters, and the last birds become low-ranked regulars — the ones with the least chance of becoming breeders at the end of winter.

This all sounds (and is) very complicated, and it may strike you as a little depressing as well. We are so used to thinking of fall and winter chickadee flocks as merry bands of carefree woodland sprites, oblivious to the cold and snow around them, that the brutal truth of their lives may seem a little sad. But, in our view, such a reaction would really be missing an important and amazing point. It is indeed true that chickadees are subject to the same necessities and laws of survival as any other creatures that have to face an Algonquin winter. In this, chickadees are in no way exceptional. But of all the Park's winter inhabitants, the Black-capped Chickadee is the only one that devotes a significant amount of its energy and behaviour not just to the immediate problem of short-term survival but to the acquisition of breeding status in the warm spring days that, we hope, lie ahead.

Surely, this is the way chickadees are truly exceptional. It is not because they can just sail effortlessly through an Algonquin winter or dispense with the need for social status — no animal can do such things.

Rather it is because, even as they struggle with winter's cruel and inescapable hardships, Black-capped Chickadees are jockeying for position in a far-off spring many of them will never live to see. What better symbol could there be of courage in the face of adversity? What better — and more real — reason to admire them than the hope they so cheerily represent. ↻

September 3, 1987, Vol. 28, No. 12 (D.S.)

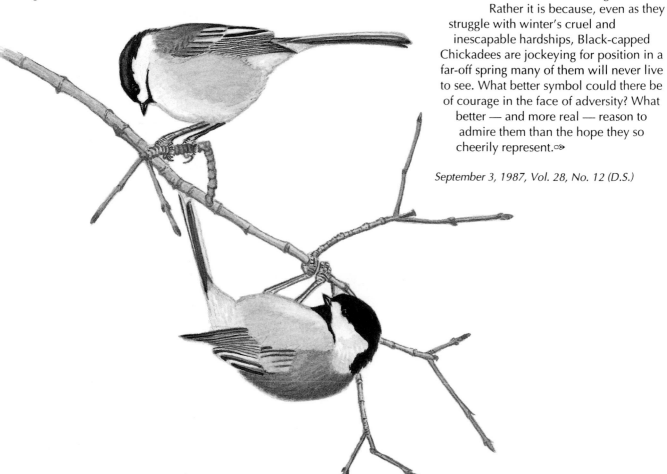

Geography Teachers Who Fly in the Sky

When you were making plans for your trip to Algonquin earlier this year, you probably told friends you would be going "up" to the Park. People say this of course because, in most cases, they have to drive north to get here. Still, as most regular visitors know, you really do have to go "up" to reach the Park, no matter from where you are coming. For years we have been pointing out that Algonquin lies on a dome of rock that is higher than the surrounding country. When you travel in from Huntsville to Canisbay Campground, for example, you rise approximately 150 metres (500 feet) to 445 metres (1,450 feet) above sea level, and there are places in the Park that are another 100 metres higher than that. Over a distance of 60 kilometres a rise of 150 metres may seem hardly noticeable, but if we look hard enough, we can find significant differences. The climate up here on the Algonquin dome is measurably cooler, for one thing. On average there are only 84 frost-free days a year on the high, west side of the Park, whereas the figure is 105 over on the east side where the elevation has dropped off again, down to less than 200 metres above sea level. The extra height of the highlands also makes for greater rain and snowfall because air masses moving east from Georgian Bay are forced to rise and lose more of their moisture in the Park than would otherwise be the case.

We have known for a long time that the colder and wetter climate of Algonquin's west side has definite, and sometimes very dramatic, effects on Park vegetation. Ontario's provincial flower, for example, the White Trillium, is virtually non-existent in the Park highlands, although it is abundant in the Huntsville area. Trees such as Basswood, American Elm, and White Ash, which are

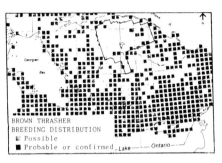

BROWN THRASHER
BREEDING DISTRIBUTION
▨ Possible
■ Probable or confirmed

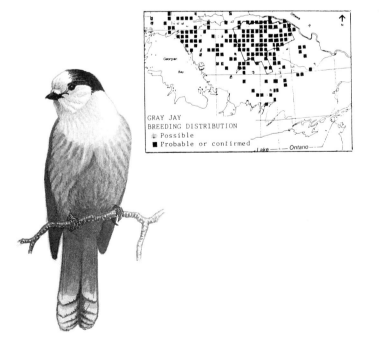

GRAY JAY
BREEDING DISTRIBUTION
▨ Possible
■ Probable or confirmed

also common there, have all just about dropped out of the picture by the time the West Gate is reached. On the other hand, there is a visible trend toward more conifers when you make the same trip. This is not surprising, of course. As you go up into an area with colder, more "northerly" conditions, you should expect to encounter more northerly vegetation.

You should also expect the same sort of effect with animal life — and we do, in fact, see such trends. Beyond just saying so and citing a few examples, however, we were never able until just last fall to graphically illustrate the Algonquin dome's effect on animal distribution.

What has happened to improve this situation is the publication of a landmark book, the *Atlas of Breeding Birds of Ontario*, edited by M.D. Cadman, P.J.F. Eagles, and F.M. Helleiner. The compilers of this work deserve a great deal of recognition, but then, even more than with many other books, so do a lot of other behind-the-scenes people. The atlas was, in fact, a giant, five-year project involving over 1,300 volunteer observers (including many Algonquin Park staff), who donated over 180,000 hours (that's right!) of their time to map the distribution of breeding birds in Ontario. Given that the province is bigger than France and Spain put together but a lot harder to get at, it is a wonder that anybody even contemplated such a project, let alone pulled it off. In the huge and remote land mass of northern Ontario, as a matter of fact, it was simply not practical to sample at a finer scale than on big blocks of land, each one measuring 100 kilometres by 100 kilometres. Even at that, some blocks were only visited once or twice during the project (1981 to '85). In southern Ontario (roughly everything south of the line joining Sault Ste. Marie, Sudbury, and North Bay), however, access is better and observers far more numerous. Here, some 1,824 squares, each 10 kilometres by 10 kilometres, were visited for a minimum of 16 hours both in the spring and in the early summer nesting season to determine what breeding birds were present. An incredible amount of data was generated, checked, and fed into computers at the University of Waterloo for final transformation into the distribution maps that appear in the atlas for Ontario's almost 300 breeding bird species. The patterns and fine detail that emerge from these maps are interesting just about everywhere in Ontario, but we think they are particularly fascinating right here in our part of the province because of the way they illustrate the Algonquin dome effect.

The distribution maps for the Gray Jay and Boreal Chickadee reproduced in this article show what we mean. At these latitudes the Boreal Chickadee is pretty well restricted as a breeding bird to the highest part of the Algonquin highlands, where there is just enough of a northern coniferous flavour to permit this northern bird to make a go of it. The Gray Jay (also known as Canada Jay or Whiskeyjack) isn't quite so restricted, but it too falls off and has a patchier distribution in the country surrounding the dome — even including areas north of (but also lower than) the Park.

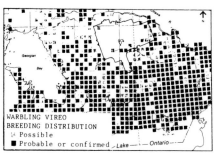

WARBLING VIREO
BREEDING DISTRIBUTION
⬚ Possible
■ Probable or confirmed Lake——Ontario---

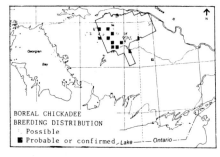

BOREAL CHICKADEE
BREEDING DISTRIBUTION
⬚ Possible
■ Probable or confirmed Lake——Ontario---

Algonquin's stronger coniferous element is not the only important difference between the Park and the surrounding country as far as many birds are concerned. The almost total lack of fields within Algonquin (but not outside, of course) is obviously very important to birds that favour open country, such as Kestrels (Sparrow Hawks) and Meadowlarks, and no one will be surprised that the atlas shows them both to be virtually absent from

the Park as breeders. Even for birds that feed in trees and shrubs, however, there are sometimes significantly more unfavourable conditions within than outside the Park. As their maps show, the Brown Thrasher and Warbling Vireo are both largely absent from the Park but found all around it. The reason seems to be that these two birds require "forest edges" of the sort that occur in towns, villages, and farm country but not in the mostly unbroken forest conditions prevailing in Algonquin.

Many other intriguing insights into the Algonquin environment are contained in the maps and text of the atlas, but the few insights here will give you a basic idea. Personally, we find it nothing short of amazing that the distribution of birds can tell us so much about differences in climate and vegetation, which we humans may barely notice even as we drive right by them on our way up into the Park. Then, too, given that birds are so sensitive to such small differences and we humans routinely bring about far bigger ones, the atlas is an excellent reminder about how important our own responsibility is in managing the environment. The geography lessons contained in the atlas may be by the birds, but they are definitely for us.◌

June 30, 1988, Vol. 29, No. 2 (D.S.)

Eggs on the Ceiling

We don't need to tell you that summer is the time of year in Algonquin Park when young animals are being brought into the world and raised to independence. And as everyone knows, the anatomy and behaviour used by some creatures to help in this task are often very sophisticated indeed. The production of milk by mammal mothers and the elaborate nests built by birds are obvious examples.

Still, in the popular consciousness, many other groups of animals are dismissed as being simple or even "primitive" when it comes to the production and raising of their young. Fish are a good case in point, as it is certainly true that many species don't do anything very elaborate. Female trout, for example, just clean off part of a suitable spawning bed and when the moment is right merely force out the eggs. The nearby male at the same time sends out a cloud of milt or sperm, which fertilizes the eggs in the water as they drift down into the cracks and crannies of the spawning bed. The adults then move on, and the eggs and resulting young are completely on their own.

There are definitely exceptions to this simple picture of fish reproduction, however, and some of them are quite remarkable indeed. One of the best examples is afforded by a very common and widespread Park species, the Fathead Minnow. While one has to concede that minnows, being small and difficult to see well, don't inspire a great deal of

awe or interest among humans, when it comes to the Fathead Minnow — at least as far as breeding males are concerned — the emotions most likely to be inspired are pity and disgust. The head, as suggested by the name, is big and fat, but, even worse, there are ugly, hard, pointed growths protruding from all over the male Fathead's face. To top that off, there is a spongy, slate-blue, wrinkled "growth" forming a pad on its back between the head and the dorsal fin.

These features certainly don't make Fathead Minnows pretty in our eyes, but since they are confined to males (and just in the breeding season at that), we can be sure that they must serve some purpose related to sex. But what could be so unusual about the Fathead's situation that it would develop such unusual structures not possessed by other fish?

The key thing is that Fathead Minnows could never just broadcast their eggs, even onto a cleaned-off spawning bed. Fatheads live in the shallow, shoreline areas of small lakes and ponds with very muddy or silty bottoms. Since any eggs deposited there would soon be buried and suffocate, the conventional means of fish egg deposition is not an option for Fathead Minnows. They might fasten their eggs to aquatic vegetation, but there they would be especially obvious to prying eyes — and vulnerable to inadvertent destruction by plant-eaters as well. What Fatheads do instead is fasten their eggs to the undersides of rocks, logs, or even floating lily pads. They hide their eggs on the ceiling, as it were, of their oozy, shallow water environment.

Accomplishing this trick is where one of the male Fathead's special anatomical features, the spongy back pad, comes into play. First, the male attracts a female, partly by making alternating,

Fathead Minnows,
fish of many talents.

vertical, deep purple and light tan bands on its sides appear and disappear (in the space of a few seconds). If the female is sufficiently impressed, she will swim closely beside the male. The two vibrate their bodies, and then the male, using his back pad, pushes the female (most often lying on her left side) up to the surface on which the eggs will be laid. Even on her side and being pushed upwards by the male, the female still needs a special, extrudable egg-laying tube to make sure that her eggs make contact with, and adhere to, the chosen spot. When she has deposited her eggs, the male fertilizes them and chases her away.

It is then that the male Fathead starts to use the other peculiar part of his anatomy, the strange, horny tubercles that adorn his face. For the five days it takes the eggs to hatch, father Fathead guards them ferociously, using his head as an armed battering ram against other neighbouring males, other minnow species, snails, and even turtles or human fingers. It also spends a lot of time circling underneath the eggs, often rubbing them with its back pad and frequently stopping to mouth and nibble at

them. These behaviours are believed to keep the eggs well supplied with oxygen and to keep them clean and free from fungus. Certainly, egg masses left on their own quickly get infected, and very few, if any, individual eggs will survive to hatching.

Under normal circumstances, with the benefit of the male Fathead's constant care and attention, most eggs do hatch and the young fish start out on their own. At best, they will only live two or three years, but at this time of year, they will develop the bizarre features and go through the finely-tuned behavioural steps that will ensure the launching of a new generation.

It is remarkable to think that such sophistication can exist in a fish, let alone one that humans have the conceit to dismiss as a "lowly" minnow. So let's not look down on the Fathead. As a matter of fact, a fish that can reproduce on its ceiling is a creature we should all look up to.

July 14, 1988, Vol. 29, No. 4 (D.S.)

Radio Turtle Is on the Air

It is quite natural for Park visitors to think of Algonquin as an important refuge for endangered wildlife. But, surprisingly, this is not really an accurate perception. To be sure, many animals are tamer and more visible inside the Park than they are outside. It is also true that Algonquin played an important role in its early years in the protection of beavers and other fur-bearing mammals against uncontrolled trapping. Nowadays, however, with modern management of hunting and trapping in Ontario, one would have trouble pointing to an Algonquin Park animal that could be considered plentiful inside Park boundaries and endangered outside. Having said all this, there actually is one exceptional wildlife species in Algonquin today whose future survival in Ontario may very well depend on the refuge afforded by the Park.

No, it's not the wolf or the loon or the bear or any of the other species we commonly associate with Algonquin. The animal is the Wood Turtle, a reptile that still occurs over a wide range in the northeastern United States and southeastern Canada but is rapidly disappearing from many localities.

Now, we have to admit at the outset that few people have ever heard of, let alone seen, a Wood Turtle, and it may be wondered why anyone should particularly care about it. Well, quite apart from the importance of preserving the full range of our natural heritage — of which the Wood Turtle is a legitimate part — there is no doubt that everyone who encounters this species is immediately intrigued by it.

To begin with, it is very attractive in appearance. Each "scute" or section of the upper shell has narrow concentric ridges that give a beautiful, sculptured effect. The lower shell is a striking yellow with irregular black blotches, and the dark neck and legs are unevenly marked with yellow or orange. But there is a lot more to the Wood Turtle than its appearance, however. This species is alone among Ontario turtles in spending much of the summer on dry land. It has the ability to move with strength and confidence and to quickly learn and remember its way around. There is nothing at all aggressive in its behaviour. Indeed, there is something in a Wood Turtle's eyes that unfailingly reawakens our childhood fascination with turtles and our notion of what a "wise old tortoise" ought to be.

All this notwithstanding, the Wood Turtle is not very well off in today's world. It lives near rivers but can't tolerate their pollution or the loss of streamside woodlands. It is vulnerable to cars and trucks, to thoughtless people and, because it spends so much time on land, to determined predators which, at the very least, often manage to chew off the ends of the turtle's legs. Every wildlife species has its own set of problems, of course, but the Wood Turtle is particularly sensitive to extra pressure because of the way it grows and reproduces. For one thing, even in the best of circumstances, most turtle eggs are found and eaten by foxes, skunks, and raccoons, and often the numbers of these predators are abnormally high in areas where man has moved in and altered the environment. Second, the few turtles that do hatch grow so slowly (not reaching sexual maturity until they are about 15 years old) that every adult is a very "rare commodity" whose loss cannot easily be tolerated by a Wood Turtle population. It doesn't take much extra pressure, therefore, to put Wood

Turtles in big trouble, so we shouldn't be too surprised to learn that they are disappearing from so many areas.

Here in Algonquin we have known for decades that they occur near the Petawawa, Bonnechère, and Opeongo Rivers on the Park's east side (with none at all in the Highway 60 Corridor), but only in a casual way as a result of chance sightings. A few years ago we began to wonder if this was really enough. After all, here was a species that was becoming increasingly rare in Canada, and the chances were good that relatively undisturbed areas such as Algonquin would become vital for its long-term prospects — and yet we really knew almost nothing about its status in the Park.

We began in 1986 with our first-ever attempt to deliberately search for Wood Turtles. The results (only one seen in a month of looking) were discouraging and alarming, to say the least, so we decided to step up our efforts the following year. Help was enlisted from over a dozen regular users of the Park's east side — they became volunteer Wood Turtle spotters — and, thanks to a grant from The Friends of Algonquin Park, six small radio transmitters were purchased so that any turtles found could be subsequently followed and relocated.

The results were most gratifying. In a very short time 14 Wood Turtles had been found and tagged. Right away this suggested that Wood Turtles were more common than we thought, at least in some areas. They also showed a good range of sizes and apparent ages, indicating that new adult turtles are coming along in a healthy population. And by relocating the six radio-fitted turtles, our summer student assigned to the project was able, for the first time, to learn just how much and what kind of ground is used by a Wood Turtle. In agreement with studies done elsewhere, he found that they didn't go far from rivers and stayed all summer in surprisingly small areas of just one or two acres — although one individual roamed over a full 115 acres near Lake Travers.

By the time this article was written, in July 1988, we had completed the better part of yet another Wood Turtle research season and have even more good news to report. This time around we discovered 21 new individual turtles, more than double the number found in 1986 and '87. This brings the grand total to 36. We now know that Wood Turtle populations are found along four separate rivers in and near Algonquin Park, namely, the Petawawa, the Barron, the Bonnechère, and the Madawaska.

The Madawaska population occurs outside the Park, but it may be the most prosperous of all. There, between the villages of Whitney and Madawaska, were found and photographed two hatchling Wood Turtles, which, as far as we know, are the first ones ever reported in Canada. As a bonus, a couple of two-year-olds turned up nearby, and we also saw signs of attemped nestings in a stretch of sandy river bank.

As for the six turtles outfitted with radios last summer, we already knew that one had died (a male at least 36 years old, which had apparently been killed and eaten by some predator), but we did relocate the five survivors. To ensure that we don't lose track of these animals because of battery failure, we removed the original transmitters and put on fresh replacements (purchased, as before, with a generous grant from The Friends of Algonquin Park). We also recruited a new turtle into our radio-equipped fleet to make up for the one that died.

We have every prospect, therefore, of learning much more about how our Algonquin Wood Turtles behave and what their habitat requirements are. For example, we hope to relocate our radioed turtles in winter and thereby find out where they hibernate and how faithful they are to those places. Even more important, we should be able to locate egg-laying sites and see how successfully our animals are reproducing. It may take several years before we have a complete picture, but we have made a promising start.

Thanks to an ingenious application of space age technology, the radios are on the turtles and the turtles are on the air, broadcasting to very interested human listeners!↝

July 21, 1988, Vol. 29, No. 5 (D.S.)

A Wood Turtle fitted out with a transmitter for radio-tracking.

Tough Wolves Don't Negotiate

August is wolf-howling season in Algonquin Park, and, by the end of this month, we hope to have taken another few thousand people out to hear the incomparably beautiful sound of wolves howling under starry skies. Last year we held Algonquin's 50th, 51st, 52nd, and 53rd public wolf howling expeditions with 4,908 people in attendance. On one occasion a breeze started up that was strong enough to prevent some of the people from hearing the wolves, but the other three attempts were unqualified successes. Everybody got to hear both pups and adults answer the imitation howls given by our naturalist staff.

There is no question that people take enormous excitement and interest from this first-hand contact between man and wolf, and Park staff are happy to make it possible. However, few of us stop to wonder why wolves bother to answer us at all. To be sure, back in 1959 when wolf researchers here in Algonquin made the startling discovery that wolves would answer recordings or human vocal imitations, they were too busy to think about why. The simple fact that they did answer was a dramatic breakthrough, enabling scientists for the first time to reliably locate wolves in the summer. The new technique made all the difference in being able to census wolves at that time of year and in studying the early stages of family life at den sites. Later, of course, the techniques became the very foundation of our present-day wolf howl programs, and, here too, it was more a case of being thankful wolves answer as readily as they do rather than worrying about why.

Still, as a general principle, we can be sure that wolves don't howl to make life simpler for wolf researchers or to oblige Park visitors who long to hear them. It is obvious that howling permits wolves to communicate with other wolves, but just what message or messages might be conveyed and under what circumstances is much less apparent.

It is also a difficult problem to study, given that one can almost never see what the wolves are, or have been, doing when they howl, much less their age, sex, individual identity, or any other information that might help us sort out who is doing the howling and why.

We now have a lot of answers to these questions, however, thanks to studies carried out over the last 15 years in Minnesota. The researchers were able to work with well-known, radio-collared wolf packs — meaning that they could always tell which wolves were out there (even if they didn't answer the researchers' howls). They could also tell where the wolves were in relationship to their territorial boundaries and whether they moved (and which way) after hearing the human howls. After many nights (and years!) of howling at wolves, the Minnesota people were able to detect several distinct patterns.

First of all, it was far from guaranteed that the wolves would answer. On over half the occasions (54 per cent) the wolves remained silent — and often they picked up and left the area as well. In another 43 per cent of the cases, however, the wolves not only stayed where they were but howled back. And some of the time at least, following the pack's answer, one or two of the adults silently approached the human observer or one wolf came within 150 feet and howled several times in a distinctive, low-pitched, gruffly-ending howl. The question is, of course, what could account for these wildly differing responses to the same stimulus (imitation wolf howls from the researchers). Several distinct patterns seem to suggest answers. There was, for example, a definite seasonal variation, with wolves being much more likely to answer in February (mating season) or August (the time of year when pups have left the den and occupy a series of temporary "rendezvous" sites). Adults are much more likely to answer when pups are present, when they are at a fresh kill, or when the pack is large. Lone adult wolves apparently never answer human imitation howls unless they are the top-ranking male in the pack. Such "alpha" males were also the individuals mentioned earlier that approached the observers and howled at them repeatedly from close distances. It seems clear from such observations that when wolves hear a howl and howl back, they are communicating (to what they not unreasonably presume is another wolf) their aggressive determination to hold their ground. This explains why they howl more readily when they have pups, a mate, or a food source to defend. It also explains why alpha males are the only lone wolves to howl back at or approach what appears to be a strange, intruding wolf that was confident enough to betray its presence by howling in the first place. Lone wolves of lower status presumably don't like the idea of a strange interloper any more than the alpha males, but they, unlike the alphas, are used to the idea of being dominated by other wolves and, for all they know, the stranger will do more than just dominate them. They could easily end up being killed because meetings with strange wolves almost invariably lead to fatal fights. Under these circumstances it is perhaps better for a less than supremely self-confident alpha male to stay silent and keep its whereabouts secret. Even whole packs apparently react this way when they hear a strange howl, especially if they have no pups or food that would be worth fighting for.

You may be struck here by the parallels between wolf psychology and our own, but it goes further than that. We humans are not particularly impressed by high, squeaky voices, but we sit up and pay attention to deep "powerful" ones, especially if they are directed toward us in an aggressive manner. The usual explanation for this instinctive reaction is that we associate low and powerful voices (produced by large vocal cords and chest cavities) with large bodies. Large-bodied people, usually males, are more of a potential physical threat if push comes to shove than small-bodied people (with high-pitched voices). Similarly, large powerful wolves have lower voices than pups or smaller adults. The Minnesota researchers got good evidence that wolves are intimidated by deep howls, whether of human or wolfish origin, and are more likely to keep quiet or move away when they hear them. This fact opens the way for a certain element of bluff in wolf confrontations and probably explains why alpha males have a special, extra low-pitched and gruffly-ending howl when they approach strange wolves (or researchers passing as such). High-pitched howls carry much better than low-pitched ones and are better for long-distance self-advertisement, but, close up, it doesn't matter. Then, it would be better to howl as low as possible so as to be more menacing to the stranger the alpha male is trying to get rid of.

We had an excellent example of this last year on our third public wolf howl when one wolf, presumably the alpha male, approached us closely and howled repeatedly. Although we will never be able to put ourselves in a wolf's skin completely, we can now, thanks to the Minnesota research, partly imagine how a real wolf would have felt if it had been where we were that night and had been foolish enough to betray its presence to the nearby pack by howling the way we did. Under the cold light of the moon and a million stars, the intruding wolf would have heard the continuous, menacing howls of the alpha male relentlessly drawing nearer. It would have heard the power and implacable hostility denoted by the deep, gruff endings. Seized by cold fear it would have left quickly, silently, and desperately.

The interloper would be gone, and the alpha male, through his howls, would have succeeded in driving away the potential threat to his pack and pups. He would not know or care that 1,244 people had just drunk in the wild beauty of his performance in awestruck silence, humbled by the dramatic contact made between man and wolf on that memorable night in Algonquin Park.✎

August 18, 1988, Vol. 29, No. 9 (D.S.)

Talk About a Canoe Trip!

We don't have to remind anyone about Algonquin Park's fame as a place to go on canoe trips. Generations of proud young canoeists have made innumerable trips in the Park, exploring its creeks, lakes, and rivers and treasuring memories of the wild and beautiful landscape they have seen.

We note with a touch of sadness, however, that many of today's canoeists all too easily take for granted the modern equipment and maps they have, not to mention the fact that help and civilization are never very far away. To be sure, we all realize in a general way that things were not always as easy as they are now, but it is still quite difficult for us to imagine the hardships endured by the first people to make canoe trips in the Algonquin highlands.

To give you just one example, let us consider the trip made in 1837 by David Thompson from Georgian Bay to the Ottawa River via the Muskoka-Oxtongue and Madawaska River systems. Thompson should be familiar to every Canadian as the man who surveyed vast areas of the Canadian West and who first explored the Columbia River down to its mouth on the Pacific Ocean. In 1837 he was engaged by the Government of Upper Canada (later Ontario) to explore and map one of three possible canal routes between Georgian Bay and the Ottawa River. Thompson set out with five other experienced woodsmen in a 25-foot canoe on August 1 from Penetanguishene. He had no map other than some rudimentary sketches of part of his proposed route, and right away he had to spend two days just looking for the mouth of the Muskoka River on Georgian Bay. Then, making detailed surveys of the Muskoka Lakes and Lake of Bays as he went, Thompson slowly worked his way up the Muskoka River system, not reaching Oxtongue Lake (a few miles outside the West Gate) until September 7 or 8. During all this time he and his party saw only two human beings, an old Indian man and a very sick boy near the present site of Bracebridge.

On September 9 they needed three hours to portage the canoe and all their gear past formidable Ragged Falls, and it took another two or three days to struggle up to Tea Lake in what is now Algonquin Park. There, having covered less than half his intended route and knowing nothing about how to get over the height of land into the easterly-flowing Madawaska River, Thompson made an astonishing, though sensible, decision. We join his diary on September 13 and present selected excerpts from the days that follow to give you a first-hand impression of the incredible resourcefulness and stamina of these men.

"*Sept. 13* — *as we are now at the 1st Lake at the height of Land, I resolved to do what I have long seen necessary from the shoal water, Rapids, etc. The necessity [for] exploring the country to know what it is according to my Instructions, etc. — and our large Canoe being too heavy for shoal Water, and also that with one Canoe we cannot separate ourselves to examine two Rivers at the same time, etc. etc. I determined to make two small Canoes which should be able to take all our Provisions, Baggage, etc.*

Sept. 14 — *dense fog — visited the Net, nothing in it. All hands at work. 3 Men knifing Timbers, 2 Men with myself split out the Gunwales for the Canoes to be 19 ft. in length. brought them to the Camp. split out 40 more Timbers. Set the net in another place.*

Sept. 15 — *cool clear morning … visited the Net. nothing. let it stand. all hands at work. by noon with two Men split out 33 Boards for the Canoe … For want of something fresh find myself weak. Took chocolate for Dinner with Crackers and much better. In the afternoon with 2 Men split out 53 Boards for the Canoe, in all 88 Boards.*

Sept. 17 — *Sunday. Each of the Men, except Antoine making himself a Shirt of the Cotton I brought …*

Sept. 18 — *SE Gale with steady rain, working hard to get all ready to begin a Canoe, when the weather permits, as we have no shelter from the Rain, etc. everything is wet.*

Sept. 23 — *Set to work on getting the rest of the Timbers in, &c. &c. which occupied all day with the 2 Canoes, pegs instead of nails, we have not one third enough of nails. picked an old piece of Line into Oakum to help the stopping the Seams of the Canoes …*

Sept. 24 — *Sunday. Men employed on the Canoes running gum into the seams, caulking slightly &c &c. We had 300 lb of Biscuit, & we have expended at the rate of about 1/8 lb per man per day, or less. The allowance is 1/2 lb per day. abt 1/2 Bag of Flour is also expended. But we have 3 Boxes of Pork abt 220 lb & abt 60 lbs of Beef remaining — Since Wednesday morning the 20th Inst. Ther 32 degrees and water frozen to Ice — The woods in all their Foliage have suddenly changed & assumed all the vivid tints of October, and begin to fall freely, one cannot help a sigh at such a quick change …*

Sept. 25 — *Sent all the Men to gather Gum, for it is a very scarce Article, & is what details us here. by 2 PM each returned with a little, altho' they have searched*

round this Lake, as there are few Pines, boiled it, & got it ready for the Canoes. But at 3 PM, Rain came on, & soon became very heavy so that we could do nothing. The season getting late.

Sept. 27 — *… Finished the Gum we have on the Canoe, which is by no means enough, but no more can be procured at this place … In the 14 days for making the Canoes we had 6 fine days — 6 days of Rain and 2 days of half Rain & half dry cloudy weather …"*

On September 29, Thompson finally set out again. Things would have gone slowly enough with the constant need to periodically stop and regum their new canoes, but there was another problem. Having no useful map they had to laboriously explore the shoreline of every lake, carefully looking for signs of long disused portages. Even when they were lucky enough to find one, they still had to clear it out before they could use it and then start the whole process all over again on the next lake. It took them a full 14 days to travel from Tea Lake to the present site of Whitney, just outside the East Gate.

Nowadays, with the benefit of good equipment, cleared portages, and knowing where they are going, modern canoeists can easily make the same trip in three or even two days.

Thompson did have one experience, however, that today's canoe-trippers will never duplicate. On October 10, at either Lake of Two Rivers or Rock Lake, he came across an Indian camp, as related in his diary:

"*… here we found an old Indian of the name Cha-un-d-e and enquiring what River we were on, he told us, we were on the middle Branch, or the proper Madawaska River, that no white man had been on it, that it was the shortest, best, and had the greatest Water of the 3 Branches which form the main Stream, had fewer Rapids, and was by far the most navigable & that we had been fortunate in finding it. I wanted him to give me a Sketch of the North Branch [Opeongo River], which he declined, but procured from him a sketch of the River Lakes and [carrying] Places for some distance. he advised us to be careful on the Rapids, adding that when you are below them all, there will be no more danger. he gave us two Joints of Deer for all of which I paid him 6/3 and some Salt and Pepper.*"

Below Whitney the Madawaska River is filled with rapids, and Thompson and his men had their work cut out for them keeping their makeshift, split cedar canoes from being battered to pieces. They even salvaged the nails from all but two of their supply boxes in order to strengthen their fragile craft. As they descended the river, they began to encounter other people — Indian trappers and lumbermen — whose push into the Algonquin highlands was well under way even at that early date.

Thompson reached the Ottawa River on October 24, almost three months after setting out. Incredibly, he immediately took on another river survey, this time on the Ottawa River itself, and he wasn't finished until

December. Even then he had yet to be paid for any of his work, and to collect he was obliged to go to Toronto by way of Montreal. That was no trifling matter in 1837, the year armed rebellions broke out in both the Upper and Lower Canadas. There was no public transportation operating at all between Ottawa and Montreal, and Thompson had to pay a king's ransom to rent a horse. He made the trip, alone, between Christmas and New Year's.

Of course, for Thompson, such a trip was probably only a minor diversion. After all, that same year he had made an arduous three-month canoe trip, with no map, a sieve-like tent, and a huge canoe that he had to stop and replace himself with two smaller ones, more suitable for the rugged Algonquin highlands he was assigned to cross.

And, oh yes, one more thing that will be of interest to the proud young canoeists who explore the modern Algonquin Park. When Thompson made his trip, he was 67 years old ... .∞

September 1, 1988, Vol. 29, No. 11 (D.S.)

Sex in the Leaves

It's hard to believe, but another summer has come and gone. The woods are quiet, the nights are nippy, and the first snow is only a couple of months away. Still, before winter comes, Algonquin will pass through what many of us consider to be the nicest season of all. Calm clear days, wildlife at its best, superb hiking — who could ask for more? And, topping off all the other attractions, of course, is the fall colour spectacle normally peaking sometime in the last week of September. We don't have to remind regular Park visitors just how dazzling the autumn shutdown of tree foliage can be in Algonquin. Still, there is another, perhaps even more captivating aspect of tree biology that is strongly hinted at by the fall colours but nevertheless goes unnoticed by almost all of us.

To explain what we mean here, we must point out that really two main tree species put on the big colour show at the end of the month, the Sugar Maple and the Red Maple. As a matter of fact — if you will allow us to digress momentarily into a bit of a sermon — it is a sad commentary on general environmental awareness in this country that we have to do this. Red and Sugar Maples are so common and so important in Ontario that everyone should know them, but, sad to say, this is far from the

Red Maple.

case, even among biology and forestry students. Not knowing these two trees apart is akin to not knowing a moose from a deer. No, that's not stating the case strongly enough. Red and Sugar Maples are far from just minor variations on the same theme; they are completely different organisms. Apart from the anatomical differences (such as those in the leaves shown here), the two trees have completely different lifestyles. Sugar Maples are the dominant tree on the moist, well-drained hills of the Park's west side. They are also "bisexual" in the sense that the flowers, produced at leaf-out time back in May, contain both male and female parts, and each tree can fertilize and be fertilized — and then produce seeds, which ripen slowly over the summer.

Red Maples, on the other hand, usually grow in places that Sugar Maples can't inhabit: dry, rocky hillsides or wet, mucky soil beside bogs and beaver ponds. They can achieve the tall size and proportions of a Sugar Maple, but, especially on the poorer sites, they tend to be small and sprawling, often with multiple trunks. Even more striking is the way they flower. To begin with, they produce their deep red, quite beautiful flowers soon after the snow disappears and well before leaf-out. And, even more different from the Sugar Maple, those flowers are almost always strictly male or strictly female. Each individual tree, furthermore, usually has flowers of only one sex, meaning that there are female Red Maple trees

Sugar Maple.

and male Red Maple trees (the males being perhaps seven times more numerous).

Now you would have to agree that these differences are about as profound as you could imagine and underscore our disappointment that so few people can distinguish between Red and Sugar Maples. Nevertheless, we have to admit that the flowering of both maples is over so early in the year that very few people have the chance to appreciate the utterly different sex lives of the two maples. The differences do show up again, however, and this is what we were alluding to when we said earlier that the brilliant fall colours hint at one of the most fascinating aspects of tree biology.

Sugar Maple leaves can turn almost any shade of yellow, orange, or red, but the colour seems to depend on the particular place on the tree occupied by the leaves, with shaded leaves ending up yellow and leaves exposed to the sun, even on the same tree, turning more orange or red. With Red Maple leaves, however, the fall colours depend on the sex of the tree. It is the male Red Maple trees that produce the brilliant scarlet or red leaves, which give the species its name, whereas the much less numerous female trees turn to a very different distinctly yellow or, at the most, orangish colour. We ourselves only learned of this spectacular sex difference a couple of years ago when a distinguished forester pointed it out to us. Since then we have taken great interest in picking out, often from great distances, male and female Red Maples during the fall colour season.

We invite you to try your hand as well, of course, but you might also like to try coming up with a reason why the two maple species should have such completely different lifestyles in the first place. As astounding as it may seem, especially for such a common tree as the Red Maple, no one really knows why it almost always has separately sexed trees, whereas the Sugar Maple never does. There is even the possibility, hinted at by the little research conducted on the subject, that individual trees may actually start their reproductive lives off as males and then gradually change over to being partly and then entirely females. This pattern has been established for a third species, the Striped Maple (also common in Algonquin Park). The advantage seems to be that, for a small tree struggling to make a living in dense shade, it is more economical at first to be purely male. All males have to do is produce pollen, as opposed to being obliged to produce big, energy-rich (and energy-draining) seeds the way females do. Seeds are more likely to produce offspring than pollen, but only when a Striped Maple is big or about to be shaded out and killed anyway does it throw energy into the costly, even life-threatening, business of producing seeds.

We don't know if this applies to the Red Maple as well but look forward to the day when someone finds out. It truly is amazing that, until now, no one has done the necessary field work and analysis. After all, it's not as if Red Maples were particularly difficult to find or study. Indeed, with the striking male reds and female yellows we will be seeing in a few weeks, these trees could hardly come up with a more flamboyant way of advertising their sex habits.

And surely there is somebody out there besides ourselves at *The Raven* who is interested in this whole concept of sex in the leaves. What are people waiting for?☞

September 8, 1988, Vol. 29, No. 12 (D.S.)

Striped Maple.

Songs to Fish by

We know that most readers of this particular *Raven* edition will already be listening to loons off in the Park interior and enjoying their first 1989 fishing trip in Algonquin. To put it mildly, we wish we were there, too!

The reality, as we write this in the middle of April, is that the lakes are still frozen, a cold rain is falling, and the opening day of fishing season is two agonizing weeks away. After a winter of deprivation, we would give our eye-teeth to hear a spring chorus of loons reverberating around a moonlit Park lake.

Under the circumstances the best we can do (as we did last night) is to get out our fishing tackle and put on our copy of *Voices of Algonquin Park*.* We think the temporary illusion probably helped a bit. But as we listened to the tape, it also occurred to us that relaying some of the information it contains might interest even those of you who are out there right now listening to the real thing. After all, as hauntingly beautiful as loon music is to our ears, you can be sure that these marvellous birds are singing not for us but for each other. And, although it is not generally known, the meanings of the four basic calls given by loons have been worked out in the last decade or two by patient observation and experiment (including some work done in Algonquin on Catfish Lake). With this basic knowledge, anyone can listen in on loon communications and gain a deeper insight into what loons are saying to each other.

Here, for your listening enjoyment, are the four basic call types:

• **The Hoot** is a quiet, single note used by family members to inform or reassure each other of their whereabouts. It is often used by the adults to bring the chicks in close for feeding.

• **The Wail**, often repeated several times, is long and drawn out, very similar to the howl of a wolf. Its function is far from completely understood, but it often seems to convey a desire to be reunited with a mate or family member. It is often given to other loons flying overhead and when a loon on a nest wants to exchange places with its mate.

• **The Tremolo** is often referred to as "laughter" but, in fact, conveys a range of emotions from what we might call "social tension," through "alarm," right up to "outright fear." The higher a tremolo's pitch, the greater the bird's sense of urgency and desire to flee.

• **The Yodel** is the wildest and most ringing call in the loon's repertoire and has even been called

maniacal and blood-curdling. It is given exclusively by males and is an aggressive attack message used in territorial defence or other social disputes. Yodels are often accompanied by threatening spread-wing postures and sometimes lead to actual fighting between rival males.

Yodels — indeed, all loon calls — are best heard in late May and early June when territorial squabbles, courtship, and preparations for nesting are at their peak. Fabulous, night-long choruses are common then and provide incomparable opportunities for hearing these marvellous wilderness sounds and to try sorting out their meanings. The well-known American wilderness writer Sigurd Olson described an evening of night chorusing on a beautiful lake in one of our sister parks, Quetico, up in northwestern Ontario: "We sat around until long after dark and listened, but instead of becoming quiet as the moon went high, the calling increased, and there again was the wild harmony, the music that comes only once a year, when it is spring on Lac la Croix."

You who are out there now know exactly what Olson meant. For our part, we can only add with a sigh, as we get our fishing tackle ready and listen to our tape, "We can hardly wait."☞

April 27, 1989, Vol. 30, No. 1 (D.S.)

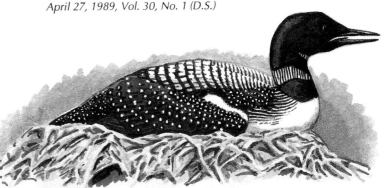

---

* *The audiocassette produced in 1986 by The Friends of Algonquin Park and featuring outstanding recordings of loons (plus wolves, moose, and Barred Owls). Available at either Park bookstore for $6.95.*

The Duck That May Not Be Much Longer

Those of us who go back a few years in the Park have come to associate many beautiful images with Algonquin: the howls of a wolf under starry skies, spring wildflowers in sun-flooded hardwood forests, and Black Ducks rising on silver-lined wings from secret beaver ponds. Quite naturally, we take it for granted that such images always have been, and will be, a part of the Park scene.

The apparently unchanging aspect of a great natural area like Algonquin is indeed one of its most attractive features, but this does not mean that no change ever occurs or that the Park is unaffected by events in the fast-paced world outside.

We may, in fact, be observing a major change in one of those "timeless" features of the Park right now. Sometimes, the duck that rises from our beaver ponds these days is not a Black Duck at all but a Mallard. Now, it may seem a little odd to you that we should say this. After all, you may have already seen a Mallard on this trip to the Park, and you are almost certainly familiar with them from city parks back home. So why would we suggest that the Mallard is something new.

Will the Black Ducks of Algonquin be replaced ...

Well, the fact is that before 1970 it was very unusual to see a Mallard in Algonquin. Two reports in a year were the most we ever had, and none at all was quite normal. In 1970, however, there were five sightings; in 1972, history was made when a female with a brood of five downy young was observed on the Little Madawaska; and by 1975, we were receiving many Mallard records each year. The first actual nest was not discovered until 1983, but since 1985 one or two broods have been seen every year just in the Highway 60 Corridor.

From "very rare" to "regularly present" in 15 years is a major change by any standard. Of course, this change raises the question of why Mallards would increase so dramatically and quickly, particularly when there were no obvious habitat changes within the Park during the period in question. In fact, the Mallard increase in the Park is just part of a much bigger picture. Mallards were once largely confined to west of the Mississippi but have been steadily moving into eastern North America for the last 30 or 40 years. This might not matter at all, except for one thing. As the Mallards roll eastwards, they replace the original Black Ducks. In area after area where Mallards have appeared, their numbers have increased, and then, simultaneously, observers have reported increasing numbers of hybrid individuals (crosses between Mallards and Blacks) and decreasing numbers of pure Black Ducks. Before long the Blacks dwindle to almost none, as do the hybrids, and what was once an area inhabited exclusively by Black Ducks is completely taken over by Mallards. This has already happened in southwestern Ontario, for example, and, while Black Ducks still seem as common in Algonquin Park as they ever have, their future here is by no means certain. Just in the last couple of years — although only in migration so far — we have had a big increase in observations of Black-Mallard hybrids. This could be the prelude to the final takeover by Mallards. Blacks still remain abundant east of here, particularly in the Maritimes, but many authorities believe it is just a question of time before the Mallards reach that last stronghold — and possibly bring about the Black Duck's complete extinction.

Needless to say, such a result would be a dramatic and rather sad ending to those of us who like Black Ducks, but scientists who have studied the matter don't find it all that mysterious. Although male Black Ducks look quite different from male Mallards, the two species are actually very closely related to each other. The Black Duck may, in fact, be just a well-marked race of the Mallard and not a separate species at all. The species probably arose fairly recently, in the last Ice Age, when a small group of Mallards was cut off from the main population out west and was forced to adapt to the forests of eastern North America. As camouflage was important in their wooded environment, so the males evolved less flamboyant plumage than the ancestral pure Mallards of the open prairies. They also evolved a resistance to avian malaria, which is transmitted to ducks by blackflies and was a serious cause of death to ducks in the east.*

If the new Black Duck population had remained physically separated from the Mallards out on the prairies for a few more thousands of years, the two might have become even more different from each other and been incapable of interbreeding, even if they did meet again some day. We'll never know because humans unintentionally arranged an end to their separation. By clearing the forests of the east, we created prairie-like habitat attractive to Mallards, and so they started to

---

* Much of the important research on avian malaria was carried out here in Algonquin at the Wildlife Research Station. The resistance of Blacks and the susceptibility of Mallards was long thought to be one of the main reasons why Blacks could live in the forested east (with all its disease-carrying blackflies) whereas Mallards apparently could not.

expand towards the Atlantic. This by itself wouldn't have meant trouble for Black Ducks except that the two species or races started to encounter each other in the same eastern wintering areas, chiefly along the Atlantic coast. Winter is the time when ducks start their courtship and pair up (which saves them from having to go through the process and lose valuable time before laying eggs when they arrive back on their breeding grounds). But because Blacks and Mallards had not yet evolved different courting behaviours during their several thousand years of separation, they still found each other quite attractive when we brought them back together again on the east coast. It turned out, in fact, that female Blacks found male Mallards to be even more interesting than males of their own species. Under these circumstances and with possibly a greater reproductive rate in Mallards, Blacks soon found themselves being genetically swamped. Also, the hybrid Black-Mallards resulting from the crossbreeding of their parents were perfectly fertile, and when they themselves bred with pure Mallards, they may have introduced the gene for resistance to avian malaria into the Mallard population.

If this is the case, it means that Mallards will have surmounted the last barrier that could have prevented

… by Mallards?

them from moving into the still forested parts of the east. We cannot predict the future with absolute certainty, of course, but it's difficult to see what could stop the Mallards from completely replacing the Black Duck everywhere.

Personally, if it comes to that, we'll greatly miss the Blacks, and Mallards somehow just won't be the same. Still, at the same time, we must admit that it is utterly fascinating to be able to witness the extinction of one species and its replacement by another in just a few years. We know that events like this have occurred hundreds of thousands of times in Earth's long history, but individual humans have such fleetingly short lifespans that we have to be very lucky to actually see such an event unfold before our eyes.

And, of course, if the Black Duck does indeed disappear from Algonquin, we can be sure that future generations of Park staff and visitors will go through the years appreciating such timeless parts of the landscape as wolves howling on starry nights, spring wildflowers in sunny woods, and Mallards rising on flashing wings from secret beaver ponds. ∞

June 29, 1989, Vol. 30, No. 2 (D.S.)

The Lesson of the Waxwing

We want to tell you about a really demoralizing experience we had on a sweltering hot day a couple of weeks ago. Two hikers, probably a mere 18 or 19 years old, whizzed past us on the climb up to the top of Lookout Trail. They made it seem as if we were standing still (which I guess we were, sort of — but just for a minute, of course). Now, passing us like that would have been bad enough, but were they content to leave it at that? Oh no! They had to cheerily add, "Nice little warm up for the Booth's Rock, eh? We're going to do it, too, this morning before we go back to Two Rivers for lunch!" Who did those kids think they were? Just because we are on the far side of 39 and have a few gray hairs to prove it is no reason for anybody to get cocky. We tried to think of a suitably caustic rejoinder to their obviously intentional putdown, but by the time we did, the two fleet-footed hikers were out of sight!

We should have replied, "Ah yes, but remember the lesson of the waxwing!" That would have stopped those little upstarts right in their tracks. And furthermore … yes, go ahead. Oh, you "remember taking something about waxwings in school but aren't sure what was so special about them or what lesson they might have for us." Well, you've come to the right place! Allow us to fix you up in both departments.

The thing that is so special about waxwings is that they have wax on their wings! Now that wasn't so hard, was it? It isn't really wax, of course, but on the ends of many waxwing inner-wing feathers are blobs of what looks for all the world like old-fashioned, bright red sealing wax. These peculiar appendages add an extra measure of beauty and distinction to what is already one of Algonquin's best-looking birds.* They also contain the "lesson" that we would like our two whiz-kid hikers to absorb, but, in fairness, this is really a very new development. Until recently, no one had the faintest idea why waxwings have waxy wings. The best anybody could

_____

There are three species of waxwing in the world, of which our local bird, the Cedar Waxwing, is abundant, particularly in boggy areas, from May to the end of August.

come up with was that the waxy tips might protect the inner-wing feathers from excessive wear or abrasion. But this theory didn't really stand up to serious examination. After all, why would so few feathers be singled out for the supposed special protection. If anything, it should be the outer-wing feathers that are favoured because they are the ones that permit flight.

To unravel the waxy, feather tip mystery, you have to know something else that is special about waxwings. To take our local example, the Cedar Waxwing is the only bird in Algonquin, or indeed in eastern North America, that lives on a mostly fruit diet. It eats wild strawberries on the ground, black cherries in the treetops, and just about every other kind of fruit in between. Even in winter they roam about, often not far south of here, looking for the fruit that persists on some ornamental shrubs. About the only times they take non-fruit foods are when they eat flowers and when, for a few days each nesting season, they capture protein-rich insects for their nestlings.

The fruit-eating lifestyle has evidently been successful for the Cedar Waxwing, even in our climate, but it does impose some particular problems. The main one is that different fruits come into season at different times and often at widely different places. What is a great place to forage one week, with more than enough food for hundreds of birds, may be quite useless the next. This means that Cedar Waxwings are best served by joining highly nomadic flocks, which can efficiently find and use the temporary rich patches of fruit as they become available. Even in the nesting season, they can't really carve out a territory the way other birds do and defend it against their neighbours while they raise their young using the food provided by the territory. What they do instead is to have a small piece of ground, strictly for nesting, that they use as a home base for forays into the surrounding country (sometimes two kilometres or farther) in search of whatever fruit is in season.

This technique obviously works, but it causes two other difficulties. One is that, perhaps more so than in many birds, a parent Cedar Waxwing must possess very good foraging skills if it is to raise young successfully. It also means that individual male and female Cedar Waxwings cannot easily assess the worthiness of other birds as possible mates. For example, in some bird species a female can check out the territory of a male to see if it has everything needed for successful family-raising before she decides to move in. Not only does she get a good territory that way, but also the male is probably no slouch either if he has been able to claim and defend a superior piece of ground against lots of male competition.

With waxwings, however, these possibilities don't exist since the nesting territories are almost trivial in value. The really important consideration is whether the prospective male or female will be able to do his or her part in the demanding job of finding food and bringing it back to the young. And how can one waxwing size up another's potential merely by looking at it beforehand? Well, it can't ever be completely sure, but its chances will be much improved if it can at least choose an older mate. In waxwings, as in humans, the best parents are those that have greater maturity and experience. One older parent is better than none, but best of all are pairs consisting of two experienced birds. It is quite important, therefore, for older waxwings to have their age recognized by prospective mates — and, in turn, to be able to recognize superior age in others. That way, older birds can mate with birds of similar high competence and not jeopardize their chances of raising young by mating with an inexperienced, youthful klutz. By now you have probably guessed it. The waxy feather tips of Cedar Waxwings are the red badge of age, usually being well developed in birds that are two years old or more. And, sure enough, the mating of waxwings is not random. Older, waxy birds mate with similarly endowed (and therefore aged) birds, leaving the younger, waxless inexperienced birds to flounder along with each other as best they can.

No doubt, our older readers with gray hair will be quick to see the delicious justice in this little story. As for us, we won't ever again be caught flat-footed out on the trail by any irreverent young speed freaks. If any try to make us look bad again, we'll zap 'em with our line about the lesson given us by waxwings. That lesson is, of course — pay attention, dammit — that the badge of age is also the badge of maturity and competence. That'll (puff puff) fix 'em. ∽

The Raven *takes great pleasure in adding that the story of why waxwings are waxy was worked out at Queen's University by Jim Mountjoy, a former Park employee who worked here as a summer naturalist from 1977 to 1987. Some of you may recall the excellent hikes and talks he gave during those years. Behind the scenes, Jim was best known for his elaborate practical jokes and, notwithstanding his youth, for being reasonably respectful to his elders.*

July 13, 1989, Vol. 30, No. 4 (D.S.)

Listening to a Fragrant Picture

One of our favourite places in Algonquin at this time of year is the wide stretch of river between Lake la Muir and Hogan Lake, very close to the centre of the Park. Our reason for liking it so much is not that it happens to be the link between two of Algonquin's best Lake Trout lakes — although that would be reason enough. Nor is it because of the beautiful little heronry on the small island at the la Muir end of the river — although that would be a good reason, too. No, the reason it is so special at this time of year is that it reveals a great deal about the natural world in so many simple and powerful ways. The river between la Muir and Hogan, you see, is the Pickerelweed capital of Algonquin Park, and right now, in the Pickerelweed flowering season, is when life there is the most dramatic and instructive.

Having said this, we have to concede that it may not mean much to many of our visitors. While every veteran canoe-tripper knows it well, Pickerelweed is unfortunately beyond most people's experience and, with "weed" in its name, is hardly likely to raise notable interest or appreciation. This is too bad because, in fact, Pickerelweed is among the most beautiful and exotic-looking of Algonquin's wildflowers. It's one that everybody should know. Found along shallow lakeshores and river banks, it emerges a foot or two above the water, often in thick, tangled beds. The large succulent leaves have a rounded arrowhead shape that help give Pickerelweed stands a lush, almost tropical appearance.*

The really attractive feature about Pickerelweed, however, is its flowers — beautiful blue flowers on spikes that poke up through the thick beds of stalks and leaves. In bloom from late July and even on into September, Pickerelweed adds something very special to our waterways. Few more beautiful sights abound in the Park than an exotic-looking jungle of Pickerelweed splashed with dashes of blue, all intricately reflected in the evening stillness of a glass-smooth lake or river.

This would be true anywhere, but on the river between Hogan and la Muir the sight is overwhelming. The Pickerelweed stand stretches up the river from Hogan Lake and out of sight to the portage, and sometimes approaches 200 yards in width. As a rough guess there might be 800,000 or a million Pickerelweed plants all in this one unbroken, tangled profusion.

A slow paddle through this vast sea of blue flower spikes leaves a strong visual impression — but that is not the only one. With a quiet breeze, the fragrance released

The midsummer spectacle of Pickerelweed, bumblebees, and kingbirds between Hogan Lake and Lake la Muir.

by those hundreds of thousands of blossoms washes over the canoeist to the point where you might imagine yourself in a huge perfume factory. And, in a way, that's exactly what the great la Muir-Hogan Pickerelweed stand really is. The perfume and colour of that infinity of flowers are powerful invitations to some special visitors needed by the Pickerelweed plants. On a good day, you won't be long in discovering who those visitors are, as the

---

* This is not at all a far-fetched image because, indeed, Pickerelweed is found from Ontario right down into South America. Hard to believe, but the same Pickerelweed that forms a beautiful and characteristic part of the northern landscapes along Algonquin canoe routes is also present along jungle streams in Venezuela.

air will be filled with a deep, buzzing drone that seems to come from nowhere — and everywhere. Then you will realize that the vast sea of vegetation stretching away to the far distant shores is roaring, vibrating, and pulsating everywhere you look with tens of thousands of bumblebees!

The spectacle is unforgettable, and it would be difficult to imagine a more beautiful vignette of the natural world. Here, in this marvellous stretch of river, the sunshine is unobstructed by trees, the water has the right depth, the bottom the right consistency, the current the right speed — everything is ideal for this one special wildflower. It grows in glorious, choking profusion, and then, needing some agent to carry pollen from one plant to another, it diverts a small fraction of the sun's energy captured by its leaves into the production of the insect-attracting and insect-bribing structures we call flowers. A huge population of bumblebees is supported by this largesse, and inadvertently they serve the Pickerelweed's "purpose" by performing the task of cross-pollination that the immobile plants cannot do for themselves.

The sun supports the Pickerelweeds, the Pickerelweeds support the bumblebees, and the bumblebees support a predator. Perched high up on isolated snags above the la Muir-Hogan Pickerelweed stand, kingbirds survey their bountiful larder. They routinely swoop down and snap up a bumblebee when the mood suits them (don't worry, they remove the stingers before they swallow the bees).

What could be simpler or more beautiful than the workings of the natural world as exemplified by this one magnificent scene? Sun, water, and soil supporting the lush growth of green plants, the intricate partnership between flowers and pollinators, the food chain of plants, plant consumers, and predators — all these themes are dramatically and beautifully represented in the great la Muir-Hogan Pickerelweed stand for anyone who takes the time to pause from their paddle to drink in its sights, sounds, and fragrance.

And yet … are things really as simple here as they seem? The truth is that beneath the scene's surface lie some astonishing complexities you probably couldn't even dream about. Next week we'll go back to the centre of Algonquin and peer into the picture more deeply.⌘

July 20, 1989, Vol. 30, No. 5 (D.S.)

Peering Into the Picture

One could spend a hundred lifetimes in Algonquin Park and never delve into all of its secrets. Last week, for example, we spoke about the breathtaking beauty of the great Pickerelweed stand up on the river between la Muir and Hogan Lakes. The lush growth, the overpowering fragrance, the roaring multitudes of foraging, pollinating bumblebees, and then, high above, fearless lords living off the land's riches — kingbirds that swoop down when the mood strikes them to snap up a meal of bumblebee. All are part of a fascinating area of the Park which, at one level, possesses what we find to be a profoundly pleasing ecological simplicity. We ended our introduction to this little world, however, by hinting that beneath the surface, things are far more complex than they seem. We promised to come back this week for a closer look.

Let's do that now, and in particular let's take a closer look at the beautiful blue flowers of Pickerelweed. Typically, flowers have a female part, called a stigma, at the end of a long stalk (called a "style" by botanists) and several pollen-producing (male) parts, called anthers, which also are borne on the ends of little stalks that hold them up above the base of the flower. Pickerelweed flowers have this basic arrangement, but they also have the added feature of possessing two distinct sets of anthers, each carried a different height above the flower base (with the female stigma at the top of the style at yet another level).

Added to this, Pickerelweed flowers can be arranged in three distinctly separate ways, as shown in the diagram. If you look at one patch of Pickerelweed, for example, you might find that the styles are the tallest structures in all the flowers and that the two sets of anthers are always at the middle and low levels below that. In another patch of flowers, however, the styles might be all of medium length with one set of anthers above and the other set below. Or, in a third patch of plants, you might find that the styles are all short and the two sets of anthers are carried at the medium and tall levels above.

Now, it is anything but obvious why Pickerelweed flowers should come in three distinct forms. Normally in nature, one form of a plant or animal is more efficient than others and comes to predominate simply because, generation after generation after generation, it leaves more descendants than any other forms until eventually only the most efficient form remains. This is really the way evolution works. So why hasn't one of the three flower forms come to predominate in Pickerelweed? After all, it would be an unbelievable coincidence if all three types were exactly equal in their abilities to produce viable seed and thus perpetuate themselves.

And yet, there it is. Pickerelweed is one of a small number of plants in several different families that have this triple-barrelled floral anatomy in roughly equal proportions throughout its range. The great Charles Darwin himself, the man who 130 years ago finally came up with a coherent theory to explain the fact of evolution, was fascinated with the problem and came up with an idea that might account for the persistence of the three forms. Darwin's basic thought was that, in common with most flowers, it is best for Pickerelweed blossoms to be fertilized by pollen that comes from another flower (that is, cross-pollination instead of self-pollination). As a matter of fact, long-styled Pickerelweed flowers are preferentially pollinated by the large pollen grain from "long" anthers. Flowers with medium-length styles need pollen from medium-length anthers. Similarly, the third form of flower, the short-styled variety, is preferentially pollinated by pollen from short-length anthers.

By definition this means that cross-pollination is favoured since a long-styled flower, for example, doesn't have the necessary long anthers (only short and medium). Therefore, the necessary pollen can only come from another medium- or short-styled flower, thus assuring cross-pollination. The same reasoning applies to the pollination of the other floral types as well.

So far, so good (we hope!), but what then guarantees that pollen, say, from a long anther on one flower will end up on the long style of another flower. Couldn't it just as easily end up on a flower with a medium or short style — in which case the pollen could not fertilize the receiving flower and would be wasted? It was Darwin's suggestion that the three types of flowers, each needing pollen from one of the other two kinds to be fertilized, had evolved their "three-level" anatomy so as to help segregate the different kinds of pollen on the bodies of visiting insects. This would help make sure that each kind of pollen ended up on the right kind (length) of style on another flower. For example, if pollen from long stamens tended to brush off on a bumblebee's head as it pushed its way into a flower to get nectar (and pollen from medium and short stamens tended to end up on different parts of the bumblebee's body), then it should work out that the pollen would only come into contact with and brush off on other long stamens (which wouldn't matter)

or on long styles (which is the "desired" result). By the same argument, pollen from medium and short anthers, picked up on their own different parts of the bumblebee's body, should be selectively transferred to medium and short styles, respectively.

It was a rather neat idea of Darwin's, and it may even be right! The only problem is that a fair bit of sophisticated scientific research has been done on the problem (including at Paugh Lake north of Barry's Bay and not far from the Park's southeast boundary) and, so far, there is little or no support for Darwin's proposed explanation. It seems that in our part of the world at least, pollen from all floral types gets slathered around rather indiscriminately. One might imagine, therefore, that many flowers might get clogged up with the wrong kinds of pollen, but this doesn't seem to happen and our Pickerelweed flowers always seem to be completely fertilized. The jury is therefore still out on the Pickerelweed flower question. One possibility is that the three-form anatomy of Pickerelweed evolved elsewhere in the plant's range with different insect pollinators that really do permit benefits to the flower along the lines proposed by Darwin. But no one knows for sure.

What we do know is that Pickerelweed is a lot more complex than it first appears! Who would have thought that such a common, albeit beautiful, plant can harbour such an intricate, unsolved mystery? But then, as we said at the outset, the Park is endlessly full of such secrets. Something to contemplate the next time you paddle up the river from Hogan Lake to Lake la Muir.∽

July 27, 1989, Vol. 30, No. 6 (D.S.)

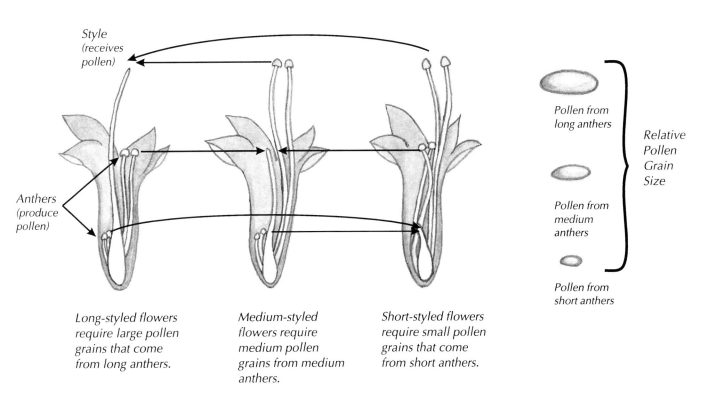

Style (receives pollen)

Anthers (produce pollen)

Pollen from long anthers

Pollen from medium anthers

Pollen from short anthers

Relative Pollen Grain Size

Long-styled flowers require large pollen grains that come from long anthers.

Medium-styled flowers require medium pollen grains from medium anthers.

Short-styled flowers require small pollen grains that come from short anthers.

Aliens in the Park

It is a common theme in science fiction that an alien life form arrives on a planet (usually ours) and then launches an assault which, if unchecked, leads to the destruction or enslavement of the original inhabitants. Whether the attack succeeds depends on any number of things. The invader may have more powerful weapons or a much greater ability to replace its casualties than the native defenders. On the other hand, the invader may be defeated because of some unforeseen flaw, such as a fatal susceptibility to a common virus or the inability to digest local food.

Stories such as these make for exciting books or films, but few people realize that struggles between native and alien species are fairly common on our planet. If anything, they are more frequent nowadays because humans travel more than ever before. In fact, it is humans who often transport alien life forms, either deliberately or accidentally, into new environments. Usually a transplant is not very well suited to its new surroundings, and it quickly dies out, unnoticed. Once in a while, however, conditions are favourable for an alien, and its numbers explode — often with devastating results for local plants and animals. Good examples of such ecological disasters are the introduction of rabbits to Australia and of Dutch Elm disease to North America.

No area is immune to alien invasions, unfortunately, and now Algonquin Park is having one as well. Last summer we found the Rusty Crayfish in Lake Travers, one of the major lakes on the Petawawa River on the east side of the Park. This species is native to Ohio, Indiana, and Illinois, but it has also appeared in recent decades in other areas to the north,

including Minnesota, Wisconsin, and parts of Ontario. We don't know how long it's been in Lake Travers or how it got there, but a good guess is that the fateful event occurred at least a few years ago, when some fisherman emptied his bait bucket into the water at the end of the day. Our presumed culprit probably didn't give the slightest thought to what he was doing. Even if someone had been there to warn him about the consequences of introducing this alien creature to a new lake, he probably wouldn't have taken it seriously. After all, one crayfish is "pretty much like any other," so what harm could it do?

Well, nobody would be very calm about introducing the Rusty Crayfish into our waters if they could see what the same species has done in similar lakes in northern Wisconsin. Once well-known fishing lakes are now almost barren of their original perch and walleye. The weed beds that fed and sheltered the fish are all gone, and in some places the lake bottom actually moves — with the army of Rusty Crayfish that have taken over the lake and achieved densities of 13 or more per square yard! There are even places where people don't swim any

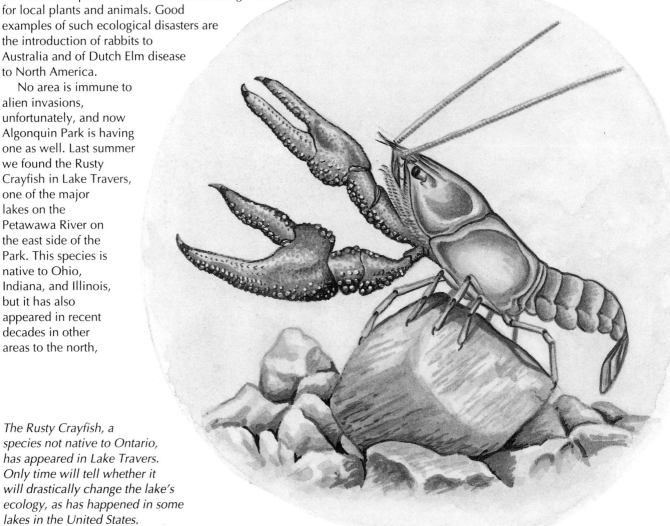

The Rusty Crayfish, a species not native to Ontario, has appeared in Lake Travers. Only time will tell whether it will drastically change the lake's ecology, as has happened in some lakes in the United States.

more because they were being constantly (and painfully) pinched by Rusty Crayfish.

Such a situation is both alarming and puzzling. Rusty Crayfish never take over so completely in their normal range, and they really don't look all that different from our five native species of crayfish. Why is it, then, that the Rusties have such an overwhelming impact in some of the northern lakes into which they have been introduced? No one really knows for sure, but one or two factors probably contribute to their success. One reason is that they lay their eggs earlier, so the young grow faster than the native species. This means that young Rusty Crayfish have an important head-start over their rivals in the competition for lake-bottom hiding places.

A second reason is that Rusty Crayfish are much more aggressive than native species. They will often drag other kinds of crayfish out of their hiding places and take over themselves. The hapless native species then lose the benefits of shelter and run a high risk of being eaten by fish — while the Rusties that evicted them are safely out of harm's way. In such a situation it's easy to see that before long the Rusties will become the predominant crayfish species.

Their extreme aggressiveness also makes Rusty Crayfish immune to attack, except from the largest of traditional crayfish-eaters, such as bass. When a fish or even a human diver approaches, they face their attacker and raise up their pincers defiantly. Unless a bass manages to strike from the rear, it may well end up retreating and violently trying to shake off the Rusty Crayfish that has clamped onto its lips.

Unfortunately, Rusty Crayfish can do much worse things to fish than give them sore mouths. They are voracious consumers of fish eggs, and they also eat the insects, snails, and weed beds that support fish populations. Rusties will eat just about anything dead or alive that they come across, even to the point of scraping algae off rocks if they have to.

Putting it simply, Rusty Crayfish have the happy (for them) faculty of making themselves at least partly immune to predation on the one hand and of completely wrecking the lake's food chain for their exclusive benefit.

By now you are probably wondering what we are going to do to save Lake Travers. Some people have suggested that we could encourage Park visitors to catch and eat crayfish (they are as delicious as lobster) or even start a commercial operation. Already Minnesota is exporting them to Sweden, where they are appreciated for the delicacy they truly are. Unfortunately, current trapping methods are much more effective for males than for females. Since the remaining males can still fertilize all the females present, trapping some males merely removes the competition they provided to the females for food and hiding places, and probably only achieves the production of even more baby crayfish ... which will grow up to be big crayfish ... which will divert even more of the lake's available food ... into the production of even more crayfish.

And if you think that's a happy prospect, think about the following. The best chance of keeping the crayfish in check would probably be to ban sport fishing in lakes where Rusties are present. Large bass, muskies, and walleyes (all present in Lake Travers) are the only predators with even a chance of making inroads into the Rusty Crayfish population. To the extent that we allow the removal of such large fish (through fishing), we are only hurting our prospects of preserving some sort of balance in the Lake Travers food chain. Unfortunately, the people most interested in solving the Rusty Crayfish problem are probably also the people most interested in continuing to catch the big fish that might be part of the solution. You really can't win with this one.

Realistically, the only thing we can do is hope that Travers will be one of those lakes (already observed in Wisconsin) where the Rusty Crayfish, for some unknown reason, fails to achieve the complete destruction of which it is capable.

Whatever the final outcome, the story of Rusty Crayfish in Lake Travers illustrates two important principles. One is that humans can't just draw a line around an area, call it a park, and assume it will automatically be "preserved" forever. The other principle, of course, is the danger involved in introducing alien creatures to a new environment. To be sure, such introductions usually fail quickly and completely, but occasionally they result in drastic ecological damage. Sadly, Lake Travers may be an example of this because we already have strong reason to believe that the walleye fishing in Travers has just about completely collapsed.

Only time will tell, and you can be sure that someday we will print a sequel to this story. In the meantime, if you will allow us to say it about such an important topic, we all have serious claws for concern.

August 10, 1989, Vol. 30, No. 8 (D.S.)

Who Said Life Was Fair?

Life, as we all know, has its small injustices. For example, just about everybody has made careful plans at one time or another, only to have the exact opposite of what was intended happen. Even worse, sometimes we pay a price for somebody else's supposedly brilliant idea that's gone wrong, even when we had nothing to do with it.

We were reminded of this sad truth last week when we drove by the big milkweed patch across from the Hardwood Hill Picnic Ground. As is so often the case, a couple of Monarch Butterflies were in the air above the flowers, and we couldn't help but think how unfair life and public opinion are when it comes to this famous plant-insect pair. After all, it's the Monarch Butterfly that gets all the admiration and attention. In a few weeks newspapers and magazines will be running articles about how beautiful they are and telling people about the best places (such as Point Pelee National Park down on Lake Erie) to see thousands of them migrating southward. Every fall, our Canadian Monarch Butterflies travel 4,000 kilometres to Mexico, where they spend the winter in incredible, massed, semi-dormant colonies up in cool, moist mountain forests. Sometimes there may be over 10 million Monarchs in just a few acres, with trees and foliage literally hidden by shoulder-to-shoulder butterflies and even bent down under their collective weight. Then, in spring, they will take wing and head back to the United States and Canada. These individual Monarchs will never again make their fantastic journey to Mexico and back because in a few weeks, after mating and egg-laying, they will die and be replaced by their offspring. Indeed, three or four generations of Monarchs may live and die on their summer feeding grounds before cool, late summer temperatures once again trigger the instinct to head south.

Now, there is no denying that "mere" insects — and gorgeous ones at that — which can bounce slowly along through the air down to Mexico and find their way, unaided, to precise, tiny locations up in the mountains, and then come all the way back again, are indeed worthy of our respect and amazement. The trouble is that hardly anybody ever thinks about the milkweeds, the plants eaten by Monarch Caterpillars and which make the whole story possible. How many tons and tons of milkweed are munched on each summer by caterpillars and turned into Monarch Butterflies without anyone stopping to consider that this is not in the milkweeds' interest?

After all, you may be sure that no organism has purposely evolved to feed another one. We have milkweeds on this planet in spite of Monarch Butterflies, not because of them. And if milkweeds were able to express an opinion about the subject, they would tell us that Monarchs are the most vile, loathsome, good-for-nothing creatures in existence: "Imagine, those horrible ugly worms attack us and eat us alive. The world would be infinitely better off without them."

Needless to say, plants cannot express an opinion about the things that eat them, but they are not completely defenceless either. Many have had accidental mutations in the past that caused them to produce chemical poisons in their tissues. The result was that the individual plants possessing the poisons were passed over by the insects that normally would have attacked them, and they (the poisonous individual plants) therefore survived and left more descendants (also poisonous) than they otherwise would have. Once in existence, such a poisonous strain of plants becomes more and more numerous with each passing generation until, eventually, all members of that species possess the ability to make the insect-deterring poison. The plant has evolved, in other words, from a tasty variety, helpless before insect attacks, to a poisonous species that, for a while at least, is immune to its former predators.

The first of two bitter ironies for milkweed in this area is that among the world's plants, milkweeds have, in fact, been outstandingly successful in evolving chemical defences against their enemies. There are 108 species in North America, for example, and many contain powerful poisons that can disrupt heart function and kill even very large animals. Cattle, mice, or insects may try them once but get violently sick, and then steer clear of milkweeds for the rest of their lives. With their enemies thus put out of commission, the milkweeds prosper and multiply — all thanks to the totally unconscious process of evolution.

The great problem for milkweeds is that one particular enemy, the Monarch Butterfly, has evolved a countermeasure against the milkweed poisons — one that, from the milkweed's "point of view," is particularly diabolical. It would be bad enough if Monarch Caterpillars merely neutralized the poisons, but they do much worse. They transfer the poison to their own skin, and this means that predators quickly learn to avoid Monarch Caterpillars. So, instead of protecting the milkweed, the poisons end up protecting the milkweed-eaters! And it doesn't end there. Even though adult butterflies consume nectar, not milkweed plant tissue, they still retain the sickening poisons they acquired as caterpillars and therefore the same protection against predators. Most birds, for example, simply will not touch Monarch Butterflies — which leaves the insects largely free to fly around, mate, and lay eggs with impunity. From all those eggs, of course, will hatch more and more milkweed-eating caterpillars, and the milkweed will be hammered even harder.

The poor old milkweed evolved its poisons in legitimate self-defence. Yet, here are those very substances being subverted into powerful protection for its worst enemy.

You might think this would be the final injustice for our unsung roadside weed, but you would be wrong. It so happens that we have two species of milkweed in Algonquin, and, unlike many of their relatives, ours are actually non-poisonous. This means that Monarch

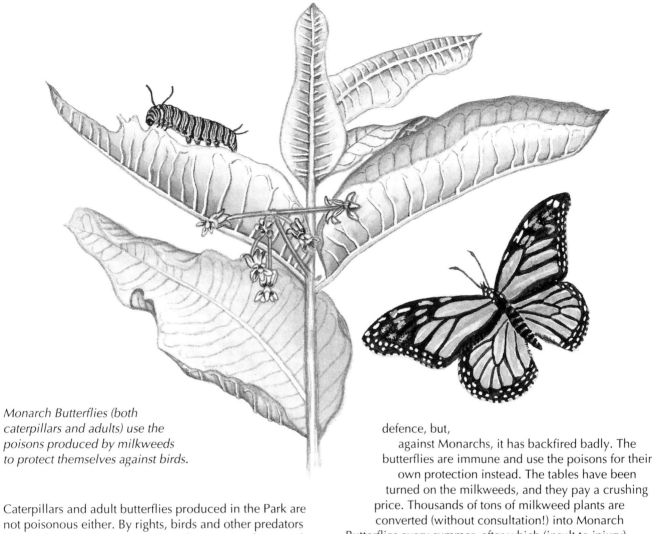

*Monarch Butterflies (both
caterpillars and adults) use the
poisons produced by milkweeds
to protect themselves against birds.*

Caterpillars and adult butterflies produced in the Park are not poisonous either. By rights, birds and other predators should therefore have no qualms about eating them, and our milkweeds should benefit from their protection. Alas, for local milkweeds this is not so. Algonquin Monarchs are almost as immune from predators as the poisonous individuals grown elsewhere on toxic species of milkweed. It only takes one stomach-turning experience with a poisonous Monarch to turn off a predator for life, and many of our local butterfly-eating birds have had that experience elsewhere, if not actually in the Park.

It seems as if milkweeds just can't win. The evolution of poisons by some species seemed like a brilliant

defence, but,
against Monarchs, it has backfired badly. The butterflies are immune and use the poisons for their own protection instead. The tables have been turned on the milkweeds, and they pay a crushing price. Thousands of tons of milkweed plants are converted (without consultation!) into Monarch Butterflies every summer, after which (insult to injury) the milkweeds are forced to fuel all those winter vacations in Mexico.

Yes, we admit a certain sense of injustice welled up in us as we drove past the Hardwood Hill milkweed patch and its arrogant, loafing Monarchs last week. But then, what could we do? One person against a billion butterflies that fight dirty? Get serious! Besides, nobody ever said life or evolution was fair.⋑

August 31, 1989, Vol. 30, No. 11 (D.S.)

Michael and the Moose

The official beginning of autumn is still two weeks away, but already there is a definite feel of fall in the Algonquin air. The nights are nippy, the woods and campgrounds have fallen silent, and here and there we already see patches of red and orange foretelling the incomparable peak of fall colours that will occur sometime in the last 10 days of this month. For many of our visitors, fall is the favourite time of year in Algonquin. We share this view ourselves. Those of us who live here year 'round, however, have a special, extra reason for appreciating late September — one that is not usually thought of by most people.

The end of this month and early October is the time of year when the rut, or mating season, of the moose occurs. It is then that Algonquin's largest animals are at their most spectacular, not only in appearance, but in behaviour as well. For the last 10 years or so, ever since moose became common in the Park, many of us have made a practice of dragging ourselves out of bed at four or five in the morning to call and observe moose at, and shortly after, dawn during the peak rutting season. It has been our privilege to see and hear many magnificent animals over this past decade, and to observe numerous fascinating sequences of behaviour, ranging from the bizarre digging of rut pits in which bulls urinate and then wallow, to actual fights between awesomely powerful rivals.

Many people have asked us about the danger involved in being too close to bull moose during the rut and, quite frankly, we had come to believe there was little or no risk at all. The moose we observed may have appeared fearless or even curious but never menacing or hostile. This may still be a valid impression, but last year, on October 6, one of our staff, Mike Runtz, had an experience that should give pause to all of us who like to "go moosing" on frosty fall mornings. Mike recorded his observations shortly afterwards, and we present excerpts here. They are among the rarest, most spectacular, and most sobering any of us have made.

To help you appreciate exactly what Mike did and saw, you should first know a few things about moose rutting behaviour and how we go about calling them. Cow moose vocalize in a very similar way to domestic cows, but bulls normally make a completely different noise, a deep, resonant grunting hiccup that we have come to refer to as a "gawunk." We normally call bull moose by imitating cow calls or by thrashing an old antler in roadside shrubbery and giving bull-like "gawunks." Mike refers to all of these practices in his account. Here it is.

"Upon turning north on the Opeongo Road, Graham and I spotted a cow and a very large bull on the east side of the road, among poplars and birches. The bull was extremely attentive to the cow, following closely behind her and licking his lips with his large, pink tongue. I gave a couple of cow calls that seemed to stimulate the bull to respond in short, bawling notes. I gave a couple of bull 'gawunks' accompanied by antler-thrashing. The bull 'gawunked' back and antler-thrashed. He then returned his attention to the cow. As he approached her from the rear, he constantly licked his lips and gave soft, bawling notes. He also raised his head and curled up his upper lip. He smelled and licked her rear frequently. The cow stood still, and the bull rested his head on tip of her rump. He slowly moved his head across her rump so that his head rested first on the right side and then on the left side of her back-end. He then quickly reared up and with a couple of short steps mounted her. He gave a couple of thrusts, and the cow moved forward. He then staggered along with her and more or less slipped off. The total time he was on top was not more than two or three seconds. This sequence was repeated two more times, and each mounting lasted at best only a few seconds. During mounting, the bull uttered a couple of guttural, short grunts. The cow was relatively quiet but did utter a few soft, moan-like calls prior to the bull mounting. The time between the first two mountings was only perhaps five to 10 minutes.

The excitement that I experienced while observing the aforementioned is really undescribable. I was aware of the rarity in observing actual copulation, and as I observed the event occur within 50 feet of me, it was a truly unforgettable experience.

After the mating, I was photographing the bull at about 40 feet. He was aware of my presence and was looking in my direction. He suddenly lowered

The Best of The Raven

his head and charged! I grabbed the tripod with mounted camera and ran in panic. The bull stopped at about 15 feet from me. With heart pounding madly, I watched from behind an aspen. I backed off but approached closer again after a few minutes and began photographing. Again, he lowered his head and charged. The sight of these huge, orangish bone structures lunging towards me, coupled with the sound of his feet thundering nearer, was indeed a terrifying situation. Again he stopped short of me as I fled.

Approximately 15 minutes later, both the bull and cow began to stare off to the east. Finally I saw a small second-year bull approaching. The large bull 'gawunked' repeatedly and began to walk towards the small bull. His head was lowered, and then he gave a short charge (about 15 to 20 feet) towards the small bull. The small bull did not leave, so after about a half a minute the large bull charged again. This time he did not stop but chased the small bull across a small hill and out of sight. The large bull returned to the cow after a full minute had passed. After about 15 minutes, he again stalked the cow. This time another cow from across the paved road approached him. The bull ignored this cow and addressed his attention solely to the receptive cow. Once again copulation took place, in the same fashion as described earlier. I was able to photograph the cows from as close as 10 feet. Both cows laid down at the edge of the trees in the open mat. The bull stayed near the female and continued to lick his lips and then her rump. I gave a few cow bawls. This seemed to entice the cow to bawl (perhaps to keep the bull near?). Finally the bull

stood near a clump of alders. He stood very still, and we were anticipating a charge when I noticed that his eyes were closed. He was apparently sleeping standing up. Graham thrashed his feet on vegetation to wake the bull. Not only did he open his eyes, but he also charged! I dived into a thick Balsam Fir patch, scratching my hands and arms and losing a piece of my tripod in the process. The bull had probably been as close as 15 feet from me before he swerved and charged a third person who had joined us by then.

Graham and I left the bog quickly as this charge seemed to be more serious than the other two. We called out to the other person, but no answer. We figured that he was either dead or else the bull was in his immediate vicinity. After a few minutes, he answered that he was alright. Apparently he fled when the bull charged and got behind a spruce. The bull stopped within six feet of him, and the fellow stood still as the bull towered above. He said he could clearly see the whites of the eyes of the bull.

As we left, we met Kevin from Barry's Bay. He wanted to photograph the moose, but I warned him not to approach the bull as it was extremely aggressive. Kevin said he would heed my warning, but I found out the next day that he had not. Apparently, according to Kevin, he had tried to photograph the bull from the open bog. The bull had charged, and while running, Kevin had tripped. The bull apparently towered over Kevin, moving his head from side to side as if he had lost sight of him. Kevin stated that he had remained motionless for several minutes. Finally he decided to run; jumping to his feet startled the bull, which jumped back, allowing Kevin to flee.

As I recall, the bull's ears were held back prior to each charge. I believe that the bull was aggressive because the female was receptive and that he was getting breeding opportunities. Also, there appeared to be a critical approach distance of about approximately 30 to 40 feet within which he would not tolerate our presence. As none of the charges did result in injury to ourselves (luckily!), these might have been bluffs designed only to frighten us away."

With this, Mike's account comes to an end. Fortunately, he and his companions of that day last fall did not do the same thing — although some people might say it wasn't for any lack of trying! The events Mike described reinforce a point he won't, and we shouldn't, ever forget. No matter how tame or indifferent to us some animals may appear, they all have limits to how much disturbance they will tolerate. For safety considerations, if nothing else, we need to respect those bounds.

After all, Michael and the rest of us have every reason to enjoy many more fall days in Algonquin when the colours and the moose are at their best.⤜

September 7, 1989, Vol. 30, No. 12 (D.S.)

Let's Face (Moose) Facts

We don't know about you, but when warm weather returns to Algonquin Park there are certain signs of spring that we especially look forward to seeing again. Trout Lilies along the portage, the flush of green poplar leaves on distant hillsides, and a few Brook Trout on the end of our line are a few obvious ones. But, for the past 10 years or so, we have become particularly fond of another one as well — the late May sight of a newborn moose calf with big, brown eyes and long, gangly legs coming down to the water's edge under the sheltering belly and watchful gaze of its giant mother. It's difficult to imagine a more appealing picture or a better symbol of life's renewal after a long winter of cold and snow.

It's difficult as well, when viewing such a beautiful scene, not to be caught up with the idea that all is happiness and bliss in the world of Algonquin Park moose. After all, this is what we want for our own families, and it's only natural to extend those feelings to other creatures and to expect that the generally happy state of human affairs should apply to them as well.

This being the case, it is also normal to be upset when we see evidence that things are not always as rosy for Park moose as the appealing cow-calf scenes might suggest. For example, especially in March and April, most of the moose we see are very scraggly-looking, with often quite large patches of bare skin around the sides and shoulders. Even more distressing, we usually find a few moose carcasses floating in our lakes every spring, and for the last few years we have found a dozen or more dead moose on land, usually emaciated and curled up where they lay down for the last time. No one likes to see such sights, and visitors who encounter them quite understandably ask what might be responsible. Sometimes, too, it happens that visitors express the idea that something should be done to prevent such losses. Here we have to part company with our concerned visitors and, at the risk of sounding heartless, point out that premature deaths among our moose are completely natural and normal.

Our intention is not to shock anyone but merely to underline certain aspects of life in the real world and to point out that facts are facts, whether we like them or not or attempt to ignore them. In the case of our Algonquin moose herd, for example, we have to realize that, even if our animals enjoyed the absolute best of health, great numbers of them would still die every year. The simple fact is that in a population numbering somewhere between 3,000 and 4,000 — as ours does — at least 1,000 calves are born every year. This is all well and good, but if the moose population is truly holding steady, the annual birth of at least 1,000 moose necessarily means the annual death of at least 1,000.

To be more specific, at least one-quarter of the Park moose alive on June 1, 1990, will be dead by June 1, 1991. We humans would be horrified at the thought of over a quarter of our friends and relatives dying over the coming year. But that is precisely what does happen, and must happen, each and every year in a moose population. Sometimes we have to pinch ourselves to realize that moose live in ways so different from our own. Moose, and almost all other forms of wildlife, die (and are born, of course) at rates so rapid that we can scarcely imagine what it would be like if we were in their position.

Seen in this light, it won't really mean very much if visitors find a dozen or two dead moose in the Park this spring. To be cold-hearted about the situation, why get excited over a few proven moose deaths when we know from undeniable, simple arithmetic the real number that have died since last spring is at least 1,000?

We are sorry if we appear brutish to you in portraying reality this way, and we will admit that we have oversimplified a bit. As a matter of fact, the real world is even more heartless than we have described. So far we have talked about the moose population as if it were stable — with the many births balancing the many deaths every year. Unfortunately, there is no guarantee that this will always be true. Obviously, if births exceed deaths, the moose population will grow. We had this sort of situation in the late '70s and early 1980s when moose rose in a few short years from being a rare animal to their present abundance. (This occurred because the Park's deer population had collapsed in the 1970s, and moose were then no longer subject to attacks from a parasitic brainworm that was carried harmlessly by deer but was fatal when transmitted to moose.) Such periods of population increase are dramatic, but they just can't continue to the point where moose totally overwhelm the environment. Long before then, something will happen to raise the death rate, lower the birth rate, or both.

As a matter of fact, we believe our moose population stabilized around 1985. Those of us who enjoy seeing moose would agree that the increase in our Park population was a desirable event. But who is to say things can't turn around again, with deaths exceeding births and the population going down as a result? At least two things could cause such a turnaround and may, in fact, actually be causing one right now.

One is the return of the White-tailed Deer inside — and definitely outside — Algonquin. We hinted earlier that moose were originally rare because deer and the brainworms they carried (fatal to moose) were so abundant. Only the virtual disappearance of deer in the 1970s allowed moose to reach the high numbers we saw in the '80s, and now there are grounds to suspect their return will again spell big trouble for our moose. So far we have no reason to think it is happening, but no one knows what level the deer population would have to reach to start pushing the moose death rate above the moose birth rate and therefore cause a decline.

The second and perhaps more immediate problem faced by Park moose is winter ticks. The larvae of these little animals get on moose in the fall (often tens of thousands on a single animal) and grow through the winter by sucking moose blood, before mating and dropping off onto the ground in April. Depending on the severity of the infestation, moose rub the hair off their hides in late winter in an effort to get rid of the irritating ticks. Having large hairless patches can put a moose at severe risk if there is cold, wet weather in late winter, and some of the dead animals we have been finding during the past few springs probably died because of their heavy tick loads. Other tick-infested areas of North America have had significant late winter die-offs of moose. Although it hasn't happened here yet, the possibility can't be ruled out, given our obviously high population of ticks.

So where does this leave us? What does the future hold for Algonquin's moose? Unfortunately, neither we nor anyone else can answer these questions because, perhaps surprisingly, so much depends on the weather. Whether deer numbers continue to rise, for example, and with them the danger of brainworm depends mostly on our winters. Strings of mild winters mean an expanding deer population and eventual risk to moose, but that can quickly be reversed by just one bad deer-killing winter with deep snow.

With ticks also, much depends on chance. When the engorged female ticks fall off moose in April, they die if

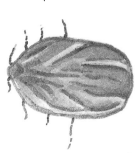
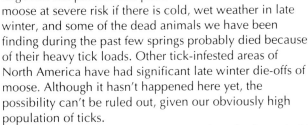

Fully-grown male Winter Tick and engorged female (about twice the life size).

they land on snow but survive if they land on dry ground. If the summer is hot, ticks may die if they are in open, sunny areas (which is where moose are most likely to bed down and possibly get reinfected in the fall). And, of course, whether tick-infested moose actually die depends very much on how cold and wet it is during their late winter "hairless period," when they are most vulnerable.

The truth is that moose, as with all wildlife, are subject to many controlling influences, some of which allow their numbers to increase and others of which may force their numbers down. Brainworms and ticks are only two of the forces that happen to act on moose.

Some people find it hard to accept we can't do anything about animals, such as ticks and brainworms, that we think of as "nasty" and help other animals, such as moose, that we happen to like. But, as we said before, moose populations can't keep growing forever at the rates they are capable of under ideal conditions. Sooner or later, deaths, whether through starvation, disease, or predators, will unavoidably equal the birth rate. This means that in any attempt we might make to play God, the best we could hope for would be to save moose from premature deaths from brainworms or ticks … only to see them die from some other premature and unpleasant agent of death.

It is not easy for everyone to accept these ideas, and yet accept them we must if we are to have a realistic notion of how the real world operates. We have always believed human beings are much better served by facing facts as they are, not as we might wish them to be, and we would even go one step further. Although it may seem like making a virtue of necessity, we would suggest that there is endless wonder and fascination to be derived from an age-old system whose underlying reality of pitiless competition, suffering, and premature death produces so much apparent harmony, beauty, and tranquility for the human observer.

Perhaps you will think about these things the next time you paddle by an appealing little newborn moose calf and its mother at the edge of your favourite fishing lake. It may not be your first instinct to dwell on the notion that the calf, very likely, and the cow, quite possibly, will be dead within the coming year. But you can also take heart from the knowledge that they will probably both be replaced as well. Death and birth in the world of Algonquin Park moose are a bittersweet combination, but they are facts, and they are as old and as real as life itself.∞

April 26, 1990 , Vol. 31, No. 1 (D.S.)

Why Fire Is Like Rain

Two years ago a horrified public watched as half the forests of Yellowstone National Park in the United States were consumed by fires so mighty that only the arrival of winter finally put them out. Last summer, devastating fires swept across northern Manitoba, forcing the evacuation of over 20,000 people and sending hazy smoke as far away as Europe. Faced with such awesomely destructive rampages, a panic-stricken press speculated about the greenhouse effect, global warming, and the disastrous consequences for North America's forests and wildlife. In the case of Yellowstone, they mourned the severe degradation, or even loss, of the world's first national park and crucified the policymakers and managers who, it turned out, had at first deliberately allowed some of the fires to burn unchecked.

Now, we daresay that if half of Algonquin Park went up in smoke one summer, the reaction here would be similar. In the popular mind it would be hard to imagine a worse calamity. The thought of centuries-old trees being destroyed in a few seconds and thousands of birds and animals supposedly choking to death or being burned alive is just too horrible for many people to contemplate. Anyone who values the natural environment, so goes the usual thinking, would be truly aghast.

And yet, quite obviously by now, here we are hinting that we don't agree with this commonly accepted view of fire. Are we seriously suggesting that forest fires are nothing to get excited about? Well, in a word and up to a point — yes! More specifically, we contend that fire in a forest is about as normal and natural as rain. Now, to say that fire is like rain may seem downright preposterous. If anything, the two appear to be complete opposites. Fire, after all, burns and sears while rain refreshes. Fire destroys life while rain makes it possible. We admit this is true, but we still aren't going to back down from our statement. Please allow us to explain.

First, let us consider why we say that fire is a normal part of the environment. This notion might seem difficult to prove. On the one hand, our modern records don't go back very far; on the other hand, humans now mask the normal situation. We do this by starting many fires ourselves but also by putting out almost all fires, including natural ones, long before they have burned their natural course. There are ways around this difficulty, however, and investigations carried out around the world leave no doubt whatsoever that fires were a common and regular occurrence in many environments long before man's influence began to be felt.

This is particularly true in more flammable forests of pine or spruce, and a study carried out on Algonquin's mainly coniferous east side provides a good example. Two records of the past fire history from that part of the Park were available. One was found in, of all places, the mud at the bottom of Greenleaf Lake. This lake is unusual in being so deep that the water does not circulate all the way to the bottom. Any oxygen originally down there was used up long ago, and no organisms can live in, and stir up, the bottom mud. This means that summer and winter layers of detritus drifting down from above are preserved in a year-by-year record that goes right back to Greenleaf's formation following the departure of the last glacier 11,000 years ago. By taking a core of the bottom mud and examining the contents of the annual layers, researchers have been able to determine what kinds of trees have grown around the lake over the years (by identifying the kinds of pollen in each layer) and also how often fires occurred. Forest fires cause the deposition of minute fragments of charcoal and increased amounts of aluminum (because of greater soil erosion after a fire). Their presence in the sediment layer was proof that fire had burned in the Greenleaf Lake basin in the year corresponding to the layer and permitted the reconstruction of the local fire history far back into the past. In addition, it was possible to get independent confirmation, at least for the last several hundred years, by examining the scars left by fires in the trunks of still-living Red Pine trees scattered around Barron Township (in which Greenleaf Lake is located). As everyone knows, trees put on visible growth rings every

year. By taking a sample from the trunks of these trees, it was possible to see how often in their lives they had been singed by fire and precisely when — right down to the exact years.

Both these approaches indicated that, on average, there was a major fire in Barron Township at least once every 45 years and that every part of the township could expect to be burned once every 70 years. (Of course, some particular areas might escape for much longer than that, but then other areas would be burned even more frequently than once every 70 years.)

No matter how you look at these figures, they indicate that fire was indeed a normal and common part of the east-side Algonquin environment. In a way, we should not be surprised. All we have to do is look at the way many plants live in order to realize that fire must always have been a normal, even necessary, part of their environment. Why do Jack Pine trees have cones that open only after exposure to great heat if it isn't to ensure that the seeds are released precisely when they have a chance to succeed — after a fire has prepared a mineral soil seedbed and killed the shade-casting parent trees? Why do aspen trees sucker profusely after a fire and grow only in direct sunlight if it isn't to take advantage of the frequent and normal destruction of old trees by forest fires? Even in Algonquin's west-side forests of Sugar Maple, where fire is much less a factor, there is evidence that at least one tree species, the Yellow Birch, depended on ground fires to burn off the dead maple leaves and prepare a seedbed suitable for its tiny seedlings. All these trees and in turn the plants and animals associated with them depended on fire for their prosperity, if not their very existence. It is difficult to imagine how such a situation could ever have evolved if fire weren't a normal part of the environment.

Another way of realizing the importance of a certain, natural frequency of fire is provided by looking at what happens when that frequency is disturbed. We know from the records left by the men who surveyed what is now Algonquin Park in the 1880s, for example, that virtually the entire watershed of the Petawawa River on the east side burned in the preceding decade or two. We know, of course, that fires were always part of that environment, but this indicated an enormous increase in their extent and frequency. Most people think that the White Pine loggers were unintentionally responsible both for starting more fires in the first place and then for providing more fuel for them (in the form of pine slash).

Whatever their exact origin, the extra fires made much more than a trivial difference to the Park area. Not only were the forests themselves greatly affected (any stands of old-growth White Pine still remaining after logging were consumed) but so were the Park's wildlife. Burned areas were soon taken over by new growth, and White-tailed Deer, formerly excluded from the Park area by the combination of little food and deep winter snow, now found conditions much more suitable. Within decades they went from being rare or altogether absent to being incredibly abundant. Some estimates had them as high as 100,000 in the Park area, and these numbers had their own secondary consequences for the environment. For years there was almost no regeneration of cedar or Yellow Birch in Algonquin — because both were preferred food items of deer. And, although the link was not recognized at the time, the advent of the deer was mostly, if not completely, responsible for the local extinction of caribou and for moose becoming rare. (Both animals are highly vulnerable to a parasitic brainworm carried by deer.)

All these drastic changes in the Park environment were caused not by something new but merely by an increase in the occurrence of the fires that had always been a normal part of the scene. Today, of course, we have almost the opposite situation. Thanks to modern equipment and highly-trained crews, we have made fire almost extinct as an influence on the Algonquin and many other environments where it formerly played an important role. Since the 1930s, Algonquin has been "deprived" of more than 600 natural fires that, without our fire suppression, would have burned varying areas of forest. As a result, and for quite some time now, the "deer bubble" has burst and moose have returned. In that sense the current almost-no-fire situation in Algonquin has recreated an environment more like the one that existed before the White Pine loggers arrived.

Still, we should not forget all those tree species and their dependent wildlife, such as beaver, deer, moose, and bear, that relied on forest fires for their prosperity. There is plenty of reason to believe that the fortunes of these plants and animals will be much different if fire is suppressed than they would be under truly natural conditions. This was explicitly recognized in Algonquin's 1974 Master Plan, which calls for a let-burn policy in the Park's wilderness and watershed nature reserve zones. The policy has never been implemented here because of certain obvious difficulties. If the object is to restore the natural fire regime, for example, how do you compensate for the effect of fires starting outside those zones that would have burned into them if we hadn't put them out? How do you stop a fire starting within the zone when it reaches the zone boundaries? Are we really ready to see valuable campsites in the affected areas incinerated?

As long as we as a society aren't ready to tackle these questions, we will have to settle for a perhaps ironic situation in which our wilderness zones are ecologically less natural than the surrounding zones — areas where logging partly compensates for the absence of fire.

Resolution of these difficult problems will have to wait for another day. For now we hope that we have made some progress in our self-appointed task of convincing you that fire is indeed like rain. Both are perfectly natural parts of the environment that have shaped our living world. And, although knowing where to draw the line is difficult, rain and fire are both things we can have too much of — but also too little. ✑

August 16, 1990, Vol. 31, No. 9 (D.S.)

Winter Roulette

September is here again, and fall is unfolding as it should. The days are clear and silent, and the nights are nippy. Birds are leaving for the south, and already we have patches of red and orange foliage foretelling the peak of colours at the end of the month. October will then see the turning of Tamaracks and Aspens, the building of winter food piles by our beaver colonies, and the closing down of the Park's staffed facilities after Thanksgiving weekend. All these things are normal and regular events, year after year, and we know that many of our fall visitors share our appreciation for their comfortable predictability.

The age-old progression of the seasons is such a familiar fact of life that you may be surprised when we point out that the one after this — winter — is not going to be predictable at all. Now it is true, just as day follows night, that the winter of 1990–91 will bring cold and snow to Algonquin. In that sense, the coming winter will be just as normal as the current season. Nevertheless, the winter will also bring events of wild randomness, and these events will have an enormous, quite unpredictable bearing on the lives and fortunes of Algonquin Park inhabitants. It is almost as if they were dragged into a casino and forced to bet everything they had on a single game of chance. Grant you, this may seem to be an exaggeration, but if you join us in following the events of a typical winter, you will see what we mean.

By the end of October the days will be noticeably shorter, and we will be having hard frosts just about every night. The cold will intensify, and the first snowstorm may occur in November. Then again, it may not, and therein lies a question of deadly importance. Algonquin's vast army of mice, voles, and shrews is a vital link in the Park's food chain. They consume insects, seeds, and snails and in turn are food for larger animals, such as weasels, foxes, martens, and owls. Shrews and most mice remain active all winter, but their own internal heat-generating capacities are just not good enough to keep their tiny bodies warm in truly cold weather. When the temperature dips to 20 below for any extended period, they are doomed to freeze solid, even if they huddle together in well-insulated underground nests. The only thing that can save them is a good, thick layer of insulating snow, but who is to say a life-saving blizzard will arrive in time? It may well be that the first storm of the year passes north or south of the Park. Even worse, we could get a big dump, the snow could all melt, thoroughly soaking the leaf litter and the underground tunnels and nests of the Park's small mammals, and then it could get really cold.

On such seemingly unimportant details about the timing and sequence of cold and snow hang the lives of literally millions of Algonquin mice and shrews. If the numbers don't turn up right in a given year, the Park's small mammal populations can be decimated, and with their collapse can come that of the predators that depend on them. Then, too, even if the mice and shrews are saved by the timely arrival of deep snow, this doesn't necessarily ensure the salvation of their predators. If the snow is too thick, the predators may not be able to get at them. As long as the snow cover is light and fluffy, the mice and shrews will be content to tunnel along on the soil surface. That, after all, is where their food is and where the snow insulation is best. Although foxes and owls can hear mice scurrying along down there and can plunge their legs unerringly down to the sound source through amazingly deep snow, there are still limits, nonetheless, especially for smaller predators. With more snowfalls the outlook for predators might seem increasingly dim, but other chance events can turn this around.

As the snow thickens and especially if a warm spell causes the upper layers to compact and lose their fluffiness, life will become less comfortable for small mammals down at the bottom of the snow. Carbon dioxide, released by the slow but continuing bacterial decay in the soil, will no longer be able to escape upward and will start to build up in the tunnel networks at the bottom of the snow. The mice and shrews will be forced to build and maintain ventilation shafts up to the surface, but when they do, of course, they again come within range of those owls and foxes. The important question once more, for both the hunters and the hunted is the precise timing of events. If deep snow comes early and cold temperatures delay compaction, the mice and shrews may be able to stay out of reach for so long that predators will either starve or wander out of the Park. It could all depend on a chance warm spell in the first week of January. If there is one, owls and foxes might live; if not, they might die.

Small mammals and their predators are far from the only creatures, of course, whose fortunes are greatly affected by snow depths. Regular Park visitors are quite familiar with the fact that deer start to have serious difficulties in moving about when the snow is 50 centimetres (20 inches) or more in depth. Indeed, severe winters, especially when there were two or three of them in a row, all but destroyed the Park's deer population on a couple of occasions. What may not be appreciated is how chancey these events were. The difference between a bad winter and an easy winter for deer can be as little as two or three snowstorms — snowstorms that might just as easily have missed the Park or not materialized at all.

Then, too, what is shaping up as a killer winter can be transformed into a paradise for deer almost overnight. It sometimes happens that a freak warm spell followed by a good hard freeze will quickly transform metre-deep snow, in which deer were floundering, into a snow "pavement," hard enough and strong enough to allow deer to move about with ease. Not only that, but the new surface may in effect elevate the deer up off the ground into range of a whole new supply of nutritious browse that was out of reach beforehand.

As in any game of chance, however, what is the lucky number for one player can be a disaster for another. The same hard-crust conditions that sometimes spell salvation for deer can spell just the opposite for grouse. Grouse escape the bitter cold of winter nights by plunging down into soft snow and hollowing out a snug, well-insulated chamber. Needless to say, grouse can't do this and may freeze to death if there is a very cold night and a rock-hard crust, or they may break their necks if they try.

Or, strictly by chance, there could be the worst of both worlds. The crust could be strong enough to prevent grouse from flying into the snow but also too weak to consistently support large animals. Under such conditions, deer and moose may irregularly break through the crust, lacerating their legs and expending great amounts of energy as they struggle to get back on top. Even worse, this may make them much more vulnerable to wolves. Many a healthy deer that otherwise would have gotten away has fallen victim to wolves just because, a few days earlier, weather conditions happened to make a crust strong enough to support wolves but not a running deer.

There is no doubt that the unpredictable interplay of snow and rain, cold spells and warm spells, can have enormous life-and-death consequences for many individual Algonquin Park inhabitants, but it goes much further than that. Depending on how deep the snow is, for example, and how easy or difficult it is for a cow moose to move around and get food, she will finish up the winter in a correspondingly better or worse nutritional state. This has an immediate bearing on the vigour of

Where will the wheel stop this year?

her calf that will be born a month or two later, and this in turn has a big influence on the calf's prospects for survival. Not only that, but cow moose are apparently unable to make up the nutritional consequences of a bad winter very quickly. In fact, a bad winter can still have a lowering influence on the survival of calves born as much as three summers later. It is almost like a person who has lost his or her life savings because of one unlucky event and then has to spend years digging out of a financial hole.

Seen in this light, the chance events of the coming winter are of much more than trivial importance. No matter how reassuringly normal the fall now appears, the inhabitants of Algonquin Park will soon be obliged to play a potentially deadly game of roulette. They have stepped up to the table (made it this far), determined the stakes (their lives and future offspring), placed their bets (chosen their lifestyles), and the wheel (winter) is about to spin. ... Good luck!↩

September 6, 1990, Vol. 31, No. 12 (D.S.)

A Toehold in the Mysterious South

Another spring is unfolding in Algonquin Park. Even as we write, in mid-April, there are signs of the coming miracle. The days are getting longer and warmer, a few ducks have already shown up in our opening lakes and rivers, and somebody even reported the first bear of the year just two days ago. Soon buds will be swelling, hillsides will be awash with the pastel pinks and greens of May, and the woods will be alive with the songs of beautiful warblers reclaiming their territories and getting ready to raise another generation of young. The Park is filled with so many fascinating events at this time of year that we are always grateful for the chance to see them. At the same time, however, we admit to being totally perplexed by some.

The aspect of puzzlement is on our minds right now because we are getting ready to go on an expedition to the extreme southern tip of Algonquin, where we hope to repeat a discovery we made there at this time last year.

What we did, not far from the shore of Kingscote Lake in the Park's southern panhandle, was to find the first two nests ever recorded in Algonquin Park of the rare Red-shouldered Hawk. We were delighted with this accomplishment, but at the same time it raised some questions we can't answer.

But before an explanation is provided, a few details of our discoveries will be of interest. With the first one, made on April 18, 1990, we had walked into an area where Red-shouldered Hawks had been observed the year before and where some of our timber technicians had noticed several large stick nests in the winter. We played a recording of a Red-shouldered Hawk's calls, and within seconds we saw and heard a male Red-shouldered flying straight towards us above the still leafless hardwoods. It screamed, dived, and swooped several times and then, having determined that we were not another Red-shouldered Hawk (and therefore of no importance), soared away out of sight. For our part, we were determined to have a close look at the area from which the hawk had come. Within minutes, we had found one of the stick nests discovered in the winter, and, best of all, a female Red-shouldered Hawk was sitting on it — presumably on eggs!

We beat a hasty retreat so as not to disturb her and went exploring elsewhere. Later on, near the north end of Kingscote, we were lucky enough to discover another Red-shouldered Hawk, which came in to our recorded calls. It was a beautiful sunny day, and that gorgeous hawk made a marvellous spectacle as it soared over the still-frozen lake and the ancient, rounded hills. We could see the narrow, white bands on the black tail, the beautiful rufous colouration on the breast, and when the bird banked, the "checkerboard" pattern of the upper wing surface and even the normally inconspicuous reddish shoulder patches from which the bird gets its name.

Our observations of that day will stay in our memory for a long time, and they are ones we hope to have repeated by the time you pick up this copy of *The Raven*. Unfortunately, it has become increasingly difficult to observe Red-shouldered Hawks in our province. The sad fact is that where the Red-shouldered Hawk was once the most common hawk in southern Ontario, now it is completely gone from many large areas and is very rare in others. What a far cry from even just 40 years ago when almost any tract of deciduous or mixed woods bordering a stream or lake in the agricultural south had its pair of Red-shouldered Hawks that returned year after year and often to the very same nest. Just to give you an idea of how abundant they were, one observer, writing in the 1930s, remarked that he knew of 30 pairs within a 15-mile radius of his home, and others estimated that Red-shouldered Hawks were four times as common as the larger Red-tailed Hawk.

No one knows for sure why Red-shouldered Hawks have dwindled from abundance to their present low numbers and patchy distribution. To be sure, there is less woodland in southern Ontario now than there used to be, but Red-shoulders have disappeared even from traditional nesting woods that still remain, and no one seriously believes that less food is available. Indeed, the Red-shouldered Hawk is a predatory generalist, taking everything from mice and squirrels to frogs, snakes, insects, and even earthworms and should be largely immune to problems with particular kinds of prey. One interesting theory (developed, incidentally, by a former Algonquin summer naturalist) makes a plausible link between the disappearance of Red-shoulders and selective logging. According to this idea, when a farmer maximizes the timber or firewood production of his woodlot by the selective removal of certain trees (thereby letting more sunlight into the gaps between remaining trees and stimulating their growth), he also brings on big trouble for the resident Red-shouldered Hawks. The bigger and less manoeuverable Red-tailed Hawk, formerly excluded from the closed canopy of the woodlot, now can move in and exploit the newly opened-up woods. And, if any Red-shouldered Hawks try to put up an argument, the larger size of the Red-tail quickly settles the issue in their favour. The theory has a definite appeal because, in general, Red-tail numbers have gone up as those of Red-shoulders have gone down. Also, the former Red-shoulder nesting areas now occupied by Red-tails tend to be woods that humans have opened up through selective logging.

The possible sensitivity of Red-shouldered Hawks to logging has led the Ministry of Natural Resources in the last several years to find as many as possible of the province's remaining nesting sites and to reserve at least the immediate surrounding areas from cutting. It was this effort that led to our discovery of the first Red-shoulder nest in Algonquin last April (and of the second not far away on May 3, 1990). Even more important, another 38 nests were found in a wide arc of central Ontario stretching from Parry Sound in the west to near Ottawa in the east. The two Algonquin nests were really just a minor part of this broad picture.

And this brings us back to the puzzling question that we alluded to at the beginning of this *Raven*. Over the years we have had a smattering of Red-shouldered Hawk observations in Algonquin Park, usually involving birds in migration, and we have known since the early 1980s that a few resident birds lived at the very southern tip of the Park and probably nested there. The actual discoveries we made last spring only confirmed those suspicions and haven't really changed the understanding we have always had of the overall hawk picture in Algonquin. As far as the big soaring hawks are concerned, that picture basically is this: there are Red-tails thinly scattered over Algonquin (probably mostly associated with thin woods or big bogs and other open areas); there are Broad-winged Hawks just about everywhere (this is the small hawk with the wide black-and-white tail bands often seen perched along Highway 60); and, finally, as we have seen, there are Red-shouldered Hawks (perhaps only two or three pairs) confined to the very southern tip of the Park. The perplexing question is, why aren't Red-shouldered Hawks found elsewhere in Algonquin? For the life of us, we can't see anything different about the woods around Kingscote Lake as opposed to those farther north — at least of the sort that could account for the presence or absence of a big, resourceful hawk like a Red-shoulder. To be sure, the woods around Kingscote Lake are richer than most Algonquin hardwoods, and even have a few ferns and wildflowers that are very rare or altogether absent from the main part of the Park.

Needless to say, it is difficult to imagine how differences as subtle as these could matter to a Red-shouldered Hawk.

Sometimes we invoke the higher altitude of the west side of Algonquin (and its correspondingly harsher climate) to explain forest or wildlife differences between there and lower surrounding areas. Several kinds of reptiles and amphibians, for example, don't make it up onto the "Algonquin dome," presumably because the winters are just too long and cold for them at the higher elevations. It might be argued that, if Red-shouldered Hawks only make it just inside the very southern edge of Algonquin, they too are somehow excluded from the bulk of the Park by something to do with climate — the later spring, for example. The trouble with this argument is that Kingscote Lake is only 50 kilometres (30 miles) as the hawk flies from Highway 60 and has exactly the same elevation as Smoke Lake and Canoe Lake (two of the highest lakes along Highway 60).

No, quite frankly, we can't see any reason at all why Red-shouldered Hawks can make a go of it at Kingscote Lake but nowhere else in the Park. We are left scratching our heads and hoping that someday somebody (maybe another Algonquin summer naturalist) will be able to make sense of it all.

In the meantime, we are getting ready to go back for another visit to the little Red-shouldered Hawk population of Kingscote Lake. We don't know why they only have such a tiny toehold deep in our mysterious south, but we're sure glad they have that much!∞

April 25, 1991, Vol. 32, No. 1 (D.S.)

No one knows why Red-shouldered Hawks nest only in the extreme southern tip of Algonquin.

Life in the Acid Vat

Although Bat Lake is highly acidic, it supports huge numbers of phantom midge larvae, preyed upon by visiting Bufflehead ducks. The lake is also a major breeding ground of the Yellow-spotted Salamander, whose gelatinous egg masses are conspicuous around the lake margin in May.

Visitors to the Park this year will have noticed that we have opened two new trails in the Highway 60 Corridor — the Track and Tower Trail, starting at kilometre 25, and the Bat Lake Trail at kilometre 30. Together they add almost 19 kilometres to our interpretive trail network. When their trail guide booklets become available next year, they will introduce many hikers to some very interesting local human history, as well as to some basic Park ecology.

In this issue, we thought we would give you a sneak preview to one of the trail guide stories by introducing you to the extra special body of water — Bat Lake — for which the shorter of the two trails is named. Bat Lake's claim to fame is that it is one of 15 lakes in Algonquin Park known to be acidic — and the only such lake in the

Corridor (and therefore the only one easily accessible to large numbers of visitors). Now, we will grant you that an acid lake conjures up images of grim sterility, and it might seem the last place to which you would want to hike. Besides, what vacationer would want such an unwelcome reminder of how vulnerable our lakes and forests are to long-range air pollution and of how meaningless park boundaries are in their ability to protect?

Well, we think you will be surprised by what Bat Lake is really like. To begin with, it is a rather pretty little lake nestled in a forest of spruce and pine. Every summer, lots of water-lilies grow in the shallower sections, and there are no outward signs of anything being amiss. So what do we really mean when we say that Bat Lake is acidic, and what is really wrong with it?

In terms of basic chemistry, Bat Lake has a pH of 4.75, meaning that it is fully 56 times as acidic as a typical, normal Park lake that might have a summertime surface pH of, say, 6.5. What's more, Bat Lake has absolutely no capacity to neutralize the acid rain and snow that now fall on Algonquin. This certainly sounds like a concrete example of the acid rain damage predicted by the countless articles and news reports we have all read and heard over the last decade, but, in fact, the truth is much more complicated. Scientists have recently learned how to read the pH history of lakes, extending back hundreds of thousands of years, by looking at the fossils of algae that have died and settled out in the layers of mud at the bottom of a lake. Different kinds of algae are closely associated with narrow ranges of acidity. On this basis, the record shows that Bat Lake has "always" been naturally acidic* (although the recent, additional input of man-caused acid rain may have increased the acidity somewhat).

Regardless of how it got that way, Bat Lake today is a fishless vat of acid. According to some water chemistry classification schemes, it would be considered "acid dead," thus encouraging the usual picture people have of acid lakes as sterile wastelands.

In fact, by anybody's standards, the lake is swarming with life. First, there are the microscopic algae mentioned above, and then there are at least five species of tiny crustaceans that graze on the algae. Preying in turn on the crustaceans are millions of phantom midge larvae, almost transparent, little insects that sometimes reach densities in Bat Lake of 800 per cubic metre. They are difficult to see in the daytime, but at night when you shine a flashlight into Bat Lake, the water seems to be a teeming "soup" of small, but still very visible, organisms. Most kinds of phantom midges hide in the bottom mud during the day to escape from fish, and only rise up into the lake at night. The kind that lives in Bat Lake, however, is a rare species that stays up in the water both day and night. Its occurrence there and its incredible numbers are both explained by the fact that Bat Lake has no fish (thanks, of course, to its high acidity).

The great crop of phantom midge larvae supports unusually large numbers of backswimmers and dytiscids (both predatory insects), and in the spring and fall, Bat Lake is one of the best places we know of in Algonquin to see migrating Buffleheads, a beautiful little northern duck that specializes in aquatic invertebrates.

The most spectacular of all visitors to Bat Lake, however, are the Yellow-spotted Salamanders. Right now they are present as tadpoles — thousands of salamander larvae preying on the crustaceans and growing rapidly until they are big enough to transform into air-breathing adults and leave the lake sometime in August. Next spring, soon after the ice is out, the adults will return to Bat Lake to court and lay their eggs. For a few nights there will be a frenzy of activity, and then, for the month of May, you will be able to see over 1,500 baseball-sized,

milky-white, gelatinous egg masses attached to underwater stems all around the shore of the lake. Each egg mass contains about 60 to 80 eggs. Notwithstanding the acidity of Bat Lake, the eggs don't seem to suffer. Indeed, one little test we did suggested that half the eggs can be expected to hatch into tadpoles.

The enormous production of Yellow-spotted Salamanders in Bat Lake is of great interest because most Yellow-spotted Salamanders aren't nearly so well off. The usual story is that they are forced to breed and lay their eggs in temporary meltwater pools in the forest because in lakes both the adults and any tadpoles that hatched from the eggs would be annihilated by fish. Bat Lake, of course, doesn't have this problem, nor is there any danger it will dry up before the tadpoles have had time to transform into air-breathing adults. Bat Lake is therefore a salamander paradise, and it may be reasonably suggested that such unusual, naturally acidic and fishless waterbodies are far more effective in populating the forest with salamanders than are the more numerous but smaller spring meltwater pools, which often dry up too soon anyway. Many people are surprised to learn that the weight of salamanders in our forests is greater than that of mice or birds — even at this time of year when bird populations are at their annual high. Even if they are usually out of sight, therefore, salamanders play a major role in the forest ecosystem. Places such as Bat Lake, which inject so many salamanders into the surrounding forest, must be seen as themselves playing a major role in that ecosystem.

To top it all off, we can assure you Algonquin Park offers few more spectacular wildlife experiences than that to be had by floating around Bat Lake with a flashlight on the right night in May. Here and there, all along the shoreline, exotic-looking, miniature dragons are wriggling up from the bottom to gulp a breath of air at the surface, and once in a while your flashlight beam illuminates a female, entwined around a submerged stem, in the act of extruding her enormous egg mass.

It is a picture of strange, primitive beauty, but, most of all, it is a picture of life — and that is the basic lesson of Bat Lake. It may be acidic and, compared to other lakes, it may be a very simple ecosystem, but it is undeniably and even astonishingly filled with life.

Needless to say, this reality is the exact opposite of the idea we would normally have of an acidified lake, and you may find it a little difficult to believe that what we have been saying is true. So by all means, take the new trail and start making your own acquaintance with pretty little Bat Lake. And, please, don't worry about disappearing in a cloud of steam if you should happen to fall in. If all those algae, crustaceans, midge larvae, ducks, and salamanders can live all or much of their lives in Bat Lake, a few minutes soaking out there with them isn't going to hurt you. Or, as a salamander might say, "Come on in, the acid's fine!"∾

*We do not mean to suggest by this that all of the 15 Park lakes are naturally acidic. Studies by researchers from Queen's University in Kingston, Ontario, on the fossil algae of Drummer Lake and Little Eastend Lake indicate that they, at least, acidified only within the last 30 years, almost certainly as a result of man-caused acid rain and snow.

June 27, 1991, Vol. 32, No. 2 (D.S.)

A World so Foreign

We aren't sure about the rest of the world, but here in North America we live in a culture that strongly blurs the lines between humans and animals. As children, we are surrounded by animals on television or in books that walk, talk, and wear clothes. Even modern documentaries about real animals often ascribe human thoughts and emotions to their subjects, making a strong, implicit suggestion that animals think and feel pretty much the way we do. Such confusion between animal fact and fiction will no doubt be with us for many years to come, and maybe it doesn't matter. Still, we personally can't help feeling that this confusion colours the way we think about and act towards the natural world. As an example, many people seem to think that if only wild animals were left alone, they would live out their lives "normally and happily" (just the way humans for the most part also do). And how many times have we been told that wild animals are "born free," and who wouldn't want to be "happy as a lark?"

These thoughts came to mind a couple of weeks ago when we were lucky enough to see a family of Ermines (also called Short-tailed Weasels) moving along the shore of Peck Lake. The adult female was in the lead, and three youngsters were close behind, sniffing in every nook and cranny but never straying very far from their mother. They were almost certainly making a move from one temporary living area to a new one where the female had found the mouse-hunting to be better. The chances were quite good, if we had waited a while, that we would have seen her come back once or twice to get the rest of her litter and lead them to the new hunting grounds as well.

A mother weasel typically raises six to eight youngsters every spring. She nurses them in the nest for a while, and then, until they are about 10 weeks old (and with no assistance from the long-gone father), she hunts all the food required for herself and the young. Toward the end of this period, her daughters will each weigh as much as she does and her sons up to 50 per cent more. Needless to say, feeding them all is a remarkable accomplishment.

Now, this seems as devoted as anything humans could ever do, and it probably reinforces the hazy notion we all have that animals — at least the "higher" ones, such as mammals and birds — are somehow quite similar to us.

If we could watch an Ermine for more than one of these rare encounters, however, we might realize that things are not all innocent bliss in their world. We aren't referring here to the fact that weasels are killers of awesome efficiency. As a matter of fact, we think most people nowadays are perfectly ready to accept and appreciate the role of predators in the natural world.

No, what we have in mind are a couple of features of weasel existence, ones that are partly imposed on them by their mouse-hunting way of life but seldom appreciated by many people, who otherwise have a pretty good idea of how weasels operate.

The first is that weasels lead a fast-paced, demanding life, which can be kept up for only so long. Being long and slinky is great for following mice down their tunnels but not good for conserving heat in a cold climate. A weasel will starve to death in just 48 hours and must kill at a high rate just to stay alive. By the age of two (if it makes it even that far) a weasel is starting to burn out. It lives so close to the edge that even the slightest infirmity means it will fail to keep up. Indeed, starvation is the leading cause of death among weasels (followed by predation by larger animals, such as foxes and owls).

Needless to say, a full lifespan that lasts just two years is very different from the human experience. But this is just one way the lives of weasels are almost unimaginably different from our own.

A second is the way they reproduce. We often talk about "survival of the fittest," but what really counts in the natural world is how many living descendants an animal produces. Suppose, for example, there were two female weasels, Weasel A and Weasel B. Weasel A takes things easy, producing just two young per year, and lives for two years, thus achieving a total lifetime production of four offspring. Weasel B, on the other hand, only lives for one year — partly because she wears herself completely out by raising eight youngsters in her one breeding season.

In the big picture it doesn't matter that Weasel A survived twice as long as Weasel B. Nor does it matter that many of the young weasels die before they become breeders themselves. Other things being equal, in the following generation there will be twice as many new weasels mothered by Weasel B than by Weasel A. And if this tendency to live a shorter life but produce more offspring is inherited, then the offspring of Weasel B will similarly out-reproduce the offspring of Weasel A. After just two generations, Weasel B will have not twice but four times as many grand-offspring as Weasel A, and after 10 generations (only 20 years), there will be more than 1,000 times as many B-type weasels as there are of the A type.

By this time, of course, both original weasels are long since dead and the fact that one survived longer than the other is utterly insignificant. All that matters is that Weasel B had an advantage over Weasel A in reproduction, and now her descendants completely dominate the population.

Advantages of one strain over another are seldom so one-sided as in this example, but it is easy to see that even a slight advantage will lead to eventual success over more slowly-reproducing, rival strains. To be sure, raising a large family all at once is hard on a mother (humans and weasels would agree on this), and in some species (like ours) it may be a better "strategy" to reproduce slowly so as to live longer and leave more offspring over the long haul. But if an animal has a short or uncertain future ahead, the victorious, "more fit" strains will be those that throw everything they have into the current year's reproduction.

Female weasels certainly seem to have this strategy. Even though the cost must be enormous, the kinds of weasels that have left the most descendants (the ones we see today) are the ones that go for broke each year. Female weasels have evolved another trait that gives them a slight edge in their unwitting race to leave the greatest possible number of descendants. They mate in the spring while still nursing their current babies, but the newly fertilized eggs stop developing very soon and are retained in the womb in a sort of suspended animation for a full 10 months. Only late the following winter do the eggs implant themselves in the wall of the mother's womb and start the true two-month-long pregnancy. The advantage of this arrangement is that the female can time the birth of her young to best suit her own nutritional needs. No need to have the young born even a little bit too late or too soon as a result of a male not coming by at exactly the right time. Thanks to the delayed implantation of her eggs, she can "turn on" her pregnancy, albeit involuntarily, at the best possible moment to maximize the health and survival prospects of her babies.

Males have an entirely different set of tricks for maximizing their own individual offspring — which they do by mating with as many females as possible. The older males, the ones that have made it to the age of two, achieve the best results by roaming widely, finding and staying with successive females for a day or two until they come into heat, and then moving on. Younger one-year old males can't compete with old males in their "roaming strategy" so they usually stay close to just one or two females. If they get to mate at all, it is because no two-year-old happens along when the females are receptive. Young or old, the males make the most of their opportunities. You will recall that, thanks to the phenomenon of delayed implantation, mating takes place a full year before the resulting young are born. This means that not only are mother weasels fertile during the spring nursing period but so are their baby daughters. That is why male weasels, after mating with the mothers, drag the helpless, still-blind female babies out of the nest and mate with them as well — before going on to look for more.*

We will admit that this behaviour, on our terms, appears unspeakably inhuman and brutish. Still, it has not been our intention here to shock or disturb anyone, much less to pass judgement on the worth of weasels. Our only point has been to illustrate that the lives of wild animals are almost unimaginably remote from our own. Their existence is neither "good" nor "bad," neither "loving" nor "cruel." They do not know or understand that they live on a planet. They do not know or understand what delayed implantation is. They do not know or understand what death is. They do not know or understand that they are slaves to the evolutionary imperative of maximum lifetime reproduction.

They live lives that, to our eyes, are fascinating, breath-taking in their finely-tuned intricacy, and often wildly beautiful — but they are most definitely not human lives. It wouldn't hurt any of us to remember this the next time we see a weasel talking and wearing clothes on television, or even when we are lucky enough — as we were last week — to see a real one in the wild leading her young to new hunting grounds. It is only too easy to ascribe human feelings and emotions to animals, especially given our limited and often artificial exposure to them. The truth is, animals live in a world so foreign to ours that, even with the greatest of efforts, we can barely begin to imagine what their lives would really be like.⤳

July 4, 1991, Vol. 32, No. 3 (D.S.)

---

* A human mother would object to this in the strongest way, but mother weasels are not human. As a matter of fact, they offer no resistance at all to the male — and why should they? It is in the mother's reproductive "interest" that the daughters have young when they are one year old (it may be their only chance), and that means they must be impregnated when they are still babies. Besides, if a male is good enough to father the mother's next litter, why would she object to the same male fathering her grand-offspring as well?

Why It Pays to Have Pink Armpits

With some justification all of us probably take for granted that Algonquin Park has many beautiful kinds of birds and that summer is the best time of year to see them. In fact, if you come along on one of our early morning bird hikes, you can expect to see Bobolinks, Chestnut-sided Warblers, Red-winged Blackbirds, and many others in a long list of outstanding Algonquin songbirds.

It's one thing to take for granted the presence of all these beautiful Park inhabitants, but it's quite another to really know why they are so colourful. To be sure, we all realize that it must have something to do with nesting, directly or indirectly. Otherwise it wouldn't be only the males that (usually) have the bright plumage and females the much duller. Still, it's far from obvious just how brilliant bird colours actually work — a fact that was brought home to us a month ago when a male Rose-breasted Grosbeak happened to fly directly overhead when we were walking the new Track and Tower Trail.

The Rose-breasted Grosbeak is an excellent example of a beautifully coloured Park bird. The female is dull brown, rather like an oversized sparrow, but the male is a real knockout. Its crisp black and white plumage is offset by a brilliant, triangular patch of red leading from the throat and pointing down onto the white breast. This, together with the enormous, whitish bill (responsible for the name grosbeak), gives the bird a truly arresting appearance, both dazzling and exotic at the same time. But the Rose-breasted Grosbeak has one more very special plumage characteristic as well. As we were able to see when our bird flew over us last month, males have bright pink armpits (or should it be wingpits?).

What on earth could they be for? Aren't male Rose-breasted Grosbeaks brilliant enough as it is? And besides, apart from exceptional situations like ours, neither we or anything else should ever be in a position to see into these hot pink secret places.

At first we thought the pink armpits might play a role similar to that of the red shoulder patches of our familiar Red-winged Blackbirds. Redwings are perfectly capable of choosing whether or not to display their famous patches — just as a Grosbeak is obviously capable of not showing off its armpits if it so chooses. In Redwings, the red patches have a definite function — they are used in territorial disputes to tell other males

that the male displaying his patches is a powerful force that must be reckoned with. We know this because male Redwings whose epaulettes have been dyed black have considerable trouble hanging onto their territories. Apparently neighbouring rivals just don't take the blackened males seriously, and sometimes even superior males are evicted from their territories if deprived of those red shoulder patches. Interestingly, female Redwings are completely indifferent to all this. If a male Redwing has a good territory, females find him desirable and they couldn't care less whether he also has fancy red shoulder patches.

But this is not to say that striking plumage in birds is always used to intimidate rival males and never to impress females. Male Ruffed Grouse often fan their tails out and erect their neck ruffs in the presence of females — even in the fall or winter — and male Meadowlarks court their females by standing in front of them as tall as they can while at the same time puffing out their yellow breasts so as to present the biggest stimulus possible.

So, returning to Rose-breasted Grosbeaks, the males' bright colours in general and their garish armpits in particular could in theory be used to terrorize rival males, to sweep females off their legs, or maybe even both. What is the true answer?

With a bird as common as the Rose-breasted Grosbeak, you might suppose that biologists would have long ago discovered the answer to such a basic question. But, as yet another indication of how little we really know about the natural world that surrounds us, it turns out that

A male Rose-breasted Grosbeak (above) displaying to a female.

no one has ever done a serious study of the Rose-breasted Grosbeak — so we don't really know the role of their bright colours. This is disappointing because Rose-breasted Grosbeaks would be quite easy to observe for anyone who put his or her mind to it. We ourselves, for example, quickly got some evidence on the subject when we found two males fighting on June 14. The dominant bird sang loudly and pursued the other vigorously. Sometimes, before launching an attack, the stronger male (who was presumably defending his territory) briefly spread his tail or flicked his wings but did nothing that could be construed as displaying any of his plumage toward the rival bird — which suggests that male Grosbeaks do not use their bright colours to intimidate opponents.

But we are still left without a positive answer as to how the colours really are used (if at all). The only clue we have been able to find comes from an account written back in 1944 by a man watching a semi-captive male whose attention had been suddenly rivetted towards a passing, apparently unmated female. The description, slightly edited, reads as follows:

"His voice now was so entrancingly beautiful that words cannot describe it, and his courtship display an exquisite tableau. He spread and dropped his rapidly quivering wings so low that their tips grazed the ground upon which he stood. His body was held in a crouching position with the breast almost touching the ground; his tail partly spread and slightly elevated; his head retracted so far that his nape lay against the feathers of his back (thereby giving maximum exposure of the red breast triangle toward the female). The mating song poured forth from his open beak as he moved toward the female, waving his head and body in an erratic dance. The downward and forward sweep of his wings revealed in striking contrast the blacks and whites of the separated wing feathers, the white of the rump, and the vivid rose of the underwing coverts" (i.e., armpits!) …

This one scrap of available evidence suggests that the male plumage of the Rose-breasted Grosbeak is used to dazzle females — not to stare down other male contenders. Still, it would be foolish to draw a definitive conclusion from just one observation, from just one person, made almost 50 years ago. We are still left wondering whether pink armpits are the Great Aphrodisiac, whether they might be the Great Intimidator instead, or as well. And we find it particularly amazing that even today, in 1991, we still don't know for sure. Obviously, there is a pressing need and a fine opportunity for further research into pink armpits. Any takers?☞

July 11, 1991, Vol. 32, No. 4 (D.S.)

A Mystery Solved

The east side of Algonquin is one of our favourite stomping grounds. If you take the Achray Road leading back into the Park from Highway 17 near Pembroke, you enter a very special part of Algonquin, quite different from the rest. There are miles and miles of pine forests, spectacular cliffs along the Barron and Petawawa Rivers, beautiful waterfalls at Carcajou Bay and High Falls Lake, gorgeous beaches on Grand Lake, and magnificent landscapes captured long ago in the classic Tom Thomson paintings "Jack Pine" and "West Wind." The list of things that make Algonquin's east side look and feel different from the west side, more familiar to Park visitors, is a long one.

There are special plants, like the endless, riverside stands of crimson-red Cardinal-flowers just now coming into bloom. There are even a few animals, that in Algonquin, are found only on the east side.

One of the most interesting is the Wood Turtle, perhaps already known to some readers from a *Raven* article three years ago. We pointed out back then that the occurrence of this provincially rare turtle along the Petawawa and Bonnechère Rivers in Algonquin had been known for a long time, but that we had little knowledge of their real range and abundance. Given increasing worry about how well Wood Turtles were doing elsewhere in Canada and the United States, we decided to take a closer look at our Algonquin population. Thanks to a research grant from The Friends of Algonquin Park, we were able to buy six little radio transmitters for tracking any turtles we might be able to find. Once we had hired a full-time summer student cum Wood Turtle watcher, we were in business. The results were gratifying; indeed, after a couple of years, we had a very reassuring picture of our Algonquin Park Wood Turtle population. Individual turtles seemed to be quite common along suitable rivers. The good variety of sizes and ages indicated that many new adult turtles were coming along in a healthy population. Those were the main things that we wanted to establish, but in the course of the study many other interesting details emerged as well. For example, the radio tracking enabled us to learn that most individuals stayed all summer in surprisingly small areas of only one or two acres, whereas others occupied more than 100 acres or even travelled right out of radio range for part of the summer.

It was a lot of fun tracking down these turtles and taking the time to watch them go about their business. With their beautiful ridged shells and yellow, orange, and black colouration elsewhere, they are attractive-looking animals, and, in keeping with their reputation for intelligence, they moved with strength and confidence, as if they always knew what they were doing and where they were going.

Of course, we could not always be certain of what the turtles were up to. It takes far more time than we had available to really acquire a thorough understanding of any animal's behaviour. For example, on one occasion we saw an old male pause and then rock from side to side, take another few steps, and then repeat the procedure. At the time we had no idea what this meant, and to the extent we tried to think of an explanation at all, we only half wondered if the animal might be sick.

As it turned out, what we were lucky enough to witness that day was an example of a then unknown but actually quite widespread behaviour pattern in Wood Turtles. Another Wood Turtle observer, John H. Kaufmann of the University of Florida, also saw similar behaviour in the United States at about the same time. The first time he saw it, Dr. Kaufmann thought as we had that the turtle might be sick, but the second time he was less convinced. The rocking motion, he observed, was caused by the turtle stomping on the ground, about eight times with one foreleg and then with the other. What's more, every once in a while, the turtle shot his head down to the ground, grabbed something, and ate it. A couple of times, Dr. Kaufmann saw that the prey was an earthworm, and then, in a flash, he understood what was going on. The Wood Turtle was grunting for worms!

Now, if you have never heard of "worm-grunting," don't feel bad — we hadn't either. Dr. Kaufmann, however, knew all about it because in his part of Florida worm-grunting is big business. Somebody way back when discovered that if they stuck a wooden stake in the ground and rasped a notched stick or spring against it, all kinds of earthworms would quickly emerge from the ground and wriggle away from the source of the vibration. It is a simple, effective way to catch earthworms, and it is used by many people, from casual fishermen right up to a few full-time professional worm-grunters. The United States Forest Service sells $30 annual permits for worm-grunting in one of its national forests, and there is even a worm-grunting championship held each year to see who can "grunt up" the most worms in a given time.

Even with his prior knowledge of worm-grunting by humans, Dr. Kaufmann at first had trouble believing, and even more trouble persuading others, that Wood Turtles were actually using the same technique. Since then, however, he has seen it 227 times in sessions lasting from 30 minutes up to seven hours and with as many as seven worms caught in eight minutes. Other people have now reported similar observations both with Wood Turtles and other creatures ranging from gulls and plovers in Europe to kiwis in New Zealand. All of them get worms to pop out in the surface either by tramping rapidly with both feet alternately or thumping just one foot rapidly on the ground. Dr. Kaufmann has even duplicated the effect by tapping on the ground with his fingers, getting four worms to emerge in the first 15 seconds.

No one knows for sure why worms react this way to vibrations in the soil. One guess is that the vibrations resemble those caused by falling rain, and the worms are programmed to emerge on the surface to avoid drowning. Another, to us more plausible, theory is that the vibrations resemble those caused by approaching moles. Moles are highly effective worm predators, and under most circumstances, it would pay earthworms to get out of their way as quickly as they could.

But whatever the true reason for the worm behaviour, the fact remains that the ground-thumping technique works like a charm for the creatures that employ it. For our part, we find it just plain awesome that our beautiful, old, slow-moving Wood Turtles have the sophistication to exploit this weakness of earthworms. We are pleased, also, to have actually witnessed an instance of Wood Turtle worm-grunting behaviour before it was understood and that the mystery has now been solved. So, if you go over to the east side of Algonquin and stop for lunch on the banks of the Petawawa or the Barron, listen carefully for the stomping of Wood Turtles back in the alders, trying to scare up some worms for dinner. And, by all means, see if you can actually observe one or more turtles performing this remarkable behaviour. If you succeed, you should be truly amazed at what the turtles are doing. On the other hand, you shouldn't really be surprised. After all, didn't we tell you in the very first sentence of this article what sort of place the east side of Algonquin is?↝

July 18, 1991, Vol. 32, No. 5 (D.S.)

This Wood Turtle has induced an earthworm to come to the surface by "stomping" on the ground.

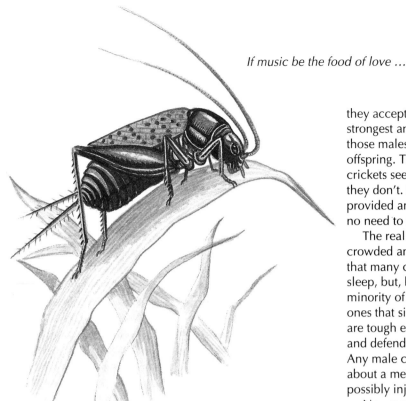

If music be the food of love ...

A Midsummer Night's Dreamboat

Who has not drifted off to sleep at this time of year listening to the pleasant chirping of crickets outside the tent or cottage? It is one of those familiar, comforting sounds of warm summer nights that tell us all is well with the world and help us forget our worries.

Most of the time we are as content as anyone else to accept the summer singing of crickets as the soothing background it is. Once in a while, however, our thoughts wander to the individual performers, and we try to picture just what is going on out there in the black warmth of the night.

If you hear a cricket calling close by, for example, you can be sure that it is a male doing his best to attract females. The male produces the sound by "stridulating" — rubbing his wings together rapidly in such a way that special, hardened bumps on their surfaces give out a remarkably loud burst of "music."

The volume of one of these songs can be as much as 90 decibels, and the reason why a male puts so much energy into his singing is not difficult to guess. The louder his song, the more attractive he is to females and the greater the distance from which he can pull them in. And it really does work. Female crickets sometimes literally run towards calling males, and they mate immediately upon arrival at the source of the sound. For a female cricket, a song in the night signifies Mr. Right — no questions asked.

You may find this a little strange because the females of most animals are normally very fussy about the males they accept as mates. In general, females choose the strongest and fittest males so that the superior qualities of those males will enhance the survival prospects of their offspring. The apparently indiscriminate females of crickets seem to violate this general pattern, but in fact they don't. For them, any male that sings has already provided ample proof of his superiority, so there is really no need to check him out any further.

The reality of life for male crickets is that they live in a crowded and competitive world. At times it may seem that many crickets (perhaps too many) are singing you to sleep, but, believe us, the ones that sing are only a small minority of the crickets that are actually out there. The ones that sing are the cream of the crop — the ones that are tough enough to seize an exclusive singing territory and defend it to the grass blade from a host of pretenders. Any male cricket that comes closer to a singer than about a metre will be viciously attacked and quite possibly injured.

No wonder, then, that females readily zero in on singing males and have them father their young. No wonder, either, that many males, apparently sensing that they can't compete with the territory-holders, refrain from singing altogether. As long as they keep their wings firmly shut, such males can wander at will, often very close to the singing males, without being attacked. As a matter of fact, they deliberately stay close to the singers (and are called "satellite males" as a result) because this gives them their one chance for success. Being silent, they can't attract females themselves, but once in a while they will waylay and forcibly mate with a female running in towards the calling male (hey, it's dark out and crickets can't talk).

Now, the fact that each calling male cricket is surrounded by several silent satellites raises an interesting question. Perceptive readers will already be wondering how such a pattern could persist. If males that sing achieve more matings, they should leave more descendants (who would also be singers) and they should have long ago come to totally predominate in the cricket population. It shouldn't matter that satellite males sometimes steal matings; as long as they father fewer offspring than the singing males, they (the silent ones) should dwindle more and more with each generation until, for all practical purposes, they have entirely disappeared. How, then, can we explain the continued presence of both singing and silent behaviours among modern crickets? There is, in fact, only one possible answer. Notwithstanding our first impression, the two types of behaviours must give rise to equal numbers of descendants. The only way for that to be true would be if singing crickets live shorter lives than silent crickets. If a singing male achieved four matings a night but lived for just three weeks, he would leave the same number of descendants as a silent male who had only two matings a night but lived for six weeks.

But why would singing males, undoubtedly the strongest, toughest, and most desirable of all, have shorter lives than their weaker competitors? There are apparently at least three reasons. To begin with, a singing cricket is exposed to sudden sneak attacks by satellite males, who may try to take over the top spot. Even if the singer beats off the attacker, he may be injured and have his life shortened as a result.

A second serious risk run by calling crickets is that they attract not only females but predators as well. Crickets partly avoid this problem by being active only at night, but studies in the United States have shown that cats are capable of homing in on the sound of crickets. Cats aren't a factor here in Algonquin, of course, but it is very likely that other night-time predators are a threat.

The most insidious danger of all faced by singing crickets is that their calls attract parasites. The females of certain flies are just as responsive to the cricket songs as are female crickets. When the flies arrive at the source of the sound, however, they deposit larvae on the doomed singer. The larvae burrow inside the cricket, feed and grow for about a week, and then emerge to pupate and transform to adult flies. You won't be surprised that this is rather hard on the male cricket. In fact, he invariably dies as the fattened-up larvae emerge from his body.

Of course, in the greater scheme of things, it doesn't really matter how a singing cricket dies as long as, on average, it is at an earlier age than for silent crickets. In that way, even though it attracts and mates with many more females in a given night than any silent satellite male, this advantage is cancelled out by the singer's shorter life, and the two types leave equal numbers of offspring over the long haul.

In actual fact, things are even more subtle than this because individual males are capable of switching back and forth from one strategy to the other depending on the circumstances. If cricket numbers are low, for example, individual males can space themselves out and all adopt the singing strategy. If the population density increases, on the other hand, many of the same males may face such stiff competition that they will do better by becoming silent satellites.

We find it intriguing to think about these things when we turn in on a midsummer night, and we recommend it to you, too. What better way to lull yourself off to sleep than by listening to their songs and pondering eternal cricket verities. The male you hear chirping away unseen in the darkness is, for the local females, a dream cricket come true. Irresistibly they are drawn to his songs, and mating takes place out there in the warm summer night. On the down side, it is true for some crickets that "the way to your lover's heart may lead to someone else's stomach," but don't lose any sleep over this. After all, there is a strong cricket tradition of living for today and not worrying about tomorrow. You know, "if music be the food of love, stridulate on!"

Good night and pleasant dreams.∞

August 8, 1991, Vol. 32, No. 8 (D.S.)

Murder in the Cathedral

As just about everybody enjoys a good mystery story, what more entertaining challenge could there be than to read along, carefully assimilating all the clues, and try to outsmart the author? And who among us has not at least daydreamed of achieving fame and fortune by inventing some ingenious plot that would leave our imagined readers utterly perplexed until the moment we finally chose to reveal who did the crime and how?

Given the general fascination with such stories, we thought it might be appropriate to present a mystery of our own for you — a real-life Algonquin Park mystery. As a matter of fact, it is quite timely that we do so, in part because this summer you can visit for the first time what we believe to be the most outstanding example in the Highway 60 Corridor of one of the "scenes of the crime." We have in mind a magnificent grove of hemlock trees on our new Bat Lake Trail, a stand we chose to call "Cathedral Grove" after the famous stand of old-growth Douglas Firs on Vancouver Island. To be sure, our hemlocks aren't nearly as big as the trees out west, but they are impressive nonetheless. At one point there are hemlock trunks almost as far as you can see — huge, thick, dark columns rising from the clear forest floor high into the canopy of lacy evergreen hemlock foliage above. And just to complete the picture, for most of the year there is a distinct hush about the place, one that is only occasionally disturbed by the sighing of branches in the treetops.

Now, here we must digress a bit — if only to set the scene of our mystery. Cathedral Grove is really just an example — albeit a large and spectacular one — of something that is very common in Algonquin. More or less pure patches of hemlock are a fairly regular hilltop feature in the hardwoods of the Park's west side. These groves are important not only because they are a distinct and beautiful element to our eyes in what would otherwise be an unbroken sea of Sugar Maples but also because, being very different little islands of conifers among the hardwoods, they contribute to the diversity and richness of Park wildlife. When you walk into a hemlock grove, for example, you immediately leave the Red-eyed Vireos and Least Flycatchers behind and start hearing the songs of Blackburnian and Black-throated Green Warblers. Or, if you visit in the evenings, you may be serenaded by a Swainson's Thrush — a bird you would never expect to find in the hardwoods just a hundred yards away.

Hemlocks are important for larger animals as well. On cold winter nights, the temperatures can be several degrees warmer under a hemlock stand than out in the surrounding, leafless hardwoods. White-tailed Deer, often pushed to the limits of tolerance here at the northern edge of their range, are quick to take advantage of such slightly warmer temperatures by preferentially bedding down under the cover of hemlocks. Deer also find that travel is easier in groves of hemlocks because so much snow is intercepted by the branches and foliage that there is noticeably less accumulation on the ground below. Deer can easily bog down in deep snow, so here is another important wintertime advantage conferred by hemlock groves and another reason why deer often congregate or "yard up" in such places for the winter.

Cathedral Grove on the Bat Lake Trail.

There is no doubt that our patches of hemlock are a beautiful and important part of the Park's forests. That is the "setting;" now comes the mystery. If you walk into Cathedral Grove on the Bat Lake Trail — or pretty well any other hemlock stand in Algonquin Park — you will be impressed by the big trees and you will find the general atmosphere to be so pleasing that you may very well fail to notice something is missing. There are few young hemlock trees beneath the old ones. Although you may well see the odd seedling-sized individuals, even these are usually very old. One forester once found a tree just 10 inches in diameter that was 359 years old, and even a two-inch tree may be as much as 200 years old. When you visit hemlock grove after hemlock grove, you see the same pattern everywhere, and when you learn that a recent, thorough search in one area failed to find a hemlock less than a century old, a mystery starts to emerge — to put it mildly! Not only that, but given the importance of hemlock to the aesthetics and wildlife of Algonquin's forests, we also have reason to be concerned. Could it be that Algonquin Park hemlocks are actually on the way out? How can it be that the groves are so common — not to mention other hemlocks that we find mixed in with different conifers around lakeshores — and yet there is often no new generation of young hemlocks coming up anywhere to replace the old trees? Has something fundamental changed in our forests? Could something be killing off hemlock reproduction before it even gets started?

Most mysteries are solved by paying careful attention to clues. In this case we might first take note of the fact that our hemlocks usually produce healthy seed crops every second year (including this one, incidentally). Since faulty seed production is obviously not a problem, we will have to look elsewhere. One factor may well be the small size of the seeds. They are so tiny that when they germinate, the little roots are incapable of penetrating the layer of dead leaves on the forest floor and the hemlock seedlings just never get established. Even if they do manage somehow, they root so shallowly that they may very well succumb to drought when the top inch of soil dries out in the would-be tree's first summer. That soil moisture may indeed be of critical importance is suggested by the places hemlocks grow. Water is obviously not much of a problem along lakeshores, and even up on hillsides the groves are usually found on north-facing slopes — places that receive a little less sunlight and are presumably less prone to drying out than other slopes.

But even if a crop of hemlock seedlings does get established and survives the first few summers to the point where the plants are robust enough to withstand drought, none of this may count if there are any deer around. Big hemlocks may be good for deer, as we have seen, but the opposite is far from true. In fact, deer love hemlock foliage so much that a few of them can move into a grove and totally wipe out any seedlings that by some miracle had managed to get that far. The fact that we actually have hemlock stands, incidentally, is a pretty strong suggestion that deer must have been very rare, if not totally absent, in the old Algonquin forests of centuries ago when our present hemlocks got started in life.

As if this weren't enough, there is still the problem of shade. Hemlock seedlings and saplings have a fantastic ability to hang on to life even in deep shade for years and years, hardly growing at all, but still having the ability to start growing rapidly (as much as 25 centimetres a year) if an overhead tree falls down or is destroyed, letting in the needed sunlight. Still, hemlock stands are so long-lived and their shade so dense that many authorities suspect a new crop of seedlings can only grow up to full tree size when some disaster removes at least part of the old stand shading the new generation.

So imagine, if you will, the following set of circumstances. A ground fire or violent windstorm kills or knocks over many individuals in an old hemlock grove. Seeds fall on the mineral soil exposed by the fire or rotting trunks of the downed trees; rainfall is above average for the next three or four summers; and there are no deer to speak of for the next 20 years.

If this is the combination of circumstances required for a new generation of hemlock to get established, is it any wonder that it apparently happens less than once a century? By the same token, if fire is important for hemlock, are we willing to restore it to Algonquin Park?

The explanation suggested here for the apparent absence of hemlock reproduction we now observe may seem reasonable, but you can probably tell that we are only making educated guesses and don't really know. Obviously, this violates all the rules of writing mysteries. At the end of the story, the author is supposed to tell you who the culprit is!

You have every right to be peeved at this failing of ours, but we hasten to add that we are still working on the case. As a matter of fact, we have even hired a plant ecologist to tackle the problem. Over the next few years, Stan Vasiliauskas, now a doctoral student at Queen's University, will be establishing plots, taking careful measurements of the trees and soil conditions, sifting through clues to local fire history, and following up any other leads that might help shed light on the great Algonquin hemlock mystery.

In the meantime, the rest of us will just have to cheer from the sidelines. Although, by all means, go right ahead if you want to try your hand at finding the solution yourself. Visit Cathedral Grove or any other hemlock stand as often as you like, and maybe you'll notice a missing clue or have a flash of inspiration. Crack this case, and your fame will be assured. Just think of it, the Agatha Christie (or T.S. Eliot?) of the forest ecology world. Go for it!✑

July 25, 1991, Vol. 32, No. 6 (D.S.)

Sweet Manipulators

We are sure most of our readers would readily agree that picking berries is one of summer's greatest pleasures. In fact, the mere thought of spending an hour or two with the family in a sunny patch of ripe blueberries or raspberries, and then turning the result into a delicious pie or other dessert, is one that no doubt brings back fond memories to us all.

Still, we daresay that we almost never stop and think of all this from the plant's "point of view." Now, to be sure, no plant has a brain, and plants can't even begin to think about our use of their berries or anything else. Nevertheless, we can also be certain — even if we aren't used to thinking in such terms — that plants produce brightly-coloured, delicious berries only because it benefits them to do so. The fact is that plants grow in a very crowded, competitive world. They all have to struggle against their neighbours for sunlight, water, and soil nutrients, and under those circumstances, the diversion of precious resources into the production of all those berries has to be seen as very "expensive." If it didn't pay the plants somehow to indulge in this apparently wasteful extravagance, things would have changed long ago. Other varieties of the same plants that weren't so wasteful, that produced less expensive, smaller, duller, and less nutritious berries, would have been more prosperous. They would have been stronger, left more descendants, and eventually have come to predominate over the varieties that "wasted" their energies on the production of flamboyant fruit. In fact, you could even ask the question as to why plants should produce any berries at all? Why feed the berry-eaters? Why not just produce "naked" seeds?

Obviously this has not happened, at least not with raspberries and blueberries, so there must be some other reason — which we haven't guessed yet — for those plants to pour so many resources into all the berry flesh that, year after year, almost all get eaten by us and other berry-lovers.

Actually, if you stop and think about the places where blueberries and raspberries grow, you can start to figure out the answer. Both live in sunny, open, disturbed areas, which under natural conditions only last for the few years it takes for trees to grow up again and shade out the blueberries or raspberries. Successful strains of these two plants are therefore those that somehow manage to broadcast their seeds far and wide, with the result that some seeds end up in, and succeed in colonizing, new open areas that are often many miles away from the parent plants. A lowly plant cannot know where new suitable areas might be, and even if it did, it would be unable to somehow project its seeds to the right location. It can, however, in a manner of speaking, manipulate other organisms into doing the job on its behalf. By surrounding its seeds with nutritious and conspicuously coloured fruit flesh, the blueberry or raspberry plants encourage birds or bears to come and have a feast. Later, often miles away, the bird or bear excretes the undigested seeds, which once in a while happens to be in a place that is suitable for a new blueberry or raspberry stand. It sounds like an awfully slim chance — and it is — but it's also a lot better than no chance at all. This, then, is the payoff to the plant for the production of all that expensive fruit.

Of course, this slender but vital reward to the plant would be totally wiped out if the seeds were unable to survive their passage through bird or bear digestive tracts. They obviously succeed, but then there is another problem. Seeds are necessarily nutritious because they contain enough energy and nutrients to get a new seedling started in life. They therefore run the risk of being attacked, either at the beginning or end of their bear-/bird-assisted voyage, by other creatures such as mice. Apparently raspberries and blueberries escape this particular threat by having seeds so small that they just aren't worth the trouble, even for a mouse. In fact, did you even know there are seeds inside a blueberry?* Other berry-producing plants have evolved the opposite solution.

Cherries, for example, have a single, large seed that is covered with an extremely hard outer casing, which discourages all but the most determined mice. They aren't called cherry stones for nothing! Birds and chipmunks usually just eat the flesh of cherries and discard the stone, whereas bears eat the whole fruit and pass the stones, just as they do with blueberry and raspberry seeds. Interestingly, there are almost no examples of berries that contain seeds intermediate in size between those of raspberries and those of cherries. It seems that berry-producing plants get around the problem of seed-destroyers either by making their seeds too tiny to be bothered with or too formidable and time-consuming to be attacked. Inbetween-sized seeds probably wouldn't work because they would be big enough to be interesting and small enough to be handled profitably.

Of course, whether the seeds are big or small, the flesh surrounding them still serves to "bribe" a bird or mammal into transporting the seeds far away from the shade of the parent plant and sometimes to a place suitable for new growth.

Now, the idea of bribery by fruit flesh brings up a second interesting point concerning the way berry-producing plants operate. So far, we have seen the approach that might be called "we'll make them an offer they can't refuse." Raspberries and blueberries are indeed highly nutritious and very likely to attract a whole host of animals — not just bears and birds. Although we normally think of them as real meat-eaters, even foxes

and martens, for example, commonly cash in on a good blueberry or raspberry crop and, of course, unwittingly end up helping the bears and the birds to transport the seeds.

There is a second general approach to bribery as well — the more parsimonious "take it or leave it" approach. Not many berry-producing plants in Algonquin have this strategy, but there are a few. In another month, especially on the east side of the Park, High Bush Cranberry will produce its berry crops, and later on the well-named Winterberry, a shrub of our low, wet alder swamps, will also produce fruit. Even though the berries are bright red and impossible for birds to miss, they will last, uneaten, for weeks or even months on the shrubs that produced them.

Unlike the fruit we love to pick in the summer, these autumn berries are not very sweet or nutritious but rather insipid and uninteresting. Because they are so low in sugars and fats, they are relatively less expensive for the plants to produce and are largely immune to bacteria that might otherwise attack them and cause them to rot. At the same time, they are not very interesting to birds either — which is why they often last for a long time on the shrubs. Even well-known fruit-eaters such as Robins and other thrushes may totally ignore the brightly-coloured Winterberries, preferring to hunt nutritious insects instead. When the cold and snow come in late fall, however, any remaining birds suddenly find themselves with no access to insects, and they are forced to turn to the low-quality berries spurned 'til then. For the birds, those berries may be a last resort, but if the plants that produced them could smile they would. It took a bit of a wait, but their "purpose" has been achieved. Their fruit has been eaten and their seeds transported far away — which, of course, was the whole point of the exercise and in this case achieved for a very small investment on the part of the plants.

It is astonishing to reflect on the idea that berries are far from being innocent, pretty little appendages put on earth for the pleasure of man and the sustenance of birds and animals. They are agents of subtle manipulation, evolved by the plants over millions of years to trick us

---

* There are indeed — about 10 usually — each one about 0.01 centimetres long!

into doing what they cannot do for themselves — namely, transport their seeds far away to new growing grounds.

---

* Not that we want to be indelicate, but perceptive readers will have already realized that humans, unlike bears and birds, are now very poor seed dispersers for raspberries and blueberries. In fact, if all animals used privies and washrooms, these berries would never have evolved … .

A Visit From Mom & Dad and Their Son Cain

Autumn is here once again in Algonquin. Most of our campers and staff are gone, and the Park suddenly feels rather empty. A few patches of red and orange leaves are giving us a preview of the peak of colours at the end of the month. There are other signs of fall as well. The nights are getting cold, many of our birds have already left for the south, and beavers will soon be laying in their food piles in anticipation of the long, cold winter to come.

All of these things have more than a touch of inevitability and sadness about them, and we suppose that is why we are always so delighted by any Park inhabitant that seems unaffected by the approach of hard times. Our best example of such a creature is the Gray Jay, which after a summer of near invisibility is now starting to come out of the woods in family groups to visit campgrounds and picnic grounds in search of handouts

Something to think about the next time you reach out, your mouth watering, for a scrumptious blueberry or raspberry. And, please, don't resent the fact that a brainless plant is about to do a number on you. After all, even if you are being used,* at least you are being used sweetly.꙳

August 15, 1991, Vol. 32, No. 9 (D.S.)

from Park visitors. There is certainly nothing sad about these birds — indeed quite the opposite. With their big, dark eyes, soft fluffy plumage and, above all, their habit of fearlessly gliding down to our picnic table and even landing on our hands to take a bit of bread or cheese, they seem entirely confident and content — and they never fail to warm our hearts. Here at least is a Park inhabitant that is unafraid of us and unafraid of winter. Of course, it's no secret to any experienced Algonquin visitor as to how the Gray Jay can stay here all year long. All those handouts we provide are methodically carried back into the bush, trip after trip, and hidden away in hundreds of little hiding places — behind pieces of bark, under tufts of lichens, or in almost any other imaginable nook or cranny — but always up in the trees where the jays can still have access to them no matter how deep the snow is later on. Gray Jays are even able to "glue" their little pieces of food into place, thanks to copious amounts of sticky saliva produced in specially enlarged glands. No one has the slightest doubt that it is these thousands of little tidbits hidden away by each pair of Gray Jays that allow them to live all winter in North America's bleak

A mated pair of Gray Jays accompanied by …

and seemingly foodless forests of spruce, from Algonquin Park in the south right up to the treeline in the far north.

It is pleasingly reassuring, therefore, to think that these friendly and confiding creatures are so successful. By caching food in times of plenty and then drawing on their stores in times of scarcity, Gray Jays have found an elegant way to smooth out the year's food supplies and thereby eliminate that nasty old problem of winter. Hats off and congratulations on a marvellous victory.

Yet, if we look closely, there's something not quite right. It may have struck you, especially if you have bumped into a lot of Gray Jays in your day, that about half of the "family groups" we encounter in the fall consist of just two birds (a territory-owning pair) while the other half have three birds (a pair plus a young). There are almost never any more than that. Now, given that most Gray Jay broods back in the spring had at least two, and much more often three, youngsters, it is extremely odd that, in the fall, it is always just one young (if any) that remains with its parents. Even more peculiar is the fact (learned through our use of coloured bands) that in about 30 per cent of our fall trios, the extra Gray Jay is not even the young of the adults it is with but rather was hatched in a completely different territory. In Gray Jay families, then, there seems to be a rule that "three's company, four's a crowd." But whatever could account for such a peculiar arrangement, and how could it have come about?

On a few occasions we have been lucky enough to see the way Gray Jay broods are reduced to just one bird. It always happens in June, when the young are about 60 days old and have just reached the age where they can feed themselves. The young start to squabble among themselves, and after about 10 days one has expelled its former nestmates from its parent's territory. The winner (usually a male) is the bird that stays with its parents through the summer, fall, and winter, and the losers are forced to leave. Sometimes these "ejectees" succeed in attaching themselves (at no more than one to a pair) to other unrelated pairs of jays who for some reason or another have no young of their own. But most ejectees aren't so lucky. Young and inexperienced, and booted out into a cruel world without the benefit of parental protection and guidance, about 80 per cent of them die before their first fall.

Knowing how Gray Jay brood reductions occur and what happens to the winners and losers only makes the whole matter even more mysterious. After all, why should the dominant bird in a brood of Gray Jays consign its brothers and sisters to a very high probability of early death? And why should the parents, who have worked extremely hard to raise the whole nestful, just watch as one of their young, in effect, kills some or all of the others?

We think we have answers to these questions, and they are very interesting from two points of view. First of all, we know that Gray Jay numbers are fairly constant, but they are spread out thinly in our northern forests. This suggests that the land is supporting all the Gray Jays it can. If this is true, it may well be that a typical territory just can't support an extra big load of four or five Gray

Jays through the winter — especially when two or three of them (the young) have contributed only a little to the winter food stores. It could also be, in fact, that a young bird can't store enough food for its own survival and requires help from the adults in order to make it through. If a pair of adults were capable of storing enough extra food for just one extra bird, then brood reduction in Gray Jays would be quite understandable.

If you were a young Gray Jay, for example, hatched along with two brothers or sisters and there was only enough food in the territory for one of you to survive the following winter, you should do your best to make sure you were the one that got to stay. Brotherly love is all

... the dominant young bird, usually a male, from their previous nesting. This juvenile ejected his weaker brothers and sisters from the territory back in June.

very well, but when your own survival is at stake a young jay has to do what he has to do!

The more diabolical souls among our readers will now be protesting that, rather than kick out your brothers and sisters in June, you would do much better to wait until fall. That way you could let the little suckers contribute to the territory's food stores all summer long, kick them out when they had outlived their usefulness, and then reap alone what you and they had invested in mom and dad's territory. Great idea! — your winter survival would be even more guaranteed!

Well, we daresay this logic might be correct if Gray Jays recover stored food by searching randomly. That way you would have just as much chance of finding food hidden by your parents and brothers and sisters as you would have of finding your own.

But suppose just for a moment that Gray Jays recover their stored food by actually remembering where they have hidden it. In that case, as a young bird, you would acquire the extra measure of stored food necessary for your winter survival either by watching and remembering where your parents hid food or by pilfering food hidden by them, rehiding it yourself, and remembering the new location. Either way, it wouldn't do you any good to wait until fall before you expelled your brothers and sisters if you really wanted to have exclusive access to the extra stored food provided by your parents. Your brothers and sisters, even if you did kick them out of the family group, could still sneak back and get the food during your unavoidable absences. No, the only way to prevent your siblings from having access to the crucial parental food subsidy would be to prevent them from ever knowing where it was located in the first place. That means kicking out your brothers and sisters at the beginning of the food storage season, not at the end.

The fact that in the real world Gray Jay dominant juveniles do kick their siblings out of the family group in June, at the earliest possible moment, suggests that Gray Jays may indeed recover their stored food through memory … .

It is awesome in the true sense of the word that the three friendly gray birds eagerly accepting your handouts, and ferrying their booty back into the bush, could actually be remembering all the exact locations involved, let alone all the ones where they must have hidden food in the previous weeks and months. Not one of us could match such an intellectual feat, and yet there is evidence,

both from the reasoning we have used here and from direct experiments in lab situations, that Gray Jays can indeed far surpass any human being in their ability to remember thousands of precise spatial locations over long periods of time.

Recovery of stored food by memory is one major implication of the fighting among broods of Gray Jays in June, but there is another. However powerful Gray Jay brains may be, and however effective food storage is as a way of dealing with winter, the fact remains that they are governed by the same cruel laws as any other animal. Many or most young must die in their first year of life, and the fact that in Gray Jays winners and losers happen to be chosen by a deadly brother-sister battle back in June is merely a detail.

But hey, we don't mean to depress you with all this talk about reality. By all means, enjoy feeding the beautiful Gray Jays gliding down to your picnic table. Perhaps, if it is a trio, you can guess which are the adults and which is the young from last spring. If you can, please don't think ill of him just because he did in his brothers and sisters last June. After all, his actions were not motivated by any sense of malice or cruelty but were merely a logical consequence of the fact that there is only so much energy to go round and only so many individuals the land can support.

This applies to all living things — to the trees turning colour, to the thrushes and warblers now heading south, to the beavers getting their food piles ready, and even to those gentle birds with the fantastic memories now visiting your picnic table. You know: mom and dad Gray Jay and their son, Cain. ✎

September 5, 1991, Vol. 32, No. 12 (D.S.)

What Can We Learn?

Most, if not all, readers of *The Raven* are aware of the tragic bear attack that took place last October 11, 1991, on Bates' Island in Lake Opeongo. Such an incident is deeply disturbing, and the Park has been flooded with calls from people all across North America, quite understandably seeking an explanation of what went wrong and some indication of what might be done to prevent a recurrence.

In this issue of *The Raven* we will try to think things through and to find answers to these important questions.

First, some facts. The attack occurred when Raymond Jakubauskas, 32 years old, and Carola Frehe, aged 48, were setting up camp not long after arriving on the island. We believe Ms. Frehe was attacked first and that Mr. Jakubauskas then tried to drive off the bear with an oar. (Long bruises were later discovered on the bear, and the oar was found broken at the scene.) Both victims were killed by a single blow to the head.

Over the following five days the bear dragged the bodies away in a series of stages, feeding on them from

time to time and covering them with leaves at each stopping place. By the time the campers were reported missing and our search revealed what happened, the remains were 375 feet away from the campsite in the fourth and last pile of leaves. The bear was destroyed not far away.*

* DID THE BEAR HAVE TO BE DESTROYED?

A number of people have asked us why the bear had to be killed. The concern of these questioners was inspired, no doubt, by the assumption that human victims had somehow intruded on the bear's space, provoked it, or otherwise brought on the attack. This kind of scenario occurs frequently in Grizzly Bear encounters, but, as far as we know, Black Bears that kill people are apparently almost always motivated by predation. We believe that is the most likely explanation for what happened in the Bates' Island incident.

In a way, however, it doesn't really matter. Whatever the exact sequence of events leading up to this attack, the bear ended up feeding on its victims. Everything we know about bears indicates they have excellent memories for a wide range of foods and their sources. We know this bear was "rewarded" for his innovative behaviour, and there is no reason to think he would forget what he had just learned — that humans are edible and easy to kill. That is why there was no question about our having to destroy this animal.

In seeking to understand why the attack occurred, most people want to know if the bear was rabid or had anything else wrong with it that might explain its highly abnormal behaviour. The simple answer is "no." A detailed examination by Ministry of Natural Resources and University of Guelph wildlife pathologists and veterinarians revealed no disease, no brain abnormality, no injury, nor indeed any other condition that might predispose a bear to attack humans. The bear was an apparently healthy eight-year-old male weighing 308 pounds.

A second major question to be asked concerns the behaviour of the people. Could it be they did something, whether deliberately or inadvertently, that could have attracted the bear or provoked it into attacking? Once again the answer appears to be "no." It is true that the campers had started to prepare a meal, and it is therefore possible the bear was attracted by food, but there are problems with this idea. For one thing, a tray of ground beef was still untouched, even five days later when we came on the scene. Besides, every day in bear country all over North America, tens of thousands of campers do basically the same thing as these people did (start getting supper ready), but that doesn't get them attacked by bears as a result. Something beyond the presence of food is necessary to account for this bear's behaviour.

Many of our callers, including half a dozen doctors, were aware that menstruation was implicated as a possible factor in two Grizzly Bear attacks out west, and they wanted to make sure that this possibility was checked out in the Bates' Island case as well. In fact, menstruation has not played a role in any of the Black Bear attacks known to us. Also, a study recently published in the *Journal of Wildlife Management* casts serious doubt on the idea that menstrual odours elicit any reaction at all from Black Bears.

Where does this leave us? If the bear was not diseased and the people did not do anything out of the ordinary to bring on the attack, how then can we explain what happened? It is here that an examination of other Black Bear attacks can be helpful. In his book *Bear Attacks*, Dr. Stephen Herrero of the University of Calgary documented a total of 26 deaths in North America from 1900 to 1983 resulting from Black Bear attacks. These include the three boys who died on May 13, 1978, in Algonquin's only other bear attack, at Lone Creek on the far east side of the Park. No two attacks were the same in all respects, but Dr. Herrero was able to detect some general trends. The attacks took place throughout the non-denning season (almost always during the day) and more often involved male bears. Only one case involved a female possibly trying to protect her cubs. Whenever the offending bear was killed and examined, it was found to be free of rabies or any other factor that might predispose it toward aggressive behaviour.

Most important of all, however, is Herrero's conclusion that in the great majority of cases the Black Bear was deliberately preying on its victims. It seems that Black Bears, unlike Grizzlies, rarely ever kill people just because the people have intruded into their space or might be a threat to their cubs. Rather, when a Black Bear kills a person it seems to be because the bear wants to eat that person. Another strong trend revealed by analysis of the extremely rare fatal attacks on people by Black Bears is that very few of the bears were already used to getting human food or garbage. In other words, a bear that kills people is almost never a "campground" or "garbage" bear that has become progressively less and less afraid of people and then "decided to go one step further," as it were, and kill somebody. On the contrary, almost all of the "killer" Black Bears were truly wild bears living in remote areas, and they had little or no prior contact with humans.**

The picture of a wild, so-called "predaceous" bear may come the closest to describing the Bates' Island bear. Certainly it was a bear that was unknown to us. It had not been handled or relocated before (in which case it would have had ear tags). Nor had there been any bear trouble on Opeongo in the summer of 1991, and almost none in the Park as a whole, which is quite understandable since last year was very good for a wide variety of bear foods.

We don't need to tell anybody how frightening it is to think that occasionally there are Black Bears that prey on human beings, but we probably do need to point out some important implications. Many people want to know what they should do to avoid an attack like the one on Bates' Island. In asking such questions, they are unconsciously assuming there is some "right way" of camping or handling food that, if followed, would eliminate or significantly reduce the possibility of an attack. The problem is that, faced with a predaceous bear, you probably can't do anything to prevent an attack. After all, if the bear is after you, how is better handling of your food going to help? Or, to take the particular case of the Bates' Island animal, if it truly was one of those mercifully rare "predaceous" Black Bears, there is probably nothing Mr. Jakubauskas and Ms. Frehe could have done to prevent the attack. They may simply have been in the wrong place at the wrong time.

Of course, whether this view is entirely correct, the question it all boils down to in most people's minds is, "Should I be afraid to go camping in Algonquin Park or anywhere else there are Black Bears?" To answer this question, we have to consider the odds of encountering a predaceous bear. Clearly, those odds are almost nil. Even here in Algonquin where we have now had two fatal bear attacks, the fact remains that there were over 8,000,000 non-fatal visits to the Park between the 1978 bear attack and the one last fall. Surely we cannot let our lives be

---

*** It may be useful for readers trying to come to grips with the Bates' Island attack to recognize that in animals, just as in humans, there exists a tremendous range of physical and mental attributes. When we see an Albert Einstein or a Wayne Gretzky among humans, we don't ask what is "wrong" with them; we just accept the existence of the occasional truly exceptional individual. Similarly, the Bates' Island Black Bear may simply have been a truly exceptional, off-the-end-of-the-scale individual bear.*

dominated by fear of remotely improbable flukes. If we really do decide never to go camping again because of the supposed danger from bears, then, to be consistent, we should also stay indoors on cloudy days. After all, we are much more likely to get hit by lightning (or killed by a bee sting for that matter) than we are to be attacked by a bear. And, needless to say, we should never cross the street or get into a car.

There is one more thing about which you should know. There is a spray whose active ingredient, capsaicin, is derived from cayenne pepper. Although it is non-lethal and causes no lasting ill effects, when delivered to an animal's eyes it causes severe and almost instantaneous pain. High-strength versions with a powerful spray propellant have been credited with saving four lives in Canada, Japan, and the United States. Because of wind conditions and other circumstances of an attack, of course, having a can of capsaicin spray could never be considered an absolute guarantee of safety.

More to the point, your chances of ever having to use it against a predaceous Black Bear are next to zero because your chances of meeting such an animal are next to zero. Nevertheless, the product does exist, is legal, and you have the right to know about it — if only for your peace of mind.

We hope the above has been of some help to you in sorting out how you should view the Bates' Island bear attack and its implications for your own safety. None of this, of course, will do anything for Carola Frehe and Raymond Jakubauskas. They died in the saddest and most unfortunate of circumstances. We did not know them, and for this we are sorry. We only hope that their deaths will help us to understand a little better the beautiful but sometimes cruel world in which we live.

This *Raven* is respectfully dedicated to their memory.☙

April 23, 1992, Vol. 33, No. 1 (D.S.)

A Song for Him and a Song for Her

We don't have to tell anybody that Algonquin Park is filled with bird songs at this time of year. Long before dawn the chorus begins; it builds to a peak just after sunrise, subsides around mid-day (especially in hot weather), then picks up again late in the afternoon and continues on to, or past, sunset.

We daresay that everybody enjoys all this singing, but probably just as a sort of general background music. Most people would probably be quite intimidated by the idea of actually identifying all the "instruments" (bird species) in the avian orchestra. And yet, there is a lot to be said for doing just that, and the task of teasing apart all those different songs is not nearly so difficult as one might think. With today's multitude of excellent bird song recordings, not to mention the numerous visual field guide books, it's surprisingly easy to get yourself started in the fun of learning to identify birds not just by sight but by sound as well. Believe us, if we can do it with our distinctly unmusical ears, you can too!

We can't emphasize too much just how much pleasure and interest can be derived from such an ability. It is rewarding in the extreme to be able to stand in one spot and put names to all the invisible songsters out there. Instead of merely being inundated by meaningless music, however beautiful it may be, you are instead surrounded by dozens of different forest creatures. And even if you can't see them all, you know they are out there, and the instantaneous name and mental image that you can attach to each song adds a whole new dimension to a walk in the forest.

There is one little catch, however. Every once in awhile you will hear a totally weird song not to be heard on the commercially available bird recordings and failing to remind you of any other bird you know. And yet, when you track it down you find that it is a very familiar bird whose song you thought you knew perfectly well.

One of the best examples of this is afforded by our common little Chestnut-sided Warbler. It is one of our prettiest warblers, with a bright yellow cap, black streaks on a greenish back, and conspicuous chestnut-coloured bands running down each side and contrasting with the white throat and breast. It is also one of the most interesting warblers in the sense that the great early naturalist, Jean Jacques Audubon, saw only three in his lifetime whereas today it is abundant. Chestnut-sided Warblers like brushy, sunny openings in the forest, and they apparently have greatly benefitted from logging and other forest-disturbing activities of man. Around Algonquin Park campgrounds, for example, they are one of the commonest of all birds, and everybody has heard hundreds of times (even if they didn't know it) the sweet song usually remembered as "please-please-pleased-to-MEET-cha." The catch is, though, as every bird-listener in Algonquin Park eventually finds out, that the Chestnut-sided Warbler also has a completely different song as well. This is a jumbly series of notes lacking the emphatic ending of the normal song (the "to-MEET-cha" part) and which must be learned separately.

Now, for a long time we just accepted the fact that Chestnut-sided Warblers had two song types without really knowing why. For all we knew, some individual males always sang the primary song (the one with MEET-cha at the end) while other males exclusively sang the other, secondary song. Or, if all males really did sing both songs, we had no idea under what circumstances one might be used instead of the other.

However, we now have a fairly good idea of what the two songs mean. Dr. Donald Kroodsma of the University of Vermont, through patient observation and experiment, has worked it all out for us. The primary song (which is the same throughout the large range of the Chestnut-sided Warbler) is sung by males to attract females. The secondary song (which varies considerably from one region to another) is used for threatening rival males in territorial disputes.

to a confusing mix of both primary and secondary songs. A few days later when the females have chosen their mate, and come to know and stay inside his territorial boundaries, the males have little reason to keep singing the female-attracting primary song. Trespass by neighbouring males, however, continues to be a serious problem, particularly because they will try to mate with the resident female in the pre-egg period when she is most fertile. The primary preoccupation of a

Armed with this knowledge, we can start to make sense of the two song types of the Chestnut-sided Warbler and of their use pattern. When males get back to the Park in mid-May, for example, they space themselves out in appropriate habitat and pour out their primary song in an effort to attract a female. They may well sing as often as 300 times an hour from sunrise to sunset — which totals up to an amazing 4,000 love songs a day. Interspersed into the otherwise almost non-stop primary songs, however, will be short bursts of the secondary songs. These occur when one male encroaches onto the territory of another.

When females finally do return to Algonquin, about a week after the males, they of course know nothing about the territorial boundaries carved out by the males — and no particular reason to respect them even if they did. They are very much in "shopping mode," and they wander about before choosing a male with whom to settle. Until they do, eager males pursue them eagerly, repeatedly singing "please-please-pleased-to-MEET-cha." These pursuits often take them into the territories of neighbouring males, who naturally respond to the intrusions by blasting the trespasser male with secondary songs. A human listener unable to see the details of such heavy-duty courtship will therefore be treated at this stage

territory-holding male at this time is defence against trespass and that is why he now sings almost non-stop secondary songs (whereas just a week earlier the same bird would have been singing almost nothing but primary songs).

Thus, the otherwise bewildering and seemingly unpredictable switching back and forth between the two song types in Chestnut-sided Warblers really does make some sort of sense. It is rather neatly explained by the shifting social circumstances in which the male warblers find themselves.

We have always appreciated the challenge of putting names on all those invisible singers, and now we have the additional possibility of actually knowing what they are doing. With Chestnut-sided Warblers at least, we can even hear the males trying to sweet-talk the females one minute and threaten rival males the next. How fascinating to think that the hundreds of individual melodies that wash over us from unseen jewels in the treetops each carry so much hidden meaning. Amongst all that soothing background music is a song for each and every species and, as we now know, sometimes even a "song for him and a song for her."☙

July 2, 1992, Vol. 33, No. 2 (D.S.)

Bliss Beneath the Bridge?

Just about everyone enjoys the long hot days of July. The water is warm, the roadside flowers are in full bloom, and birds and animals are busy raising families all through the Park. It's perfectly normal and natural for us to be a little lulled by the bounty and bliss of the summer season, and very easy to forget that in the natural world, competition and strife can never really be far away.

We were reminded of this the other day when we saw a couple of Cliff Swallows at the Portage Store. As they usually do, these birds were putting on a fascinating show, swooping and gliding over the water, scooping up invisible insects, twisting and turning, and giving us plenty of opportunity to see the white foreheads, orange rumps, and square tails that distinguish them from other kinds of swallow. We don't see Cliff Swallows all that often in Algonquin Park, and we wondered if these two might be nesting on a cottage or other building around Canoe Lake. Cliff Swallows are really birds of western North America, named for their habit of building their often quite large nesting colonies on cliff faces. With settlement they moved into the eastern part of the continent as well, taking advantage of bridges and buildings.

In the Park, small colonies come and go in such places as Opeongo and the old mill site at Rock Lake. Right now, however, the best place to see Cliff Swallows in the Algonquin area is probably just west of the Park where Highway 60 crosses the north arm of Oxtongue Lake on its way to Dwight and Huntsville. There, under the bridge, you can see a colony of 15 to 20 Cliff Swallow nests, along with about 30 built by Barn Swallows.*

Now, if you take a canoe and drift under the bridge to get a good look at the swallows and their nests, you will almost certainly get the impression of a peaceful and prosperous little community. The birds come and go with their characteristic grace, the air is filled with their soft, pleasing chatters, and large youngsters can be seen at each entrance hole waiting to be fed. Soon they will make their first flights and join their parents in coursing through the air, feeding on aerial insects, and getting ready for their long flight to winter quarters in Argentina. The whole situation might seem to be ideal. The enclosed mud nests located above water under the overhead protection of the bridge are about as secure from

predators as could be imagined, and, just for good measure, the adults seem almost to thrive on each other's company. Indeed, it has been shown that Cliff Swallow nesting colonies are almost like "information centres." Adults spread out looking for food, and if they discover a (usually temporary) rich patch of flying insects, they come back to the colony with their throats and bills bulging with food for their nestlings. Adults that have had poor luck notice this and then follow the successful foragers back to the good hunting grounds. In this way the entire colony benefits from the original discovery of food.

Still, if you were able to spend more than just a few minutes enjoying the sights and sounds of the Cliff Swallow colony, you might pick up a few clues that things are not quite so blissful and harmonious as they might first appear.

For one thing, not every nest will have big healthy young, and if you could peer inside you might see why. Cliff Swallows are prey to blood-sucking insects, particularly one called the "swallow bug," which hides in cracks in or near nests during the day and crawls out at night to attack its hosts. These formidable little insects can spread throughout a colony either under their own power or by riding on the adults. Worst of all, when the swallows leave in late summer, the swallow bugs can hide in the nests and survive for as long as three years waiting for the birds to come back. The swallows may derive enormous benefits from their habit of living in beautifully constructed protective nests in sheltered colonies, but they must pay a terrible price as well. It is not at all unusual for half of the nestlings in a colony to be killed by the bugs, and there is almost nothing the swallows can do short of completely abandoning the colony.

Faced with such an awful problem, Cliff Swallows are under particularly intense pressure to come up with any tactic at all that might improve the survival of their young. If you were an adult swallow, for example, and were born with the tendency to do something that improved your offspring's chances by even 10 per cent or less, you could expect that within just a few generations your descendants (who inherited the same ability) would vastly outnumber those of your neighbours who didn't have your "secret" technique. And what might such a method be that could so improve your chances of leaving surviving young Cliff Swallows?

Perhaps the most obvious strategy would be to lay some of your eggs in the nests of your neighbours. That way, even if your own nest were overwhelmed by swallow bugs, your neighbours' nests might be luckier

---

* Barn Swallows, the familiar blue-backed birds with the long, forked tails, build shelf-like nests of mud open at the top. Cliff Swallow nests, although also built of mud, are completely closed-in, resembling gourds, with an entrance hole at the narrow end.

and, at little cost to yourself, you would have a much better overall chance of leaving a few surviving offspring. Amazingly, female Cliff Swallows do indeed try to lay eggs in as many nests as they can besides their own, but it goes much further than this. For example, it's all very well to lay eggs in nearby nests, but the owners of these nests do their best to prevent this from happening. Males and females take turns guarding their nests and vigorously repel any attempted visit by a female who wants to lay an egg. Egg-laying takes place over just a few days, and it may well be, if you are a would-be egg dumper, that you don't get the chance to unload all the eggs you would like. In these circumstances you may have little choice but to lay those eggs in your own nest. But perhaps all is not lost. After all the eggs are laid, your neighbours' nests will still occasionally be left unguarded for a moment or two. Theoretically, you could take advantage of those opportunities to carry one or more of your eggs to the unattended nests, and the result would be the same as if you had been able to lay them there in the first place.

A nice idea, you may say, but does anybody seriously think a mere swallow could or would indulge in such sophisticated behaviour? Well, if you watch long enough and are really lucky, you might see the answer for yourself. Incredible as it may seem, Cliff Swallows from time to time actually do appear at their nest entrance holding an egg in their bill and then, if they get the chance, fly to an unattended neighbouring nest, disappear inside, and emerge a few seconds later without the egg. Thus, even if they don't manage to lay the egg elsewhere in the first place, many Cliff Swallows still manage to spread their eggs around by other means and thereby increase their chances of eventual reproductive success.

But even that is not the whole story. It's all very well to lay one of your eggs in a neighbour's nest or carry one there later on. There is still going to be a problem. Birds almost always lay the precise number of eggs (four in the case of the Cliff Swallow) that will give rise to the greatest possible number of surviving young. In other words, even if a female Cliff Swallow laid five eggs, there will be fewer eventual survivors than from four eggs because the adult swallows simply can't gather enough food to properly feed five nestlings. Even if all of them survive to fledging, they will be underweight and prime candidates for an early death. That is why it is better to lay only four eggs (in your own nest) and raise just four healthy youngsters that have a correspondingly better prospect for long-term survival. The problem, therefore, with adding a fifth egg to one of your neighbour's nests is that none of the five resulting nestlings will do very well. This includes the four nestlings coming from your neighbour's eggs as well as the one coming from the egg you managed to sneak in there.

So what do you do to get around this problem? ... That's right, before you start sticking any of your eggs into neighbouring nests, you visit those same nests and remove one of the eggs. You might spear the egg with your bill or pick it up and drop it in the lake — anything to get rid of it. That way, when you come back later to lay your own egg, you will be bringing the number of eggs not up to five, which is too many, but up to four, which is just right.

You may be interested to know that Cliff Swallows tend to do all this in "husband and wife" teams. The males are usually the ones that wreck the neighbours' eggs, the females are the ones that transfer the illicit replacement eggs, and both sexes fight to prevent other pairs from doing the same thing to them. Astonishingly, that is about the only note of co-operation, at least in the early stages, in a Cliff Swallow colony. Far from being the blissful and harmonious little communities that we usually imagine, such colonies are the scenes of incredible beneath-the-surface strife and conflict. Theft, deceit, and baby-killing are everyday events in an unconscious but ruthless competition to extract the utmost from colony life, to beat the swallow bugs, and to leave more descendants than the neighbours do.

Something to think about on a hot July day as you drive over the Oxtongue Lake bridge on your way home or paddle under for a first-hand look at the "peaceful" Cliff Swallow colony. What better demonstration that, no matter how benign outward appearances may be in nature, deadly serious competition is never far away.

We shouldn't have to point out that the world of Cliff Swallows is a literal demonstration of the old saying about being wise not to put all your eggs in one basket. And, of course, it also shows that to succeed in life, you have to get an egg up on the competition.❧

July 16, 1992, Vol. 33, No. 4 (D.S.)

Female Cliff Swallow about to put one of its eggs in a neighbour's nest.

You Want "Bad"?

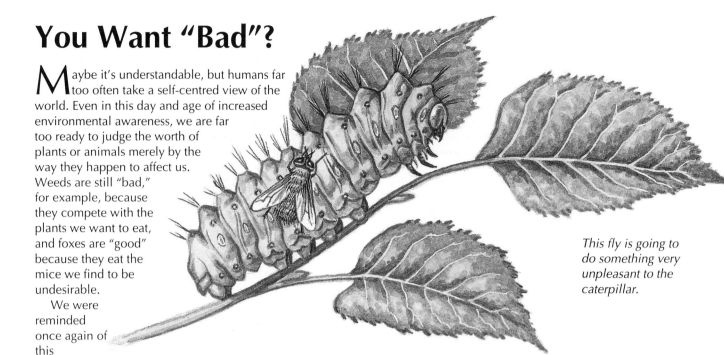

This fly is going to do something very unpleasant to the caterpillar.

Maybe it's understandable, but humans far too often take a self-centred view of the world. Even in this day and age of increased environmental awareness, we are far too ready to judge the worth of plants or animals merely by the way they happen to affect us. Weeds are still "bad," for example, because they compete with the plants we want to eat, and foxes are "good" because they eat the mice we find to be undesirable.

We were reminded once again of this unfortunate tendency just last week when some of our staff came in from working on the new Centennial Ridges Trail that we will be opening next year. "Boy, the flies were bad," the crew leader said, and we will concede that some of the lads really did have a few blood stains. Apparently they had encountered the odd deer fly up on the high ridge, and some of them even muttered about "almost being carried away."

Now, we weren't actually up there to experience the so-called attack ourselves, but we have seen a few deer flies, blackflies, and mosquitoes in our day. Frankly, we haven't yet seen anything to get excited about. To be sure, we have seen a few people swell up with bad, individual reactions, and we do remember an evening in June, 20 years ago, coming in off Grand Lake on the east side of the Park when the blackflies were unusually thick. As a matter of fact, we'll always recall looking over at one of our co-workers who was frantically trying to tie the canoe on our truck. The fact that shoulder-to-shoulder blackflies actually hid large areas of his shirt was really quite impressive. Later on, when we got indoors, we all found that our navels were filled and our bodies smeared with blood. We even wondered on that occasion how long we would have lasted if we had to stay outside.

Still, as attention-getting as such incidents might be, they really don't amount to much. After all, did any of us die from loss of blood on the notorious "night of the blackflies" and didn't every single one of our complaining work crew make it back last week from their little run-in with the deer flies? Quite frankly, even under the worst imaginable circumstances, we just have no business grumbling about how "bad" the flies might be. The fact is, humans are extraordinarily lucky when it comes to flies and should be embarrassed to even bring up the subject.

By contrast, thousands of animals in this world have real problems with flies — problems that put ours to complete and utter shame. Perhaps mentioning a few of them might put our paltry complaints into some sort of realistic perspective.

If you have seen the movie "Alien" or its successor "Aliens," you will have some idea of what we mean. In these films, human beings encounter a creature from another solar system that is able to use people for the development of its embryos. When the baby alien is ready to emerge, it rips its way out of the host human and goes on its merry way. Fine for the alien but very hard — fatal, in fact — for the human.

The films may be science fiction, but almost the exact same scenario is an everyday occurrence here on our planet Earth. The only real differences are that the victims are not (usually) humans and the creatures who do the embryo insertions are not terrifying aliens but quite ordinary-looking flies.

The main group, called "tachinids," has about 8,000 species (700 in Canada), and many of them would be passed over as normal, run-of-the-mill house flies. Indeed, their day-to-day existence is rather benign. They don't bite like deer flies and mosquitoes, for example, but feed on honeydew and flower nectar. When it comes to reproducing themselves, however, they are every bit as ghastly as the alien creature in the films. The hosts they choose for their young are usually other insects, often soft-bodied caterpillars but sometimes tough adult insects as well. Some tachinids fasten their eggs onto the outside of their victims and depend on the larvae hatching and burrowing inside all on their own. Other species actually insert their eggs inside the host's body to begin with. Tachinids that specialize in well-armoured hosts such as beetles have an egg-laying apparatus that looks, and works, like a can opener. Still other tachinids just lay their eggs in places where the hosts are likely to pass by. In this case the larvae themselves ambush the host and saw their way into its body. In yet another interesting twist, the host "eats" the tachinid eggs. Having been swallowed, the eggs then hatch and begin to consume the host's body from the inside out. Quite ingenious, don't you think?

Of course, there are real problems with living in, and devouring, a victim this way. For one thing, the fly larva should avoid killing its host until the last possible moment. For another, there is the little problem of breathing. Some tachinid fly larvae are able to chemically over-ride the host's wound-healing process in such a way that, instead of sealing off the entry hole, the scab forms a tube leading from the fly larvae to the outside air. Other larvae are able to tap into the internal air supply of their victims. This amounts, as one authority described it, to the alien "sticking a breathing tube into your lung while feeding on your other internal organs."

Alas, all good things must come to an end, and it's no different with tachinid larvae. When a larva has exhausted the nutritive possibilities of its unwilling, living host, it crawls out, leaving the host to die or killing it in the process. The mature larva then turns into a pupa and some time later emerges as an adult fly ready to start the cycle all over again.

The tachinid flies are the most prominent of these "parasitoid" flies (the term referring to the fact that, unlike ordinary parasites, these ones kill their hosts). They are far from the only ones, however.

Another family of flies, the small-headed flies, contains many species that employ a similar strategy, except that they seem to specialize on spiders. Small-headed fly larvae burrow into a spider's body, attach themselves to the spider's lung, and sometimes remain there for years without doing it any harm. Then, quite suddenly, they start to feed and develop rapidly, sometimes causing the death of the spider in as little as 24 hours.

Not to be outdone, there is another fly family, the "big-headed flies," that specializes in searching out leafhoppers and planthoppers and spiriting them off into the air. There they insert a deadly egg into the body of each victim before dropping it back into the vegetation. Then, too, there are the "thick-headed flies," these ones specializing in wasps and bees that they ambush near flowers. They insert their eggs into the victim's abdomen, and the larvae consume that part first before crawling forward into the wasp or bee's thorax and finally killing it.

If you are a bit squeamish at the idea of being eaten from the inside out, perhaps you would find the "bee-fly" family more to your liking. They specialize on bees and wasps as well, but on the larvae rather than the adults.

Another perhaps appealing difference is that they don't burrow inside their host's body the way most parasitoids do. Instead, they have apparently perfected the technique of sucking the victims' bodies entirely dry from the outside.

If you think we must be getting near the end of our list of — dare we say it — "unpleasant" flies, think again! We have yet to mention Blow Flies, for example. Most members of this family lay their eggs in rotting meat but some attack earthworms and even small reptiles and amphibians, always using the tried-and-true method of eating the living victim from the inside out.

Then, too, there are the snail-killing flies and also the flesh flies. The latter deposit their larvae mostly on already dead insects, but some species go after hosts that are — to begin with — perfectly alive and healthy. One flesh fly, the so-called Friendly Fly, attacks Tent Caterpillars. When we have an outbreak of Tent Caterpillars, as we did just a few years ago in the Muskoka Region, the population of Friendly Flies builds up quickly and becomes very noticeable. Indeed, it is the attacks of the Friendly Flies that are at least partly responsible for bringing Tent Caterpillars under control.

Did we mention Coffin Flies? Well, maybe you don't want to know about them, except we should mention that at least one species of this family doesn't like the contents of coffins at all. It specializes instead on eating the heads off living ants — but that's another story.

We hope you will forgive us if we have seemed to emphasize the gruesome and the macabre in this little tour of the known parasitoid flies. We emphasize the word "known" because all the authorities are unanimous in stating there are many thousands more parasitoid fly species out there that haven't even been described, let alone studied enough to know what other species they victimize. What a fantastic demonstration of how little we know about the natural world and of how so many bizarre opportunities for making a living in that world are exploited — even if usually unknown by us.

And, of course, we hope we have made the point by now that humans have a laughably easy time of it when it comes to contending with flies. There is just no comparison between the trifling inconvenience flies cause for us and the real problems they pose for thousands of other species. So, if you ever hear somebody complaining about how supposedly "bad" the flies are, just smile indulgently and send them to us. If they want to talk about "bad," we'll tell them about "**real** bad." ❧

July 23, 1992, Vol. 33, No. 5 (D.S.)

Worlds Within Worlds

One of our favourite places along the MacDougall Parkway (Highway 60) in Algonquin Park is Post 10 on the return trail of the Spruce Bog Boardwalk. There, the trail guide invites us to walk up to the top of the rock cut beside the highway and contemplate the environment through which the trail has just taken us.

It really is a fine view. On the southern horizon we can see the roof of the new, ridgetop visitor centre we will be opening next year. To the north, we can see tiny, faraway people going in on the trail as they cross over the Sunday Creek bog on the trail's main boardwalk. And, most of all, we can see the marvellous world within a world that is an Algonquin Park spruce bog stretching out before us. What a great place to sit on a summer evening listening to the sunset serenades of Swamp Sparrows and Yellowthroats and admiring the wild northern beauty of Sunday Creek meandering through the open bog between forests of gaunt and lonely Black Spruce.

We never cease to marvel at this Park environment that has grown up in just the past 11,000 years following the melting of the last glacier. At first there was just open water, but this was slowly invaded from each side by floating mats of vegetation. Generations of sedges, mosses, and shrubs grew and died, sinking down to form semi-decayed layers of peat. Eventually the floating mats reached the bottom of the pond, at least near its original edges, and the mat was solid enough to support trees — Tamarack at first and then eventually Black Spruce.

The original open water would have long since turned into solid, forested land from one side of the valley to the other, except that the creek itself and periodic flooding by beavers prevent completion of the process. So it is that we trail users of 1992 can sit and contemplate a spruce bog arrested in mid-development and wonder at its intricate beauty.

But if spruce bogs are whole little worlds unto themselves within the wider world of Algonquin Park, so too within spruce bogs we can find even smaller, more intricate worlds. One of our favourite examples is provided by the famous "carnivorous" bog plant, the Purple Pitcher-plant.

As many Park visitors already know, the Pitcher-plant is basically a green plant that makes its own food (sugar) using carbon dioxide, water, and the energy of sunlight. In addition, however, it has the bizarre "behaviour" of actually trapping insects in its enclosed, pitcher-like leaves. Sweet-smelling nectar and possibly the purplish-red veins and blotches in the leaves attract hapless victims. If they alight on the pitcher's "hood," or entrance structure, insects encounter stiff, downward-pointing hairs and then, below that, a slippery waxy area. Many a small insect loses its footing there and tumbles down into the pool of combined rain water and Pitcher-plant juice that lies below. Escape up the slippery walls is almost impossible. The insect drowns in the deadly pool and then is digested by enzymes released into the liquid by the pitcher's walls.

What a marvellous way for the Pitcher-plant to get around a major ecological problem presented by life in a bog. After all, bog plants do not grow in mineral soil the way most plants do but on peat, the semi-decayed remains of previous plant generations. Such "soil" is desperately poor in minerals — substances such as potassium, calcium, and especially nitrogen that all plants (and we animals, too) need to make vital body chemicals, particularly proteins. Instead of trying to extract almost non-existent nitrogen and other minerals from the bog, Pitcher-plants tap into the much richer supply contained in insects. The proteins of doomed bugs are broken down in the death pools, absorbed by the pitcher walls, and then reassembled to make Pitcher-plant proteins. Very convenient for the Pitcher-plants, less convenient for the insects!

And yet, as fascinating as this little story is, it by no means ends there. The so-called death pool within a Pitcher-plant leaf is a whole little world of its own. If you stop and think about it, there are some possibly quite attractive features about living there. Here is a warm, sheltered little body of liquid, constantly enriched by the digestion of insect victims. To be sure, for any would-be inhabitant of a Pitcher-plant pool there is the little problem of all those digestive enzymes, but apparently many organisms are quite capable of resisting them. Flesh-fly maggots hang from the pool's surface waiting to feed on incoming dead insects. Pieces sink down to the bottom of the pitcher and are further eaten by midge larvae lying hidden in the black sludge of chewed-up corpses. Many particles are too small to be seen with the naked eye, but they are quite suitable food for the bacteria that flourish in the nutrient-rich soup. The bacteria themselves are eaten by microscopic, one-celled animals, and these in turn are swept up and eaten by the brush-like "arms" of the larvae of a very special insect.

This is the Pitcher-plant Mosquito, a species whose larvae are not only immune to the digestive enzymes in which they swim but, in fact, are never found anywhere else. Those little Pitcher-plant pools have a lot of things going for the enzyme-proof mosquito larvae. There are obviously no fish to contend with, and the enclosing leaf even performs a sort of "aquarium maintenance service." Being an otherwise normal green leaf, it produces oxygen, some of which is released into the liquid and becomes available to sustain the lives of the mosquito larvae and other insects. Pitcher-plant pools are so rich in oxygen, in fact, that the Pitcher-plant Mosquito is thought to be the only species in the world that doesn't need to get oxygen by sticking a little breathing tube from the water up to the outside air. Of course, as the midge, fly, and mosquito larvae consume oxygen they produce carbon dioxide — and nitrogen-rich ammonia — as waste products. Both of these are useful to the Pitcher-plant, however, so rather than accumulating in the Pitcher-plant pool and gradually poisoning it, both are steadily removed, maintaining more or less ideal conditions for the insects.

Pitcher-plant leaves provide a haven for the mosquito larvae in another important way as well. The Pitcher-plant Mosquito is basically a tropical species (all its 300 relatives live in hot climates), and its larvae are especially sensitive to freezing. It often turns out, however, that deep snow blankets our northern bogs and insulates the little Pitcher-plant pools from the deadly cold outside. The temperature may dip to 40 below, but the Pitcher-plant pools may still not freeze. The larvae are in suspended animation in the cold water but are not entombed in lethal ice.

When spring comes the snow melts, of course, and increasing day length triggers renewed development in the mosquito larvae. They turn into pupae from which adults soon emerge into the outside air. The timing of these events and especially of the subsequent egg-laying shows an amazing precision. Pitcher-plant pools may be a mosquito larvae heaven, but there is a premium on being first. The earliest larvae to hatch will find the most food and grow fastest into the healthiest possible adults, who will then lay the greatest number of eggs in the following generation. Later-hatching larvae will find slim pickings in the pool, grow more slowly, and develop into stunted adults that will lay fewer (and later) eggs for the season's second crop of larvae.

In terms of their offspring's survival, therefore, it pays for female Pitcher-plant Mosquitoes to be quick off the mark in laying their eggs. It also pays for them to be able to recognize the best, most productive, Pitcher-plant leaves in which to lay. Pitcher-plant leaves are pale green in their first seven to 10 days of life while they expand and fill out. Only then do they harden, darken, and start producing their insect-attracting odours. From two to four weeks of age a Pitcher-plant leaf is a highly effective insect predator, but then its ability to attract prey drops off and remains low for the rest of the leaf's 15-month existence. The best strategy for a female Pitcher-plant

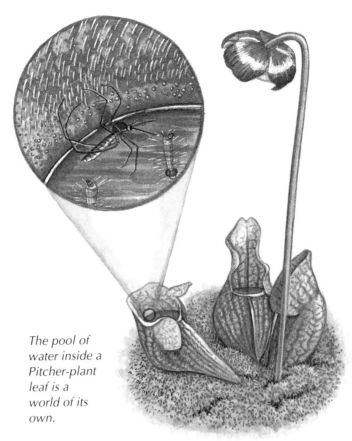

The pool of water inside a Pitcher-plant leaf is a world of its own.

Mosquito, therefore, is to lay her eggs in a young leaf so that when they hatch, the leaf will just be coming into its most productive period as an insect trap.

And, as amazing as it may seem, female Pitcher-plant Mosquitoes actually can distinguish young leaves from older ones. Egg-laying females flying up to a cluster of Pitcher-plant leaves invariably choose the youngest one to lay their eggs. Flying into the leaf, they hover over the water and, without actually touching it, delicately deposit their tiny white eggs, one at a time, right on the surface.*

We think it marvellous to sit on the rock cut at the Spruce Bog Boardwalk Post 10 as the sun goes down and to contemplate the breathtaking intricacy of the worlds within worlds that stretch out before us. Within the vastness of Algonquin Park itself lie innumerable smaller worlds, such as this one fascinating spruce bog. And then, within that bog lie even other worlds, including that contained within a single, hidden leaf of a single Pitcher-plant. …

It is a picture of almost overwhelming beauty and symmetry well worth our admiration. You could even say that some parts are pitcher perfect.

July 30, 1992, Vol. 33, No. 6 (D.S.)

---

* If you find all this talk about mosquitoes less than inspiring, you will be glad to learn that the Pitcher-plant Mosquito does not drink blood — at least not here in Algonquin. Females of some mosquito species need a meal of blood to acquire enough protein to form eggs, but in the north the Pitcher-plant Mosquito can get by without such meals.

In other areas (from New Jersey southward), however, female Pitcher-plant Mosquitoes do require blood meals and have been observed to bite both humans and turtles. Here in Algonquin, if you are a human being, a turtle, or presumably anything in between, you can breathe easy (and worry about the Park's other 27 kinds of mosquito).

It's Yer Genuwine High-Tech

We daresay that most people are fascinated by new gadgets. This being so, what an age to be living in! With today's digital sound, versatile computers, and powerful microchips, the sky seems to be the limit. New and better devices are coming out all the time, and the old saying about "building a better mousetrap and having the world beat a path to your doorstep" has never seemed to be truer.

We confess to being as impressed and amazed by all the new gadgetry as anyone else, but sometimes we get the feeling that the supposedly unsophisticated natural world is getting short shrift. This was brought home to us with special vividness one day last week when we were riding down to the new visitor centre with a visiting journalist. The man was proudly showing off his new cellular phone when a Short-tailed Shrew about two inches long ran across the highway right in front of us. And do you know something? Without a word of a lie, the man never even stopped talking about his phone and, as far as we could tell, didn't even look at the shrew.

Incredible! After all, a cellular phone is a nice example of some pretty fancy high-tech, but it can't hold a candle to a Short-tailed Shrew! There's just no comparison.

Now, we want to say right away that no one should feel bad if they have to own up to knowing as little about Short-tailed Shrews as our newspaper friend. In fact, we bet there are lots of folks in exactly the same boat. It's not a crime not to know about Short-tailed Shrews, but it certainly is a shame because they are about as interesting and as "high-tech" as can be. So, if you are in

the dark about these little creatures, allow us to take a few minutes and fill you in.

First of all, these particular shrews are just one among hundreds of kinds found throughout the world and one among the five found here in Algonquin Park. Most people are at least vaguely aware that shrews superficially resemble mice but are much smaller and lack the big, constantly growing front teeth of a rodent. Several of our Algonquin shrews weigh around five grams whereas most mice would be four or five times as big (20 to 25 grams). Being so tiny, shrews lose heat very quickly to the surrounding air and are famous for killing prey and burning up energy at truly prodigious rates. Small shrews must eat their own weight in food every 24 hours and will starve to death in a day if they are unable to keep up this rate of intake. Imagine what it would be like to eat 150 pounds of insects, snails, slugs, and earthworms every single day on pain of starvation and you will have some idea of what it would be like to be a shrew.*

The above generalities apply more or less to the Short-tailed Shrew as well, but there are also important differences. For one thing, Short-tails are much bigger than most shrews. They weigh in at 10 to 20 grams, making them almost as big as some mice. Short-tails also seem to be much more common than our smaller shrews. On average there may be 10 Short-tailed Shrews per acre although, as with many small mammals, populations can fluctuate dramatically. A few Algonquin oldtimers can still remember the fantastic summer of 1947 when Short-tailed Shrews may have reached densities of 100 per acre or even higher. All in all, this particular shrew is sufficiently different, more plentiful, and more important than the other smaller kinds that many naturalists prefer to use the Latin name "Blarina" (instead of "shrew") to reflect its distinctiveness.

Now, when any animal is obviously more successful than its relatives, we may legitimately suspect it has one or more special adaptations that give it an edge over the competition.

In fact, Blarinas have three special adaptations that account for their success. The simplest of all is that Blarinas smell bad — and presumably taste about the same. This has the effect of protecting them from all but the hungriest of predators and apparently allows them to proliferate much more rapidly than would otherwise be the case.

The second key to the Short-tailed Shrew's success was inadvertently discovered back in 1889 when a man named Maynard was bitten by a Short-tail he was trying to capture. The skin of his hand was barely punctured —

A Short-tailed Shrew closing in on a Deer Mouse.

---

* With a diet like that you might prefer starvation, especially when the best you could hope for would be one or two years of life. By then your teeth would be worn out and your body an ancient wreck, and you would starve to death anyway. Such is the short life of a shrew.

but within 30 seconds he felt a burning sensation followed by intense shooting pains in his arm. The pain and swelling reached a maximum after an hour, but he still felt considerable discomfort more than a week later. Mr. Maynard had learned first-hand that the saliva of the Short-tailed Shrew is deadly poisonous! Subsequent studies have shown that the poison is produced by the salivary glands in the Blarina's lower jaw (saliva produced by two other sets of glands in the animal's mouth is completely harmless). Very little of the saliva is sufficient to kill a mouse, and this enables Blarinas to tap into a major food supply that is completely unavailable to smaller, non-poisonous shrews. Even though a Blarina is still appreciably smaller than a mouse, all it has to do is get in a few nips and wait for the deadly saliva to do its work. Within a few minutes the hapless mouse is dead or so lethargic that it can't resist when the Short-tail starts to devour it. The idea of being paralyzed and then eaten alive is not particularly interesting for the victim, but the advantage to the shrew is considerable. You will remember that shrews risk starving to death if they don't eat their own weight in food every day. The problem is that they aren't guaranteed to find the necessary steady supply every single day. Under these circumstances, the ability to store excess food for later use could make the difference between life and death. Short-tailed Shrews do indeed paralyze mice and smaller prey with their saliva, bury them for safekeeping, and then return a day or two later. Being still alive, the victims have not rotted, and the shrew can derive maximum nutritional benefit from its surplus food supply.

As macabre as this little twist may be, however, it is nothing compared to the final, ultra-sophisticated feature of our supreme little mouse-killing machine. Shrews operate mostly at night and in tunnels under the soil and leaf litter. Their keen sense of smell helps them zero in on prey under these conditions, but neither this sense nor their small eyes help much with the more basic problem of getting around through complicated underground tunnel networks in almost complete darkness. Most shrews do indeed blunder into things and uselessly poke their way up blocked tunnels — at least until they have memorized the local travel routes. The Short-tailed and a few other shrews, however, have made a major breakthrough, enabling them to navigate in total darkness in completely unfamiliar surroundings. As with bats, these shrews can "see" their environment through "echolocation." By sending out high-pitched clicks and then listening to the echoes, the Short-tailed Shrew generates in its brain a three-dimensional picture of its underground world, which it can then use to make navigation decisions. Like all shrews, Short-tails lack the big, sound-collecting external ears of bats (not very practical in a world of narrow underground tunnels), but they can nevertheless distinguish some very small features of their environment. Even from a foot away, for example, a Blarina can detect an opening of just a quarter of an inch wide. Even more amazing, by sending a burst of ultrasonic clicks down a tunnel from its entrance, a Short-tailed Shrew can "see" if the tunnel is blocked farther down, and can do this even if the tunnel is bent or curved. In other words, shrews can use their echolocation capabilities to almost literally see around corners.

Imagine being a mouse "safely" curled up in your subterranean nest when a Blarina comes into your tunnel network. We don't know if mice can hear the ultrasonic clicks of an approaching Short-tail, but if they can it must be something like one of those Second World War submarine scenes where the crew members all hold their breath listening to the sonar "pings" from the dreaded destroyer passing overhead. The trouble is, in the case of a cowering mouse, the echolocation signals and data processors (brains) of a Short-tailed Shrew can distinguish between different surfaces such as soil, leaves, and fur. …

We think it nothing less than astounding that a minuscule 10-gram package of flesh can so completely eclipse the capabilities of the high-tech gadgets about which everybody gets so excited these days. Imagine paying more attention to a crude trinket like a cellular phone than to a sophisticated marvel like a Short-tailed Shrew. And if anybody from Sony, IBM, or Mitsubishi comes along with some hype about a better mousetrap, you might just ask them a few questions. Do their high-tech gadgets contain enough toxin to kill 200 mice? Can their mouse traps actually track down their victims and then clean up the mess? Is their technology capable of seeing around corners in complete darkness and resolving the data into a useful, three-dimensional picture on a computer screen tiny enough to fit inside a shrew's skull?

When these companies begin to manufacture products with even some of the abilities of a Short-tailed Shrew, then we'll start to take them seriously. In the meantime we will always pay keen and respectful attention whenever we're lucky enough to see a Short-tailed Shrew run across the highway. They may look simple and unsophisticated, but they truly are the world's best and most awesomely high-tech mouse trap.

Or, as people always say in these parts, "If it's a better mouse trap you want, then gettin' some of them there Blarinas would be a shrewd move."✑

August 6, 1992, Vol. 33, No. 7 (D.S.)

A Visit From the Caped Fungus-Eater

A couple of weeks ago we had a most unusual visit. We were sitting around our campfire on Shirley Lake telling stories when something white caught our eyes as it streaked over our heads.

We had a pretty good idea it must be a flying squirrel and quickly mounted a search. Sure enough, we soon found it in our flashlight beam and got a good look at it sitting on the branch of a big hemlock. For half a minute we could see its bright white belly, tan upperparts, and big, dark eyes as it nibbled away on a piece of fungus held in its front paws in typical squirrel fashion. Then, almost as suddenly as it had arrived, our little visitor launched itself into space and swooped off in a long glide into the darkness of the surrounding forest.

We greatly appreciated this sighting, short though it was, because we only rarely get to see flying squirrels. They are abundant in the forests of Algonquin Park — at least as common as the familiar daytime Red Squirrel — but, because they are strictly nocturnal, we are almost always unaware of their presence.

On this occasion we not only got a reasonably good look at a flying squirrel itself, we also got — almost without knowing it — an indication of this little animal's unique and important role in the ecology of northern forests.

The fact that our little visitor happened to be eating a mushroom is much more than a trivial coincidence. The flying squirrel we have here in Algonquin, technically called the Northern Flying Squirrel, is one of the few animals that can subsist on a diet of lichens all winter long and fungi (mushrooms) in the summer and fall. Apparently this ability is the key factor permitting Northern Flying Squirrels to inhabit the coniferous forests of North America (right up to the tree line in the far north).

Surprisingly, the relationship between flying squirrels and mushrooms also has important implications for the health of the forest. Many of the squirrel's preferred fungi form close and mutually beneficial associations with tree roots. The fungi obtain sugar (energy) from the roots but return the favour by providing the tree roots with extra nutrients that make a major difference in how well the tree grows.

Now, the parts of the fungi eaten by the flying squirrels are not the microscopic thread-like structures wrapped around the roots of trees but the bigger, fleshy bodies that we often call mushrooms. These are the parts of the fungus that produce the tiny spores that normally float away in the air and occasionally land in a place suitable for the growth of a new fungus. Some species of fungi,

however, produce "mushrooms" that remain hidden underground. These kinds are obviously going to have a problem in the dissemination of their spores, and it is here that Northern Flying Squirrels play an especially important role. They can actually smell those underground mushrooms, dig them up, and eat them. The squirrels derive nourishment from these fungi, of course, but they also provide a vital service to the mushroom in return. The spores of the underground mushrooms pass unharmed through the digestive system of the flying squirrels. Often, the spores (conveniently expelled by the squirrels in little packages of fertilizer) land in places

suitable for the growth of a new underground fungus. Thus, the cycle is completed to the benefit of all the players. To be sure, some of the fungus has been consumed by the flying squirrel, but the fungus has profited at the same time by the "free" dispersal of its spores to new growing places. Perhaps even more important, the forest itself has profited because, as we have seen, the health of its trees depends on the close association of their roots with the fungi.

Thus, our sighting of the flying squirrel at our Shirley Lake campsite sitting on the branch and munching away on a piece of mushroom was a marvellous little vignette of a fascinating and very important ecological relationship in our Algonquin forests.

We also had another, more personal, reason for appreciating the visit from the Shirley Lake flying squirrel. Many years ago, we were lucky enough to have had the experience of actually raising a baby flying squirrel and getting to know this fascinating creature in a way that few people ever can. And so, our sighting of two weeks ago revived some special memories.

It was way back in May 1968, when we were presented with a furred, but still helpless and blind baby flying squirrel. Our maintenance staff had discovered a nest earlier in the day in a stack of swimming buoys piled up for the winter beside one of the buildings at Lake of Two Rivers. Once they realized there were five babies in the nest, the workers backed off and watched as the mother carried off four of them, one at a time, to an alternate nest in a nearby tree cavity. After several hours, however, she had still not returned for the last baby and the decision was made to turn it over to the Museum.

Now, raising babies is a demanding task at the best of times, but in this case the timing could hardly have been better. Its eyes opened the very next day, making it about 33 days old and meaning that the most difficult part of its babyhood was nearing an end. We had to feed it with an eyedropper at first, but soon it was able to drink and take solid food on its own, so we had a comparatively easy time of it. At the same time, because it had never actually seen its own mother or any other flying squirrel, this youngster grew up thoroughly imprinted on humans, accepting and trusting us totally.

"It" turned out to be a "he," and somebody was quick to point out that the name "Wilbur" (after the Wright brothers) was particularly appropriate for a male flying squirrel. Wilbur it was, then, and he became an inseparable part of our lives. In the daytime he considered us as his "hollow tree," sleeping down inside our shirt (just above the belt and always on the left side — don't ask us why!) or sticking his head out of our collar to watch the world go by.

Just as with normal, wild flying squirrels, however, he became truly active only at night. He immediately took to an exercise wheel and would run in it full tilt and non-stop for minutes at a time and with his legs moving so fast they were literally a blur.

It shouldn't come as any surprise, however, that Wilbur's most amazing performances involved his prowess in the air. Flying squirrels don't really fly, of course, but they are masterful and manoeuvrable gliders, and we never got tired of watching Wilbur show us what he could do. After running up to the top of a curtain and bobbing his head a few times (apparently to accurately judge the distance of his intended landing spot), he would leap out into the air, instantly spreading out all four legs and starting his glide. The gliding surface of a flying squirrel is provided mostly by the "patagium," a fold of furred skin that stretches from the wrist of the forearm back to the ankle of the hind foot. When a flying squirrel is airborne, it stretches out its limbs in a "spread-eagle" position and thus achieves maximum deployment of the patagia between the wrists and the ankles. The gliding surface is further increased thanks to the flat, feather-like tail and to two cartilaginous spurs, one at each wrist, that actually extend the leading edge of each membrane a couple of centimetres out beyond each wrist.

Flying squirrels have often been compared to modern hang gliders, and we think the comparison is quite apt. Both allow a certain amount of billowing in their gliding membranes (this prevents side-slipping), both are more or less manoeuvrable, and in their glides both can cover horizontally as much as three times the vertical distance lost. In other words, both might cover 300 horizontal feet while descending just 100 feet.

We often showed people just how agile Wilbur was by throwing him (underhand) across a room. He routinely swerved around obstacles or changed course so as to reach a suitable landing surface (such as a curtain instead of a wall). He seemed to enjoy such exhibitions, incidentally, because, having landed, he typically ran up to the top of the curtain and glided back to the thrower, apparently looking for another throw.

Watching such displays, you couldn't help but be amazed that something as bizarre as a "living hang glider" could actually have evolved. And yet, the truth is that the gliding habit has appeared in many different places all over the world. At least four different mammal families have come up with this way of life, including a group of little nectar- and pollen-eating marsupials in Australia. Then there is the famous "flying frog" of Borneo (which actually uses its huge webbed feet as a sort of parachute or gliding surface) and the "flying dragon," or "lizard" (which extends flaps from its rib cage to increase its air-catching surface area when leaping out of a tree).

Of course, when you stop and think about it, it is an obvious advantage for any creature that lives in trees to have gliding ability. This will be true whether the creature eats nuts, insects, nectar, or fungi. If you see something good to eat in a neighbouring tree, you will benefit enormously if you can dispense with going all the way down to the ground and then back up the other tree to the food item. For a tree-dweller, in other words, the shortest distance between two points is a straight glide, and perhaps we shouldn't be too surprised that such a marvellous ability has evolved more than once on this planet.

Or, to take the particular example of our own Northern Flying Squirrel and to repeat what one of our companions (really) said after the departure of our little mushroom-nibbling visitor two weeks ago at Shirley Lake, "Ah, yes, nothing beats hang-gliding in the dark for fungus and profit." ∽

August 20, 1992, Vol. 33, No. 9 (D.S.)

A Poacher Meets His Match

Most everyone knows that Algonquin Park will be celebrating its 100th birthday in 1993 and, with it, a whole century of wildlife protection and conservation. Few people realize, however, just how difficult it has often been to carry out that protection in conditions that are often demanding and sometimes dangerous. Nor do many people know that the people responsible for fish and wildlife protection in Algonquin Park and throughout Ontario, the province's conservation officers, are observing their centennial right now, in 1992.

It is always appropriate when celebrating an important milestone to reflect on the traditions and contributions of those who have gone before. Along these lines we would like to reprint a fascinating account we came across a few weeks ago of a true event in the history of Algonquin Park and of Ontario's conservation officers, an account that we believe exemplifies the proud conservation traditions of both. We found the story in one of the 1948 issues of *Sylva*, a marvellous magazine that used to be put out by the old Department of Lands and Forests, forerunner of today's Ministry of Natural Resources. It was written by Nelson T. Jones, a conservation officer who worked on the north side of the Park, and it describes his rather harrowing run-in with a poacher in Algonquin Park the year before. We are sure you will find it as interesting as we did. Here then are excerpts from Officer Jones's story, entitled simply "Law Enforcement."

"On the morning of November 30, 1947, I was getting ready to leave my cabin when a knock came on the door. Opening it, I found the caller to be the holder of Trap Line Area #27, in the east part of Head Township, who informed me that someone unknown to him had cut out the top of a beaver house on his zone and set a trap inside. I left the cabin with the trapper, who took me back along an old road south of Mackey. After driving about eight miles on this road, we left the car and walked the rest of the way to the beaver house.

My companion left me there and I concealed myself in some small spruce to watch. As it was Sunday morning, I thought perhaps the person who had set the trap might return.

After waiting several hours and having seen no one, I decided to move around some as I was getting cold. While doing so, I met the trapper who had been back further looking over his zone.

Eventually we found the tracks of a man and a small dog in the snow. As they appeared to be fresh tracks, we followed them to a point where they entered Algonquin Park, having crossed the blaze line on a rabbit trail. Making certain the tracks continued on into the Park, we returned to the car as it was getting too late in the day to go on.

The trapper, on learning that I was going to return the next morning to follow out the tracks, said he would like to accompany me. I told him I would be glad to have him as he is a good bushman and would be a very good guide. The next morning I arose early and proceeded to a point behind Mackey where we had agreed to meet. Strapping our packsacks on our backs, we started out to see where these tracks led. From the place where we had to leave the car, it was about two and one half miles to the blaze line.

We crossed the blaze line on a rabbit trail, picking up the tracks inside the Park. We had walked about six miles when we came out on the ice at a large beaver lake. As we were crossing this lake we noticed the fresh tracks of a man in the centre of a much used trail. Gazing around we noticed a thatched shelter built on the south bank; we had approached from the north. Carrying on, we circled by a beaver dam on which two traps were set. Blood on the snow by a beaver house with the top nearly cut out told us a beaver had been taken. We found no one at the shelter when we arrived there about 11:30 a.m. It looked quite cosy, containing a sleeping bag, wool blankets and a considerable supply of food and traps.

I lifted up the sleeping bag and under it I found two beaver pelts. They had not been skinned very long. The trapper waited with me until about 1 p.m. when he left, following the tracks leading south from the shelter. These tracks were found to circle a large area with many traps set for beaver and otter.

At approximately 2:05 p.m. as I sat on the sleeping bag waiting, the sound of someone breaking wood put me on the alert. Finally, I saw a man approaching carrying an armful of wood, an axe and a bag of traps, also a gun slung from a shoulder strap. As he came nearer, I saw he was quite large in stature with a heavy growth of whiskers.

I walked out a few feet to meet him and spoke. Until this time, he had not noticed me. Stopping abruptly, and before I had time to speak again, he asked with a frown, 'Are you a game warden?' I replied that I was and showed him my credentials. As I did this I informed him he was under arrest and that he would have to go out with me. I asked to see the gun he was carrying. At this he said, 'You stay back 'fore you get hurt, you see no gun.' He threw the wood, axe and bag of traps on the ground. I then told him it would be better to talk to me and not try getting rough. He then said, 'I am big man, seen bigger men than you couldn't handle me,' and added, 'I go now, but not with you.' At this, he started to run towards the beaver lake. Running about 25 or 30 ft. on the snow-covered ice, I caught up to him, grabbing him by the left shoulder. He wheeled and shoved the rifle, which later proved to be a 44-40 Winchester, in my stomach. I pulled the blackjack from my pocket and struck the gun, knocking it to one side. He said, 'Be careful, this gun is loaded,' and began to run again. After another spring, I caught up and as I did, he swung the gun as a club, striking me on the right side of the ribs, breaking the 6th and 8th ribs. He ran on and, when in the centre of the lake, as I was again almost upon him, he swung with the gun again striking me on the nose and causing it to bleed. With another swing he caught me across the left shoulder and the back of the left hand, as I attempted to protect my body from the blow. He again ran on and by this time we had almost crossed the lake.

He started up the bank into the bush with me right behind him and I struck at his arm holding the gun. As I swung, he lowered his head in an attempt to knock me down off the bank. The blackjack struck him a hard blow on the head, inflicting a wound which bled freely. This, however, did not slow him down. He ran towards a large jack pine. I came around the tree and he swung the axe which buried itself in the tree as I jumped back. By this time I was in a state of anger and more determined than ever that he was not going to get away. As he ran around another tree some yards on, I closed in on him before he had a chance to swing again. Seizing him by the arm, I used a Judo hold, throwing him to the ground on his back. He fell heavily and the rifle flew up striking him over the left eye, causing a laceration which allowed blood to drain into his eye. I held him on his back in the snow and the blood interfered with the vision of his eye.

I said I would let him up as soon as he told me who he was and where he was from. He readily acceded to my request.

I got up and stepped back out of his reach. He got to his feet and stooped to pick up his gun. I spoke again and told him I would carry the axe and gun and that he would walk ahead. He said, 'Alright.' He said he was sorry he had battled me the way he had. I told him it was a little late for that and reminded him that I had tried to talk to him telling him it would be worse for him if I had to use force. He told me that he thought when he first saw me, he could push me over easily and get away and that I didn't look to be a tough man. He knew I didn't know him.

Arriving back at the camp, I built a fire, boiled some water for tea, bathed and bandaged his head and gave him some sandwiches left from lunch. I then had him do up his belongings, all of which I seized. We waited until my friend returned at about 3:20 p.m. The three of us then started the long hike out to my car some eight miles away.

The surrounding country was very rough going, but the prisoner carried his pack, which was quite heavy, the whole distance and didn't stop to rest until he reached my car. He filled his pipe and lit it three times as he trudged along.

We arrived at the car at 7:35 p.m., more than half of our trip being made after dark, and started the trip of fifty-one miles to Pembroke where I called for Mr. E.L. Skuce, Fish and Wildlife Specialist. After a late supper we went to the office, as Mr. Skuce wanted some information about the prisoner. The prisoner was then taken to a doctor and from there he was lodged in the county jail to await trial.

Several charges were laid, two of which were laid under the criminal code; one of resisting arrest, pointing a firearm, carrying a firearm in the Park, hunting in the park, killing two beaver in closed season and destroying beaver houses.

On December 4, 1947, the prisoner was convicted and sentenced to serve three months in jail on the obstruction charges and a fine of $500.00 or an additional five months on the other charges.

The poacher is now serving eight months in Guelph Reformatory as the cost of poaching in Algonquin Park."☞

August 27, 1992, Vol. 33, No. 10 (D.S.)

Are They Kings or Slaves?

We humans have many popular and pleasing interpretations of the natural world. A mother duck leading her brood across a beaver pond is the perfect image of motherly devotion. A chipmunk taking food from our hand conveys a comforting picture of gratitude and friendliness. And, of course, one of the most appealing of all ideas is the picture of the noble and all-powerful top predator in the ecosystem. Whether it is a lion in Africa or a wolf in Algonquin Park, we contemplate the "king of the jungle" (or forest) with a mixture of respectful admiration and downright envy of creatures that are in apparently total control of their destiny.

Now, just like anybody else, we get shivers down our spine whenever we hear the howl of a wolf. We will also agree that nature offers few spectacles more stirring than a fierce-eyed eagle proudly surveying the winter Algonquin landscape from a lofty perch or a pack of wolves setting out on the hunt. Still, for all the wild beauty and perfection of the world's great predators we think many people tend to exaggerate their powers and to misunderstand the realities of their difficult lives.

It may come as a surprise, for example, that many seemingly masterful predators, often resort to eating carrion. Maybe it is relatively well known that the Bald Eagle, striking enough to be chosen the emblem of the United States, routinely eats dead fish or robs other, lesser predators of their kills. But how many people realize that this behaviour is also true for many other "masterful" mammals or birds of prey? Wolves here in Algonquin Park, for example, sometimes draw a significant part of their late winter sustenance from the emaciated carcasses of moose that have been killed by heavy infestations of blood-sucking ticks. Even the Peregrine Falcon, long a favourite of royalty for its awesome, 250 kilometre an hour dives on helpless prey from high in the sky, will shoo gulls and crows away from a flattened road kill if it thinks it can scrounge a meal that way.

The picture of an eagle or a wolf picking over smelly, half-rotten carcasses somehow clashes with the popular idea of how "noble" predators should behave, but this only underscores how unrealistic we sometimes become in our attitudes about wildlife. After all, it's fine for us armchair humans to decide how an eagle should behave; it's quite another thing to be actually out there and to have to make a living in an unforgiving world. As a matter of fact, a predator would have to be a fool (to use another human term) to pass up a free meal just because it was already dead. No predator knows from where its next meal is coming, or even if there will be a next meal. Moreover, and this is also often not appreciated by many people, attacking live prey can be downright dangerous. Not only is there a chance of getting a twig in the eye during a hot pursuit through the forest but also many

Hawk Owl.

"victims" are not nearly so helpless as they might seem. One well-placed kick from a moose can crush a wolf's skull or fracture a couple of ribs, and a wolf should obviously do anything it can to avoid such unpleasantness. This includes never turning up its nose at dead animals (think of them as "pre-killed" prey) even if this doesn't happen to fit the human definition of noble behaviour.

Another common myth about the behaviour of nature's top predators is that they kill their prey quickly and cleanly. The thinking seems to be that "yes, wolves and lions must kill to live, but they dispatch their victims quickly and with a minimum of suffering." This pleases our human sensibilities and helps keep alive the idea of "nobility," but once again it has more to do with wishful thinking than reality. The fact is, predators often take a long time to kill their prey simply because many prey animals are powerful in their own right and the predator has a difficult time with them. Indeed, unpleasant as it seems to us humans — and no doubt for the victim — many predators do not deliberately kill their victims at all but only achieve this result when they have eaten enough of them or the right parts. A few years ago we had an excellent illustration of this when we came around a curve in the highway near Cache Lake and saw a wolf excitedly sniffing on the pavement up ahead and then disappearing over the embankment. When we stopped and got out to see if the wolf was still visible, you can imagine our amazement when we saw that it was only 15 metres away violently pulling at a deer lying at the edge of the forest. The wolf saw us, lifted its head and, seemingly with great reluctance, slowly moved off into the bush.

Then the incredible happened. The deer stood up! Bleeding from the neck and its rear end, it then staggered into the bush.* The wolf had actually been "feeding" on a helpless, still-living deer!

We have related this incident to many people over the years and have observed two types of reaction. The first type, coming from those who are convinced of the "nobility" of predators in general and wolves in particular, is one of displeasure because, in their eyes, it doesn't enhance the wolf's image. The second sort of reaction, coming from people who dislike wolves or even from those who have no particular opinion on the subject, is one of disgust. What could be more

---

* We soon put the deer out of its misery and also learned that it had first been hit by a truck earlier that morning. Apparently the wolf had come along just before we did, had smelled the blood on the pavement, quickly discovered the deer down the embankment, and was just starting to feed when we got out of our car and interrupted the proceedings.

unspeakably cruel, goes this school of thought, than to eat your prey alive?

Well, we beg to offer the opinion that both these reactions are wrong, and both are rooted in our stubbornly misplaced insistence on trying to see the natural world through human eyes. To begin with, we hope by now that we have disposed once and for all of the idea that wolves are "noble." That is a uniquely human concept and has nothing to do with wolves in the real world, who are merely trying to eat and survive.

But neither are wolves "cruel," even when they eat their prey alive. It is simply not reasonable to expect that a wolf can understand the concepts of "life" and "death" or the feelings of its victims. After all, these are difficult notions to grasp. Our own human children do not fully appreciate what is meant by death until they are three or four, and they often take much longer to realize that some of their actions hurt others.

Why should we think that wolves and other non-human animals can conceptualize better than small children? To be "cruel" a wolf would have to realize that its victim could (a) feel pain, (b) be "dead" instead of "alive," and (c) not feel pain if it were dead. Even then, for us to call it "cruel," the wolf would have to deliberately choose not to kill

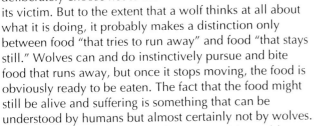
Scrawny young wolf.

its victim. But to the extent that a wolf thinks at all about what it is doing, it probably makes a distinction only between food "that tries to run away" and food "that stays still." Wolves can and do instinctively pursue and bite food that runs away, but once it stops moving, the food is obviously ready to be eaten. The fact that the food might still be alive and suffering is something that can be understood by humans but almost certainly not by wolves.

If wolves and other top predators are neither noble nor cruel in the ways that we have often imagined them to be, what about the notion that they are "all powerful" and in total control of their lives? Here again, facts contradict the popular picture. Several recent studies have shown that even the most devastatingly efficient predators have surprisingly low success rates. In the famous study of wolves and moose on Isle Royale in Lake Superior, for example, it turned out that the wolves killed only eight per cent of the moose they chased. Even this low figure doesn't reflect the fact that the wolves chased only about 58 per cent of the moose they encountered. The other 42 per cent stood their ground at the approach of the wolves, and the wolves soon left, apparently sensing that they had no hope at all against such confident moose. The wolves, supposed "monarchs" of the north woods, had to look elsewhere for an animal they might be lucky enough to tackle successfully.

The reality of a predator's life is not one of casually choosing its next meal and then effortlessly picking off the

defenceless victim. Instead, the predator must first find the prey, then hope that the particular individual it encounters is old enough, young enough, or sick enough to be caught. Obviously, only a certain fraction of prey animals are vulnerable in these ways, and the predator's problem is to find these scarce catchable individuals at a fast enough rate to avoid starvation. If there are many individual predators competing for the same, limited number of catchable prey, it is inevitable that some of the predators will fail to find their next meal on time. When an old wolf or an inexperienced young hawk goes hungry and dies, it eases the competition among the remaining predators. But even that doesn't guarantee their survival. Factors totally out of the predators' control may destroy their food supply and reduce them to beggardom. For example, climatic conditions in the far north may cause the collapse of mouse populations, and even the most accomplished mouse hunters may suddenly find themselves in serious trouble. Last winter was a good example of such a situation, and many hungry northern owls drifted into southern Ontario, including Algonquin Park. Hundreds of human wildlife viewers delighted in their first sightings of Northern Hawk Owls and Great Gray Owls and, as usual, were impressed by the magnificence of these superb predators. Still, the underlying reality of last winter's owl show was that the individual birds had been forced to leave the north woods because of desperate food conditions. Many of them were terribly weak, and even down here only a few would survive the winter.

Obviously, these refugees were nowhere near to enjoying anything that could be called "masterful control" of their environment. As with falcons, wolves, and eagles — as indeed with all predators in the world — it would be truer to say that they were hanging on for dear life. Their survival was not as much a question of how alert and skillful they were as it was of the availability of catchable animals. Needless to say, there could never be any room in their minds for "nobly surveying the landscape" or showing "genteel compassion" toward their prey.

Lofty thoughts and total control of the world are the domain of human fairy tales. Nature's top predators, the "kings" of the jungle and forest in our popular imagination, are really prisoners of their own imperatives and of the unavoidable truths of the real world in which they live. They are certainly not the kings of their environment. If anything, it would be truer to say they are its slaves.☜

September 3, 1992, Vol. 33, No. 11 (D.S.)

The Last Colour Is the Best Colour

There is, however, one more fall colour in Algonquin. Although we believe it is the most beautiful of all, we have to concede that few people are aware of its existence. You have to be in the Park in the first week of November and you have to be at the right place on the shores of the right lakes. There, preferably on a bright, cloudless day when the cold sunlight of late fall bathes the gray dormant landscape of Algonquin, you might look down into the water and see before you one of nature's most colourful and breathtaking spectacles — the annual spawning of Brook Trout. Dozens of brilliantly coloured fish are milling

We always feel somewhat sad after Labour Day. The campgrounds are shutting down, summer staff are going back to school, and we won't see most of our regular visitors again until next summer.

To be sure, lots of people will be coming in for a few hours or even going on one last canoe trip during the peak of fall colours in the final 10 days of September, but even then there is a touch of melancholy in the air. No matter how brilliant the reds and oranges of Algonquin's vast west-side Sugar Maple forests, the knowledge is never far away that we are witnessing the shut-down of nature itself. The lives of trillions of leaves are coming to an end. For four months they have captured energy from the warm summer sun and made the sugars that directly or indirectly power all the plant and animal life in Algonquin. But now their intricate chemical mechanisms are breaking down. Green chlorophyll is disappearing to reveal yellows hidden until then. In some trees, such as maples and cherries, new red pigments are being manufactured, but their sole purpose is to assist in the final salvage and transport of sugars and minerals back into the tree before the leaves detach and flutter lifelessly down to the forest floor. This sombre note will be accentuated by the less flamboyant colours of the trees that turn colour later in the fall. The yellows of the birches and aspens, the rusty brown of Red Oak, and finally the gold of Tamarack are all beautiful in their own way, but there is no avoiding the fact that each brings us that much closer to the drab semi-death of the winter landscape.

about in shallow water, occasionally catching the sunlight in just the right way for you to see the dazzling orange-red flanks of the males to best advantage.

Everyone knows that Brook Trout are beautiful fish. Indeed, the other common name for this species, "Speckled Trout," is inspired by the red spots surrounded by bluish halos along their sides and providing a pleasing contrast with the deep olive green of the back. But in fall the already beautiful colours are greatly intensified, especially in the males that develop those deep red sides and a black border underneath separating the flank colour from the still white belly. Indeed, the Park probably has few other creatures as beautiful as a mature male Brook Trout in the first week of November.

As good as the colours are, however, that is just part of the spectacle. After all, here is a fish for which Algonquin is famous, found in at least 230 lakes and of which we nevertheless rarely ever get more than a glimpse — at least in their wild state. And yet here they are, before our eyes, sometimes in just a foot or two of water, oblivious to our presence and exhibiting not only their most brilliant colours of the year but also their most fascinating behaviour — that associated with spawning.

Brook Trout have very exacting requirements for successful reproduction. The spawning beds must be made of sand or gravel that the female can stir up after laying her eggs in such a way that the material covers the eggs and hides them from would-be egg-eaters. At the same time, precisely because they do end up being buried in gravel, the eggs are liable to run out of oxygen at some point during the winter-long "incubation" period or be poisoned by their own waste products. This problem is countered by choosing beds of gravel that have an upwelling of spring water. Percolating up through the gravel, this water will bring new oxygen to the buried eggs and flush away the waste products.

Female Brook Trout are very sensitive to the presence of these crucial upwellings and return year after year to the exact same spots on the spawning beds. When they first arrive, they clean off any debris accumulated over the summer and prepare "redds" — shallow depressions in the gravel where the eggs will be deposited. As this happens, the closely following male ejects his milt, which fertilizes the eggs that then float down to the gravel and are subsequently buried there by the female's vigorous tail-fanning movements. If all goes well, the eggs will hatch sometime between February and April, and a month later, after the yolk sacs have been absorbed, the little Brook Trout fry will emerge from the gravel and start their lives as free-swimming fish.*

All this is extremely interesting, particularly if you're lucky enough to see any of the process with your own eyes, but we continue to be fascinated by one particular aspect of spawning in Brook Trout, namely the bright colours that attracted our attention in the first place. Now, you might suppose, just as with many birds, that the bright colours of breeding males simply serve to make the males more attractive to females. This is indeed one of the roles proposed for the red pigments in Brook Trout, but others have been suggested as well — and they may well be more important.

Fish are not capable of manufacturing the orange and red pigments themselves but derive them instead from pigments contained in the bodies of certain tiny crustaceans on which they prey. For much of the year the pigment is stored in the muscles of the fish — accounting for the beautiful orange colour of Brook Trout flesh so much appreciated by Algonquin Park fishermen. With the approach of spawning season, however, the pigment moves from the muscles to the skin in males, as we have seen, and in females to the ovaries and eventually the eggs. Professional hatchery managers and fish farmers have long known that the trout or salmon eggs with the deepest red or orange colour were the ones that survived best and gave rise to the most, and healthiest, young fry, but even today no one knows why for sure. There is some

suggestion that heavily pigmented eggs can withstand higher temperatures and concentrations of ammonia — one of the poisonous products of egg development that must eventually be flushed away from the egg if it is to survive. Other evidence suggests that strongly coloured eggs are better able than pale eggs to withstand conditions of low oxygen. This, too, might explain why heavily pigmented eggs have a higher survival rate when you remember that the eggs end up buried in gravel, where water circulation may be inadequate to keep the eggs constantly supplied with fresh oxygen. Then, too, before they are laid, thousands of eggs are kept in the female's body cavity at quite some distance from any blood supply. Here, too, an increased capacity to withstand low oxygen would help the eggs to remain viable for a longer time.

Other explanations have been proposed as well, including the idea that the pigment plays a role as a fertility hormone or that it may be used by the fish to make Vitamin A. In this regard it's no coincidence that the pigments in Brook Trout are the same colour as those in carrots! Both groups are called "carotenoids," and both can be easily transformed into Vitamin A — which in humans is especially important for good night vision. Could it be that the orange/red pigment in Brook Trout indirectly helps them see in the deep dark world they inhabit for most of the year?

We may not yet have definitive answers to these questions but pondering them adds an extra, pleasurable dimension to what is already a fascinating experience. Indeed, we can't think of anything we would rather do than sit above a Brook Trout spawning bed on a bright November day and drink in the beauty of the Park's last fall colours. To us, the sight of all those brilliant orange and red fish roiling and milling about in the shallows is the finest picture of fall imaginable. And even though it is the very last truly colourful scene offered by an Algonquin autumn it somehow doesn't affect us in the same, slightly saddening way that the "normal" fall colours do. As we hinted earlier, the reds, yellows, and oranges of fall foliage signify the death of countless leaves, the shutting down of the great Algonquin forests for another year. The colours of spawning Brook Trout, on the other hand, signify vigorous animals in the very prime of their existence. They signify life and the renewal of life. They hold the promise of a new generation of beautiful Brook Trout, of warm spring days, and of more unforgettable fishing expeditions in the years to come.

Maybe that is why the last colour of fall, the little known brilliance of spawning Brook Trout, is also the best colour of them all.∞

September 10, 1992, Vol. 33, No. 12 (D.S.)

---

* By way of contrast, the spawning habits of Lake Trout, the Park's other famous game fish, are quite different. They spawn earlier than Brook Trout, usually in the last two weeks of October and at night, never in the day. They also choose a quite different type of spawning bed — rock rubble instead of the gravel beds with spring seepage required by Brook Trout.